OUR DOCUMENTS

OUR DOCUMENTS

100 Milestone Documents
from the National Archives

Foreword by Michael Beschloss

OXFORD
UNIVERSITY PRESS

ACKNOWLEDGMENTS

Our Documents is the result of the contributions of many talented and devoted individuals. Special thanks go to those responsible for selecting the documents. The team included National Archives staff members, Stacey Bredhoff, John Constance, Susan Cooper, Lori Lisowski, Lee Ann Potter, Milton Gustufson, and Walter Hill; and Cathy Gorn and Maria Mazzenga from National History Day. The individuals who researched, wrote drafts, and compiled information for the contextual essays were Daniel Rulli, Lee Ann Potter, and Mary Jo Maralit. Other NARA staff members who provided editorial review for the essays included Lori Lisowski, Chris Rudy Smith, Mary Ryan, James Worsham, and Lisa Bainer. Jim Zeender was instrumental in locating the documents and ensuring the accuracy of their citations. Steve Puglia, Jeffery Reed, and Erin Rhodes scanned the documents. Darlene McClurkin, Kahlil Chism, and Kevin Bradley identified historical photos to complement the text. Finally, Jennifer Nelson, Darren Cole, and Theo Welch were responsible for posting the materials on the *Our Documents* web site. The fact that so many individuals were part of this effort places significant emphasis on the "Our" in *Our Documents*.

Editors:
CHRISTINE COMPSTON
RACHEL FILENE SEIDMAN

Design and layout:
ALEXIS SIROC

Library of Congress Cataloging-in-Publication Data

United States. National Archives and Records Administration.
  Our documents : 100 milestone documents from the National Archives.
    p. cm.
Summary: A collection of one hundred documents that were important in
the development of the United States from its founding to 1965, including the Declaration of Independence, Constitution, and lesser-known writings.
Includes bibliographical references and index.
  ISBN 0-19-517206-X (alk. paper) – ISBN 0-19-517207-8 (pbk. : alk. paper)
  1. United States–History–Sources–Juvenile literature. 2. United States–Politics and government–Sources–Juvenile literature. [1. United States–History–Sources. 2. United States–Politics and government–Sources.] I. Title.
  E173.U62 2003
  973–dc22

                                2003015080

Printing number: 9 8 7 6 5 4 3 2 1

Printed in the United States on acid-free paper

Frontis: *This engraving commemorated the committee that drafted the Declaration of Independence: Benjamin Franklin, Thomas Jefferson, John Adams, Robert R. Livingston, and Roger Sherman.*

FOREWORD

When I was a ten-year-old boy growing up in Illinois, I read in an encyclopedia about how the Constitution and the Declaration of Independence were displayed at the National Archives Building in Washington, D.C. To a boy that age, it was thrilling—the hermetically sealed cases filled with inert helium gas, the device that would plunge the documents into an underground vault at the first hint of impending vandalism, fire, or nuclear war. State-of-the-art technology was deployed to protect those Charters of Freedom from the dangers of the nuclear age. George Washington and James Madison could never have dreamt that these documents would one day have to be protected from something called the hydrogen bomb.

As I grew older and became a historian, I realized that the display at the National Archives was a perfect metaphor for what the Constitution meant to every American. For twenty-one decades, we had protected those pieces of parchment, and for twenty-one decades, the basic ideas they embodied had protected all of us.

As proud as the Founders were of what they had created, they knew that if the American experiment succeeded, the Constitution would be augmented and changed by other documents—treaties, Presidential pronunciamentos, Acts of Congress, Supreme Court decisions. Everyone who attended the Constitutional Convention at Philadelphia wondered how it would all turn out.

If Benjamin Franklin or James Madison were to return to life today, he could find no better way to discover how their handiwork finally developed than to read the hundred documents in this book. You may read this volume as a kind of autobiography of America. It begins with the optimism of the American Revolutionaries and the more skeptical designs of the Founders,

going on to the expansion of the Louisiana Purchase, the struggles with Native Americans, the agonies over slavery and race. You will discover the promise of new inventions like the cotton gin and the electric lamp and an interstate system of highways, the conflicts over states' rights and, in the twentieth century, the rise of the United States to world responsibility that finally showed how prophetic Thomas Jefferson was when he insisted that the "contagion" of democracy would one day spread throughout the world.

What the Founders would particularly cherish about this book is that it is autobiography, not biography. It allows you to experience the excitement of the American story by listening to the voices of those who shaped it. It was not that the Founders lacked respect for scholarship (fortunately for those of us who earn our living writing history). Many were scholars themselves. But one of the many ways they wanted to distinguish America from the kingly empires of Europe was this: in the eighteenth century, most Englishmen or Spaniards unquestioningly absorbed the history that their rulers handed down to them. In contrast, Franklin and Madison and their comrades knew that in the America of the future, the most meaningful assessment of American history would not be that of the leaders but that of the people. It would be theirs to judge how well the grand experiment was working.

For that, there are few better tools than this book. As the twenty-first century unfolds, it gives us access to some of the most important historical treasures we Americans possess in order to reach—through the filter of our own generation's traumas, joys and preoccupations—such a verdict for our time.

Michael Beschloss
Washington, D.C.
July 4, 2003

PREFACE

O n September 17, 2002, I was honored to join President George W. Bush and other national leaders in the Rose Garden of the White House as the President announced a nationwide civics initiative in which the National Archives and Records Administration is playing a key role. This book is one of the results of that initiative.

Our Documents is a collaboration among the National Archives, National History Day, the Corporation for National and Community Service, and the USA Freedom Corps. The purpose of *Our Documents* is to encourage all Americans to participate in a series of events and programs to get us thinking, talking, and teaching about the rights and responsibilities of citizens in our democracy. Such an exploration of our nation's civic legacy can encourage everyone to strengthen their understanding and appreciation of the records and values that undergird our democracy.

Our Documents revolves around 100 milestone documents drawn primarily from the public laws, Supreme Court decisions, speeches, treaties, constitutional amendments, and millions of other documents that have influenced the course of U.S. history and are held by the National Archives.

The list begins with the Lee Resolution of June 7, 1776, a simple document resolving that the United Colonies "are, and of right, ought to be free and independent States." Richard Henry Lee introduced this resolution in the Second Continental Congress, and it was approved on July 2, setting in motion the adoption of the Declaration of Independence on July 4. Although virtually all Americans are familiar with the Declaration of Independence, far fewer know of the role the Lee Resolution played in the history of our country. *Our Documents* features well-known historical documents such as the Constitution and the Bill of Rights, as well as less-familiar documents such as the Lee Resolution and De Lôme letter.

In his remarks on September 17, President Bush said, "Our history is not a story of perfection. It is a story of imperfect people working toward great ideas." *Our Documents* bears this out. For example, while the Supreme Court's ruling in *Plessy* v. *Ferguson* (1896) upheld "equal but separate accommodations for the white and colored races," the case of *Brown* v. *Board of Education* overturned this ruling in 1954, signaling the end of legalized racial segregation in U.S. schools.

Likewise, the Constitution as originally written in 1787 mentions little about the right to vote. At the time it was thought that only a privileged few (meaning white men who owned property) should have that right. But through the years, Americans fought passionately for the right to vote, a process illustrated by the Fifteenth Amendment to the Constitution, which in 1870 enfranchised African-American men; the Nineteenth Amendment, which granted women the right to vote in 1920; and the Voting Rights Act of 1965, which outlawed discriminatory voting practices.

All of these documents have helped shape our national character, and they reflect our diversity, our unity, and our commitment as a nation to continue our work toward forming "a more perfect union." Understanding these foundations on which our nation is built is crucial to participating in our democracy in a meaningful way.

JOHN W. CARLIN
ARCHIVIST OF THE UNITED STATES

Why These 100 Documents?

A team of historians, archivists, educators, and curators from the National Archives and Records Administration and National History Day selected the documents included in the list of 100 milestones. Given that the National Archives holds literally billions of documents, identifying 100 was a difficult task made possible by the establishment of certain criteria. The team first narrowed down the time span of the list. The decision not to include milestone documents since 1965 was a deliberate acknowledgment of the difficulty in examining more recent history. As stated in the guidelines for the National History Standards, developed by the National Center for History in the Schools, "Historians can never attain complete objectivity, but they tend to fall shortest of the goal when they deal with current or very recent events."

Next, the team chose to focus primarily on documents of political, rather than economic or social, significance. The team was, however, keenly aware of the economic and social factors that both prompted and resulted from the chosen documents. Furthermore, the team referred to textbooks, state and national standards, and personal experience and knowledge to determine which documents and themes are typically taught in the nation's history and government classrooms. These factors prompted the team to include a few documents on the list that are not in the holdings of the National Archives: *The Federalist Papers* No. 10 and No. 51, President George Washington's Farewell Address, President Abraham Lincoln's Second Inaugural Address, and the Gettysburg Address.

Finally, the team considered how each of the documents provided a point of entry into a discussion about the rights and responsibilities of citizens in American democracy. As the list developed, the team was encouraged by the many connections that exist among the documents and found it gratifying to see how the spirit of one document appeared in later documents and how the documents taken as a whole reflect democratic ideals in action. These revelations were ones that the team hoped all Americans, particularly teachers and students, would discover as well.

The fact that virtually all of the documents reside in the holdings of the National Archives and Records Administration is not surprising. In fact, it is most fitting that these highly significant documents are in the hands of the federal government agency whose mission is to preserve and provide access to essential evidence documenting the rights of American citizens, the actions of federal officials, and the national experience.

1776

LEE RESOLUTION

ew England was already in rebellion against the British and Thomas Paine's pamphlet "Common Sense," urging Americans to break away from the monarchy, had sold more than 100,000 copies by the spring of 1776. On June 7, 1776, in the Second Continental Congress, Richard Henry Lee, a Virginia delegate, introduced this resolution, which proposed independence for the American colonies. The Lee Resolution contained three parts: a declaration of independence, a call to form foreign alliances, and "a plan for confederation." On June 11, the Congress appointed three committees to undertake these three tasks. They did not approve the plan for alliances until September 1776 and delayed action on the plan of confederation until November 1777. But on July 2, 1776, Congress adopted the first part of Lee's resolution, leading to the creation of the United States of America.

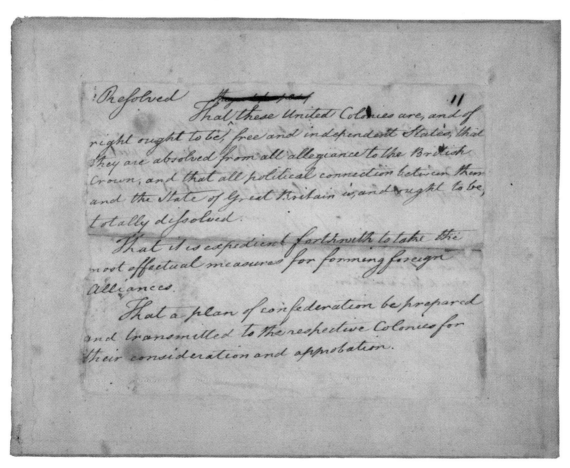

RESOLVED, That these United Colonies are, and of right ought to be, free and independent States, that they are absolved from all allegiance to the British Crown, and that all political connection between them and the State of Great Britain is, and ought to be, totally dissolved.

That it is expedient forthwith to take the most effectual measures for forming foreign Alliances.

That a plan of confederation be prepared and transmitted to the respective Colonies for their consideration and approbation.

1776

DECLARATION OF INDEPENDENCE

On June 10, 1776, Congress appointed a committee of Thomas Jefferson, John Adams, Benjamin Franklin, Robert R. Livingston, and Roger Sherman to draft a statement of independence for the colonies. Jefferson worked on the statement from June 11 to 28 and submitted drafts to Adams and Franklin, who made some changes. He presented the draft to Congress following the adoption of the independence section of the Lee Resolution on July 2. Congress took all of July 3 and most of July 4 to revise the document. Finally, on the afternoon of July 4, Congress adopted the Declaration. Under the supervision of the Jefferson committee, the approved Declaration was printed on July 4 and a copy was attached to the "rough journal of the Continental Congress for July 4th." These printed copies, bearing only the names of John Hancock, President, and Charles Thomson, secretary, were distributed to state assemblies, conventions, committees of safety, and commanding officers of the Continental troops.

On July 19, Congress ordered an engrossed copy of the Declaration—that is, one copied out in a large hand on parchment—with a new title, "The unanimous Declaration of the thirteen united States of America," and "that the same, when engrossed, be signed by every member of Congress." On August 2 John Hancock, the president of the Congress, signed the copy with a bold signature that became a landmark in history. The list of other delegate signatures, following custom, began at the right, in geographic order of states, from northernmost New Hampshire to southernmost Georgia.

IN CONGRESS, July 4, 1776.

The unanimous Declaration of the thirteen united States of America,

When in the Course of human events, it becomes necessary for one people to dissolve the political bands which have connected them with another, and to assume among the powers of the earth, the separate and equal station to which the Laws of Nature and of Nature's God entitle them, a decent respect to the opinions of mankind requires that they should declare the causes which impel them to the separation.

We hold these truths to be self-evident, that all men are created equal, that they are endowed by their Creator with certain unalienable Rights, that among these are Life, Liberty and the pursuit of Happiness.—That to secure these rights, Governments are instituted among Men, deriving their just powers from the consent of the governed,—That whenever any Form of Government becomes destructive of these ends, it is the Right of the People to alter or to abolish it, and to institute new Government, laying its foundation on such principles and organizing its powers in such form, as to them shall seem most likely to effect their Safety and Happiness. Prudence, indeed, will dictate that Governments long established should not be changed for light and transient causes; and accordingly all experience hath shewn, that mankind are more disposed to suffer, while evils are sufferable, than to right themselves by abolishing the forms to which they are accustomed. But when a long train of abuses and usurpations, pursuing invariably the same Object evinces a design to reduce them under absolute Despotism, it is their right, it is their duty, to throw off such Government, and to provide new Guards for their future security.—Such has been the patient sufferance of these Colonies; and such is now the necessity which constrains them to alter their former Systems of Government. The history of the present King of Great Britain is a history of repeated injuries and usurpations, all having in direct object the establishment of an absolute Tyranny over these States. To prove this, let Facts be submitted to a candid world.

He has refused his Assent to Laws, the most wholesome and necessary for the public good.

He has forbidden his Governors to pass Laws of immediate and pressing importance, unless suspended in their operation till his Assent should be obtained; and when so suspended, he has utterly neglected to attend to them.

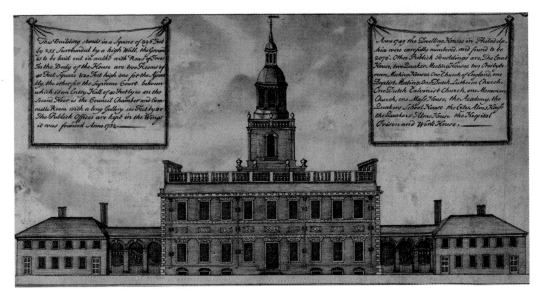

The Pennsylvania State House in a 1752 engraving. It would become known as Independence Hall after an 1824 visit from the Marquis de Lafayette rekindled interest in the site of the Declaration's signing as an appropriate place to officially greet the aging French veteran of the American Revolution.

He has refused to pass other Laws for the accommodation of large districts of people, unless those people would relinquish the right of Representation in the Legislature, a right inestimable to them and formidable to tyrants only.

He has called together legislative bodies at places unusual, uncomfortable, and distant from the depository of their public Records, for the sole purpose of fatiguing them into compliance with his measures.

He has dissolved Representative Houses repeatedly, for opposing with manly firmness his invasions on the rights of the people.

He has refused for a long time, after such dissolutions, to cause others to be elected; whereby the Legislative powers, incapable of Annihilation, have returned to the People at large for their exercise; the State remaining in the mean time exposed to all the dangers of invasion from without, and convulsions within.

He has endeavoured to prevent the population of these States; for that purpose obstructing the Laws for Naturalization of Foreigners; refusing to pass others to encourage their migrations hither, and raising the conditions of new Appropriations of Lands.

He has obstructed the Administration of Justice, by refusing his Assent to Laws for establishing Judiciary powers.

He has made Judges dependent on his Will alone, for the tenure of their offices, and the amount and payment of their salaries.

He has erected a multitude of New Offices, and sent hither swarms of Officers to harrass our people, and eat out their substance.

He has kept among us, in times of peace, Standing Armies without the Consent of our legislatures.

He has affected to render the Military independent of and superior to the Civil power.

He has combined with others to subject us to a jurisdiction foreign to our constitution, and unacknowledged by our Laws; giving his Assent to their Acts of pretended Legislation:

For Quartering large bodies of armed troops among us:

For protecting them, by a mock Trial, from punishment for any Murders which they should commit on the Inhabitants of these States:

For cutting off our Trade with all parts of the world:

For imposing Taxes on us without our Consent:

For depriving us in many cases, of the benefits of Trial by Jury:

For transporting us beyond Seas to be tried for pretended offences:

For abolishing the free System of English Laws in a neighbouring Province, establishing therein an Arbitrary government, and enlarging its Boundaries so as to render it at once an example and fit instrument for introducing the same absolute rule into these Colonies:

For taking away our Charters, abolishing our most valuable Laws, and altering fundamentally the Forms of our Governments:

For suspending our own Legislatures, and declaring themselves invested with power to legislate for us in all cases whatsoever.

He has abdicated Government here, by declaring us out of his Protection and waging War against us.

He has plundered our seas, ravaged our Coasts, burnt our towns, and destroyed the lives of our people.

He is at this time transporting large Armies of foreign Mercenaries to compleat the works of death, desolation and tyranny, already begun with circumstances of Cruelty & perfidy scarcely paralleled in the most barbarous ages, and totally unworthy the Head of a civilized nation.

He has constrained our fellow Citizens taken Captive on the high Seas to bear Arms against their Country, to become the executioners of their friends and Brethren, or to fall themselves by their Hands.

He has excited domestic insurrections amongst us, and has endeavoured to bring on the inhabitants of our frontiers, the merciless Indian Savages, whose known rule of warfare, is an undistinguished destruction of all ages, sexes and conditions.

In every stage of these Oppressions We have Petitioned for Redress in the most humble terms: Our repeated Petitions have been answered only by repeated injury. A Prince whose character is thus marked by every act which may define a Tyrant, is unfit to be the ruler of a free people.

Nor have We been wanting in attentions to our Brittish brethren. We have warned them from time to time of attempts by their legislature to extend an unwarrantable jurisdiction over us. We have reminded them of the circumstances of our emigration and settlement here. We have appealed to their native justice and magnanimity, and we have conjured them by the ties of our common kindred to disavow these usurpations, which would inevitably interrupt our connections and correspondence. They too have been deaf to the voice of justice and of consanguinity. We must, therefore, acquiesce in the necessity, which denounces our Separation, and hold them, as we hold the rest of mankind, Enemies in War, in Peace Friends.

We, therefore, the Representatives of the united States of America, in General Congress, Assembled, appealing to the Supreme Judge of the world for the rectitude of our intentions, do, in the Name, and by Authority of the good People of these Colonies, solemnly publish and declare, That these United Colonies are, and of Right ought to be Free and Independent States; that they are Absolved from all Allegiance to the British Crown, and that all political connection between them and the State of Great Britain, is and ought to be totally dissolved; and that as Free and Independent States, they have full Power to levy War, conclude Peace, contract Alliances, establish Commerce, and to do all other Acts and Things which Independent States may of right do. And for the support of this Declaration, with a firm reliance on the protection of divine Providence, we mutually pledge to each other our Lives, our Fortunes and our sacred Honor.

GEORGIA	NORTH CAROLINA	MASSACHUSETTS	PENNSYLVANIA	NEW YORK	NEW HAMPSHIRE
BUTTON GWINNETT	WILLIAM HOOPER	JOHN HANCOCK	ROBERT MORRIS	WILLIAM FLOYD	JOSIAH BARTLETT
LYMAN HALL	JOSEPH HEWES		BENJAMIN RUSH	PHILIP LIVINGSTON	WILLIAM WHIPPLE
GEORGE WALTON	JOHN PENN	**MARYLAND**	BENJAMIN FRANKLIN	FRANCIS LEWIS	
		SAMUEL CHASE	JOHN MORTON	LEWIS MORRIS	**MASSACHUSETTS**
	SOUTH CAROLINA	WILLIAM PACA	GEORGE CLYMER		SAMUEL ADAMS
	EDWARD RUTLEDGE	THOMAS STONE	JAMES SMITH	**NEW JERSEY**	JOHN ADAMS
	THOMAS HEYWARD, JR.	CHARLES CARROLL OF CARROLLTON	GEORGE TAYLOR	RICHARD STOCKTON	ROBERT TREAT PAINE
	THOMAS LYNCH, JR.		JAMES WILSON	JOHN WITHERSPOON	ELBRIDGE GERRY
	ARTHUR MIDDLETON	**VIRGINIA**	GEORGE ROSS	FRANCIS HOPKINSON	
		GEORGE WYTHE		JOHN HART	**RHODE ISLAND**
		RICHARD HENRY LEE	**DELAWARE**	ABRAHAM CLARK	STEPHEN HOPKINS
		THOMAS JEFFERSON	CAESAR RODNEY		WILLIAM ELLERY
		BENJAMIN HARRISON	GEORGE READ		
		THOMAS NELSON, JR.	THOMAS MCKEAN		**CONNECTICUT**
		FRANCIS LIGHTFOOT LEE			ROGER SHERMAN
		CARTER BRAXTON			SAMUEL HUNTINGTON
					WILLIAM WILLIAMS
					OLIVER WOLCOTT
					NEW HAMPSHIRE
					MATTHEW THORNTON

1777

ARTICLES OF CONFEDERATION

Following the Lee Resolution, which had been introduced to the Continental Congress a few days earlier and proposed independence for the colonies, on June 11, 1776, the Second Continental Congress appointed a committee to determine the form of a confederation of the colonies. Composed of one representative from each colony, the committee chose as the principal writer John Dickinson, a delegate from Delaware.

The Dickinson Draft of the Articles of Confederation named the Confederation "the United States of America," based congressional representation on the population of each state, and gave to the national government all powers not designated to the states. In this "first constitution of the United States," each state retained "every Power...which is not by this confederation expressly delegated to the United States," and each state had one vote in Congress. Instead of forming a strong national government, the states entered into "a firm league of friendship with each other." After considerable debate and alteration, the Continental Congress adopted the Articles of Confederation on November 15, 1777.

Ratification by all thirteen states was necessary to set the Confederation into motion. Because of disputes over representation, voting, and the western lands claimed by some states, ratification followed a lengthy four years later when Maryland agreed to the new plan on March 1, 1781, and the Congress of the Confederation came into being. Thus was born the first constitution of the United States, which prevailed from March 1, 1781, until 1789, when the present Constitution replaced it.

To all to whom these Presents shall come, we the undersigned Delegates of the States affixed to our Names send greeting.

Articles of Confederation and perpetual Union between the states of New Hampshire, Massachusetts-bay, Rhode Island and Providence Plantations, Connecticut, New York, New Jersey, Pennsylvania, Delaware, Maryland, Virginia, North Carolina, South Carolina and Georgia.

I.

The Stile of this Confederacy shall be "The United States of America".

II.

Each state retains its sovereignty, freedom, and independence, and every power, jurisdiction, and right, which is not by this Confederation expressly delegated to the United States, in Congress assembled.

III.

The said States hereby severally enter into a firm league of friendship with each other, for their common defense, the security of their liberties, and their mutual and general welfare, binding themselves to assist each other, against all force offered to, or attacks made upon them, or any of them, on account of religion, sovereignty, trade, or any other pretense whatever....

V.

For the most convenient management of the general interests of the United States, delegates shall be annually appointed in such manner as the legislatures of each State shall direct, to meet in Congress on the first Monday in November, in every year, with a power reserved to each State to recall its delegates, or any of them, at any time within the year, and to send others in their stead for the remainder of the year.

No State shall be represented in Congress by less than two, nor more than seven members; and no person shall be capable of being a delegate for more than three years in any term of six years; nor shall any person, being a delegate, be capable of holding any office under the United States, for which he, or another for his benefit, receives any salary, fees or emolument of any kind.

Each State shall maintain its own delegates in a meeting of the States, and while they act as members of the committee of the States.

In determining questions in the United States in Congress assembled, each State shall have one vote.

Freedom of speech and debate in Congress shall

"The said States hereby severally enter into a firm league of friendship with each other, for their common defense, the security of their liberties, and their mutual and general welfare..."

not be impeached or questioned in any court or place out of Congress, and the members of Congress shall be protected in their persons from arrests or imprisonments, during the time of their going to and from, and attendance on Congress, except for treason, felony, or breach of the peace....

XIII....

And Whereas it hath pleased the Great Governor of the World to incline the hearts of the legislatures we respectively represent in Congress, to approve of, and to authorize us to ratify the said Articles of Confederation and perpetual Union. Know Ye that we the undersigned delegates, by virtue of the power and authority to us given for that purpose, do by these presents, in the name and in behalf of our respective constituents, fully and entirely ratify and confirm each and every of the said Articles of Confederation and perpetual Union, and all and singular the matters and things therein contained: And we do further solemnly plight and engage the faith of our respective constituents, that they shall abide by the determinations of the United States in Congress assembled, on all questions, which by the said Confederation are submitted to them. And that the Articles thereof shall be inviolably observed by the States we respectively represent, and that the Union shall be perpetual.

In Witness whereof we have hereunto set our hands in Congress. Done at Philadelphia in the State of Pennsylvania the ninth day of July in the Year of our Lord One Thousand Seven Hundred and Seventy-Eight, and in the Third Year of the independence of America.

Agreed to by Congress 15 November 1777

In force after ratification by Maryland, 1 March 1781

1778

TREATY OF ALLIANCE WITH FRANCE

*B*elieving that they would benefit militarily by allying themselves with a powerful nation, the revolutionary colonies formed an alliance with France against Great Britain. According to this first military treaty of the new nation, the United States would provide military assistance to France if England attacked, and neither France nor the United States would make peace with England until it recognized the independence of the United States. Alexander Gerard on behalf of the king of France and Benjamin Franklin of Pennsylvania, along with his fellow commissioners Silas Deane and Arthur Lee, signed this military treaty on February 6, 1778. France went to war against England four months later, soon adding Spain and Holland as allies. England faced these adversaries unassisted. The treaty is divided into two columns, with the English on the left and the French on the right.

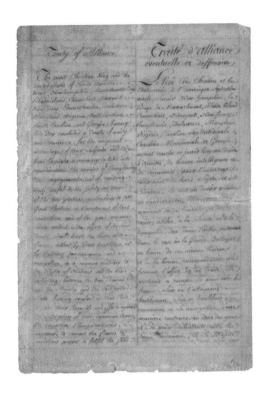

The most Christian King and the United States of North America, to wit, New Hampshire, Massachusetts Bay, Rhodes island, Connecticut, New York, New Jersey, Pennsylvania, Delaware, Maryland, Virginia, North Carolina, South Carolina, and Georgia, having this Day concluded a Treaty of amity and Commerce, for the reciprocal advantage of their Subjects and Citizens have thought it necessary to take into consideration the means of strengthening those engagements and of rondring them useful to the safety and tranquility of the two parties, particularly in case Great Britain in Resentment of that connection and of the good correspondence which is the object of the said Treaty, should break the Peace with France, either by direct hostilities, or by hindering her commerce and navigation, in a manner contrary to the Rights of Nations, and the Peace subsisting between the two Crowns; and his Majesty and the said united States having resolved in that Case to join their Councils and efforts against the Enterprises of their common Enemy, the respective Plenipotentiaries, impower'd to concert the Clauses & conditions proper to fulfil the said Intentions, have, after the most mature Deliberation, concluded and determined on the following Articles.

ART. 1.

If War should break out between France and Great Britain, during the continuance of the present War between the United States and England, his Majesty and the said united States, shall make it a common cause, and aid each other mutually with their good Offices, their Counsels, and their forces, according to the exigence of Conjunctures as becomes good & faithful Allies.

ART. 2.

The essential and direct End of the present defensive alliance is to maintain effectually the liberty, Sovereignty, and independence absolute and unlimited of the said united States, as well in Matters of Gouvernement as of commerce....

Done at Paris, this sixth Day of February, one thousand seven hundred and seventy eight.

C. A. GERARD

B FRANKLIN

SILAS DEANE

ARTHUR LEE

1782

ORIGINAL DESIGN OF THE GREAT SEAL OF THE UNITED STATES

A few hours after the Continental Congress ratified the Declaration of Independence on July 4, 1776, it appointed a committee to design a seal for the United States that would symbolize its national sovereignty. The committee members—Benjamin Franklin, Thomas Jefferson, and John Adams—prepared a very complicated design that Congress failed to act on. However, one prominent feature survived in the version Congress ultimately approved—the motto E Pluribus Unum, Latin for "Out of Many, One."

In 1780 a second committee—James Lovell of Massachusetts and John Morin Scott and William Churchill Houston of Virginia—developed a second design, but Congress tabled that also. Some of the features of this design also persisted in the final seal, including the olive branch, the constellation of 123 stars, and the shield of red and white stripes on a blue field. A third committee was appointed in May of 1782. This committee's design added the eagle for the first time, to the crest of the seal.

Early in 1782 Congress referred the three designs to the secretary of the Continental Congress, Charles Thompson. Thompson contributed a fourth design, and William Barton, a Philadelphia student of heraldry, made revisions. Thompson submitted a written description of his final version to the Continental Congress that explained its symbolism. The colors on the shield are those used in the U.S. flag; white signifies purity and innocence, red signifies hardiness and valor, and blue signifies vigilance, perseverance, and justice. The olive branch and arrows denote the powers of peace and war, powers vested in Congress. The constellation of stars indicates a new state taking its place among other sovereign powers, and the shield is shown on the breast of a lone eagle to denote that the United States ought to rely on its own virtue. The Continental Congress officially approved the design of the national seal on June 20, 1782.

The seal's obverse appears on all official documents, to authenticate the signature of the President, and also on proclamations, warrants, treaties, and commissions of high officials of the government. The Great Seal, which doubles as our national coat of arms, is also the official decoration on military uniform buttons, and on plaques above the entrances to U.S. embassies and consulates and other places of national importance. Both the obverse and the less familiar reverse, which never appears as a seal, are standard and time-honored features of the U.S. one-dollar bill.

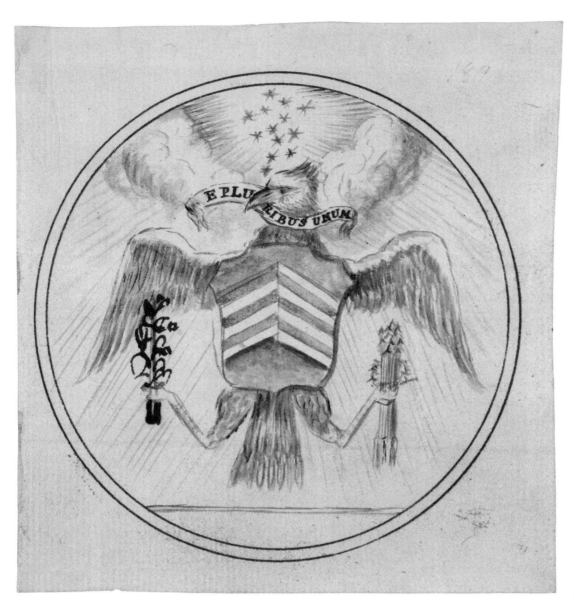

A report to the Continental Congress explains the pyramid on the reverse of the Seal: "[It] signifies Strength and Duration: The Eye over it & the Motto allude to the many signal interpositions of providence in favour of the American cause. The date underneath is that of the Declaration of Independence and words under it signify the beginning of the New American Æra, which commences from that date."

1783

TREATY OF PARIS

*T**he American War for Independence was actually a world conflict involving not only the United States and Great Britain but also France, Spain, and the Netherlands. The peace process brought a vaguely formed, newly born United States into the arena of international diplomacy, pitting it against the largest, most sophisticated, and most established powers on earth.*

The three American negotiators, John Adams, Benjamin Franklin, and John Jay, proved to be masters of the game, outmaneuvering their counterparts and clinging fiercely to the interests most vital to the future of the United States. Two crucial provisions of the treaty were British recognition of U.S. independence and the delineation of boundaries that would allow for American western expansion.

This treaty between the American colonies and Great Britain, which four negotiators signed on September 3, 1783, ended the American Revolution and formally recognized the United States as an independent nation. The Treaty of Paris is named for the city in which it was negotiated and signed. The last page bears the signatures of David Hartley, a member of Parliament who represented Great Britain, and the three American negotiators, who signed their names in alphabetical order.

THE DEFINITIVE TREATY OF PEACE 1783

In the Name of the most holy and undivided Trinity.

It having pleased the Divine Providence to dispose the hearts of the most serene and most potent Prince George the Third, by the grace of God, king of Great Britain, France, and Ireland, defender of the faith, duke of Brunswick and Lunebourg, arch-treasurer and prince elector of the Holy Roman Empire etc., and of the United States of America, to forget all past misunderstandings and differences that have unhappily interrupted the good correspondence and friendship which they mutually wish to restore, and to establish such a beneficial and satisfactory intercourse, between the two countries upon the ground of reciprocal advantages and mutual convenience as may promote and secure to both perpetual peace and harmony; and having for this desirable end already laid the foundation of peace and reconciliation by the Provisional Articles signed at Paris on the 30th of November 1782, by the commissioners empowered on each part, which articles were agreed to be inserted in and constitute the Treaty of Peace proposed to be concluded between the Crown of Great Britain and the said United States, but which treaty was not to be concluded until terms of peace should be agreed upon between Great Britain and France and his Britannic Majesty should be ready to conclude such treaty accordingly; and the treaty between Great Britain and France having since been concluded, his

Britannic Majesty and the United States of America, in order to carry into full effect the Provisional Articles above mentioned, according to the tenor thereof, have constituted and appointed, that is to say his Britannic Majesty on his part, David Hartley, Esqr., member of the Parliament of Great Britain, and the said United States on their part, John Adams, Esqr., late a commissioner of the United States of America at the court of Versailles, late delegate in Congress from the state of Massachusetts, and chief justice of the said state, and minister plenipotentiary of the said United States to their high mightinesses the States General of the United Netherlands; Benjamin Franklin, Esqr., late delegate in Congress from the state of Pennsylvania, president of the convention of the said state, and minister plenipotentiary from the United States of America at the court of Versailles; John Jay, Esqr., late president of Congress and chief justice of the state of New York, and minister plenipotentiary from the said United States at the court of Madrid; to be plenipotentiaries for the concluding and signing the present definitive treaty; who after having reciprocally communicated their respective full powers have agreed upon and confirmed the following articles.

ARTICLE 1

His Brittanic Majesty acknowledges the said United States, viz., New Hampshire, Massachusetts Bay, Rhode Island and Providence Plantations, Connecticut, New

without Difficulty and without requiring any Compensation.

Article 10th..

The solemn Ratifications of the present Treaty expedited in good & due Form shall be exchanged between the contracting Parties in the Space of Six Months or sooner if possible to be computed from the Day of the Signature of the present Treaty. In Witness whereof we the undersigned their Ministers Plenipotentiary have in their Name and in Virtue of our Full Powers signed with our Hands the present Definitive Treaty, and caused the Seals of our Arms to be affix'd thereto.

Done at Paris, this third Day of September, In the Year of our Lord one thousand seven hundred & eighty three. —

D Hartley   John Adams.   B Franklin   John Jay —

This painting by Benjamin West commemorates the signing of the peace treaty. It includes, from left to right, John Jay, John Adams, Benjamin Franklin, Henry Laurens, and Franklin's grandson, William Temple Franklin, secretary to the American delegation. West intended for his painting to include the British delegation, but they refused to sit for it.

York, New Jersey, Pennsylvania, Maryland, Virginia, North Carolina, South Carolina and Georgia, to be free sovereign and independent states, that he treats with them as such, and for himself, his heirs, and successors, relinquishes all claims to the government, propriety, and territorial rights of the same and every part thereof.

Article 2

And that all disputes which might arise in future on the subject of the boundaries of the said United States may be prevented, it is hereby agreed and declared, that the following are and shall be their boundaries, viz.; from the northwest angle of Nova Scotia, viz., that angle which is formed by a line drawn due north from the source of St. Croix River to the highlands; along the said highlands which divide those rivers that empty themselves into the river St. Lawrence, from those which fall into the Atlantic Ocean, to the northwesternmost head of Connecticut River; thence down along the middle of that river to the forty-fifth degree of north latitude; from thence by a line due west on said latitude until it strikes the river Iroquois or Cataraquy; thence along the middle of said river into Lake Ontario; through the middle of said lake until it strikes the communication by water between that lake and Lake Erie; thence along the middle of said communication into Lake Erie, through the middle of said lake until it arrives at the water communication between that lake and Lake Huron; thence along the middle of said water communication into Lake Huron, thence through the middle of said lake to the water communication between that lake and Lake Superior; thence through Lake Superior northward of the Isles Royal and Phelipeaux to the Long Lake; thence through the middle of said Long Lake and the water communication between it and the Lake of the Woods, to the said Lake of the Woods; thence through the said lake to the most northwesternmost point thereof, and from thence on a due west course to the river Mississippi; thence by a line to be drawn along the middle of the said river Mississippi until it shall intersect the northernmost part of the thirty-first degree of north latitude, South, by a line to be drawn due east from the determination of the line last mentioned in the latitude of thirty-one degrees of the equator, to the middle of the river Apalachicola or Catahouche; thence along the middle thereof to its junction with the Flint River, thence straight to the head of Saint Mary's River; and thence down along the middle of Saint Mary's River to the Atlantic Ocean; east, by a line to be drawn along the middle of the river Saint Croix, from its mouth in the Bay of Fundy to its source, and from its source directly north to the aforesaid highlands which divide the rivers that fall into the Atlantic Ocean from those which fall into the river Saint Lawrence; comprehending all islands within twenty leagues of any part of the shores of the United States, and lying between lines to be drawn due east from the points where the aforesaid boundaries between Nova Scotia on the one part and East Florida on the other shall, respectively, touch the Bay of Fundy and the Atlantic Ocean, excepting such islands as now are or heretofore have been within the limits of the said province of Nova Scotia....

Done at Paris, this third day of September in the year of our Lord, one thousand seven hundred and eighty-three.

D. Hartley (Seal)

John Adams (Seal)

B. Franklin (Seal)

John Jay (Seal)

1787

VIRGINIA PLAN

*T*he fifty-five delegates who gathered in Philadelphia for the Constitutional Convention in May 1787 recognized that the Articles of Confederation would not serve as a practical plan for the new government—that document was too weak to hold a country together under attack or over time. The delegates faced the challenge of devising a new approach. Two Virginia delegates were key to the process—James Madison, who drafted the plan, and Edmund Randolph, who presented it to the Constitutional Convention on May 29, 1787. The appropriately named Virginia Plan proposed a strong central government composed of three branches: legislative, executive, and judicial.

   The Virginia Plan revealed a bold approach, replacing the confederation of state governments with a centralized national government. Randolph and Madison called for representation in both houses of the legislature to be proportional to each state's population. This quickly angered other delegates who recognized that Virginia was the largest state. The Virginia Plan further described the two congressional houses: one with members elected by the people for three-

James Madison in 1783, four years before the Virginian helped draft a plan for a long-standing U.S. government. This gold-cased miniature portrait is by Philadelphia artist Charles Willson Peale.

year terms and the other composed of older leaders elected by the state legislatures for seven-year terms. The two houses would jointly name the new nation's President and judges and would have the power of legislation and taxation as well as the ability to veto state laws. The Virginia Plan traced the broad outlines of what would become the U.S. Constitution: a national government consisting of three branches, all subject to the checks and balances that prevent the abuse of power.

State of the resolutions submitted to the consideration of the House by the honorable Mr. Randolph, as altered, amended, and agreed to, in a Committee of the whole House.

   1. Resolved that it is the opinion of this Committee that a national government ought to be established consisting of a Supreme Legislative, Judiciary, and Executive.

   2. Resolved. [T]hat the national Legislature ought to consist of Two Branches.

   3. Resolved that the members of the first branch of the national Legislature ought to be elected by the People of the several States for the term of Three years; to receive fixed stipends, by which they may be compensated for the devotion of their time to public service

to be paid out of the National Treasury; to be ineligible to any Office established by a particular State or under the authority of the United-States (except those peculiarly belonging to the functions of the first branch) during the term of service, and under the national government for the space of one year after it's expiration.

   4. Resolved. [T]hat the members of the second Branch of the national Legislature ought to be chosen by the individual Legislatures; to be of the age of thirty years at least; to hold their offices for a term sufficient to ensure their independency, namely seven years; to receive fixed stipends, by which they may be compensated for the devotion of their time to public service— to be paid out of the National Treasury to be ineligible

State of the resolutions submitted to the consideration of the House
by the honorable Mr. Randolph, as altered, amended, and agreed to
in a committee of the whole House.

1. Resolved   that it is the opinion of this committee that a national
              government ought to be established consisting of
                  a Supreme Legislative, Judiciary, and Executive.

2. Resolved   that the national legislature ought to consist of
                  Two Branches.

3. Resolved   that the members of the first branch of the national
              Legislature ought to be elected by
                  the People of the several States
                  for the term of Three years.
                  to receive fixed Stipends, by which they may
                      be compensated for the devotion of their time
                      to public service
                  to be paid out of the National Treasury.
                  to be ineligible to any Office established by a
                      particular State or under the authority of the
                      United States (except those peculiarly belonging to
                      the functions of the first branch) during the term
                      of service, and under the national government
                      for the space of one year after its expiration.

4. Resolved. that the members of the second Branch of the
              national Legislature ought to be chosen by
                  the individual Legislatures.
                  to be of the age of thirty years at least.
                  to hold their offices for a term sufficient to
                      ensure their independency, namely
                      Seven years.
                  to receive fixed stipends, by which they may be
                      compensated for the devotion of their time to public
                      service — to be paid out of the National Treasury.
                  to be ineligible to any office established by a
                      particular State, or under the authority of
                      the United States (except those peculiarly be-
                      -longing to the functions of the second branch)
                      during the term of service, and under the
                      national government, for the space of One
                      year after its expiration.

to any office established by a particular State, or under the authority of the United States (except those peculiarly belonging to the functions of the second branch) during the term of service, and under the national government, for the space of one year after its expiration.

5. Resolved that each branch ought to possess the right of originating acts.

6. Resolved. [T]hat the national Legislature ought to be empowered to enjoy the legislative rights vested in Congress by the confederation—and moreover to legislate in all cases to which the separate States are incompetent: or in which the harmony of the United States may be interrupted by the exercise of individual legislation. to negative all laws passed by the several States contravening, in the opinion of the national Legislature, the articles of union, or any treaties subsisting under the authority of the union.

7. Resolved. [T]hat the right of suffrage in the first branch of the national Legislature ought not to be according to the rule established in the articles of confederation: but according to some equitable ratio of representation—namely, in proportion to the whole number of white and other free citizens and inhabitants of every age, sex, and condition including those bound to servitude for a term of years, and three fifths of all other persons not comprehended in the foregoing description, except Indians, not paying taxes in each State.

8. Resolved. [T]hat the right of suffrage in the second branch of the national Legislature ought to be according to the rule established for the first.

9. Resolved. [T]hat a national Executive be instituted to consist of a single person to be chosen by the National Legislature for the term of seven years with power to carry into execution the national Laws, to appoint to Offices in cases not otherwise provided for to be ineligible a second time, and to be removable on impeachment and conviction of mal practice or neglect of duty; to receive a fixed stipend, by which he may be compensated for the devotion of his time to public service to be paid out of the national Treasury.

10. Resolved. [T]hat the national executive shall have a right to negative any legislative act: which shall not be afterwards passed unless by two third parts of each branch of the national Legislature.

11. Resolved. [T]hat a national Judiciary be established to consist of One Supreme Tribunal. The Judges of which to be appointed by the second Branch of the National Legislature to hold their offices during good behaviour to receive, punctually, at stated times, a fixed compensation for their services: in which no encrease or

diminution shall be made so as to affect the persons actually in office at the time of such encrease or diminution.

12. Resolved. That the national Legislature be empowered to appoint inferior Tribunals.

13. Resolved. That the jurisdiction of the national Judiciary shall extend to cases which respect the collection of the national revenue: impeachments of any national officers: and questions which involve the national peace and harmony.

14. Resolved. [T]hat provision ought to be made for the admission of States, lawfully arising within the limits of the United States, whether from a voluntary junction of government and territory, or otherwise, with the consent of a number of voices in the national Legislature less than the whole.

15. Resolved. [T]hat provision ought to be made for the continuance of Congress and their authorities until a given day after the reform of the articles of Union shall be adopted; and for the completion of all their engagements.

16. Resolved [T]hat a republican constitution, and its existing laws, ought to be guaranteed to each State by the United States.

17. Resolved. [T]hat provision ought to be made for the amendment of the articles of Union, whensoever it shall seem necessary.

18. Resolved. [T]hat the Legislative, Executive, and Judiciary powers within the several States ought to be bound by oath to support the articles of Union.

19. Resolved. [T]hat the amendments which shall be offered to the confederation by the Convention, ought at a proper time or times, after the approbation of Congress to be submitted to an assembly or assemblies of representatives, recommended by the several Legislatures, to be expressly chosen by the People to consider and decide thereon.

Received this sheet from the President of the United States, with the journals of the general Convention, March 19th, 1796.

TIMOTHY PICKERING

SECY OF STATE

State of the Resolutions submitted by Mr. Randolph to the Consideration of the House, as altered, amended and agreed to in a committee of the whole House.

Received from the President of the U. States, March 19, 1796. by

TIMOTHY PICKERING

SECY OF STATE

1787

NORTHWEST ORDINANCE

N*ew lands to the West constituted a serious challenge for the new government. Whites were eager to take possession of the land, against the wishes of Native Americans. Following the procedures outlined in the Ordinance of 1785 (including one that towns be six miles square, subdivided into thirty-six 640-acre sections, and that the community reserve the income from one section for the support of public schooling), the authors of the Northwest Ordinance (probably jurist Nathan Dane of Massachusetts and politician Rufus King of New York) formulated a plan that was subsequently put to good and frequent use as the country expanded to the Pacific.*

Three principal provisions were ordained in the document: (1) a division of the Northwest Territory into "not less than three nor more than five States"; (2) a three-stage method for admitting a new state to the Union—with Congress appointing a governor, secretary, and three judges in the first phase; election of an assembly and one nonvoting delegate to Congress in the second phase; and the drafting of a state constitution and request for admission to the Union in the third phase, when the population reached sixty thousand; and (3) a bill of rights protecting religious freedom and other individual rights. In addition, the ordinance encouraged education and forbade slavery. Officially titled "An Ordinance for the Government of the Territory of the United States North-West of the River Ohio," the Northwest Ordinance became law on July 13, 1787, in the Second Continental Congress. The Ordinance provided a method for admitting new states to the union from the territory and promised settlers of the Northwest Territory the same individual liberties that had been fought for in the Revolution.

AN ORDINANCE FOR THE GOVERNMENT OF THE TERRITORY OF THE UNITED STATES NORTHWEST OF THE RIVER OHIO.

SECTION 1. Be it ordained by the United States in Congress assembled, That the said territory, for the purposes of temporary government, be one district, subject, however, to be divided into two districts, as future circumstances may, in the opinion of Congress, make it expedient....

SEC. 3. Be it ordained by the authority aforesaid, That there shall be appointed from time to time by Congress, a governor, whose commission shall continue in force for the term of three years, unless sooner revoked by Congress; he shall reside in the district, and have a freehold estate therein in 1,000 acres of land, while in the exercise of his office....

SEC. 5. The governor and judges, or a majority of them, shall adopt and publish in the district such laws of the original States, criminal and civil, as may be necessary and best suited to the circumstances of the district, and report them to Congress from time to time: which laws shall be in force in the district until the organization of the General Assembly therein, unless disapproved of by Congress; but afterwards the Legislature shall have authority to alter them as they shall think fit.

SEC. 6. The governor, for the time being, shall be commander in chief of the militia, appoint and commission all officers in the same below the rank of general officers; all general officers shall be appointed and commissioned by Congress....

SEC. 9. So soon as there shall be five thousand free male inhabitants of full age in the district, upon giving proof thereof to the governor, they shall receive authority, with time and place, to elect a representative from their counties or townships to represent them in the general assembly: Provided, That, for every five hundred free male inhabitants, there shall be one representative, and so on progressively with the number of free male inhabitants shall the right of representation increase, until the number of representatives shall amount to twenty five; after which, the number and proportion of representatives shall be regulated by the legislature: Provided, That no person be eligible or qualified to act as a representative unless he shall have been a citizen of one of the United States three years, and be a resident in the district, or unless he shall have resided in the district three years; and, in either case, shall likewise hold in his own right, in fee simple, two hundred acres of land within the same; Provided, also, That a freehold in fifty acres of land in the district, having been a citizen of one of the states, and being resident in the district, or the like freehold and two years residence in the district, shall be necessary to qualify a man as an elector of a representative....

SEC. 11. The general assembly or legislature shall consist of the governor, legislative council, and a house of representatives.... And the governor, legislative council, and house of representatives, shall have authority to make laws in all cases, for the good government of the district, not repugnant to the principles and articles in this ordinance established and declared. And all bills, having passed by a majority in the house, and by a majority in the council, shall be referred to the governor for his assent; but no bill, or legislative act whatever, shall be of any force without his assent. The governor shall have power to convene, prorogue, and dissolve the general assembly, when, in his opinion, it shall be expedient....

SEC. 14. ART. 1. No person, demeaning himself in a peaceable and orderly manner, shall ever be molested on account of his mode of worship or religious sentiments, in the said territory....

ART. 3. Religion, morality, and knowledge, being necessary to good government and the happiness of mankind, schools and the means of education shall forever be encouraged. The utmost good faith shall always be observed towards the Indians; their lands and property shall never be taken from them without their consent; and, in their property, rights, and liberty, they shall never be invaded or disturbed, unless in just and lawful wars authorized by Congress; but laws founded in justice and humanity, shall from time to time be made for preventing wrongs being done to them, and for preserving peace and friendship with them....

ART. 5. There shall be formed in the said territory, not less than three nor more than five States; and the boundaries of the States, as soon as Virginia shall alter her act of cession, and consent to the same, shall become fixed and established.... Provided, however, and it is further understood and declared, that the boundaries of these three States shall be subject so far to be altered, that, if Congress shall hereafter find it expedient, they shall have authority to form one or two States in that part of the said territory which lies north of an east and west line drawn through the southerly bend or extreme of Lake Michigan. And, whenever any of the said States shall have sixty thousand free inhabitants therein, such State shall be admitted, by its delegates, into the Congress of the United States, on an equal footing with the original States in all respects whatever, and shall be at liberty to form a permanent constitution and State government: Provided, the constitution and government so to be formed, shall be republican, and in conformity to the principles contained in these articles; and, so far as it can be consistent with the general interest of the confederacy, such admission shall be allowed at an earlier period, and when there may be a less number of free inhabitants in the State than sixty thousand.

ART. 6. There shall be neither slavery nor involuntary servitude in the said territory, otherwise than in the punishment of crimes whereof the party shall have been duly convicted: Provided, always, That any person escaping into the same, from whom labor or service is lawfully claimed in any one of the original States, such fugitive may be lawfully reclaimed and conveyed to the person claiming his or her labor or service as aforesaid.

Be it ordained by the authority aforesaid, That the resolutions of the 23rd of April, 1784, relative to the subject of this ordinance, be, and the same are hereby repealed and declared null and void.

Done by the United States, in Congress assembled, the 13th day of July, in the year of our Lord 1787, and of their sovereignty and independence the twelfth.

1787

CONSTITUTION OF THE UNITED STATES

The Federal Convention convened in the State House (Independence Hall) in Philadelphia on May 14, 1787, to revise the Articles of Confederation, which, as many recognized, did not provide a sufficiently durable model for the new country. The delegates, including George Washington, Benjamin Franklin, Alexander Hamilton, and James Madison, believed that without revision, the Articles of Confederation would not protect the new country from foreign aggression or from simply disintegrating. Through discussion and debate it became clear by mid-June that rather than amend the existing Articles, the Convention would need to draft an entirely new frame of government, following the recommendations for a strong national government in the Virginia Plan. All through the summer the delegates debated and redrafted the articles of the new Constitution. Among the chief points at issue were how much power to allow the central government, how many representatives in Congress to allow each state, and how these representatives should be elected—directly by the people or by the state legislators. The work of many minds, the Constitution stands as a model of cooperative statesmanship and the art of compromise. Delegates to the Constitutional Convention drafted this four-page document secretly during the summer of 1787 and signed it into law on September 17, 1787, establishing the government of the United States.

We the People of the United States, in Order to form a more perfect Union, establish Justice, insure domestic Tranquility, provide for the common defense, promote the general Welfare, and secure the Blessings of Liberty to ourselves and our Posterity, do ordain and establish this Constitution for the United States of America.

ARTICLE. I.

SECTION. 1.

All legislative Powers herein granted shall be vested in a Congress of the United States, which shall consist of a Senate and House of Representatives.

SECTION. 2.

The House of Representatives shall be composed of Members chosen every second Year by the People of the several States, and the Electors in each State shall have the Qualifications requisite for Electors of the most numerous Branch of the State Legislature.

No Person shall be a Representative who shall not have attained to the Age of twenty five Years, and been seven Years a Citizen of the United States, and who shall not, when elected, be an Inhabitant of that State in which he shall be chosen.

Representatives and direct Taxes shall be apportioned among the several States which may be included within this Union, according to their respective Numbers, which shall be determined by adding to the whole Number of free Persons, including those bound to Service for a Term of Years, and excluding Indians not taxed, three fifths of all other Persons. The actual Enumeration shall be made within three Years after the first Meeting of the Congress of the United States, and within every subsequent Term of ten Years, in such Manner as they shall by Law direct. The Number of Representatives shall not exceed one for every thirty Thousand, but each State shall have at Least one Representative; and until such enumeration shall be made, the State of New Hampshire shall be entitled to chuse three, Massachusetts eight, Rhode-Island and Providence Plantations one, Connecticut five, New-York six, New Jersey four, Pennsylvania eight, Delaware one, Maryland six, Virginia ten, North Carolina five, South Carolina five, and Georgia three.

When vacancies happen in the Representation from any State, the Executive Authority thereof shall issue Writs of Election to fill such Vacancies.

The House of Representatives shall chuse their Speaker and other Officers; and shall have the sole Power of Impeachment.

SECTION. 3.

The Senate of the United States shall be composed of two Senators from each State, chosen by the

Legislature thereof for six Years; and each Senator shall have one Vote.

Immediately after they shall be assembled in Consequence of the first Election, they shall be divided as equally as may be into three Classes. The Seats of the Senators of the first Class shall be vacated at the Expiration of the second Year, of the second Class at the Expiration of the fourth Year, and of the third Class at the Expiration of the sixth Year, so that one third may be chosen every second Year; and if Vacancies happen by Resignation, or otherwise, during the Recess of the Legislature of any State, the Executive thereof may make temporary Appointments until the next Meeting of the Legislature, which shall then fill such Vacancies.

No Person shall be a Senator who shall not have attained to the Age of thirty Years, and been nine Years a Citizen of the United States, and who shall not, when elected, be an Inhabitant of that State for which he shall be chosen.

The Vice President of the United States shall be President of the Senate, but shall have no Vote, unless they be equally divided.

The Senate shall chuse their other Officers, and also a President pro tempore, in the Absence of the Vice President, or when he shall exercise the Office of President of the United States.

The Senate shall have the sole Power to try all Impeachments. When sitting for that Purpose, they shall be on Oath or Affirmation. When the President of the United States is tried, the Chief Justice shall preside: And no Person shall be convicted without the Concurrence of two thirds of the Members present.

Judgment in Cases of Impeachment shall not extend further than to removal from Office, and disqualification to hold and enjoy any Office of honor, Trust or Profit under the United States: but the Party convicted shall nevertheless be liable and subject to Indictment, Trial, Judgment and Punishment, according to Law.

Section. 4.

The Times, Places and Manner of holding Elections for Senators and Representatives, shall be prescribed in each State by the Legislature thereof; but the Congress may at any time by Law make or alter such Regulations, except as to the Places of chusing Senators.

The Congress shall assemble at least once in every Year, and such Meeting shall be on the first Monday in December, unless they shall by Law appoint a different Day.

Section. 5.

Each House shall be the Judge of the Elections, Returns and Qualifications of its own Members, and a Majority of each shall constitute a Quorum to do Business; but a smaller Number may adjourn from day to day, and may be authorized to compel the Attendance of absent Members, in such Manner, and under such Penalties as each House may provide.

Each House may determine the Rules of its Proceedings, punish its Members for disorderly Behaviour, and, with the Concurrence of two thirds, expel a Member.

Each House shall keep a Journal of its Proceedings, and from time to time publish the same, excepting such Parts as may in their Judgment require Secrecy; and the Yeas and Nays of the Members of either House on any question shall, at the Desire of one fifth of those Present, be entered on the Journal.

Neither House, during the Session of Congress, shall, without the Consent of the other, adjourn for more than three days, nor to any other Place than that in which the two Houses shall be sitting.

Section. 6.

The Senators and Representatives shall receive a Compensation for their Services, to be ascertained by Law, and paid out of the Treasury of the United States. They shall in all Cases, except Treason, Felony and Breach of the Peace, be privileged from Arrest during their Attendance at the Session of their respective Houses, and in going to and returning from the same; and for any Speech or Debate in either House, they shall not be questioned in any other Place.

No Senator or Representative shall, during the Time for which he was elected, be appointed to any civil Office under the Authority of the United States, which shall have been created, or the Emoluments whereof shall have been encreased during such time; and no Person holding any Office under the United States, shall be a Member of either House during his Continuance in Office.

Section. 7.

All Bills for raising Revenue shall originate in the House of Representatives; but the Senate may propose or concur with Amendments as on other Bills.

Every Bill which shall have passed the House of Representatives and the Senate, shall, before it become a Law, be presented to the President of the United States: If he approve he shall sign it, but if not he shall return it, with his Objections to that House in which it shall have originated, who shall enter the Objections at

large on their Journal, and proceed to reconsider it. If after such Reconsideration two thirds of that House shall agree to pass the Bill, it shall be sent, together with the Objections, to the other House, by which it shall likewise be reconsidered, and if approved by two thirds of that House, it shall become a Law. But in all such Cases the Votes of both Houses shall be determined by yeas and Nays, and the Names of the Persons voting for and against the Bill shall be entered on the Journal of each House respectively. If any Bill shall not be returned by the President within ten Days (Sundays excepted) after it shall have been presented to him, the Same shall be a Law, in like Manner as if he had signed it, unless the Congress by their Adjournment prevent its Return, in which Case it shall not be a Law.

Every Order, Resolution, or Vote to which the Concurrence of the Senate and House of Representatives may be necessary (except on a question of Adjournment) shall be presented to the President of the United States; and before the Same shall take Effect, shall be approved by him, or being disapproved by him, shall be repassed by two thirds of the Senate and House of Representatives, according to the Rules and Limitations prescribed in the Case of a Bill.

SECTION. 8.

The Congress shall have Power To lay and collect Taxes, Duties, Imposts and Excises, to pay the Debts and provide for the common Defence and general Welfare of the United States; but all Duties, Imposts and Excises shall be uniform throughout the United States;

To borrow Money on the credit of the United States;

To regulate Commerce with foreign Nations, and among the several States, and with the Indian Tribes;

To establish an uniform Rule of Naturalization, and uniform Laws on the subject of Bankruptcies throughout the United States;

To coin Money, regulate the Value thereof, and of foreign Coin, and fix the Standard of Weights and Measures;

To provide for the Punishment of counterfeiting the Securities and current Coin of the United States;

To establish Post Offices and post Roads;

To promote the Progress of Science and useful Arts, by securing for limited Times to Authors and Inventors the exclusive Right to their respective Writings and Discoveries;

To constitute Tribunals inferior to the supreme Court;

To define and punish Piracies and Felonies committed on the high Seas, and Offences against the Law of Nations;

To declare War, grant Letters of Marque and Reprisal, and make Rules concerning Captures on Land and Water;

To raise and support Armies, but no Appropriation of Money to that Use shall be for a longer Term than two Years;

To provide and maintain a Navy;

To make Rules for the Government and Regulation of the land and naval Forces;

To provide for calling forth the Militia to execute the Laws of the Union, suppress Insurrections and repel Invasions;

To provide for organizing, arming, and disciplining, the Militia, and for governing such Part of them as may be employed in the Service of the United States, reserving to the States respectively, the Appointment of the Officers, and the Authority of training the Militia according to the discipline prescribed by Congress;

To exercise exclusive Legislation in all Cases whatsoever, over such District (not exceeding ten Miles square) as may, by Cession of particular States, and the Acceptance of Congress, become the Seat of the Government of the United States, and to exercise like Authority over all Places purchased by the Consent of the Legislature of the State in which the Same shall be, for the Erection of Forts, Magazines, Arsenals, dockYards, and other needful Buildings;—And

To make all Laws which shall be necessary and proper for carrying into Execution the foregoing Powers, and all other Powers vested by this Constitution in the Government of the United States, or in any Department or Officer thereof.

SECTION. 9.

The Migration or Importation of such Persons as any of the States now existing shall think proper to admit, shall not be prohibited by the Congress prior to the Year one thousand eight hundred and eight, but a Tax or duty may be imposed on such Importation, not exceeding ten dollars for each Person.

The Privilege of the Writ of Habeas Corpus shall not be suspended, unless when in Cases of Rebellion or Invasion the public Safety may require it.

No Bill of Attainder or ex post facto Law shall be passed.

No Capitation, or other direct, Tax shall be laid, unless in Proportion to the Census or enumeration herein before directed to be taken.

No Tax or Duty shall be laid on Articles exported from any State.

No Preference shall be given by any Regulation of Commerce or Revenue to the Ports of one State over those of another; nor shall Vessels bound to, or from, one State, be obliged to enter, clear, or pay Duties in another.

No Money shall be drawn from the Treasury, but in Consequence of Appropriations made by Law; and a regular Statement and Account of the Receipts and Expenditures of all public Money shall be published from time to time.

No Title of Nobility shall be granted by the United States: And no Person holding any Office of Profit or Trust under them, shall, without the Consent of the Congress, accept of any present, Emolument, Office, or Title, of any kind whatever, from any King, Prince, or foreign State.

SECTION. 10.

No State shall enter into any Treaty, Alliance, or Confederation; grant Letters of Marque and Reprisal; coin Money; emit Bills of Credit; make any Thing but gold and silver Coin a Tender in Payment of Debts; pass any Bill of Attainder, ex post facto Law, or Law impairing the Obligation of Contracts, or grant any Title of Nobility.

No State shall, without the Consent of the Congress, lay any Imposts or Duties on Imports or Exports, except what may be absolutely necessary for executing it's inspection Laws: and the net Produce of all Duties and Imposts, laid by any State on Imports or Exports, shall be for the Use of the Treasury of the United States; and all such Laws shall be subject to the Revision and Controul of the Congress.

No State shall, without the Consent of Congress, lay any Duty of Tonnage, keep Troops, or Ships of War in time of Peace, enter into any Agreement or Compact with another State, or with a foreign Power, or engage in War, unless actually invaded, or in such imminent Danger as will not admit of delay.

ARTICLE. II.

SECTION. 1.

The executive Power shall be vested in a President of the United States of America. He shall hold his Office during the Term of four Years, and, together with the Vice President, chosen for the same Term, be elected, as follows:

Each State shall appoint, in such Manner as the Legislature thereof may direct, a Number of Electors, equal to the whole Number of Senators and Represen-tatives to which the State may be entitled in the Congress: but no Senator or Representative, or Person holding an Office of Trust or Profit under the United States, shall be appointed an Elector.

The Electors shall meet in their respective States, and vote by Ballot for two Persons, of whom one at least shall not be an Inhabitant of the same State with themselves. And they shall make a List of all the Persons voted for, and of the Number of Votes for each; which List they shall sign and certify, and transmit sealed to the Seat of the Government of the United States, directed to the President of the Senate. The President of the Senate shall, in the Presence of the Senate and House of Representatives, open all the Certificates, and the Votes shall then be counted. The Person having the greatest Number of Votes shall be the President, if such Number be a Majority of the whole Number of Electors appointed; and if there be more than one who have such Majority, and have an equal Number of Votes, then the House of Representatives shall immediately chuse by Ballot one of them for President; and if no Person have a Majority, then from the five highest on the List the said House shall in like Manner chuse the President. But in chusing the President, the Votes shall be taken by States, the Representation from each State having one Vote; A quorum for this purpose shall consist of a Member or Members from two thirds of the States, and a Majority of all the States shall be necessary to a Choice. In every Case, after the Choice of the President, the Person having the greatest Number of Votes of the Electors shall be the Vice President. But if there should remain two or more who have equal Votes, the Senate shall chuse from them by Ballot the Vice President.

The Congress may determine the Time of chusing the Electors, and the Day on which they shall give their Votes; which Day shall be the same throughout the United States.

No Person except a natural born Citizen, or a Citizen of the United States, at the time of the Adoption of this Constitution, shall be eligible to the Office of President; neither shall any Person be eligible to that Office who shall not have attained to the Age of thirty five Years, and been fourteen Years a Resident within the United States.

In Case of the Removal of the President from Office, or of his Death, Resignation, or Inability to discharge the Powers and Duties of the said Office, the Same shall devolve on the Vice President, and the Congress may by Law provide for the Case of Removal, Death, Resignation or Inability, both of the President and Vice

This mural of the signing of the U.S. Constitution decorates the rotunda of the National Archives and Records Administration.

President, declaring what Officer shall then act as President, and such Officer shall act accordingly, until the Disability be removed, or a President shall be elected.

The President shall, at stated Times, receive for his Services, a Compensation, which shall neither be increased nor diminished during the Period for which he shall have been elected, and he shall not receive within that Period any other Emolument from the United States, or any of them.

Before he enter on the Execution of his Office, he shall take the following Oath or Affirmation:—"I do solemnly swear (or affirm) that I will faithfully execute the Office of President of the United States, and will to the best of my Ability, preserve, protect and defend the Constitution of the United States."

Section. 2.

The President shall be Commander in Chief of the Army and Navy of the United States, and of the Militia of the several States, when called into the actual Service of the United States; he may require the Opinion, in writing, of the principal Officer in each of the executive Departments, upon any Subject relating to the Duties of their respective Offices, and he shall have Power to grant Reprieves and Pardons for Offences against the United States, except in Cases of Impeachment.

He shall have Power, by and with the Advice and Consent of the Senate, to make Treaties, provided two thirds of the Senators present concur; and he shall nominate, and by and with the Advice and Consent of the Senate, shall appoint Ambassadors, other public Ministers and Consuls, Judges of the supreme Court, and all other Officers of the United States, whose Appointments are not herein otherwise provided for, and which shall be established by Law: but the Congress may by Law vest the Appointment of such inferior Officers, as they think proper, in the President alone, in the Courts of Law, or in the Heads of Departments.

The President shall have Power to fill up all Vacancies that may happen during the Recess of the Senate, by granting Commissions which shall expire at the End of their next Session.

Section. 3.

He shall from time to time give to the Congress Information of the State of the Union, and recommend to their Consideration such Measures as he shall judge necessary and expedient; he may, on extraordinary Occasions, convene both Houses, or either of them, and in Case of Disagreement between them, with Respect to the Time of Adjournment, he may adjourn them to such Time as he shall think proper; he shall receive Ambassadors and other public Ministers; he shall take Care that the Laws be faithfully executed, and shall Commission all the Officers of the United States.

Section. 4.

The President, Vice President and all civil Officers of the United States, shall be removed from Office on Impeachment for, and Conviction of, Treason, Bribery, or other high Crimes and Misdemeanors.

ARTICLE. III.

Section. 1.

The judicial Power of the United States shall be vested in one supreme Court, and in such inferior Courts as the Congress may from time to time ordain and establish. The Judges, both of the supreme and inferior Courts, shall hold their Offices during good Behaviour, and shall, at stated Times, receive for their Services a Compensation, which shall not be diminished during their Continuance in Office.

Section. 2.

The judicial Power shall extend to all Cases, in Law and Equity, arising under this Constitution, the Laws of the United States, and Treaties made, or which shall be made, under their Authority;—to all Cases affecting Ambassadors, other public Ministers and Consuls;—to all Cases of admiralty and maritime Jurisdiction;—to Controversies to which the United States shall be a Party;—to Controversies between two or more States;—between a State and Citizens of another State;—between Citizens of different States;—between Citizens of the same State claiming Lands under Grants of different States, and between a State, or the Citizens thereof, and foreign States, Citizens or Subjects.

In all Cases affecting Ambassadors, other public Ministers and Consuls, and those in which a State shall be Party, the supreme Court shall have original Jurisdiction. In all the other Cases before mentioned, the supreme Court shall have appellate Jurisdiction, both as to Law and Fact, with such Exceptions, and under such Regulations as the Congress shall make.

The Trial of all Crimes, except in Cases of Impeachment, shall be by Jury; and such Trial shall be held in the State where the said Crimes shall have been committed; but when not committed within any State, the Trial shall be at such Place or Places as the Congress may by Law have directed.

SECTION. 3.

Treason against the United States, shall consist only in levying War against them, or in adhering to their Enemies, giving them Aid and Comfort. No Person shall be convicted of Treason unless on the Testimony of two Witnesses to the same overt Act, or on Confession in open Court.

The Congress shall have Power to declare the Punishment of Treason, but no Attainder of Treason shall work Corruption of Blood, or Forfeiture except during the Life of the Person attainted.

ARTICLE. IV.

SECTION. 1.

Full Faith and Credit shall be given in each State to the public Acts, Records, and judicial Proceedings of every other State. And the Congress may by general Laws prescribe the Manner in which such Acts, Records and Proceedings shall be proved, and the Effect thereof.

SECTION. 2.

The Citizens of each State shall be entitled to all Privileges and Immunities of Citizens in the several States.

A Person charged in any State with Treason, Felony, or other Crime, who shall flee from Justice, and be found in another State, shall on Demand of the executive Authority of the State from which he fled, be delivered

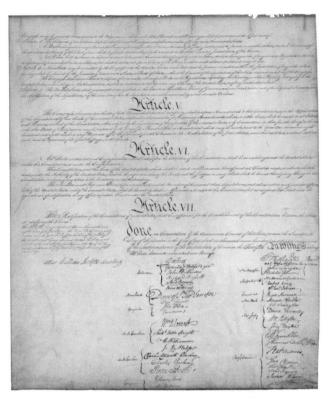

The signatures on the Constitution are organized by state.

up, to be removed to the State having Jurisdiction of the Crime.

No Person held to Service or Labour in one State, under the Laws thereof, escaping into another, shall, in Consequence of any Law or Regulation therein, be discharged from such Service or Labour, but shall be delivered up on Claim of the Party to whom such Service or Labour may be due.

SECTION. 3.

New States may be admitted by the Congress into this Union; but no new State shall be formed or erected within the Jurisdiction of any other State; nor any State be formed by the Junction of two or more States, or Parts of States, without the Consent of the Legislatures of the States concerned as well as of the Congress.

The Congress shall have Power to dispose of and make all needful Rules and Regulations respecting the Territory or other Property belonging to the United States; and nothing in this Constitution shall be so construed as to Prejudice any Claims of the United States, or of any particular State.

SECTION. 4.

The United States shall guarantee to every State in this Union a Republican Form of Government, and shall protect each of them against Invasion; and on Application of the Legislature, or of the Executive (when the Legislature cannot be convened), against domestic Violence.

ARTICLE. V.

The Congress, whenever two thirds of both Houses shall deem it necessary, shall propose Amendments to this Constitution, or, on the Application of the Legislatures of two thirds of the several States, shall call a Convention for proposing Amendments, which, in either Case, shall be valid to all Intents and Purposes, as Part of this Constitution, when ratified by the Legislatures of three fourths of the several States, or by Conventions in three fourths thereof, as the one or the other Mode of Ratification may be proposed by the Congress; Provided that no Amendment which may be made prior to the Year One thousand eight hundred and eight shall in any Manner affect the first and fourth Clauses in the Ninth Section of the first Article; and that no State, without its Consent, shall be deprived of its equal Suffrage in the Senate.

ARTICLE. VI.

All Debts contracted and Engagements entered into, before the Adoption of this Constitution, shall be as valid against the United States under this Constitution, as under the Confederation.

This Constitution, and the Laws of the United States which shall be made in Pursuance thereof; and all Treaties made, or which shall be made, under the Authority of the United States, shall be the supreme Law of the Land; and the Judges in every State shall be bound thereby, any Thing in the Constitution or Laws of any State to the Contrary notwithstanding.

The Senators and Representatives before mentioned, and the Members of the several State Legislatures, and all executive and judicial Officers, both of the United States and of the several States, shall be bound by Oath or Affirmation, to support this Constitution; but no religious Test shall ever be required as a Qualification to any Office or public Trust under the United States.

ARTICLE. VII.

The Ratification of the Conventions of nine States, shall be sufficient for the Establishment of this Constitution between the States so ratifying the Same.

The Word, "the," being interlined between the seventh and eighth Lines of the first Page, the Word "Thirty" being partly written on an Erazure in the fifteenth Line of the first Page, The Words "is tried" being interlined between the thirty second and thirty third Lines of the first Page and the Word "the" being interlined between the forty third and forty fourth Lines of the second Page.

ATTEST WILLIAM JACKSON SECRETARY

Done in Convention by the Unanimous Consent of the States present the Seventeenth Day of September in the Year of our Lord one thousand seven hundred and Eighty seven and of the Independence of the United States of America the Twelfth In witness whereof We have hereunto subscribed our Names,

G. WASHINGTON
Presidt and deputy from Virginia

DELAWARE
GEO: READ
GUNNING BEDFORD JUN
JOHN DICKINSON
RICHARD BASSETT
JACO: BROOM

MARYLAND
JAMES MCHENRY
DAN OF ST THOS. JENIFER
DANL. CARROLL

VIRGINIA
JOHN BLAIR
JAMES MADISON JR.

NORTH CAROLINA
WM. BLOUNT
RICHD. DOBBS SPAIGHT
HU WILLIAMSON

SOUTH CAROLINA
J. RUTLEDGE
CHARLES COTESWORTH PINCKNEY
CHARLES PINCKNEY
PIERCE BUTLER

GEORGIA
WILLIAM FEW
ABR BALDWIN

NEW HAMPSHIRE
JOHN LANGDON
NICHOLAS GILMAN

MASSACHUSETTS
NATHANIEL GORHAM
RUFUS KING

CONNECTICUT
WM. SAML. JOHNSON
ROGER SHERMAN

NEW YORK
ALEXANDER HAMILTON

NEW JERSEY
WIL: LIVINGSTON
DAVID BREARLEY
WM. PATERSON
JONA: DAYTON

PENNSYLVANIA
B FRANKLIN
THOMAS MIFFLIN
ROBT. MORRIS
GEO. CLYMER
THOS. FITZSIMONS
JARED INGERSOLL
JAMES WILSON
GOUV MORRIS

1787–1788

FEDERALIST PAPERS, No. 10 & No. 51

*U*rging the citizens of New York to support ratification of the proposed U.S. Constitution, the Federalist Papers *were a series of eighty-five essays, published anonymously under the pen name "Publius," which appeared primarily in two New York state newspapers: the* New York Packet *and the* Independent Journal. *"Publius" was a made-up name that purposefully invoked the Latin* publicus—*"of the people." Authors James Madison, Alexander Hamilton, and John Jay used these essays to provide detailed explanations of particular provisions of the Constitution.*

The printers J. and A. McLean published a bound edition of the essays, with revisions and corrections by Hamilton, in 1788. In 1818 printer Jacob Gideon published a later edition with revisions and corrections by Madison, and this was the first edition to specify the authorship of each essay. The assignment of authorship, numbering of essays, and exact wording vary with different editions of The Federalist.

Because the purpose of the Federalist Papers *was to promote the ratification of the Constitution, people often consult them today to better understand the intentions of the original drafters of the Constitution. The essays included here are* Federalist No. 10 *and* Federalist No. 51. *The former, written by James Madison, refuted the belief that it was impossible to extend a republican government over a large territory and argued that in fact its large size would impede efforts by factions or special interest groups to pass legislation. The latter emphasized the importance of checks and balances within a government. Although they did not seriously affect the vote in New York, the insightful essays enhance understanding of those who framed the Constitution and have deeply influenced later interpretations.*

The Same Subject Continued: The Union as a Safeguard Against Domestic Faction and Insurrection

THE FEDERALIST No. X

TO THE PEOPLE OF THE STATE OF NEW YORK:

AMONG the numerous advantages promised by a well constructed Union, none deserves to be more accurately developed than its tendency to break and control the violence of faction. The friend of popular governments never finds himself so much alarmed for their character and fate, as when he contemplates their propensity to this dangerous vice. He will not fail, therefore, to set a due value on any plan which, without violating the principles to which he is attached, provides a proper cure for it. The instability, injustice, and confusion introduced into the public councils, have, in truth, been the mortal diseases under which popular governments have everywhere perished; as they continue to be the favorite and fruitful topics from which the adversaries to liberty derive their most specious declamations. The valuable improvements made by the American constitutions on the popular models, both ancient and modern, cannot certainly be too much admired; but it would be an unwarrantable partiality, to contend that they have as effectually obviated the danger on this side, as was wished and expected....a pure democracy, by which I mean a society consisting of a small number of citizens, who assemble and administer the government in person, can admit of no cure for the mischiefs of faction. A common passion or interest will, in almost every case, be felt by a majority of the whole;

"[W]hat is government itself, but the greatest of all reflections on human nature?"

The Federalist No. 51, entitled
"The Structure of the Government Must
Furnish the Proper Checks and Balances
Between the Different Departments,"
was published in the New York Packet
on February 8, 1788.

different prospect, and promises the cure for which we are seeking. Let us examine the points in which it varies from pure democracy, and we shall comprehend both the nature of the cure and the efficacy which it must derive from the Union.

The two great points of difference between a democracy and a republic are: first, the delegation of the government, in the latter, to a small number of citizens elected by the rest; secondly, the greater number of citizens, and greater sphere of country, over which the latter may be extended....

The question resulting is, whether small or extensive republics are more favorable to the election of proper guardians of the public weal; and it is clearly decided in favor of the latter by two obvious considerations:

In the first place, it is to be remarked that, however small the republic may be, the representatives must be raised to a certain number, in order to guard against the cabals of a few; and that, however large it may be, they must be limited to a certain number, in order to guard against the confusion of a multitude. Hence, the number of representatives in the two cases not being in proportion to that of the two constituents, and being proportionally greater in the small republic, it follows that, if the proportion of fit characters be not less in the large than in the small republic, the former will present a greater option, and consequently a greater probability of a fit choice.

In the next place, as each representative will be chosen by a greater number of citizens in the large than in the small republic, it will be more difficult for

a communication and concert result from the form of government itself; and there is nothing to check the inducements to sacrifice the weaker party or an obnoxious individual. Hence it is that such democracies have ever been spectacles of turbulence and contention; have ever been found incompatible with personal security or the rights of property; and have in general been as short in their lives as they have been violent in their deaths....

A republic, by which I mean a government in which the scheme of representation takes place, opens a unworthy candidates to practice with success the vicious arts by which elections are too often carried; and the suffrages of the people being more free, will be more likely to centre in men who possess the most attractive merit and the most diffusive and established characters.

It must be confessed that in this, as in most other cases, there is a mean, on both sides of which inconveniences will be found to lie. By enlarging too much the number of electors, you render the representatives too little acquainted with all their local circumstances and lesser interests; as by reducing it too much, you render him unduly attached to these, and too little fit to comprehend and pursue great and national objects. The federal Constitution forms a happy combination in this respect; the great and aggregate interests being referred to the national, the local and particular to the State legislatures....

In the extent and proper structure of the Union, therefore, we behold a republican remedy for the diseases most incident to republican government. And according to the degree of pleasure and pride we feel in being republicans, ought to be our zeal in cherishing the spirit and supporting the character of Federalists.

Publius.

The Structure of the Government Must Furnish the Proper Checks and Balances Between the Different Departments

The Federalist No. 51

To the People of the State of New York:

TO WHAT expedient, then, shall we finally resort, for maintaining in practice the necessary partition of power among the several departments, as laid down in the Constitution? The only answer that can be given is, that as all these exterior provisions are found to be inadequate, the defect must be supplied, by so contriving the interior structure of the government as that its several constituent parts may, by their mutual relations, be the means of keeping each other in their proper places....

In order to lay a due foundation for that separate and distinct exercise of the different powers of government, which to a certain extent is admitted on all hands to be essential to the preservation of liberty, it is

"In framing a government which is to be administered by men over men, the great difficulty lies in this: you must first enable the government to control the governed; and in the next place oblige it to control itself."

evident that each department should have a will of its own; and consequently should be so constituted that the members of each should have as little agency as possible in the appointment of the members of the others....

It is equally evident, that the members of each department should be as little dependent as possible on those of the others, for the emoluments annexed to their offices. Were the executive magistrate, or the judges, not independent of the legislature in this particular, their independence in every other would be merely nominal. But the great security against a gradual concentration of the several powers in the same department, consists in giving to those who administer each department the necessary constitutional means and personal motives to resist encroachments of the others. The provision for defense must in this, as in all other cases, be made commensurate to the danger of attack. Ambition must be made to counteract ambition. The interest of the man must be connected with the constitutional rights of the place. It may be a reflection on human nature, that such devices should be necessary to control the abuses of government. But what is government itself, but the greatest of all reflections on human nature? If men were angels, no government would be necessary. If angels were to govern men, neither external nor internal controls on government would be necessary. In framing a government which is to be administered by men over men, the great difficulty lies in this: you must first enable the government to control the governed; and in the next place oblige it to control itself.

Publius.

1789

PRESIDENT GEORGE WASHINGTON'S
FIRST INAUGURAL SPEECH

O n April 16, 1789, two days after receiving official notification of his election as President, George Washington left his home in Virginia for New York City, which was then the capital of the United States. All along his route, artillery roared salutes of honor and the citizens and officials presented him with tokens of affection and respect, so that his trip became a triumphal procession. On April 23 he crossed the bay from Bridgetown, New Jersey, to New York City in a magnificent barge built especially for the occasion. On inauguration day the city was crowded with townspeople and visitors. At half past noon, Washington rode alone in the state coach from his quarters in Franklin Square to Federal Hall on the corner of Wall and Nassau Streets. Troops of the city, members of Congress appointed to escort the President, and heads of executive departments of the government under the Confederation preceded the President's coach, while to the rear followed ministers of foreign countries and local citizenry.

On the balcony, before the assembled crowd of spectators, Robert Livingston, chancellor of the State of New York, administered the oath of office prescribed by the Constitution: "I do solemnly swear that I will faithfully execute the office of President of the United States, and will, to the best of my ability, preserve, protect, and defend the Constitution of the United States." The law required no further ceremonies, but, in the Senate chamber, the President read an inaugural address. Washington knew that many feared the new role of president and worried that the country could become a new monarchy. In his inaugural address, he tried to reassure citizens of his own honesty and prevent fears of unlimited executive power.

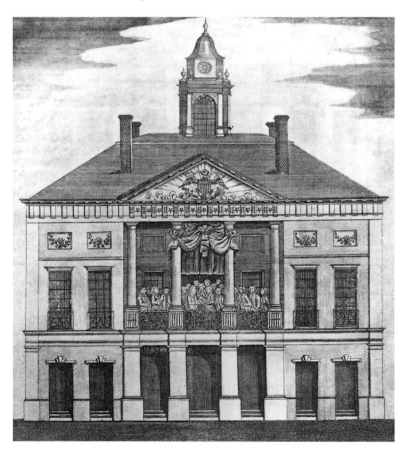

The chancellor of the State of New York, Robert Livingston, administered the oath of office to George Washington on the balcony of Federal Hall, the first seat of Congress, on April 30, 1789. The Congressional committee that planned the inauguration instructed that the oath be administered "in the most public manner, and that the greatest number of people of the United States, and without distinction, may witness the solemnity."

FELLOW-CITIZENS OF THE SENATE AND OF THE HOUSE OF REPRESENTATIVES:

Among the vicissitudes incident to life no event could have filled me with greater anxieties than that of which the notification was transmitted by your order, and received on the 14th day of the present month. On the one hand, I was summoned by my Country, whose voice I can never hear but with veneration and love, from a retreat which I had chosen with the fondest predilection, and, in my flattering hopes, with an immutable decision, as the asylum of my declining years—a retreat which was rendered every day more necessary as well as more dear to me by the addition of habit to inclination, and of frequent interruptions in my health to the gradual waste committed on it by time. On the other hand, the magnitude and difficulty of the trust to which the voice of my country called me, being sufficient to awaken in the wisest and most experienced of her citizens a distrustful scrutiny into his qualifications, could not but overwhelm with despondence one who (inheriting inferior endowments from nature and unpracticed in the duties of civil administration) ought to be peculiarly conscious of his own deficiencies. In this conflict of emotions all I dare aver is that it has been my faithful study to collect my duty from a just appreciation of every circumstance by which it might be affected. All I dare hope is that if, in executing this task, I have been too much swayed by a grateful remembrance of former instances, or by an affectionate sensibility to this transcendent proof of the confidence of my fellow-citizens, and have thence too little consulted my incapacity as well as disinclination for the weighty and untried cares before me, my error will be palliated by the motives which mislead me, and its consequences be judged by my country with some share of the partiality in which they originated.

Such being the impressions under which I have, in obedience to the public summons, repaired to the pres-

"[T]here exists in the economy and course of nature an indissoluble union between virtue and happiness; between duty and advantage; between the genuine maxims of an honest and magnanimous policy and the solid rewards of public prosperity and felicity. . . ."

ent station, it would be peculiarly improper to omit in this first official act my fervent supplications to that Almighty Being who rules over the universe, who presides in the councils of nations, and whose providential aids can supply every human defect, that His benediction may consecrate to the liberties and happiness of the people of the United States a Government instituted by themselves for these essential purposes, and may enable every instrument employed in its administration to execute with success the functions allotted to his charge. In tendering this homage to the Great Author of every public and private good, I assure myself that it expresses your sentiments not less than my own, nor those of my fellow-citizens at large less than either. No people can be bound to acknowledge and adore the Invisible Hand which conducts the affairs of men more than those of the United States. . . .

By the article establishing the executive department it is made the duty of the President "to recommend to your consideration such measures as he shall judge necessary and expedient." The circumstances under which I now meet you will acquit me from entering into that subject further than to refer to the great constitutional charter under which you are assembled, and which, in defining your powers, designates the objects to which your attention is to be given. It will be more consistent with those circumstances, and far more congenial with the feelings which actuate me, to substitute, in place of a recommendation of particular measures, the tribute that is due to the talents, the rectitude, and the patriotism which adorn the characters selected to devise and adopt them. In these honorable qualifications I behold the surest pledges that as on one side no local prejudices or attachments, no separate views nor party animosities, will misdirect the comprehensive and equal eye which ought to watch over this great assemblage of communities and interests, so, on another, that the foundation of our national policy will be laid in the pure and immutable principles of private morality, and the preeminence of free government be exemplified by all the attributes which can win the affections of its citizens and command the respect of the world. I dwell on this prospect with every satisfaction which an ardent love for my country can inspire, since there is no truth more thoroughly established than that there exists in the economy and course of nature an indissoluble union between virtue and happiness; between duty and advantage; between the genuine maxims of an honest and magnanimous policy and the solid rewards of public prosperity and felicity; since we ought to be no less persuaded that the propitious smiles of Heaven can never

Fellow Citizens of the Senate
and
of the House of Representatives.

Among the vicissitudes incident to life, no event could have filled me with greater anxieties than that of which the notification was transmitted by your order, and received on the fourteenth day of the present month:—On the one hand, I was summoned by my Country, whose voice I can never hear but with veneration and love, from a retreat which I had chosen with the fondest predilection, and, in my flattering hopes, with an immutable decision, as the asylum of my declining years: a retreat which was rendered every day more necessary as well as more dear to me, by the addition of habit to inclination, and of frequent interruptions in my health to the gradual waste committed on it by time.—On the other hand, the magnitude and difficulty of the trust to which the voice of my Country called me, being sufficient to awaken in the wisest and most experienced of her citizens, a distrustful

fifth article of the Constitution is rendered expedient at the present juncture by the nature of objections which have been urged against the system, or by the degree of inquietude which has given birth to them. Instead of undertaking particular recommendations on this subject, in which I could be guided by no lights derived from official opportunities, I shall again give way to my entire confidence in your discernment and pursuit of the public good; for I assure myself that whilst you carefully avoid every alteration which might endanger the benefits of an united and effective government, or which ought to await the future lessons of experience, a reverence for the characteristic rights of freemen and a regard for the public harmony will sufficiently influence your deliberations on the question how far the former can be impregnably fortified or the latter be safely and advantageously promoted.

To the foregoing observations I have one to add, which will be most properly addressed to the House of Representatives. It concerns myself, and will therefore be as brief as possible. When I was first honored with a call into the service of my country, then on the eve of an arduous struggle for its liberties, the light in which I contemplated my duty required that I should renounce every pecuniary compensation. From this resolution I have in no instance departed; and being still under the impressions which produced it, I must decline as inapplicable to myself any share in the personal emoluments which may be indispensably included in a permanent provision for the executive department, and must accordingly pray that the pecuniary estimates for the station in which I am placed may during my continuance in it be limited to such actual expenditures as the public good may be thought to require....

be expected on a nation that disregards the eternal rules of order and right which Heaven itself has ordained; and since the preservation of the sacred fire of liberty and the destiny of the republican model of government are justly considered, perhaps, as deeply, as finally, staked on the experiment entrusted to the hands of the American people.

Besides the ordinary objects submitted to your care, it will remain with your judgment to decide how far an exercise of the occasional power delegated by the

1789

FEDERAL JUDICIARY ACT

*T*he founders of the new nation believed that the establishment of a national judiciary was one of their most important tasks. Yet Article III of the Constitution of the United States, which focuses on the judiciary branch of government, is markedly smaller than Articles I and II, which created the legislative and executive branches. The generalizations of Article III raised questions that remained for Congress to address. One of the first acts of the new Congress was to establish a federal court system through the Judiciary Act, which President Washington signed into law on September 24, 1789. The First Congress decided that it could regulate the jurisdiction of all federal courts, and the Judiciary Act established in great detail a limited jurisdiction for the district and circuit courts.

It gave the Supreme Court the original jurisdiction provided for in the Constitution and granted the Court appellate jurisdiction in cases from the federal circuit courts and from the state courts where rulings had rejected federal claims. With minor adjustments, today's federal court system closely resembles the one created in 1789. Although opinions on the proper balance between federal and state concerns vary no less today than they did two centuries ago, the fact that today's federal court system closely resembles the one created in 1789 suggests that the First Congress performed its job admirably.

CHAP. XX. An Act to establish the Judicial Courts of the United States.

SECTION 1. Be it enacted by the Senate and House of Representatives of the United States of America in Congress assembled, That the supreme court of the United States shall consist of a chief justice and five associate justices, any four of whom shall be a quorum, and shall hold annually at the seat of government two sessions, the one commencing the first Monday of February, and the other the first Monday of August. . . .

SEC. 2. And be it further enacted, That the United States shall be, and they hereby are divided into thirteen districts. . . .

SEC. 3. And be it further enacted, That there be a court called a District Court, in each of the aforemen-tioned districts, to consist of one judge, who shall reside in the district for which he is appointed, and shall be called a District Judge, and shall hold annually four sessions, . . .

SEC. 4. And be it further enacted, That the before mentioned districts, except those of Maine and Kentucky, shall be divided into three circuits, and be called the eastern, the middle, and the southern circuit. . . . and that there shall be held annually in each district of said circuits, two courts, which shall be called Circuit Courts, and shall consist of any two justices of the Supreme Court, and the district judge of such districts, any two of whom shall constitute a quorum: Provided, That no district judge shall give a vote in any case of appeal or error from his own decision. . . .

SEC. 9. And be it further enacted, That the district courts shall have, exclusively of the courts of the several States, cognizance of all crimes and offences that shall be cognizable under the authority of the United States, committed within their respective districts, or upon the high seas; where no other punishment than whipping, not exceeding thirty stripes, a fine not exceeding one hundred dollars, or a term of imprisonment not exceeding six months, is to be inflicted; . . .

SEC. 11. And be it further enacted, That the circuit courts shall have original cognizance, concurrent with the courts of the several States, of all suits of a civil nature at common law or in equity, where the matter in dispute exceeds, exclusive of costs, the sum or value of five hundred dollars, and the United States are plaintiffs, or petitioners; or an alien is a party, or the suit is between a citizen of the State where the suit is brought, and a citizen of another State. . . .

SEC. 13. And be it further enacted, That the Supreme Court shall have exclusive jurisdiction of all controversies of a civil nature, where a state is a party, except between a state and its citizens; and except also between a state and citizens of other states, or aliens, in which latter case it shall have original but not exclusive jurisdiction. . . .

SEC. 24. And be it further enacted, That when a judgment or decree shall be reversed in a circuit court, such court shall proceed to render such judgment or pass such decree as the district court should have rendered or passed; and the Supreme Court shall do the same on reversals therein, except where the reversal is in favour of the plaintiff, or petitioner in the original suit, and the damages to be assessed, or matter to be decreed, are uncertain, in which case they shall remand the cause for a final decision. . . .

SEC. 29. And be it further enacted, That in cases punishable with death, the trial shall be had in the county where the offence was committed, or where that cannot be done without great inconvenience, twelve petit jurors at least shall be summoned from thence. And jurors in all cases to serve in the courts of the United States shall be designated by lot or otherwise in each State respectively according to the mode of forming juries therein now practised, so far as the laws of the same shall render such designation practicable by the courts or marshals of the United States; and the jurors shall have the same qualifications as are requisite for jurors by the laws of the State of which they are citizens, to serve in the highest courts of law of such State, and shall be returned as there shall be occasion for them, from such parts of the district from time to time as the court shall direct, so as shall be most favourable to an impartial trial, and so as not to incur an unnecessary expense, or unduly to burthen the citizens of any part of the district with such services. . . .

SEC. 30. And be it further enacted, That the mode of proof by oral testimony and examination of witnesses in open court shall be the same in all the courts of the United States, as well in the trial of causes in equity and of admiralty and maritime jurisdiction, as of actions at common law. . . .

SEC. 33. And be it further enacted, That for any crime or offence against the United States, the offender may, by any justice or judge of the United States, or by any justice of the peace, or other magistrate of any of the United States where he may be found agreeably to the usual mode of process against offenders in such state, and at the expense of the United States, be arrested, and imprisoned or bailed, as the case may be, for trial before such court of the United States as by this act has cognizance of the offence. . . .

SEC. 35. And be it further enacted, That in all courts of the United States, the parties may plead and manage their own causes personally or by assistance of such counsel or attorneys at law as by the rules of the said courts respectively shall be permitted to manage and conduct causes therein. And there shall be appointed in each district a meet person learned in the law to act as attorney for the United States in such district, who shall be sworn or affirmed to the faithful execution of his office, whose duty it shall be to prosecute in such district all delinquents for crimes and offences. . . . And there shall also be appointed a meet person, learned in the law, to act as attorney-general for the United States, who shall be sworn or affirmed to a faithful execution of his office; whose duty it shall be to prosecute and conduct all suits in the Supreme Court in which the United States shall be concerned, and to give his advice and opinion upon questions of law when required by the President of the United States, or when requested by the heads of any of the departments, touching any matters that may concern their departments, and shall receive such compensation for his services as shall by law be provided.

FREDERICK AUGUSTUS MUHLENBERG, SPEAKER OF THE HOUSE OF REPRESENTATIVES

JOHN ADAMS, VICE-PRESIDENT OF THE UNITED STATES, AND PRESIDENT OF THE SENATE

APPROVED, SEPTEMBER THE TWENTY FOURTH, 1789.

GEORGE WASHINGTON, PRESIDENT OF THE UNITED STATES

1791

BILL OF RIGHTS

During the debates on the adoption of the Constitution, its opponents repeatedly charged that the document would open the way to tyranny by the central government. Richard Henry Lee, for one, despaired at the absence of protection of "those essential rights of mankind without which liberty cannot exist." Still fresh in the delegates' minds was the British violation of civil rights before and during the Revolution. They demanded a "bill of rights" that would specify the immunities of individual citizens. Several state conventions in their formal ratification of the Constitution requested such amendments; others ratified the Constitution with the understanding that the amendments would come later.

On September 25, 1789, the First Congress of the United States therefore proposed to the state legislatures twelve amendments to the Constitution that addressed the most frequent criticisms. Articles 3 to 12, which three-fourths of the state legislatures ratified on December 15, 1791, constitute the first ten amendments of the Constitution and are known as the Bill of Rights. The original second article, concerning the compensation of members of Congress, finally became law on May 7, 1992. Congress never passed the original first amendment, which concerned the number of constituents for each representative. The Bill of Rights defined citizens' rights in relation to the government newly established under the Constitution. These ten amendments include guarantees many Americans now understand as central to their way of life: the four freedoms of speech, religion, the press, and political activity. The Bill of Rights also encompasses principles fundamental to the American legal system: the rights to due process of law, trial by jury, and protection from cruel and unusual punishment and self-incrimination.

THE Conventions of a number of the States, having at the time of their adopting the Constitution, expressed a desire, in order to prevent misconstruction or abuse of its powers, that further declaratory and restrictive clauses should be added: And as extending the ground of public confidence in the Government, will best ensure the beneficent ends of its institution.

RESOLVED by the Senate and House of Representatives of the United States of America, in Congress assembled, two thirds of both Houses concurring, that the following Articles be proposed to the Legislatures of the several States, as amendments to the Constitution of the United States, all, or any of which Articles, when ratified by three fourths of the said Legislatures, to be valid to all intents and purposes, as part of the said Constitution; viz.

ARTICLES in addition to, and Amendment of the Constitution of the United States of America, proposed by Congress, and ratified by the Legislatures of the several States, pursuant to the fifth Article of the original Constitution.

Article the first...After the first enumeration required by the first article of the Constitution, there shall be one Representative for every thirty thousand, until the number shall amount to one hundred, after which the proportion shall be so regulated by Congress, that there shall be not less than one hundred Representatives, nor less than one Representative for every forty thousand persons, until the number of Representatives shall amount to two hundred; after which the proportion shall be so regulated by Congress, that there shall not be less than two hundred Representatives, nor more than one Representative for every fifty thousand persons.

Article the second...No law, varying the compensation for the services of the Senators and Representatives, shall take effect, until an election of Representatives shall have intervened.

Article the third...Congress shall make no law respecting an establishment of religion, or prohibiting the free exercise thereof; or abridging the freedom of speech, or of the press; or the right of the people peace-

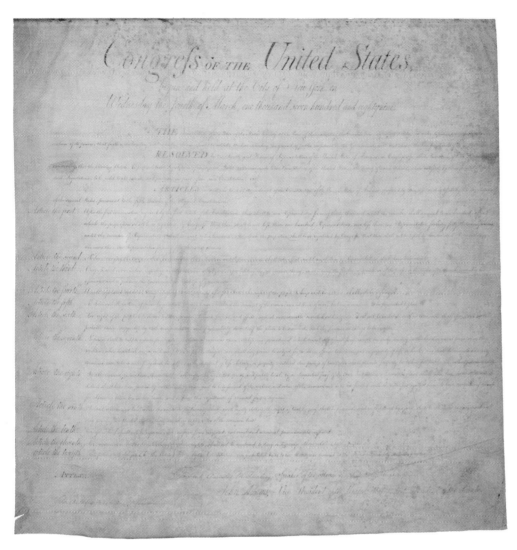

the Militia, when in actual service in time of War or public danger; nor shall any person be subject for the same offence to be twice put in jeopardy of life or limb; nor shall be compelled in any criminal case to be a witness against himself, nor be deprived of life, liberty, or property, without due process of law; nor shall private property be taken for public use, without just compensation.

Article the eighth... In all criminal prosecutions, the accused shall enjoy the right to a speedy and public trial, by an impartial jury of the State and district wherein the crime shall have been committed, which district shall have been previously ascertained by law, and to be informed of the nature and cause of the accusation; to be confronted with the witnesses against him; to have compulsory process for obtaining witnesses in his favor, and to have the Assistance of Counsel for his defence.

ably to assemble, and to petition the Government for a redress of grievances.

Article the fourth... A well regulated Militia, being necessary to the security of a free State, the right of the people to keep and bear Arms, shall not be infringed.

Article the fifth... No Soldier shall, in time of peace be quartered in any house, without the consent of the Owner, nor in time of war, but in a manner to be prescribed by law.

Article the sixth... The right of the people to be secure in their persons, houses, papers, and effects, against unreasonable searches and seizures, shall not be violated, and no Warrants shall issue, but upon probable cause, supported by Oath or affirmation, and particularly describing the place to be searched, and the persons or things to be seized.

Article the seventh... No person shall be held to answer for a capital, or otherwise infamous crime, unless on a presentment or indictment of a Grand Jury, except in cases arising in the land or naval forces, or in

Article the ninth... In Suits at common law, where the value in controversy shall exceed twenty dollars, the right of trial by jury shall be preserved, and no fact tried by a jury, shall be otherwise re-examined in any Court of the United States, than according to the rules of the common law.

Article the tenth... Excessive bail shall not be required, nor excessive fines imposed, nor cruel and unusual punishments inflicted.

Article the eleventh... The enumeration in the Constitution, of certain rights, shall not be construed to deny or disparage others retained by the people.

Article the twelfth... The powers not delegated to the United States by the Constitution, nor prohibited by it to the States, are reserved to the States respectively, or to the people.

1794
PATENT FOR COTTON GIN

*E*li Whitney's cotton gin was the first machine able to clean short-staple cotton, the one variety that grew well inland. Its sticky green seeds were time-consuming to pick out of the fluffy white cotton bolls, but his device, designed to separate cotton fiber from seed, yielded up to fifty pounds of cleaned cotton in a day. Cotton thus became a profitable crop for the first time. Whitney received a patent for his cotton gin on March 14, 1794.

After this invention, the yield of cleaned cotton doubled in each decade after 1800. Subsequent inventions, such as the machines to spin and weave cotton and the steamboats to transport it, further increased the demand for cotton. By mid-century, the United States was growing three-quarters of the world's supply of cotton, most of which was shipped to England or New England, where manufacturers converted it to cloth. At mid-century the South provided three-fifths of the country's exports—most of these in cotton.

While it was true that the cotton gin reduced the labor of removing seeds, it did not reduce the need for slaves to grow and pick the cotton. In fact, the opposite occurred. Cotton growing became so profitable for the planters that it greatly increased their demand for both land and slave labor. In 1790 there were six slave states; in 1860 there were 15. From 1790 until Congress banned the importation of slaves from Africa in 1808, Southerners imported 80,000 Africans. By 1860 approximately one in three Southerners was a slave.

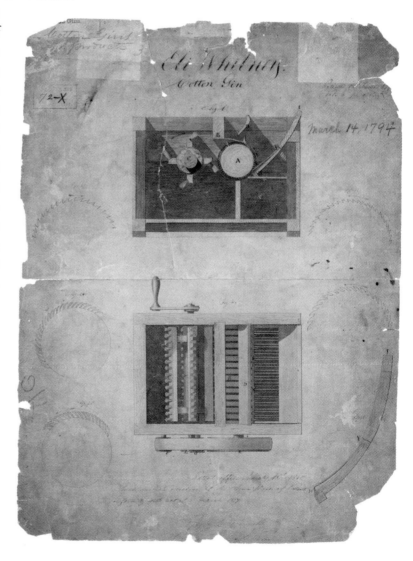

Whitney's patent application described how the device worked: "The cotton gin cranked cotton through rollers with teeth made of wire. The wire teeth tore the green seeds from the cotton. Iron slits let the cotton pass through, but not the seeds. A second rotating cylinder of bristles removed the seedless cotton from the wires. Through a simple arrangement of belts, the same crank turned both the cylinder with wires and another smaller one with bristles."

1796

PRESIDENT GEORGE WASHINGTON'S FAREWELL ADDRESS

*I*n early 1796 President George Washington decided not to seek reelection for a third term and began drafting this farewell address to the American people. The thirty-two-page handwritten address went through numerous drafts, in large part due to suggestions from Alexander Hamilton. The address was printed in Philadelphia's American Daily Advertiser on September 19, 1796. In his farewell Presidential address, George Washington advised U.S. citizens to view themselves as a cohesive unit and to avoid aligning themselves with political parties. He issued a special warning to be wary of attachments and entanglements with other nations. Washington's goal to keep the United States separate from foreign affairs remained an important aspect of foreign policy for another century.

FRIENDS AND FELLOW CITIZENS: . . .

The unity of government which constitutes you one people is also now dear to you. It is justly so, for it is a main pillar in the edifice of your real independence, the support of your tranquility at home, your peace abroad; of your safety; of your prosperity; of that very liberty which you so highly prize. But as it is easy to foresee that, from different causes and from different quarters, much pains will be taken, many artifices employed to weaken in your minds the conviction of this truth; as this is the point in your political fortress against which the batteries of internal and external enemies will be most constantly and actively (though often covertly and insidiously) directed, it is of infinite moment that you should properly estimate the immense value of your national union to your collective and individual happiness; that you should cherish a cordial, habitual, and immovable attachment to it; accustoming yourselves to think and speak of it as of the palladium of your political safety and prosperity; watching for its preservation with jealous anxiety; discountenancing whatever may suggest even a suspicion that it can in any event be abandoned; and indignantly frowning upon the first dawning of every attempt to alienate any portion of our country from the rest, or to enfeeble the sacred ties which now link together the various parts. . . .

The North, in an unrestrained intercourse with the South, protected by the equal laws of a common government, finds in the productions of the latter great additional resources of maritime and commercial enterprise and precious materials of manufacturing industry. The South, in the same intercourse, benefiting by the agency of the North, sees its agriculture grow and its commerce expand. Turning partly into its own channels the seamen of the North, it finds its particular navigation invigorated; and, while it contributes, in different ways, to nourish and increase the general mass of the national navigation, it looks forward to the protection of a maritime strength, to which itself is unequally adapted. The East, in a like intercourse with the West, already finds, and in the progressive improvement of interior communications by land and water, will more and more find a valuable vent for the commodities which it brings from abroad, or manufactures at home. The West derives from the East supplies requisite to its growth and comfort, and, what is perhaps of still greater consequence, it must of necessity owe the secure enjoyment of indispensable outlets for its own productions to the weight, influence, and the future maritime strength of the Atlantic side of the Union, directed by an indissoluble community of interest as one nation. Any other tenure by which the West can hold this essential advantage, whether derived from its own separate strength, or from an apostate and unnatural connection with any foreign power, must be intrinsically precarious.

While, then, every part of our country thus feels an immediate and particular interest in union, all the parts combined cannot fail to find in the united mass of means and efforts greater strength, greater resource, proportionably greater security from external danger, a less frequent interruption of their peace by foreign nations; and, what is of inestimable value, they must derive from union an exemption from those broils and wars between themselves, which so frequently afflict neighboring countries not tied together by the same governments, which their own rival ships alone would be sufficient to produce, but which opposite foreign alliances, attachments, and intrigues would stimulate and embitter....

In contemplating the causes which may disturb our Union, it occurs as matter of serious concern that any ground should have been furnished for characterizing parties by geographical discriminations, Northern and Southern, Atlantic and Western; whence designing men may endeavor to excite a belief that there is a real difference of local interests and views....

To the efficacy and permanency of your Union, a government for the whole is indispensable. No alliance, however strict, between the parts can be an adequate substitute; they must inevitably experience the infractions and interruptions which all alliances in all times have experienced. Sensible of this momentous truth, you have improved upon your first essay, by the adoption of a constitution of government better calculated than your former for an intimate union, and for the efficacious management of your common concerns. This government, the offspring of our own choice, uninfluenced and unawed, adopted upon full investigation and mature deliberation, completely free in its principles, in the distribution of its powers, uniting security with energy, and containing within itself a provision for its own amendment, has a just claim to your confidence and your support. Respect for its authority, compliance with its laws, acquiescence in its measures, are duties enjoined by the fundamental maxims of true liberty. The basis of our political systems is the right of the people to make and to alter their con-

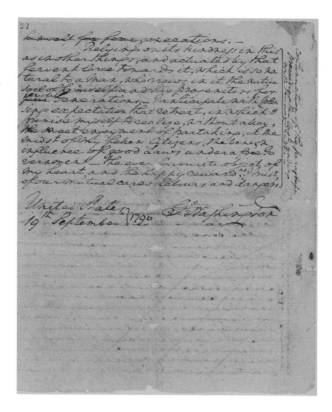

stitutions of government. But the Constitution which at any time exists, till changed by an explicit and authentic act of the whole people, is sacredly obligatory upon all. The very idea of the power and the right of the people to establish government presupposes the duty of every individual to obey the established government....

[N]othing is more essential than that permanent, inveterate antipathies against particular nations, and passionate attachments for others, should be excluded; and that, in place of them, just and amicable feelings towards all should be cultivated. The nation which indulges towards another a habitual hatred or a habitual fondness is in some degree a slave....

So likewise, a passionate attachment of one nation for another produces a variety of evils. Sympathy for the favorite nation, facilitating the illusion of an imaginary common interest in cases where no real common interest exists, and infusing into one the enmities of the other, betrays the former into a participation in the quarrels and wars of the latter without adequate inducement or justification....

In offering to you, my countrymen, these counsels of an old and affectionate friend, I dare not hope they will make the strong and lasting impression I could wish; that they will control the usual current of the passions, or prevent our nation from running the course which has hitherto marked the destiny of nations. But, if I may even flatter myself that they may be productive of some partial benefit, some occasional good; that they may now and then recur to moderate the fury of party spirit, to warn against the mischiefs of foreign intrigue, to guard against the impostures of pretended patriotism; this hope will be a full recompense for the solicitude for your welfare, by which they have been dictated....

19TH SEPTEMBER, 1796

GEO. WASHINGTON

1798

ALIEN AND SEDITION ACTS

*I*n 1798 the United States stood on the brink of war with France. The Federalists believed that Democratic-Republican criticism of Federalist policies was disloyal and feared that aliens living in the United States would sympathize with the French during a war. As a result, a Federalist-controlled Congress passed four laws, known collectively as the Alien and Sedition Acts. These laws raised the residency requirements for citizenship from five to fourteen years, authorized the President to deport aliens, and permitted their arrest, imprisonment, and deportation during wartime. The Sedition Act made it a crime for American citizens to "print, utter, or publish . . . any false, scandalous, and malicious writing" about the government.

The laws were directed against Democratic-Republicans, the party typically favored by new citizens, and the only journalists prosecuted under the Sedition Act were editors of Democratic-Republican newspapers. Sedition Act trials, along with the Senate's use of its contempt powers to suppress dissent, set off a firestorm of criticism against the Federalists and contributed to their defeat in the election of 1800, after which the acts were repealed or allowed to expire. The controversies surrounding them, however, tested the limits of freedom of speech and the press.

AN ACT CONCERNING ALIENS.

SECTION 1. Be it enacted by the Senate and the House of Representatives of the United States of America in Congress assembled, That it shall be lawful for the President of the United States at any time during the continuance of this act, to order all such aliens as he shall judge dangerous to the peace and safety of the United States, or shall have reasonable grounds to suspect are concerned in any treasonable or secret machinations against the government thereof, to depart out of the territory of the United States. . . . And in case any alien, so ordered to depart, shall be found at large within the United States after the time limited in such order for his departure, and not having obtained a license from the President to reside therein, or having obtained such license shall not have conformed thereto, every such alien shall, on conviction thereof, be imprisoned for a term not exceeding three years, and shall never after be admitted to become a citizen of the United States. . . .

SEC. 2. . . . And if any alien so removed or sent out of the United States by the President shall voluntarily return thereto, unless by permission of the President of the United States, such alien on conviction thereof, shall be imprisoned so long as, in the opinion of the President, the public safety may require.

AN ACT RESPECTING ALIEN ENEMIES.

SECTION 1. Be it enacted by the Senate and House of Representatives of the United States of America in Congress assembled, That whenever there shall be a declared war between the United States and any foreign nation or government, or any invasion or predatory incursion shall be perpetrated, attempted, or threatened against the territory of the United States, by any foreign nation or government, and the President of the United States shall make public proclamation of the event, all natives, citizens, denizens, or subjects of the hostile nation or government, being males of the age of fourteen years and upwards, who shall be within the United States, and not actually naturalized, shall be liable to be apprehended, restrained, secured and removed, as alien enemies. . . .

AN ACT IN ADDITION TO THE ACT, ENTITLED "AN ACT FOR THE PUNISHMENT OF CERTAIN CRIMES AGAINST THE UNITED STATES."

SECTION 1. Be it enacted by the Senate and House of Representatives of the United States of America, in Congress assembled, That if any persons shall unlawfully combine or conspire together, with intent to oppose any measure or measures of the government of the United States, which are or shall be directed by proper authority, or to impede the operation of any law of the United States, or to intimidate or prevent any person holding a place or office in or under the government of the United States, from undertaking, performing or executing his trust or duty, and if any person or persons, with intent as aforesaid, shall counsel, advise or attempt to procure any insurrection, riot, unlawful assembly, or combination, whether such conspiracy, threatening, counsel, advice, or attempt shall have the proposed effect or not, he or they shall be deemed guilty of a high misdemeanor, and on conviction, before any court of the United States having jurisdiction thereof, shall be punished by a fine not exceeding five thousand dollars, and by imprisonment during a term not less than six months nor exceeding five years....

SEC. 2. And be it farther enacted, That if any person shall write, print, utter or publish, or shall cause or procure to be written, printed, uttered or published, or shall knowingly and willingly assist or aid in writing, printing, uttering or publishing any false, scandalous and malicious writing or writings against the government of the United States, or either house of the Congress of the United States, or the President of the United States, with intent to defame the said government, or either house of the said Congress, or the said President, or to bring them, or either of them, into contempt or disrepute; or to excite against them, or either or any of them, the hatred of the good people of the United States, or to stir up sedition within the United States, or to excite any unlawful combinations therein, for opposing or resisting any law of the United States, or any act of the President of the United States, done in pursuance of any such law, or of the powers in him vested by the constitution of the United States, or to resist, oppose, or defeat any such law or act, or to aid, encourage or abet any hostile designs of any foreign

"[I]t shall be lawful for the president of the United States . . . to order all such aliens as he shall judge dangerous to [its] peace and safety . . . to depart. . . ."

nation against United States, their people or government, then such person, being thereof convicted before any court of the United States having jurisdiction thereof, shall be punished by a fine not exceeding two thousand dollars, and by imprisonment not exceeding two years....

1803

JEFFERSON'S SECRET MESSAGE TO CONGRESS REGARDING THE LEWIS AND CLARK EXPEDITION

*A*lthough the territory beyond the Mississippi River did not belong to the United States before the Louisiana Purchase in April 1803, on January 18 President Jefferson quietly asked Congress for $2,500 to explore the West all the way to the Pacific Ocean. His message was kept secret because some might interpret sending an expedition into territory that belonged to France as a hostile act.

Congress agreed to fund the expedition. Although Jefferson modestly focused his remarks on possible economic benefits, he was fascinated with the West and perhaps most interested in acquiring new scientific knowledge—about climate, vegetation, Indian culture, and animal life—that the explorers would collect. He also cherished the vision of a United States that would cover the entire continent. Jefferson chose Captain Meriwether Lewis, his personal secretary, to lead the expedition along with second in command Captain William Clark. Their 8,000-mile expedition, guided by the young Indian woman Sacajawea, provided the U.S. government with a tantalizing first glimpse of the vast lands west of the Mississippi River and helped spur further exploration and development of those lands.

CONFIDENTIAL.

GENTLEMEN OF THE SENATE AND OF THE HOUSE OF REPRESENTATIVES: ...

The Indian tribes residing within the limits of the United States, have, for a considerable time, been growing more and more uneasy at the constant diminution of the territory they occupy, although effected by their own voluntary sales: and the policy has long been gaining strength with them, of refusing absolutely all further sale, on any conditions; insomuch that, at this time, it hazards their friendship, and excites dangerous jealousies and perturbations in their minds to make any overture for the purchase of the smallest portions of their land. A very few tribes only are not yet obstinately in these dispositions. In order peaceably to counteract this policy of theirs, and to provide an extension of territory which the rapid increase of our numbers will call for, two measures are deemed expedient. First: to encourage them to abandon hunting, to apply to the raising stock, to agriculture and domestic manufacture, and thereby prove to themselves that less land and labor will maintain them in this, better than in their former mode of living. The extensive forests necessary in the hunting life, will then become useless, and they will see advantage in exchanging them for the means of improving their farms, and of increasing their domestic comforts. Secondly: to multiply trading houses among them, and place within their reach those things which will contribute more to their domestic comfort, than the possession of extensive, but uncultivated wilds. Experience and reflection will develop to them the wisdom of exchanging what they can spare and we want, for what we can spare and they want. In leading them to agriculture, to manufactures, and civilization; in bringing together their and our settlements, and in preparing them ultimately to participate in the benefits of our governments, I trust and believe we are acting for their greatest good. At these trading houses we have pursued the principles of the act of Congress, which directs that the commerce shall be carried on liberally, and requires only that the capital stock shall not be diminished. We consequently undersell private traders, foreign and domestic, drive them from the competition; and thus, with the good will of the Indians, rid ourselves of a description of men who are

Confidential.

Gentlemen of the Senate and of the House of Representatives.

    As the continuance of the Act for establishing trading houses with the Indian tribes will be under the consideration of the legislature at it's present session, I think it my duty to communicate the views which have guided me in the execution of that act; in order that you may decide on the policy of continuing it, in the present or any other form, or to discontinue it altogether if that shall, on the whole, seem most for the public good.

    The Indian tribes residing within the limits of the US. have for a considerable time been growing more & more uneasy at the constant diminution of the territory they occupy, altho' effected by their own voluntary sales: and the policy has long been gaining strength with them of refusing absolutely, all further sale on any conditions. insomuch that, at this time, it hazards their friendship, and excites dangerous jealousies & perturbations in their minds to make any overture for the purchase of the smallest portions of their land. a very few tribes only are not yet obstinately in these dispositions.   In order peaceably to counteract this policy of theirs, and to provide an extension of territory which the rapid increase of our numbers will call for, two measures are deemed expedient. First, to encourage them to abandon hunting, to apply to the raising stock, to agriculture and domestic manufacture, and thereby prove to themselves that less land & labour will maintain them in this, better than in their former mode of living. the extensive forests necessary in the hunting life, will then become useless, & they will see advantage in exchanging them for the means of improving their farms, & of increasing their domestic comforts. Secondly to multiply trading houses among them, & place within their reach those things which will contribute more to their domestic comfort than the possession of extensive, but uncultivated wilds. experience & reflection will develope to them the wisdom of exchanging what they can spare & we want, for what we can spare and they want. in leading them thus to agriculture, to constantly endeavoring to excite in the Indian mind suspicions, fears, and irritations towards us. A letter now enclosed, shows the effect of our competition on the operations of the traders, while the Indians, perceiving the advantage of purchasing from us, are soliciting generally, our establishment of trading houses among them. In one quarter this is particularly interesting. The Legislature, reflecting on the late occurrences on the Mississippi, must be sensible how desirable it is to possess a respectable breadth of country on that river, from our Southern limit to the Illinois at least; so that we may present as firm a front on that as on our Eastern border. We possess what is below the Yazoo, and can probably acquire a certain breadth from the Illinois and Wabash to the Ohio; but between the Ohio and Yazoo, the country all belongs to the Chickasaws, the most friendly tribe within our limits, but the most decided against the alienation of lands. The portion of their country most important for us is exactly that which they do not inhabit. Their settlements are not on the Mississippi, but in the interior country. They have lately shown a desire to become agricultural; and this leads to the desire of buying implements and comforts. In the strengthening and gratifying of these wants, I see the only prospect of planting on the Mississippi itself, the means of its own safety. Duty has required me to submit these views to the judgment of the Legislature; but as their disclosure might embarrass and defeat their effect, they are committed to the special confidence of the two Houses.

While the extension of the public commerce among the Indian tribes, may deprive of that source of profit such of our citizens as are engaged in it, it might be worthy the attention of Congress, in their care of individual as well as of the general interest, to point, in another direction, the enterprise of these citizens, as profitably for themselves, and more usefully for the public. The river Missouri, and the Indians inhabiting it, are not as well known as is rendered desirable by their connexion with the Mississippi, and consequently with us. It is, however, understood, that the country on that river is inhabited by numerous tribes, who furnish great supplies of furs and peltry to the trade of another nation, carried on in a high latitude, through an infinite number of portages and lakes, shut up by ice through a long season. The commerce on that line could bear no competition with that of the Missouri, traversing a moderate climate, offering according to the best accounts, a continued navigation from its source,

and possibly with a single portage, from the Western Ocean, and finding to the Atlantic a choice of channels through the Illinois or Wabash, the lakes and Hudson, through the Ohio and Susquehanna, or Potomac or James rivers, and through the Tennessee and Savannah, rivers. An intelligent officer, with ten or twelve chosen men, fit for the enterprise, and willing to undertake it, taken from our posts, where they may be spared without inconvenience, might explore the whole line, even to the Western Ocean, have conferences with the natives on the subject of commercial intercourse, get admission among them for our traders, as others are admitted, agree on convenient deposits for an interchange of articles, and return with the information acquired, in the course of two summers. Their arms and accoutrements, some instruments of observation, and light and cheap presents for the Indians, would be all the apparatus they could carry, and with an expectation of a soldier's portion of land on their return, would constitute the whole expense. Their pay would be going on, whether here or there. While other civilized nations have encountered great expense to enlarge the boundaries of knowledge by undertaking voyages of discovery, and for other literary purposes, in various parts and directions, our nation seems to owe to the same object, as well as to its own interests, to explore this, the only line of easy communication across the continent, and so directly traversing our own part of it. The interests of commerce place the principal object within the constitutional powers and care of Congress, and that it should incidentally advance the geographical knowledge of our own continent, cannot be but an additional gratification. The nation claiming the territory, regarding this as a literary pursuit, which is in the habit of permitting within its dominions, would not be disposed to view it with jealousy, even if the expiring state of its interests there did not render it a matter of indifference. The appropriation of two thousand five hundred dollars, "for the purpose of extending the external commerce of the United States," while understood and considered by the Executive as giving the legislative sanction, would cover the undertaking from notice, and prevent the obstructions which interested individuals might otherwise previously prepare in its way.

TH. JEFFERSON

JAN. 18. 1803.

1803

LOUISIANA PURCHASE TREATY

*W*ith no idea of the extent of their acquisition—one of the greatest bargains in history—Robert Livingston and James Monroe signed the Louisiana Purchase Treaty in Paris. The $15 million price tag was well worth it. Congress had authorized them to pay France up to $10 million for the port of New Orleans and the Floridas. Planning further warfare in Europe, Napoleon needed cash and so offered to sell the entire Louisiana territory—an area larger than Great Britain, France, Germany, Italy, Spain, and Portugal combined—and the American negotiators swiftly agreed. Under the terms of this treaty, concluded on April 30, 1803, the United States purchased 828,000 square miles of land west of the Mississippi River for roughly four cents an acre. The United States doubled its size, reaching westward toward the Pacific Ocean.

President Thomas Jefferson was somewhat unsure he had the authority to add such a vast new territory to the existing republic, but his momentous decision would further his vision of an "empire for liberty" that would stretch from coast to coast.

TREATY BETWEEN THE UNITED STATES OF AMERICA AND THE FRENCH REPUBLIC

The President of the United States of America and the First Consul of the French Republic in the name of the French People desiring to remove all Source of misunderstanding relative to objects of discussion mentioned in the Second and fifth articles of the Convention of the 8th Vendé miaire an 9/30 September 1800 relative to the rights claimed by the United States in virtue of the Treaty concluded at Madrid the 27 of October 1795, between His Catholic Majesty & the Said United States, & willing to Strengthen the union and friendship which at the time of the Said Convention was happily reestablished between the two nations have respectively named their Plenipotentiaries to wit The President of the United States, by and with the advice and consent of the Senate of the Said States; Robert R. Livingston Minister Plenipotentiary of the United States and James Monroe Minister Plenipotentiary and Envoy extraordinary of the Said States near the Government of the French Republic; And the First Consul in the name of the French people, Citizen Francis Barbé Marbois Minister of the public treasury who after having respectively exchanged their full powers have agreed to the following Articles.

ARTICLE I
Whereas by the Article the third of the Treaty concluded at St Ildefonso the 9th Vendé miaire an 9/1st October

1800 between the First Consul of the French Republic and his Catholic Majesty it was agreed as follows.

"His Catholic Majesty promises and engages on his part to cede to the French Republic six months after the full and entire execution of the conditions and Stipulations herein relative to his Royal Highness the Duke of Parma, the Colony or Province of Louisiana with the Same extent that it now has in the hand of Spain, & that it had when France possessed it; and Such as it Should be after the Treaties subsequently entered into between Spain and other States."

And whereas in pursuance of the Treaty and particularly of the third article the French Republic has an incontestible title to the domain and to the possession of the said Territory—The First Consul of the French Republic desiring to give to the United States a strong proof of his friendship doth hereby cede to the United States in the name of the French Republic for ever and in full Sovereignty the said territory with all its rights and appurtenances as fully and in the Same manner as they have been acquired by the French Republic in virtue of the above mentioned Treaty concluded with his Catholic Majesty.

ARTICLE II
In the cession made by the preceeding article are included the adjacent Islands belonging to Louisiana all public lots and Squares, vacant lands and all public buildings, fortifications, barracks and other edifices

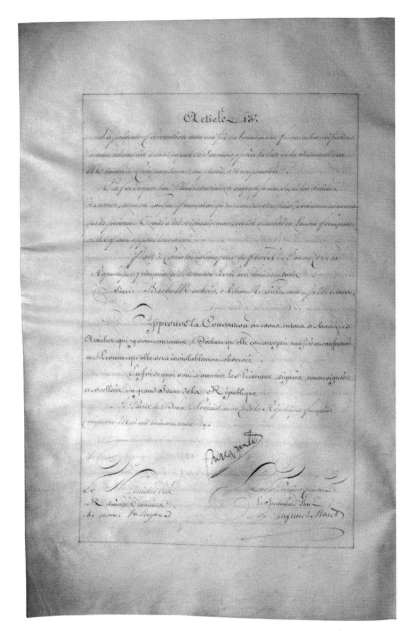

and protected in the free enjoyment of their liberty, property and the Religion which they profess. . . .

DONE AT PARIS THE TENTH DAY OF FLOREAL IN THE ELEVENTH YEAR OF THE FRENCH REPUBLIC; AND THE 30TH OF APRIL 1803.

ROBT R LIVINGSTON [SEAL]

JAS. MONROE [SEAL]

BARBÉ MARBOIS [SEAL]

In addition to this Treaty of Cession, the Louisiana Purchase Agreement comprises two conventions specifying the financial aspects of the agreement, one calling for the payment of 60 million francs ($11,250,000), the other for claims U.S. citizens had made against France for 20 million francs ($3,750,000).

A CONVENTION BETWEEN THE UNITED STATES OF AMERICA AND THE FRENCH REPUBLIC

ARTICLE 1
The Government of the United States engages to pay to the French Government in the manner Specified in the following article the sum of Sixty millions of francs independant of the Sum which Shall be fixed by another Convention for the payment of the debts due by France to citizens of United States. . . .

DONE AT PARIS THE TENTH OF FLOREAL ELEVENTH YEAR OF THE FRENCH REPUBLIC

30TH APRIL 1803.

ROBT R LIVINGSTON [SEAL]

JAS. MONROE [SEAL]

BARBÉ MARBOIS [SEAL]

which are not private property.—The Archives, papers & documents relative to the domain and Sovereignty of Louisiana and its dependances will be left in the possession of the Commissaries of the United States, and copies will be afterwards given in due form to the Magistrates and Municipal officers of such of the said papers and documents as may be necessary to them.

ARTICLE III
The inhabitants of the ceded territory shall be incorporated in the Union of the United States and admitted as soon as possible according to the principles of the federal Constitution to the enjoyment of all these rights, advantages and immunities of citizens of the United States, and in the mean time they shall be maintained

1803

MARBURY V. MADISON

President Thomas Jefferson and his Republican Party were deeply suspicious of the Federalist Party's efforts to fill the federal judiciary with its members. Outgoing Federalist President John Adams made a series of "midnight appointments" to that effect, among them William Marbury as a justice of the peace. Adams, however, did not deliver the actual commission before leaving office, and the new secretary of state, James Madison, in a move that heightened the partisan wrangling, refused to deliver it. Marbury then sued to obtain it, asking the Supreme Court to grant him a "writ of mandamus"—an order from a higher court commanding that a specified action be taken—to force Madison to turn over the commission.

"A Law repugnant to the Constitution is void." The Supreme Court chief justice argued that Marbury could not get a writ of mandamus because in 1789 the members of Congress had overstepped their authority when they passed the law that granted the Court the authority to issue such a writ. Significantly, for the first time, the Supreme Court declared unconstitutional a law passed by Congress and signed by the President. The writers of the Constitution had given the executive and legislative branches powers that would limit each other as well as the judiciary branch but had left undefined, within this intricate system, the role of the Supreme Court. It therefore fell to a strong chief justice like John Marshall to complete the triangular structure of checks and balances by establishing the principle of judicial review. Although no other law was declared unconstitutional until the Dred Scott decision of 1857, the role of the Supreme Court to invalidate federal and state laws that are contrary to the Constitution has never been seriously challenged.

John Marshall wrote 509 of the 1,100 decisions issued by the Supreme Court during his thirty-four-year tenure as Chief Justice. Associate Justice Joseph Story said of his career, "Your expositions of constitutional law . . . constitute a monument of fame far beyond the ordinary memorials of political glory. They are destined to enlighten, instruct and convince future generations. . . ."

The constitution vests the whole judicial power of the United States in one Supreme Court, and such inferior courts as congress shall, from time to time, ordain and establish. This power is expressly extended to all cases arising under the laws of the United States; and, consequently, in some form, may be exercised over the present case; because the right claimed is given by a law of the United States....

In the distribution of this power it is declared that "the Supreme Court shall have original jurisdiction in all cases affecting ambassadors, other public ministers and consuls, and those in which a state shall be a party. In all other cases, the Supreme Court shall have appellate jurisdiction."

It has been insisted, at the bar, that as the original grant of jurisdiction, to the supreme and inferior courts, is general, and the clause, assigning original jurisdiction to the Supreme Court, contains no negative or restrictive words, the power remains to the legislature, to assign original jurisdiction to that court in other cases than those specified in the article which has been recited; provided those cases belong to the judicial power of the United States.

If it had been intended to leave it in the discretion of the legislature to apportion the judicial power between the supreme and inferior courts according to the will of that body, it would certainly have been useless to have proceeded further than to have defined the judicial power, and the tribunals in which it should be vested. The subsequent part of the section is mere surplusage, is entirely without meaning, if such is to be the construction....

When an instrument organizing fundamentally a judicial system, divides it into one supreme, and so many inferior courts as the legislature may ordain and establish; then enumerates its powers, and proceeds so far to distribute them, as to define the jurisdiction of the supreme court by declaring the cases in which it

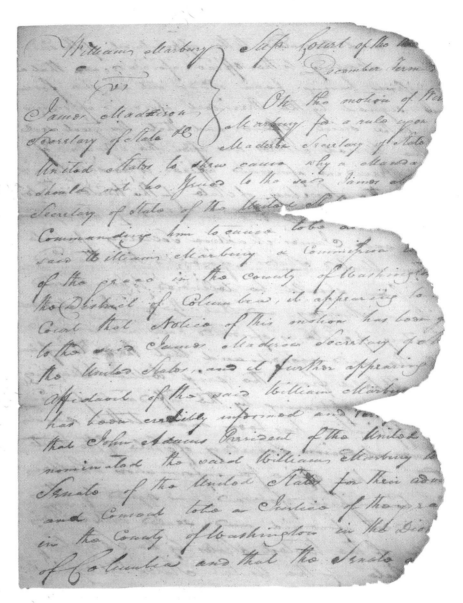

shall take original jurisdiction, and that in others it shall take appellate jurisdiction; the plain import of the words seems to be, that in one class of cases its jurisdiction is original, and not appellate; in the other it is appellate, and not original. If any other construction would render the clause inoperative, that is an additional reason for rejecting such other construction, and for adhering to their obvious meaning....

The question, whether an act, repugnant to the constitution, can become the law of the land, is a question deeply interesting to the United States; but happily, not of an intricacy proportioned to its interest. It seems only necessary to recognize certain principles, supposed to have been long and well established, to decide it.

That the people have an original right to establish, for their future government, such principles as, in their opinion, shall most conduce to their own happiness, is the basis on which the whole American fabric has been erected....

This original and supreme will organizes the government, and assigns to different departments their respective powers. It may either stop here, or establish certain limits not to be transcended by those departments.

The government of the United States is of the latter description. The powers of the legislature are defined and limited; and that those limits may not be mistaken, or forgotten, the constitution is written.... It is a proposition too plain to be contested, that the constitution controls any legislative act repugnant to it; or, that the legislature may alter the constitution by an ordinary act.

Between these alternatives there is no middle ground. The constitution is either a superior, paramount law, unchangeable by ordinary means, or it is on a level with ordinary legislative acts, and, like other acts, is alterable when the legislature shall please to alter it.

If the former part of the alternative be true, then a legislative act contrary to the constitution is not law: if the latter part be true, then written constitutions are absurd attempts, on the part of the people, to limit a power in its own nature illimitable.

Certainly all those who have framed written constitutions contemplate them as forming the fundamental and paramount law of the nation, and consequently, the theory of every such government must be, that an act of the legislature, repugnant to the constitution, is void....

If an act of the legislature, repugnant to the constitution, is void, does it, notwithstanding its invalidity, bind the courts, and oblige them to give it effect? Or, in other words, though it be not law, does it constitute a rule as operative as if it was a law? This would be to overthrow in fact what was established in theory; and would seem, at first view, an absurdity too gross to be insisted on. It shall, however, receive a more attentive consideration.

"That the people have an original right to establish, for their future government, such principles as, in their opinion, shall most conduce to their own happiness, is the basis on which the whole American fabric has been erected...."

It is emphatically the province and duty of the judicial department to say what the law is. Those who apply the rule to particular cases, must of necessity expound and interpret that rule. If two laws conflict with each other, the courts must decide on the operation of each.

So if a law be in opposition to the constitution; if both the law and the constitution apply to a particular case, so that the court must either decide that case conformably to the law, disregarding the constitution; or conformably to the constitution, disregarding the law; the court must determine which of these conflicting rules governs the case. This is of the very essence of judicial duty.

If, then, the courts are to regard the constitution, and the constitution is superior to any ordinary act of the legislature, the constitution, and not such ordinary act, must govern the case to which they both apply.

Those then who controvert the principle that the constitution is to be considered, in court, as a paramount law, are reduced to the necessity of maintaining that the courts must close their eyes on the constitution, and see only the law.

This doctrine would subvert the very foundation of all written constitutions....

That it thus reduces to nothing what we have deemed the greatest improvement on political institutions—a written constitution—would of itself be sufficient, in America, where written constitutions have been viewed with so much reverence, for rejecting the construction. But the peculiar expressions of the constitution of the United States furnish additional arguments in favour of its rejection.

The judicial power of the United States is extended to all cases arising under the constitution.

Could it be the intention of those who gave this power, to say that in using it the constitution should not be looked into? That a case arising under the constitution should be decided without examining the instrument under which it arises?

This is too extravagant to be maintained....

Thus, the particular phraseology of the constitution of the United States confirms and strengthens the principle, supposed to be essential to all written constitutions, that a law repugnant to the constitution is void; and that courts, as well as other departments, are bound by that instrument.

The rule must be discharged.

1814
TREATY OF GHENT

During the early decades of the nation's history, relations between the United States and Great Britain remained strained and then deteriorated sharply with the outbreak of war in Europe in 1803. England imposed a blockade on neutral countries such as the United States. In addition, the British took American sailors from their ships and "impressed" them into the British Navy. On June 1, 1812, President James Madison asked for a declaration of war. Shortly afterward, Congress, despite the opposition of every Federalist, approved the declaration.

The War of 1812 produced a string of U.S. military disasters. The most shocking of these was the British Army's burning of the Capitol, the President's house, and other public buildings in Washington on August 24 and 25, 1814.

By the end of that year, both sides agreed to discuss peace terms. A meeting in Belgium of U.S. delegates and British commissioners ended with the signing of the Treaty of Ghent on December 24, 1814. Great Britain agreed to relinquish claims to the Northwest Territory, and both countries pledged to work toward ending the slave trade. News of the treaty spread slowly, and word of peace did not reach the American and British armies for some time.

U.S. forces, led by Andrew Jackson, won the Battle of New Orleans on January 8, 1815, ending the hostilities after the official peace.

The British Army captured the city of Washington in August 1814. This illustration of a burning building was published just a few years later in an updated edition of The History of England *by Paul Rapin de Thoyras.*

Treaty of Peace and Amity between His Britannic Majesty and The United States of America.

His Britannic Majesty and the United States of America desirous of terminating the war which has unhappily subsisted between the two Countries, and of restoring upon principles of perfect reciprocity, Peace, Friendship, and good Understanding between them, have for that purpose appointed their respective Plenipotentiaries...who, after a reciprocal communication of their respective Full Powers, have agreed upon the following Articles.

Article the First.

There shall be a firm and universal Peace between His Britannic Majesty and the United States, and between their respective Countries, Territories, Cities, Towns, and People of every degree without exception of places or persons. All hostilities both by sea and land shall cease as soon as this Treaty shall have been ratified by both parties as hereinafter mentioned. All territory, places, and possessions whatsoever taken by either party from the other during the war, or which may be taken after the signing of this Treaty, excepting only the Islands hereinafter mentioned, shall be restored without delay and without causing any destruction or carrying away any of the Artillery or other public property originally captured in the said forts or places, and which shall remain therein upon the Exchange of the Ratifications of this Treaty, or any Slaves or other private property; And all Archives, Records, Deeds, and Papers, either of a public nature or belonging to private persons, which in the course of the war may have fallen into the hands of the Officers of either party, shall be, as far as may be practicable, forthwith restored and delivered to the proper authorities and persons to whom they respectively belong. Such of the Islands in the Bay of Passamaquoddy as are claimed by both parties shall remain in the possession of the party in whose occupation they may be at the time of the Exchange of the Ratifications of this Treaty until the decision respecting the title to the said Islands shall have been made in conformity with the fourth Article of this Treaty. No disposition made by this Treaty as to such possession of the Islands and territories claimed by both parties shall in any manner whatever be construed to affect the right of either....

1819

McCulloch v. Maryland

*I*n 1816 Congress established the Second National Bank to help control the amount of unregulated currency issued by state banks. Many states questioned the constitutionality of the national bank, and Maryland set a precedent by requiring taxes from all banks that the state had not chartered. In 1818 the State of Maryland approved legislation to impose taxes on the Second National Bank, because Congress had chartered it.

James W. McCulloch, a cashier at the Baltimore branch of the U.S. bank, refused to pay the taxes the state was demanding. In response, Maryland filed a suit against McCulloch. McCulloch v. Maryland became a major challenge to the Constitution: Does the federal government hold sovereign power over states? The proceedings added two questions: Does the Constitution empower Congress to create a bank? And could individual states ban or tax the bank? The court decided that the federal government had the right and power to set up a federal bank and that states did not have the power to tax the federal government. Chief Justice John Marshall ruled in favor of the federal government and concluded, "[T]he power to tax involves the power to destroy." In this landmark Supreme Court case, Chief Justice Marshall handed down one of his most important decisions regarding the expansion of federal power. McCulloch v. Maryland is one of the foundations of the division of powers between state and federal governments.

CHIEF JUSTICE MARSHALL DELIVERED
THE OPINION OF THE COURT.

In the case now to be determined, the defendant, a sovereign State, denies the obligation of a law enacted by the legislature of the Union, and the plaintiff, on his part, contests the validity of an act which has been passed by the legislature of that State. The constitution of our country, in its most interesting and vital parts, is to be considered; the conflicting powers of the government of the Union and of its members, as marked in that constitution, are to be discussed; and an opinion given, which may essentially influence the great operations of the government. No tribunal can approach such a question without a deep sense of its importance, and of the awful responsibility involved in its decision. But it must be decided peacefully, or remain a source of hostile legislation, perhaps of hostility of a still more serious nature; and if it is to be so decided, by this tribunal alone can the decision be made. On the Supreme Court of the United States has the constitution of our country devolved this important duty.

The first question made in the cause is, has Congress power to incorporate a bank? . . .

This government is acknowledged by all to be one of enumerated powers. The principle, that it can exercise only the powers granted to it, [is] now universally admitted. But the question respecting the extent of the powers actually granted, is perpetually arising, and will probably continue to arise, as long as our system shall exist. . . .

Among the enumerated powers, we do not find that of establishing a bank or creating a corporation. But there is no phrase in the instrument which, like the articles of confederation, excludes incidental or implied powers; and which requires that everything granted shall be expressly and minutely described. Even the 10th amendment, which was framed for the purpose of quieting the excessive jealousies which had been excited, omits the word "expressly," and declares only that the powers "not delegated to the United States, nor prohibited to the States, are reserved to the States or to the people"; thus leaving the question, whether the particular power which may become the subject of contest has been delegated to the one government, or prohibited to the other, to depend on a fair construction of the whole instrument. The men who drew and adopted this amendment had experienced the embarrassments resulting from the insertion of this word in the articles of confederation, and probably omitted it to avoid those embarrassments. A constitution, to contain an accurate detail of all the subdivisions of which its great powers

The decision in
McCulloch v.
Maryland *was recorded
in the minutes of the
U.S. Supreme Court.*

(84) February Term 1819 — (Judgments

Henry Astor
53
vs
Bazaliel Wells & the
Heirs and Representatives of
Arnold H. Dorhman dec.d

This cause came on to be heard on
the transcript of the Record and was
argued by Counsel on consideration whereof— It is Decreed and
ordered, that the Decree of the Circuit
Court for the District of Ohio in this
case be and the same is hereby
affirmed with Costs— March 6th

James W. McCulloch
66
vs
The State of Maryland &
John James, as well for the
State as for himself

This cause came on to be heard on
the transcript of the Record of the
Court of Appeals of the State of
Maryland, and was argued by Counsel,
on consideration whereof, It is the
opinion of this Court, that the act of the Legislature of Maryland
entitled " An act to impose a tax on all Banks or Branches thereof
in the State of Maryland not chartered by the Legislature" is
contrary to the Constitution of the United States and void, and
therefore that the said Court of Appeals of the State of Maryland
erred in affirming the Judgment of the Baltimore County Court
in which Judgment was rendered against James W. McCulloch
but that the said Court of Appeals of Maryland ought to have
reversed the said Judgment of the said Baltimore County Court
and to have given Judgment for the said appellant McCulloch—
It is therefore adjudged and ordered, that the said Judgment of the
said Court of Appeals of the State of Maryland in this case be
and the same is hereby reversed and annulled— and this Court
proceeding to render such Judgment as the said Court of Appeals
should have rendered; It is further adjudged and ordered, that
the judgment of the said Baltimore County Court be reversed
and annulled, and that Judgment be entered in the said Baltimore County Court for the said James W. McCulloch.—
March 6th

will admit, and of all the means by which they may be carried into execution, would partake of the prolixity of a legal code, and could scarcely be embraced by the human mind. It would probably never be understood by the public. Its nature, therefore, requires, that only its great outlines should be marked, its important objects designated, and the minor ingredients which compose those objects be deduced from the nature of the objects themselves....

After the most deliberate consideration, it is the unanimous and decided opinion of this Court, that the act to incorporate the Bank of the United States is a law made in pursuance of the constitution, and is a part of the supreme law of the land....

[W]e proceed to inquire—

2. Whether the State of Maryland may, without violating the constitution, tax that branch?

That the power of taxation is one of vital importance; that it is retained by the States; that it is not abridged by the grant of a similar power to the government of the Union; that it is to be concurrently exercised by the two governments: are truths which have never been denied. But, such is the paramount character of the constitution, that its capacity to withdraw any subject from the action of even this power, is admitted. The States are expressly forbidden to lay any duties on imports or exports, except what may be absolutely necessary for executing their inspection laws. If the obligation of this prohibition must be conceded, the same paramount character would seem to restrain, as it certainly may restrain, a State from such other exercise of this power; as is in its nature incompatible with, and repugnant to, the constitutional laws of the Union....

On this ground the counsel for the bank place its claim to be exempted from the power of a State to tax its operations. There is no express provision for the case, but the claim has been sustained on a principle which so entirely pervades the constitution, is so intermixed with the materials which compose it, so interwoven with its web, so blended with its texture, as to be incapable of being separated from it, without rending it into shreds.

This great principle is, that the constitution and the laws made in pursuance thereof are supreme; that they control the constitution and laws of the respective States, and cannot be controlled by them. From this, which may be almost termed an axiom, other propositions are deduced as corollaries, on the truth or error of which, and on their application to this case, the cause has been supposed to depend. These are, **1ST.** that a power to create implies a power to preserve. **2ND.** That a power to destroy, if wielded by a different hand, is hostile to,

"[T]he constitution and the laws made in pursuance thereof are supreme; that they control the constitution and laws of the respective States, and cannot be controlled by them."

and incompatible with these powers to create and to preserve. **3D.** That where this repugnancy exists, that authority which is supreme must control, not yield to that over which it is supreme....

That the power of taxing by the States may be exercised so as to destroy it, is too obvious to be denied. But taxation is said to be an absolute power, which acknowledges no other limits than those expressly prescribed in the constitution, and like sovereign power of every other description, is trusted to the discretion of those who use it. But the very terms of this argument admit that the sovereignty of the State, in the article of taxation itself, is subordinate to, and may be controlled by, the constitution of the United States....

In the legislature of the Union alone, are all represented. The legislature of the Union alone, therefore, can be trusted by the people with the power of controlling measures which concern all, in the confidence that it will not be abused....

If we apply the principle for which the State of Maryland contends, to the constitution generally, we shall find it capable of changing totally the character of that instrument. We shall find it capable of arresting all the measures of the government, and of prostrating it at the foot of the States. The American people have declared their constitution, and the laws made in pursuance thereof, to be supreme; but this principle would transfer the supremacy, in fact, to the States....

The Court has bestowed on this subject its most deliberate consideration. The result is a conviction that the States have no power, by taxation or otherwise, to retard, impede, burden, or in any manner control, the operations of the constitutional laws enacted by Congress to carry into execution the powers vested in the general government. This is, we think, the unavoidable consequence of that supremacy which the constitution has declared.

We are unanimously of opinion, that the law passed by the legislature of Maryland, imposing a tax on the Bank of the United States, is unconstitutional and void....

1820

MISSOURI COMPROMISE

issouri applied for statehood as a slave state in 1819. Admitting Missouri as a slave state would upset the balance between the number of slave and free states, tipping political power—particularly in the Senate—toward the slave states. Controversy flared within Congress, which finally compromised by admitting Missouri as a slave state and creating the free state of Maine out of a piece of Massachusetts to maintain the balance. The conference committee's report on the Missouri Compromise further proposed to prohibit slavery above the 36° 30´ latitude line in the remainder of the Louisiana Territory. Although regional controversies had plagued the country before, the debate over Missouri represented a new phase, with slavery now paramount over other economic issues. The compromise held for thirty-four years and managed to contain the increasing tensions over slavery.

An Act to authorize the people of the Missouri territory to form a constitution and state government, and for the admission of such state into the Union on an equal footing with the original states, and to prohibit slavery in certain territories.

Be it enacted by the Senate and House of Representatives of the United States of America, in Congress assembled, That the inhabitants of that portion of the Missouri territory included within the boundaries herein-after designated, be, and they are hereby, authorized to form for themselves a constitution and state government, and to assume such name as they shall deem proper; and the said state, when formed, shall be admitted into the Union, upon an equal footing with the original states, in all respects whatsoever.

SEC. 2. And be it further enacted, That the said state shall consist of all the territory included within the following boundaries, to wit: Beginning in the middle of the Mississippi river, on the parallel of thirty-six degrees of north latitude; thence west, along that parallel of latitude, to the St. Francois river; thence up, and following the course of that river, in the middle of the main channel thereof, to the parallel of latitude of thirty-six degrees and thirty minutes; thence west, along the same, to a point where the said parallel is intersected by a meridian line passing through the middle

of the mouth of the Kansas river, where the same empties into the Missouri river, thence, from the point aforesaid north, along the said meridian line, to the intersection of the parallel of latitude which passes through the rapids of the river Des Moines, making the said line to correspond with the Indian boundary line; thence east, from the point of intersection last afore-

In 1861, the Union Fire Company of Lancaster, Pennsylvania, sent Congress this patriotically colorful petition, captioned "In Union there is strength." It supported a constitutional amendment ensuring the existence of slavery unless it was prohibited by state law and extending the line dividing free and slaveholding states to the Pacific Ocean from the boundary specified in the Missouri Compromise.

The committee of conference of
the Senate and of the House of Representatives, on the subject of the disa-
greeing votes of the Two Houses, upon the
Bill entitled an "Act for the admission
of the State of Maine into the Union"—
Report the following Resolution.

Resolved.

1.st That they recommend to the
Senate to recede from their amendments
to the said Bill

2.d That they recommend to the
two Houses to agree to strike
out of the fourth Section of the Bill from
the House of Representatives now pending in the Senate, entitled an "Act
to authorize the people of the Missouri
Territory to form a Constitution and State
Government and for the admission of
such State into the Union upon an equal
footing with the original States" The
following proviso in the following words—
and shall ordain and establish, that
there shall be neither Slavery nor involuntary Servitude otherwise than in the

The conference committee on the Missouri Compromise submitted its report to Congress on March 1, 1820.

day of election, and all other persons qualified to vote for representatives to the general assembly of the said territory, shall be qualified to be elected and they are hereby qualified and authorized to vote, and choose representatives to form a convention, . . .

SEC. 7. And be it further enacted, That in case a constitution and state government shall be formed for the people of the said territory of Missouri, the said convention or representatives, as soon thereafter as may be, shall cause a true and attested copy of such constitution or frame of state government, as shall be formed or provided, to be transmitted to Congress.

SEC. 8. And be it further enacted. That in all that territory ceded by France to the United States, under the name of Louisiana, which lies north of thirty-six degrees and thirty minutes north latitude, not included within the limits of the state, contemplated by this act, slavery and involuntary servitude, otherwise than in the punishment of crimes, whereof the parties shall have been duly convicted, shall be, and is hereby, for-ever prohibited: Provided always, That any person escaping into the same, from whom labour or service is lawfully claimed, in any state or territory of the United States, such fugitive may be lawfully reclaimed and conveyed to the person claiming his or her labour or service as aforesaid.

APPROVED, MARCH 6, 1820.

said, along the said parallel of latitude, to the middle of the channel of the main fork of the said river Des Moines; thence down and along the middle of the main channel of the said river Des Moines, to the mouth of the same, where it empties into the Mississippi river; thence, due east, to the middle of the main channel of the Mississippi river; thence down, and following the course of the Mississippi river, in the middle of the main channel thereof, to the place of beginning. . . .

SEC. 3. And be it further enacted, That all free white male citizens of the United States, who shall have arrived at the age of twenty-one years, and have resided in said territory: three months previous to the

1823

MONROE DOCTRINE

*I*n response to a potential French threat to restore the Spanish monarchy in exchange for Cuba, Britain's foreign minister suggested that the United States and Great Britain sign a joint pledge that opposed intervention in Spanish America. Secretary of State John Quincy Adams refused, hoping to annex both Texas and Cuba to his country. Soon thereafter, hearkening back to Washington's 1796 farewell address, Adams wrote what has become known as the Monroe Doctrine. Buried in a routine annual message delivered to Congress by President James Monroe in December 1823, the doctrine warned European nations that the United States would not tolerate further colonization or puppet monarchs. The European powers, according to Monroe, must respect the Western Hemisphere as the U.S. sphere of interest.

The Monroe Doctrine was invoked in 1865 when the U.S. government exerted diplomatic and military pressure in support of the Mexican President Benito Juárez's revolt against Maximilian, the emperor of Mexico. Almost forty years later, in 1904, European creditors of a number of Latin American countries threatened armed intervention to collect the debts. President Theodore Roosevelt promptly proclaimed the right of the United States to exercise an "international police power" to curb such "chronic wrongdoing." As a result, he and future Presidents dispatched U.S. Marines into Santo Domingo in 1904, Nicaragua in 1911, and Haiti in 1915, ostensibly to keep the Europeans out.

Other Latin American nations viewed these interventions with misgiving, fearing that the true motive had more to do with asserting control than protecting these countries, and relations between the United States and its southern neighbors remained strained. Conceived to meet major concerns of the moment, the doctrine soon became a watchword of U.S. policy in the Western Hemisphere.

At the proposal of the Russian Imperial Government, made through the minister of the Emperor residing here, a full power and instructions have been transmitted to the minister of the United States at St. Petersburg to arrange by amicable negotiation the respective rights and interests of the two nations on the northwest coast of this continent. A similar proposal has been made by His Imperial Majesty to the Government of Great Britain, which has likewise been acceded to. The Government of the United States has been desirous by this friendly proceeding of manifesting the great value which they have invariably attached to the friendship of the Emperor and their solicitude to cultivate the best understanding with his Government. In the discussions to which this interest has given rise and in the arrangements by which they may terminate the occasion has been judged proper for asserting, as a principle in which the rights and interests of the United States are involved, that the American continents, by the free and independent condition which they have assumed and maintain, are henceforth not to be considered as subjects for future colonization by any European powers....

It was stated at the commencement of the last session that a great effort was then making in Spain and Portugal to improve the condition of the people of those countries, and that it appeared to be conducted with extraordinary moderation. It need scarcely be remarked that the results have been so far very different from what was then anticipated. Of events in that quarter of the globe, with which we have so much intercourse and from which we derive our origin, we have always been anxious and interested spectators. The citizens of the United States cherish sentiments the most friendly in favor of the liberty and happiness of their fellow-men on that side of the Atlantic. In the wars of the European powers in matters relating to themselves we have never taken any part, nor does it comport with our policy to do so. It is only when our rights are invaded or seriously menaced that we resent injuries or make preparation for our defense. With the movements in this hemisphere we are of necessity more immediately connected, and by causes which must be obvious to all enlightened and impartial observers. The political system of the allied powers is essentially different in this respect from that of America. This difference proceeds from that which exists in their respective Governments; and to the defense of our own, which has been achieved by the loss of so much blood and treasure, and matured by the wisdom of their most enlightened citizens, and under which we have enjoyed unexampled felicity, this whole nation is devoted. We owe it, therefore, to candor and to the amicable relations existing between the United States and those powers to declare that we should consider any attempt on their part to extend their system to any portion of this hemisphere as dangerous to our peace and safety. With the existing colonies or dependencies of any European power we have not interfered and shall not interfere. But with the Governments who have declared their independence and maintain it, and whose independence we have, on great consideration and on just principles, acknowledged, we could not view any interposition for the purpose of oppressing them, or controlling in any other manner their destiny, by any European power in any other light than as the manifestation of an unfriendly disposition toward the United States. In the war between those new Governments and Spain we declared our neutrality at the time of their recognition, and to this we have adhered, and shall continue to adhere, provided no change shall occur which, in the judgement of the competent authorities of this Government, shall make a corresponding change on the part of the United States indispensable to their security....

Our policy in regard to Europe, which was adopted at an early stage of the wars which have so long agitated that quarter of the globe, nevertheless remains the same, which is, not to interfere in the internal concerns of any of its powers; to consider the government de facto as the legitimate government for us; to cultivate friendly relations with it, and to preserve those relations by a frank, firm, and manly policy, meeting in all instances the just claims of every power, submitting to injuries from none....

It is impossible that the allied powers should extend their political system to any portion of either continent without endangering our peace and happiness; nor can anyone believe that our southern brethren, if left to themselves, would adopt it of their own accord. It is equally impossible, therefore, that we should behold such interposition in any form with indifference....

1824

GIBBONS V. OGDEN

*I*n 1807 Robert Fulton and Robert Livingston opened up steamboat travel on the Hudson River, and soon the State of New York passed a law giving them a monopoly "navigating all boats that might be propelled by steam, on all waters within the territory, or jurisdiction of the State, for the term of twenty years." Fulton and Livingston issued permits to steamboat operators and seized competitors' boats that operated without their endorsement. Aaron Ogden had a license under the Fulton-Livingston monopoly from the State of New York to navigate between New York City and New Jersey. Ogden found himself competing with Thomas Gibbons, who had received permission from the federal government to use the waterways. After the State of New York denied Gibbons access to Hudson Bay, he sued Ogden. Ogden tried to persuade the court to bar Gibbons from operating his boats, with his lawyer arguing that the states had jurisdiction over this issue of interstate commerce. Gibbons's lawyer countered that Congress should control interstate commerce.

The case progressed to the Supreme Court, where Chief Justice Marshall's opinion carried out the clear original intent of the Constitution that Congress, not the states, should regulate interstate commerce. Marshall's decision sustained the theme that the federal government should have more power than the states—and ruled that Congress could constitutionally regulate many activities that affected interstate commerce. In the wake of this decision, the federal government, with continual reference to the Constitution's commerce clause, increasingly exercised its authority by legislation and judicial decision over the whole range of the nation's economic life.

[Decided March 2, 1824]

MR. CHIEF JUSTICE MARSHALL DELIVERED THE OPINION OF THE COURT, AND, AFTER STATING THE CASE, PROCEEDED AS FOLLOWS: . . .

The words are: *Congress shall have power to regulate commerce with foreign nations, and among the several states, and with the Indian tribes.* The subject to be regulated is commerce; and our Constitution being, as was aptly said at the bar, one of enumeration and not of definition, to as certain the extent of the power it becomes necessary to settle the meaning of the word.

Commerce, undoubtedly, is traffic, but it is something more—it is intercourse. It describes the commercial intercourse between nations, and parts of nations, in all its branches, and is regulated by prescribing rules for carrying on that intercourse. The mind can scarcely conceive a system for regulating commerce between nations which shall exclude all laws concerning navigation, which shall be silent on the admission of the vessels of the one nation into the ports of the other, and be confined to prescribing rules for the conduct of individuals in the actual employment of buying and selling or of barter. If commerce does not include navigation,

the government of the Union has no direct power over that subject, and can make no law prescribing what shall constitute American vessels, or requiring that they shall be navigated by American seamen.

Yet this power has been exercised from the commencement of the government, has been exercised with the consent of all, and has been understood by all to be a commercial regulation. All America understands, and has uniformly understood, the word commerce to comprehend navigation. . . .

If Congress has the power to regulate it, that power must be exercised whenever the subject exists. If it exists within the states, if a foreign voyage may commence or terminate at a port within a state, then the power of Congress may be exercised within a state. . . .

The power of Congress, then, whatever it may be, must be exercised within the territorial jurisdiction of the several states. . . .

We are now arrived at the inquiry—What is this power? It is the power to regulate, that is, to prescribe the rule by which commerce is to be governed. . . .

But it has been urged with great earnestness that, although the power of Congress to regulate commerce with foreign nations and among the several states be coextensive with the subject itself, and have no other limits than are prescribed in the Constitution, yet the states may severally exercise the same power within their respective jurisdictions....

The appellant...contends that full power to regulate a particular subject implies the whole power and leaves no residuum; that a grant of the whole is incompatible with the existence of a right in another to any part of it. Both parties have appealed to the Constitution, to legislative acts, and judicial decisions; and have drawn arguments from all these sources to support and illustrate the propositions they respectively maintain....

The sole question is—Can a state regulate commerce with foreign nations and among the states while Congress is regulating it?

The counsel for the respondent answer this question in the affirmative, and rely very much on the restrictions in the 10th Section as supporting their opinion. They say, very truly, that limitations of a power furnish a strong argument in favor of the existence of that power, and that the section which prohibits the states from laying duties on imports or exports proves that this power might have been exercised had it not been expressly forbidden; and, consequently, that any other commercial regulation, not expressly forbidden, to which the original power of the state was competent, may still be made....

Decree

This court is of opinion that so much of the several laws of the state of New York as prohibits vessels, licensed according to the laws of the United States, from navigating the waters of the state of New York, by means of fire or steam, is repugnant to the said Constitution and void. This court is, therefore, of opinion that the decree of the court of New York for the trial of impeachments and the correction of errors, affirming the decree of the chancellor of that state is erroneous and ought to be reversed, and the same is hereby reversed and annulled. And this court doth further direct, order, and decree that the bill of the said Aaron Ogden be dismissed, and the same is hereby dismissed accordingly.

1830

PRESIDENT ANDREW JACKSON'S MESSAGE TO CONGRESS "ON INDIAN REMOVAL"

*I*n the early nineteenth century, U.S. citizens were eager to settle those lands that Indians still held in states east of the Mississippi River, primarily Georgia, Tennessee, Alabama, Mississippi, and North Carolina. White inhabitants of Georgia were particularly eager to uproot the Cherokees from the state because they had discovered gold on tribal lands. Violence was commonplace in Georgia, and in all likelihood, local whites would have decimated a portion of the tribe had the Indians not relocated. On December 6, 1830, in a message to Congress, President Andrew Jackson called for the removal of eastern Native American tribes to land west of the Mississippi River, to open new land for settlement by citizens of the United States. Clearing Alabama and Mississippi of their Indian populations, he said, would "enable those states to advance rapidly in population, wealth, and power." Jackson's message rationalized the removal policy already in place since the enactment of the Indian Removal Act of May 28, 1830. Referring to what was then the edge of white-settled territory, Jackson declared that removal would "incalculably strengthen the southwestern frontier." His militant approach to Indian removal clearly rejected tribe-by-tribe treaties and sought the power to remove the Native Americans by force.

Removal of the Indian tribes continued beyond Jackson's tenure as President. The most infamous of the removals took place between 1835 and 1838, two years after the end of Jackson's second term, when the U.S. military forcibly removed 16,000 Cherokee Indians after a fraudulent treaty by unauthorized individuals had signed away most of their remaining lands. Their journey west became known as the "Trail of Tears," because of the approximately four thousand deaths from sickness and starvation along the way. By 1850 most native people east of the Mississippi River had reluctantly taken up residence in "Indian Territory."

It gives me pleasure to announce to Congress that the benevolent policy of the Government, steadily pursued for nearly thirty years, in relation to the removal of the Indians beyond the white settlements is approaching to a happy consummation. Two important tribes have accepted the provision made for their removal at the last session of Congress, and it is believed that their example will induce the remaining tribes also to seek the same obvious advantages.

The consequences of a speedy removal will be important to the United States, to individual States, and to the Indians themselves. The pecuniary advantages which it promises to the Government are the least of its recommendations. It puts an end to all possible danger of collision between the authorities of the General and State Governments on account of the Indians. It will place a dense and civilized population in large tracts of country now occupied by a few savage hunters. By opening the whole territory between Tennessee on the north and Louisiana on the south to the settlement of the whites it will incalculably strengthen the southwestern frontier and render the adjacent States strong enough to repel future invasions without remote aid. It will relieve the whole State of Mississippi and the western part of Alabama of Indian occupancy, and enable those States to advance rapidly in population, wealth, and power. It will separate the Indians from immediate contact with settlements of whites; free them from the power of the States; enable them to pursue happiness in their own way and under their own rude institutions; will retard the progress of decay, which is lessening their numbers, and perhaps cause them gradually, under the protection of the Government and through the influence of good counsels, to cast off their savage habits and become an interesting, civilized, and Christian community.

What good man would prefer a country covered with forests and ranged by a few thousand savages to our extensive Republic, studded with cities, towns, and prosperous farms embellished with all the improvements which art can devise or industry execute, occupied by more than 12,000,000 happy people, and filled with all the blessings of liberty, civilization and religion?

The present policy of the Government is but a continuation of the same progressive change by a milder process. The tribes which occupied the countries now constituting the Eastern States were annihilated or have melted away to make room for the whites. The waves of population and civilization are rolling to the westward, and we now propose to acquire the countries occupied by the red men of the South and West by a fair exchange, and, at the expense of the United States, to send them to land where their existence may be prolonged and perhaps made perpetual. Doubtless it will be painful to leave the graves of their fathers; but what do they more than our ancestors did or than our children are now doing? To better their condition in an unknown land our forefathers left all that was dear in earthly objects. Our children by thousands yearly leave the land of their birth to seek new homes in distant regions. Does Humanity weep at these painful separations from everything, animate and inanimate, with which the young heart has become entwined? Far from it. It is rather a source of joy that our country affords scope where our young population may range unconstrained in body or in mind, developing the power and facilities of man in their highest perfection. These remove hundreds and almost thousands of miles at their own expense, purchase the lands they occupy, and support themselves at their new homes from the moment of their arrival. Can it be cruel in this Government when, by events which it can not control, the Indian is made discontented in his ancient home to purchase his lands, to give him a new and extensive territory, to pay the expense of his removal, and support him a year in his new abode? How many thousands of our own people would gladly embrace the opportunity of removing to the West on such conditions! If the offers made to the Indians were extended to them, they would be hailed with gratitude and joy.

And is it supposed that the wandering savage has a stronger attachment to his home than the settled, civilized Christian? Is it more afflicting to him to leave the graves of his fathers than it is to our brothers and children? Rightly considered, the policy of the General Government toward the red man is not only liberal, but generous. He is unwilling to submit to the laws of the States and mingle with their population. To save him from this alternative, or perhaps utter annihilation, the General Government kindly offers him a new home, and proposes to pay the whole expense of his removal and settlement.

1848

Treaty of Guadalupe Hidalgo

With the defeat of its army and the fall of the capital, Mexico City, in September 1847, the Mexican government surrendered to the United States and began negotiations to end the war that had started in May 1846. The Mexican War had begun over a combination of factors, central among them the annexation of Texas. With thousands of slave-owning Americans in residence, Texas had seceded from Mexico to become an independent republic after the battle of Santa Anna in 1836. In 1845 Congress passed a resolution to annex Texas. To win over Texans who feared a war on their own soil between Mexico and the United States, President James K. Polk supported their claim that the border between Texas and Mexico was the Rio Grande, not the Nueces River. Thus the Texas that President Polk proposed to annex was far larger than the original republic.

Mexico fought for the territory, but the United States won a resounding victory. Nicholas Trist, chief clerk of the State Department, who had accompanied General Winfield Scott as a diplomat and President Polk's representative, negotiated the peace talks. In this treaty, signed on February 2, 1848, Mexico ceded 55 percent of its territory, including parts of present-day Arizona, California, New Mexico, Texas, Colorado, Nevada, and Utah, to the United States. The United States, in return, paid Mexico $15 million and assumed several million dollars of American claims against Mexico.

At the Battle of Molino del Rey in September 1847, the U.S. Army blows up the Mexican cannon foundry, an event commemorated in a celebratory lithograph, published the next year.

Treaty of Peace, Friendship, Limits, and Settlement between the United States of America and the United Mexican States Concluded at Guadalupe Hidalgo, February 2, 1848; Ratification Advised by Senate, with Amendments, March 10, 1848; Ratified by President, March 16, 1848; Ratifications Exchanged at Queretaro, May 30, 1848; Proclaimed, July 4, 1848.

In the Name of Almighty God

The United States of America and the United Mexican States animated by a sincere desire to put an end to the calamities of the war which unhappily exists between the two Republics and to establish Upon a solid basis relations of peace and friendship, which shall confer reciprocal benefits upon the citizens of both, and assure the concord, harmony, and mutual confidence wherein the two people should live, as good neighbors have for that purpose appointed their respective plenipotentiaries...Who, after a reciprocal communication of their respective full powers, have, under the protection of Almighty God, the author of peace, arranged, agreed upon, and signed the following: Treaty of Peace, Friendship, Limits, and Settlement between the United States of America and the Mexican Republic.

Article I
There shall be firm and universal peace between the United States of America and the Mexican Republic, and between their respective countries, territories, cities, towns, and people, without exception of places or persons....

Article V
The boundary line between the two Republics shall commence in the Gulf of Mexico, three leagues from

land, opposite the mouth of the Rio Grande, otherwise called Rio Bravo del Norte, or Opposite the mouth of its deepest branch, if it should have more than one branch emptying directly into the sea; from thence up the middle of that river, following the deepest channel, where it has more than one, to the point where it strikes the southern boundary of New Mexico; thence, westwardly, along the whole southern boundary of New Mexico (which runs north of the town called Paso) to its western termination; thence, northward, along the western line of New Mexico, until it intersects the first branch of the river Gila; (or if it should not intersect any branch of that river, then to the point on the said line nearest to such branch, and thence in a direct line to the same); thence down the middle of the said branch and of the said river, until it empties into the Rio Colorado; thence across the Rio Colorado, following the division line between Upper and Lower California, to the Pacific Ocean.

The southern and western limits of New Mexico, mentioned in the article, are those laid down in the map entitled "Map of the United Mexican States, as organized and defined by various acts of the Congress of said republic, and constructed according to the best authorities. Revised edition. Published at New York, in 1847, by J. Disturnell," of which map a copy is added to this treaty, bearing the signatures and seals of the undersigned Plenipotentiaries. And, in order to preclude all difficulty in tracing upon the ground the limit separating Upper from Lower California, it is agreed that the said limit shall consist of a straight line drawn from the middle of the Rio Gila, where it unites with the Colorado, to a point on the coast of the Pacific Ocean, distant one marine league due south of the southernmost point of the port of San Diego, according to the plan of said port made in the year 1782 by Don Juan Pantoja, second sailing-master of the Spanish fleet, and published at Madrid in the year 1802, in the atlas to the voyage of the schooners Sutil and Mexicana; of which plan a copy is hereunto added, signed and sealed by the respective Plenipotentiaries. . . .

The boundary line established by this article shall be religiously respected by each of the two republics, and no change shall ever be made therein, except by the express and free consent of both nations, lawfully given by the General Government of each, in conformity with its own constitution. . . .

ARTICLE XXIII

This treaty shall be ratified by the President of the United States of America, by and with the advice and consent of the Senate thereof; and by the President of the Mexican Republic, with the previous approbation of its general Congress; and the ratifications shall be exchanged in the City of Washington, or at the seat of Government of Mexico, in four months from the date of the signature hereof, or sooner if practicable. In faith whereof we, the respective Plenipotentiaries, have signed this treaty of peace, friendship, limits, and settlement, and have hereunto affixed our seals respectively. Done in quintuplicate, at the city of Guadalupe Hidalgo, on the second day of February, in the year of our Lord one thousand eight hundred and forty-eight.

N. P. TRUST

LUIS P. CUEVAS

BERNARDO COUTO

MIGL. ATRISTAIN

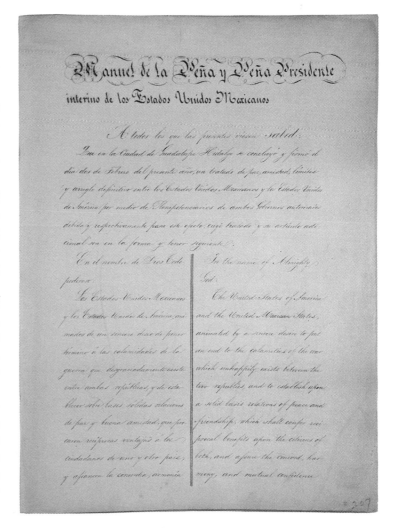

1850

COMPROMISE OF 1850

By 1850 regional disagreements over slavery strained the bonds of union between the North and South. These tensions became especially acute when Congress began to consider whether western lands acquired after the Mexican War would permit slavery. In 1849 California requested permission to enter the Union as a free state. Adding more free-state senators to Congress would destroy the balance between slave and free states that had existed since the Missouri Compromise of 1820. Because everyone looked to the Senate to defuse the growing crisis, Senator Henry Clay of Kentucky proposed a series of resolutions designed to "[a]djust amicably all existing questions of controversy... arising out of the institution of slavery."

In one of the most momentous congressional debates in American history, the Senate discussed Clay's solution for seven months. His original resolutions did not pass, but Congress eventually enacted five statutes in September of 1850. These called for the admission of California as a "free state," provided for a territorial government for Utah and New Mexico, established a boundary between Texas and the United States, called for the abolition of the slave trade in Washington, D.C., and amended the Fugitive Slave Act. With the Compromise of 1850, Congress addressed the immediate crisis resulting from territorial expansion. But one aspect of the compromise—a stronger fugitive slave act—soon began to tear at sectional peace.

CLAY'S RESOLUTIONS JANUARY 29, 1850

It being desirable, for the peace, concord, and harmony of the Union of these States, to settle and adjust amicably all existing questions of controversy between them arising out of the institution of slavery upon a fair, equitable and just basis: therefore,

1. Resolved, That California, with suitable boundaries, ought, upon her application to be admitted as one of the States of this Union, without the imposition by Congress of any restriction in respect to the exclusion or introduction of slavery within those boundaries.

2. Resolved, That as slavery does not exist by law, and is not likely to be introduced into any of the territory acquired by the United States from the republic of Mexico, it is inexpedient for Congress to provide by law either for its introduction into, or exclusion from, any part of the said territory; and that appropriate territorial governments ought to be established by Congress in all of the said territory, not assigned as the boundaries of the proposed State of California, without the adoption of any restriction or condition on the subject of slavery.

3. Resolved, That the western boundary of the State of Texas ought to be fixed on the Rio del Norte, commencing one marine league from its mouth, and running up that river to the southern line of New Mexico; thence with that line eastwardly, and so continuing in the same direction to the line as established between the United States and Spain, excluding any

portion of New Mexico, whether lying on the east or west of that river.

4. Resolved, That it be proposed to the State of Texas, that the United States will provide for the payment of all that portion of the legitimate and bona fide public debt of that State contracted prior to its annexation to the United States,... and upon the condition, also, that the said State of Texas shall, by some solemn and authentic act of her legislature or of a convention, relinquish to the United States any claim which it has to any part of New Mexico.

5. Resolved, That it is inexpedient to abolish slavery in the District of Columbia whilst that institution continues to exist in the State of Maryland, without the consent of that State, without the consent of the people of the District, and without just compensation to the owners of slaves within the District.

6. But, resolved, That it is expedient to prohibit, within the District, the slave trade in slaves brought into it from States or places beyond the limits of the District, either to be sold therein as merchandise, or to be transported to other markets without the District of Columbia.

7. Resolved, That more effectual provision ought to be made by law, according to the requirement of the constitution, for the restitution and delivery of persons bound to service or labor in any State, who may escape into any other State or Territory in the Union. And,

8. Resolved, That Congress has no power to promote or obstruct the trade in slaves between the slaveholding States; but that the admission or exclusion of slaves brought from one into another of them, depends exclusively upon their own particular laws....

An Act to amend, and supplementary to, the Act entitled "An Act respecting Fugitives from Justice, and Persons escaping from the Service of their Masters," approved February twelfth, one thousand seven hundred and ninety-three.

Be it enacted by the Senate and House of Representatives of the United States of America in congress assembled, That the persons who... are authorized to exercise the powers that any justice of the peace, or other magistrate of any of the United States, may exercise in respect to offenders for any crime or offence against the United States, by arresting, imprisoning, or bailing the same under and by virtue of the thirty-third section of the act of the twenty-fourth of September seventeen hundred and eighty-nine, entitled "An Act to establish the Judicial courts of the United States," shall be, and are hereby, authorized and required to exercise and discharge all the powers and duties conferred by this act....

SEC. 5. And be it further enacted, That it shall be the duty of all marshals and deputy marshals to obey and execute all warrants and precepts issued under the provisions of this act, when to them directed; and should any marshal or deputy marshal refuse to receive such warrant... he shall, on conviction thereof, be fined in the sum of one thousand dollars... and... the said commissioners... are hereby authorized and empowered... to appoint, in writing under their hands, anyone or more suitable persons, from time to time, to execute all such warrants and other process as may be issued by them in the lawful performance of their respective duties... to summon and call to their aid the bystanders, or posse comitatus of the proper county, when necessary... and all good citizens are hereby commanded to aid and assist in the prompt and efficient execution of this law, whenever their services may he required....

SEC. 6. And be it further enacted, That when a person held to service or labor in any State or Territory of the United States, has heretofore or shall hereafter escape into another State or Territory of the United States, the person or persons to whom such service or labor may be due, or his, her, or their agent or attorney ... may pursue and reclaim such fugitive person, either by procuring a warrant... or by seizing and arresting such fugitive, where the same can be done without process, and by taking, or causing such person to be taken, forthwith before such court, judge, or commissioner, whose duty it shall be to hear and determine the case of such claimant in a summary manner; and upon satisfactory proof being made, by deposition or affidavit, in writing... to use such reasonable force and restraint as may be necessary... to take and remove such fugitive person back to the State or Territory whence he or she may have escaped as aforesaid. In no trial or hearing under this act shall the testimony of such alleged fugitive be admitted in evidence; and the certificates in this and the first [fourth] section mentioned, shall be conclusive of the right of the person or persons in whose favor granted, to remove such fugitive to the State or Territory from which he escaped....

SEC. 7. And be it further enacted, That any person who shall knowingly and willingly obstruct, hinder, or prevent such claimant, his agent or attorney,... from arresting such a fugitive from service or labor,... shall, for either of said offences, be subject to a fine not exceeding one thousand dollars, and imprisonment not exceeding six months....

Approved, September 18, 1850.

1854

KANSAS-NEBRASKA ACT

*U*nder the terms of the Missouri Compromise of 1820, slavery became illegal in territories above the 36° 30´ latitude line. Nevertheless, in January 1854 Senator
Stephen Douglas introduced a bill that divided the land north of this line and west
of Missouri into two territories, Kansas and Nebraska. He argued for popular sovereignty, which
would allow the settlers of the new territories to decide for themselves whether slavery would be legal
there. Antislavery advocates were outraged at this attack on the Missouri Compromise. After months
of debate, the Kansas-Nebraska Act passed on May 30, 1854. Pro-slavery and anti-slavery settlers
rushed to Kansas, each side hoping to determine the results of the first election after the law went
into effect. The conflict turned violent, aggravating the split between North and South until reconciliation was virtually impossible. Opponents of the Kansas-Nebraska Act helped found the
Republican Party, which opposed the spread of slavery into the territories. As a result of the Kansas-
Nebraska Act, the United States moved closer to civil war.

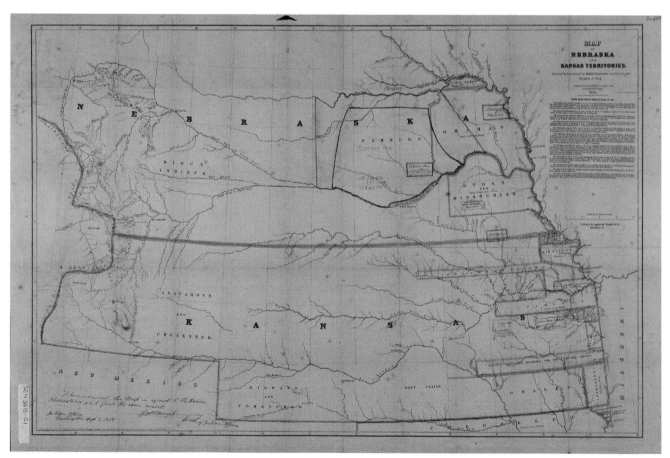

This 1854 map shows the location of the Indian reserves as well as the division of the Kansas and Nebraska territories.

"[I]t being the true intent and meaning of this act not to legislate slavery into any Territory or State, nor to exclude it therefrom, but to leave the people thereof perfectly free to form and regulate their domestic institutions in their own way, . . ."

Be it enacted by the Senate and House of Representatives of the United States of America in Congress assembled, That all that part of the territory of the United States included within the following limits, except such portions thereof as are hereinafter expressly exempted from the operations of this act, to wit: beginning at a point in the Missouri River where the fortieth parallel of north latitude crosses the same; then west on said parallel to the east boundary of the Territory of Utah, the summit of the Rocky Mountains; thence on said summit northwest to the forty-ninth parallel of north latitude; thence east on said parallel to the western boundary of the territory of Minnesota; thence southward on said boundary to the Missouri River; thence down the main channel of said river to the place of beginning, be, and the same is hereby, created into a temporary government by the name of the Territory Nebraska; and when admitted as a State or States, the said Territory or any portion of the same, shall be received into the Union with or without slavery, as their constitution may prescribe at the time of the admission: Provided, That nothing in this act contained shall be construed to inhibit the government of the United States from dividing said Territory into two or more Territories, in such manner and at such time as Congress shall deem convenient and proper, or from attaching a portion of said Territory to any other State or Territory of the United States: Provided further, That nothing in this act contained shall be construed to impair the rights of person or property now pertaining the Indians in said Territory so long as such rights shall remain unextinguished by treaty between the United States and such Indians, or include any territory which, by treaty with any Indian tribe, is not, without the consent of said tribe, to be included within the territorial line or jurisdiction of any State or Territory; but all such territory shall be out of the boundaries, and constitute no part of the Territory of Nebraska, until said tribe shall signify their assent to the President of the United States to be included within the said Territory of Nebraska, or to affect the authority of the government of the United States to make any regulations respecting such Indians, their lands, property, or other rights, by treaty, law, or otherwise, which it would have been competent to the government to make if this act had never passed. . . .

SEC. 14. And be it further enacted, That a delegate to the House of Representatives of the United States, to serve for the term of two years, who shall be a citizen of the United States, may be elected by the voters qualified to elect members of the Legislative Assembly, who shall be entitled to the same rights and privileges as are exercised and enjoyed by the delegates from the several other Territories of the United States to the said House of Representatives, but the delegate first elected shall hold his seat only during the term of the Congress to which he shall be elected. . . . That the Constitution, and all Laws of the United States which are not locally inapplicable, shall have the same force and effect within the said Territory of Nebraska as elsewhere within the United States, except the eighth section of the act preparatory to the admission of Missouri into the Union approved March sixth, eighteen hundred and twenty, which, being inconsistent with the principle of non-intervention by Congress with slaves in the States and Territories, as recognized by the legislation of eighteen hundred and fifty, commonly called the Compromise Measures, is hereby declared inoperative and void; it being the true intent and meaning of this act not to legislate slavery into any Territory or State, nor to exclude it therefrom, but to leave the people thereof perfectly free to form and regulate their domestic institutions in their own way, subject only to the Constitution of the United States: Provided, That nothing herein contained shall be construed to revive or put in force any law or regulation which may have existed prior to the act of sixth March, eighteen hundred and twenty, either protecting, establishing, prohibiting, or abolishing slavery. . . .

SEC. 19. And be it further enacted, That all that part of the Territory of the United States included within the following limits, except such portions thereof as are hereinafter expressly exempted from the operations of this act, to wit, beginning at a point on the western boundary of the State of Missouri, where the thirty-seventh parallel of north latitude crosses the same; thence west on said parallel to the eastern boundary of New Mexico; thence north on said boundary to latitude thirty-eight; thence following said boundary westward to the east boundary of the Territory of Utah, on the summit of the Rocky Mountains; thence northward on said summit to the fortieth parallel of latitude, thence east on said parallel to the western boundary of the State of Missouri; thence south with the western boundary of said State to the place of beginning, be, and the same is hereby, created into a temporary government by the name of the Territory of Kansas; and when admitted as a State or States, the said Territory, or any portion of the same, shall be received into the Union with or without slavery, as their Constitution may prescribe at the time of their admission....

SEC. 32. And be it further enacted, That a delegate to the House of Representatives of the United States, to serve for the term of two years, who shall be a citizen of the United States, may be elected by the voters qualified to elect members of the Legislative Assembly.... That the Constitution, and all laws of the United States which are not locally inapplicable, shall have the same force and effect within the said Territory of Kansas as elsewhere within the United States, except the eighth section of the act preparatory to the admission of Missouri into the Union, approved March sixth, eighteen hundred and twenty, which, being inconsistent with the principle of non-intervention by Congress with slavery in the States and Territories, as recognized by the legislation of eighteen hundred and fifty, commonly called the Compromise Measures, is hereby declared inoperative and void; it being the true intent and meaning of this act not to legislate slavery into any Territory or State, nor to exclude it therefrom, but to leave the people thereof perfectly free to form and regulate their domestic institutions in their own way, subject only to the Constitution of the United States: Provided, That nothing herein contained shall be construed to revive or put in force any law or regulation which may have existed prior to the act of sixth of March, eighteen hundred and twenty, either protecting, establishing, prohibiting, or abolishing slavery.

APPROVED, MAY 30, 1854.

1857

SCOTT V. SANDFORD

*I*n 1846 a slave named Dred Scott and his
wife, Harriet, sued for their freedom in a
St. Louis city court. The odds were in their
favor. They had lived with their owner, an army
surgeon, in the free state of Illinois and then at
Fort Snelling, then in the free territory of
Wisconsin. The Scotts' right to freedom rested
on their having been in bondage for extended
periods in a free territory and then returned to a
slave state. Courts had ruled this way in the
past. However, what appeared to be a straightforward lawsuit between two private parties
became an eleven-year legal struggle that culmi-
nated in one of the most notorious decisions ever
issued by the U.S. Supreme Court, with enormous political implications for the entire
nation. On March 6, 1857, Chief Justice Roger
B. Taney read the majority opinion of the Court,
which stated that slaves were not citizens of the
United States and, therefore, could not expect
protection from the federal government or the
courts. The opinion also stated that Congress
had no authority to ban slavery from a federal

*During his twenty-eight years as Chief Justice of the United
States, Roger Taney was vigilant in his concern with states'
rights. His belief that the power to maintain slavery or free slaves
belonged exclusively to the states was at the root of his infamous
decision in the Dred Scott case.*

territory. This decision advanced the nation even closer to civil war. The Thirteenth and Fourteenth
Amendments to the Constitution, which abolished slavery and declared all persons born in the
United States to be U.S. citizens, overturned the decision in Scott v. Sandford.

DRED SCOTT, PLAINTIFF IN ERROR, V. JOHN F. A. SANDFORD.

Mr. Chief Justice TANEY delivered the opinion of the court....

There are two leading questions presented by the record:

1. Had the Circuit Court of the United States jurisdiction to hear and determine the case between these parties? And

2. If it had jurisdiction, is the judgment it has given erroneous or not?...

The question is simply this: Can a negro whose ancestors were imported into this country, and sold as slaves, become a member of the political community

formed and brought into existence by the Constitution of the United States, and as such become entitled to all the rights and privileges and immunities guaranteed to the citizen? One of which rights is the privilege of suing in a court of the United States in the cases specified in the Constitution....

The words "people of the United States" and "citizens" are synonymous terms, and mean the same thing. They both describe the political body who, according to our republican institutions, form the sovereignty, and who hold the power and conduct the Government through their representatives. They are what we familiarly call the "sovereign people," and every citizen is one of this people and a constituent member of this

Chief Justice Roger B. Taney wrote and signed this judgment remanding the Dred Scott case to the Circuit Court of the United States for the district of Missouri.

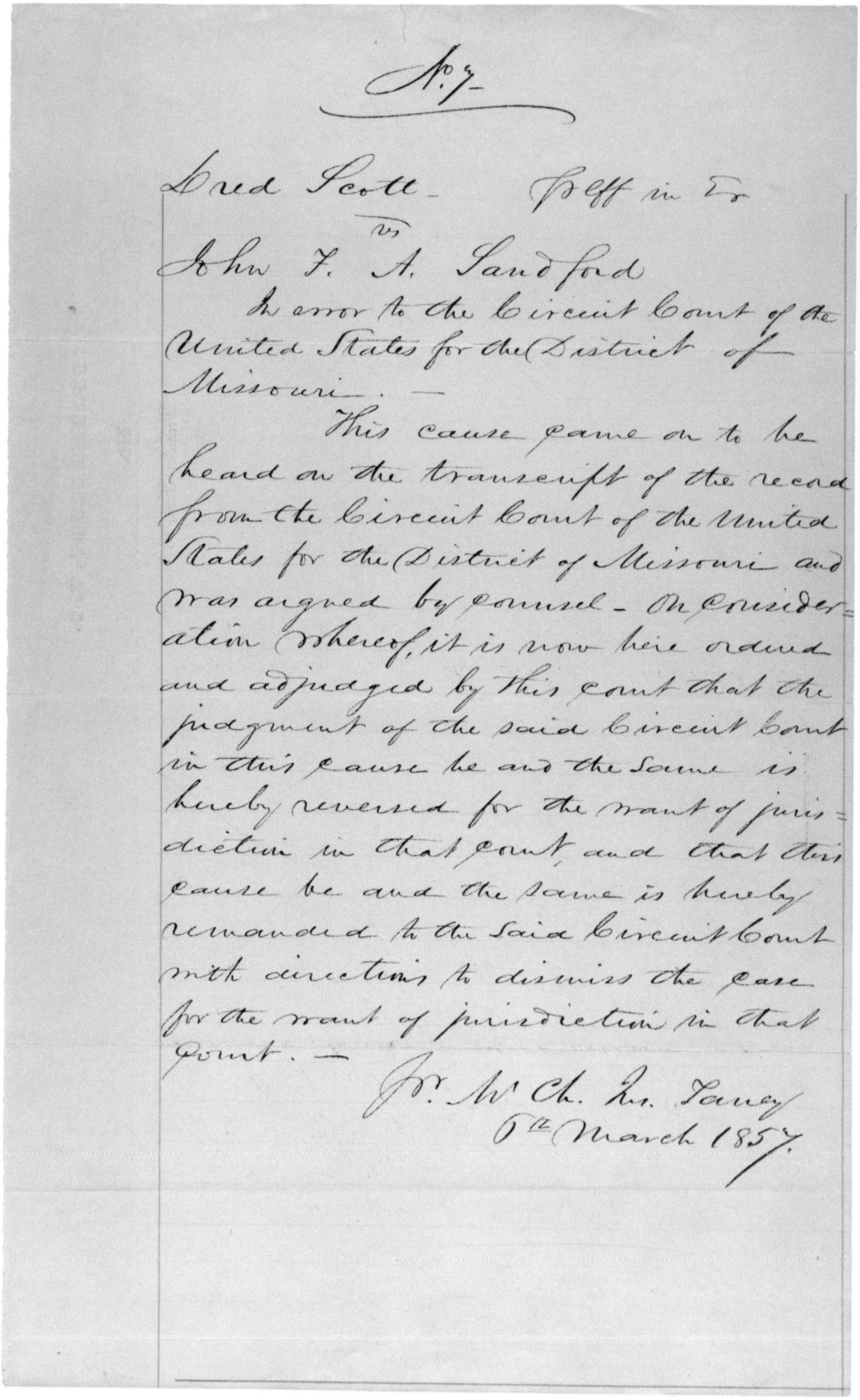

No. 7

Dred Scott   Plff in Er

vs

John F. A. Sandford

In error to the Circuit Court of the United States for the District of Missouri. —

    This cause came on to be heard on the transcript of the record from the Circuit Court of the United States for the District of Missouri and was argued by counsel. On consideration whereof, it is now here ordered and adjudged by this court that the judgment of the said Circuit Court in this cause be and the same is hereby reversed for the want of jurisdiction in that court, and that this cause be and the same is hereby remanded to the said Circuit Court with directions to dismiss the case for the want of jurisdiction in that court. —

Pr W Ch Js Taney
6th March 1857

> *"Can a negro whose ancestors were imported into this country, and sold as slaves, become a member of the political community formed and brought into existence by the Constitution of the United States, and as such become entitled to all the rights and privileges and immunities guaranteed to the citizen?"*

sovereignty. The question before us is, whether the class of persons described in the plea in abatement compose a portion of this people, and are constituent members of this sovereignty? We think they are not, and that they are not included, and were not intended to be included, under the word "citizens" in the Constitution, and can therefore claim none of the rights and privileges which that instrument provides for and secures to citizens of the United States. On the contrary, they were at that time considered as a subordinate and inferior class of beings, who had been subjugated by the dominant race, and, whether emancipated or not, yet remained subject to their authority, and had no rights or privileges but such as those who held the power and the government might choose to grant them....

The language of the Declaration of Independence is equally conclusive:

It begins by declaring "that when in the course of human events it becomes necessary for one people to dissolve the political bands which have connected them with another, and to assume among the powers of the earth the separate and equal station to which the laws of nature and nature's God entitle them, a decent respect for the opinions of mankind requires that they should declare the causes which impel them to the separation."

It then proceeds to say: "We hold these truths to be self-evident: that all men are created equal; that they are endowed by their Creator with certain unalienable rights; that among them is life, liberty, and the pursuit of happiness; that to secure these rights, Governments are instituted, deriving their just powers from the consent of the governed."

The general words above quoted would seem to embrace the whole human family, and if they were used in a similar instrument at this day would be so understood. But it is too clear for dispute, that the enslaved African race were not intended to be included, and formed no part of the people who framed and adopted this declaration; for if the language, as understood in that day, would embrace them, the conduct of the distinguished men who framed the Declaration of Independence would have been utterly and flagrantly inconsistent with the principles they asserted; and instead of the sympathy of mankind, to which they so confidently appealed, they would have deserved and received universal rebuke and reprobation....

And upon a full and careful consideration of the subject, the court is of opinion, that, upon the facts stated in the plea in abatement, Dred Scott was not a citizen of Missouri within the meaning of the Constitution of the United States, and not entitled as such to sue in its courts; and, consequently, that the Circuit Court had no jurisdiction of the case, and that the judgment on the plea in abatement is erroneous....

This brings us to examine by what provision of the Constitution the present Federal Government, under its delegated and restricted powers, is authorized to acquire territory outside of the original limits of the United States, and what powers it may exercise therein over the person or property of a citizen of the United States, while it remains a Territory, and until it shall be admitted as one of the States of the Union....

Upon these considerations, it is the opinion of the court that the act of Congress which prohibited a citizen from holding and owning property of this kind in the territory of the United States north of the line therein mentioned, is not warranted by the Constitution, and is therefore void; and that neither Dred Scott himself, nor any of his family, were made free by being carried into this territory; even if they had been carried there by the owner, with the intention of becoming a permanent resident....

1861

TELEGRAM ANNOUNCING
THE SURRENDER OF FORT SUMTER

On April 10, 1861, Brig. Gen. Pierre G. T. Beauregard, in command of the provisional Confederate forces at Charleston, South Carolina, demanded the surrender of the U.S. garrison of Fort Sumter in Charleston Harbor. Garrison commander Robert Anderson refused. On April 12 Confederate batteries opened fire on the fort, which was unable to reply effectively. At 2:30 P.M. on April 13, Major Anderson surrendered Fort Sumter, evacuating the garrison on the following day. This telegram from Anderson to the Secretary of War, Simon Cameron, announced his withdrawal from Fort Sumter and the start of the Civil War, which would last until April 1865. From 1863 to 1865, the Confederates at Fort Sumter withstood a twenty-two-month siege by Union forces. During this time, most of the fort was reduced to rubble.

S.S.BALTIC.OFF SANDY HOOK APR.EIGHTEENTH.TEN THIRTY A.M. .VIA NEW YORK. . HON.S.CAMERON, SECY.WAR. WASHN. HAVING DEFENDED FORT SUMTER FOR THIRTY FOUR HOURS UNTIL THE QUARTERS WERE ENTIRELY BURNED THE MAIN GATES DESTROYED BY FIRE.THE GORGE WALLS SERIOUSLY INJURED.THE MAGAZINE SURROUNDED BY FLAMES AND ITS DOOR CLOSED FROM THE EFFECTS OF HEAT .FOUR BARRELLS AND THREE CARTRIDGES OF POWDER ONLY BEING AVAILABLE AND NO PROVISIONS REMAINING BUT PORK.I ACCEPTED TERMS OF EVACUATION OFFERED BY GENERAL BEAUREGARD BEING ON SAME OFFERED BY HIM ON THE ELEVENTH INST.PRIOR TO THE COMMENCEMENT OF HOSTILITIES AND MARCHED OUT OF THE FORT SUNDAY AFTERNOON THE FOURTEENTH INST.WITH COLORS FLYING AND DRUMS BEATING.BRINGING AWAY COMPANY AND PRIVATE PROPERTY AND SALUTING MY FLAG WITH FIFTY GUNS. ROBERT ANDERSON.MAJOR FIRST ARTILLERY.COMMANDING.

1862

Homestead Act

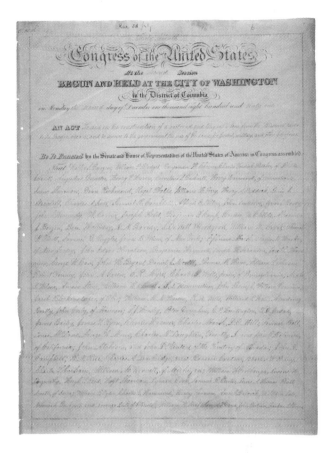

*M*any nineteenth-century Americans considered westward migration a solution for the increasing congestion in eastern cities. In 1860 the Republican Party platform called for an act that would address this problem. Two years later the Homestead Act, which Congress passed in the midst of the Civil War, provided that any adult citizen, or intended citizen, who had never borne arms against the U.S. government could claim 160 acres of surveyed government land. The law required claimants to improve the plot by building a dwelling and cultivating the land. After five years on the land, the original filer owned the property, free and clear, except for a small registration fee.

However, comparatively few urban laborers could afford to build a farm or acquire the necessary tools, seed, and livestock. In the end most of those who purchased land under the act came from areas close to their new homesteads (Iowans moved to Nebraska, Minnesotans to South Dakota, and so on). Unfortunately, the act was framed so ambiguously that it seemed to invite fraud, and early modifications by Congress only compounded the problem. Most of the land went to speculators, cattlemen, miners, lumbermen, and railroads. Of some 500 million acres dispersed by the General Land Office between 1862 and 1904, only 80 million acres went to homesteaders. Indeed, small farmers acquired more land under the Homestead Act in the 20th century than in the 19th.

CHAP. LXXV. — AN ACT TO SECURE HOMESTEADS TO ACTUAL SETTLERS ON THE PUBLIC DOMAIN.

Be it enacted by the Senate and House of Representatives of the United States of America in Congress assembled, That any person who is the head of a family, or who has arrived at the age of twenty-one years, and is a citizen of the United States, or who shall have filed his declaration of intention to become such, as required by the naturalization laws of the United States, and who has never borne arms against the United States Government or given aid and comfort to its enemies, shall, from and after the first January, eighteen hundred and sixty-three, be entitled to enter one quarter section or a less quantity of unappropriated public lands, upon which said person may have filed a preemption claim, or which may, at the time the application is made, be subject to preemption at one dollar and twenty-five cents, or less, per acre; or eighty acres or less of such unappropriated lands, at two dollars and fifty cents per acre, to be located in a body, in conformity to the legal subdivisions of the public lands, and after the same shall have been surveyed: Provided, That any person owning and residing on land may, under the provisions of this act, enter other land lying contiguous to his or her said land, which shall not, with the land so already owned and occupied, exceed in the aggregate one hundred and sixty acres.…

APPROVED, MAY 20, 1862.

1862

PACIFIC RAILWAY ACT

*I*n the 1850s Congress commissioned several topographical surveys across the West to determine the best route for a railroad to the Pacific coast, but private corporations were reluctant to undertake the task without federal assistance. Southern states saw the railroads as a northern interest and refused to support them. After the South seceded, northern politicians no longer had to consider southern concerns. During the Civil War they passed a series of pro-business measures. In an effort to aid business in the construction of a railroad and telegraph line from the Missouri River to the Pacific Ocean and to

This iconic photograph records the moment when the tracks of the Central Pacific and Union Pacific Railroads were joined at Promontory, Utah, on May 10, 1869. Champagne flowed as the engineers shook hands. As one newspaper headline reported, there was "Universal Rejoicing, Enthusiasm, and Jubilee."

secure government use of that line, in 1862 Congress passed the Pacific Railway Act, which designated the thirty-second parallel as the initial transcontinental route and gave railroad companies huge grants of lands for rights-of-way.

The legislation authorized two railroad companies, the Union Pacific and the Central Pacific, to construct the lines. Beginning in 1863 the Union Pacific, employing more than eight thousand Irish, German, and Italian immigrants, built westward from Omaha, Nebraska; the Central Pacific, whose workforce included more than ten thousand Chinese laborers, built eastward from Sacramento, California. Each company faced unprecedented construction problems—mountains, severe weather, and the hostility of Native Americans. On May 10, 1869, in a ceremony at Promontory, Utah, workers laid the last rails and drove in the last spike. Congress eventually authorized four transcontinental railroads and granted 174 million acres of public lands for rights-of-way.

CHAP. CXX.—AN ACT TO AID IN THE CONSTRUCTION OF A RAILROAD AND TELEGRAPH LINE FROM THE MISSOURI RIVER TO THE PACIFIC OCEAN, AND TO SECURE TO THE GOVERNMENT THE USE OF THE SAME FOR POSTAL, MILITARY, AND OTHER PURPOSES.

Be it enacted by the Senate and House of Representatives of the United States of America in Congress assembled That Walter S. Burgess, William P. Blodget, Benjamin H. Cheever, Charles Fosdick Fletcher, [and many others], together with commissioners to be

appointed by the Secretary of the Interior, and all persons who shall or may be associated with them, and their successors, are hereby created and erected into a body corporate and politic in deed and in law, by the name, style, and title of "The Union Pacific Railroad Company";...and the said corporation is hereby authorized and empowered to layout, locate, construct, furnish, maintain, and enjoy a continuous railroad and telegraph, with the appurtenances, from a point on the one hundredth meridian of longitude west from

Greenwich, between the south margin of the valley of the Republican River and the north margin of the valley of the Platte River, in the Territory of Nebraska, to the western boundary of Nevada Territory, upon the route and terms hereinafter provided, and is hereby vested with all the powers, privileges, and immunities necessary to carry into effect the purposes of this act as herein set forth. . . .

SEC. 2. And be it further enacted, That the right of way through the public lands be, and the same is hereby, granted to said company for the construction of said railroad and telegraph line; and the right, power, and authority is hereby given to said company to take from the public lands adjacent to the line of said road, earth, stone, timber, and other materials for the construction thereof; said right of way is granted to said railroad to the extent of two hundred feet in width on each side of said railroad where it may pass over the public lands, including all necessary grounds for stations, buildings, workshops, and depots, machine shops, switches, side tracks, turntables, and, water stations. The United States shall extinguish as rapidly as may be the Indian titles to all lands falling under the

operation of this act and required for the said right of way and; grants hereinafter made.

SEC. 3. And be it further enacted, That there be, and is hereby, granted to the said company, for the purpose of aiding in the construction, of said railroad and telegraph line, and to secure the safe and speedy transportation of the mails, troops, munitions of war, and public stores thereon, every alternate section of public land, designated by odd numbers, to the amount of five alternate sections per mile on each side of said railroad, on the line thereof, and within the limits often miles on each side of said road, not sold, reserved, or otherwise disposed of by the United States, and to which a preemption or homestead claim may not have attached, at the time the line of said road is definitely fixed: Provided, That all mineral lands shall be excepted from the operation of this act; but where the same shall contain timber, the timber thereon is hereby granted to said company. And all such lands, so granted by this section, which shall not be sold or disposed of by said company within three years after the entire road shall have been completed, shall be subject to settlement and preemption, like other lands, at a price not exceeding one dollar and twenty-five cents per acre, to be paid to said company.

SEC. 4. And be it further enacted, That whenever said company shall have completed forty consecutive miles of any portion of said railroad and telegraph line, ready for the service contemplated by this act, and supplied with all necessary drains, culverts, viaducts, crossings, sidings, bridges, turnouts, watering places, depots, equipments, furniture, and all other appurtenances of a first class railroad, the rails and all the other iron used in the construction and equipment of said road to be American manufacture of the best quality, the President of the United States shall appoint three commissioners to examine the same and report to him in relation thereto; and if it shall appear to him that forty consecutive miles of said railroad and telegraph line have been completed and equipped in all respects as required by this act, then, upon certificate of said commissioners to that effect, patents shall issue conveying the right and title to said lands to said company, on each side of the road as far as the same is completed, to the amount aforesaid, . . .

APPROVED, JULY 1, 1862.

1862

MORRILL ACT

*W*hen they came into power during the Civil War, Republicans eagerly set out to infuse their ideals into the country's economy through new laws. The Morrill Act reflected the Republican belief in the importance of public education, in particular practical education for farmers and workers. Senator Justin Morrill of Vermont sponsored this "Act Donating Public Lands to the several States and Territories which may provide Colleges for the Benefit of Agriculture and Mechanic Arts." It marked the first federal aid to higher education.

The Morrill Act committed the federal government to grant each state thirty thousand acres of public land per representative and senator in Congress, so that the allocation would be roughly in proportion to each state's population. Many states sold the land grants, which grew to an allocation of over 100 million acres, and squandered the revenue. Nevertheless, this endowment laid the foundation for a national system of state colleges and universities. In some cases, sales of the land financed existing institutions; in others, states chartered new schools and built their campuses on the land grants. Major universities such as Nebraska, Washington State, Clemson, and Cornell gained charters as land-grant schools. State colleges brought higher education to millions of students, a development that inevitably reshaped the nation's social and economic fabric.

Be it enacted by the Senate and House of Representatives of the United States of America in Congress assembled, That there be granted to the several States, for the purposes hereinafter mentioned, an amount of public land, to be apportioned to each State a quantity equal to thirty thousand acres for each senator and representative in Congress to which the States are respectively entitled by the apportionment under the census of eighteen hundred and sixty: Provided, That no mineral lands shall be selected or purchased under the provisions of this Act. . . .

SEC. 3. And be it further enacted, That all the expenses of management, superintendence, and taxes from date of selection of said lands, previous to their sales, and all expenses incurred in the management and disbursement of the moneys which may be received therefrom, shall be paid by the States to which they may belong, out of the Treasury of said States, so that the entire proceeds of the sale of said lands shall be applied without any diminution whatever to the purposes hereinafter mentioned.

SEC. 4. And be it further enacted, That all moneys derived from the sale of the lands aforesaid by the States to which the lands are apportioned, and from the sales of land scrip hereinbefore provided for, shall be invested in stocks of the United States, or of the States, or some other safe stocks, yielding not less than five per centum upon the par value of said stocks; and that the moneys so invested shall constitute a perpetual fund, the capital of which shall remain forever undiminished, (except so far as may be provided in section fifth of this act,) and the interest of which shall be inviolably appropriated, by each State which may take and claim the benefit of this act, to the endowment, support, and maintenance of at least one college where the leading object shall be, without excluding other scientific and classical studies, and including military tactics, to teach such branches of learning as are related to agriculture and the mechanic arts, in such manner as the legislatures of the States may respectively prescribe, in order to promote the liberal and practical education of the industrial classes in the several pursuits and professions in life. . . .

"[E]ach State . . . may take and claim the benefit of this act, to the endowment, support, and maintenance of at least one college. . . ."

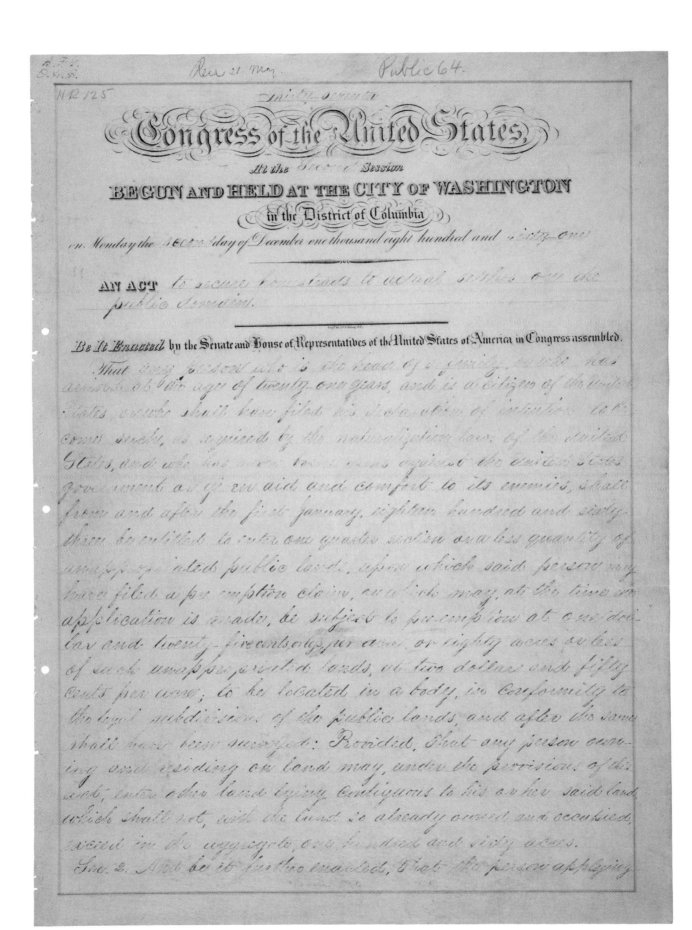

1863

EMANCIPATION PROCLAMATION

E ven though sectional conflicts over slavery had been a major cause of the Civil War, ending slavery was not an original goal of the war. Initially, the North fought this war with the South to prevent the secession of the southern states and preserve the Union. However, to build military momentum after the Union victory in the Battle of Antietam, Abraham Lincoln changed the character of the war. On January 1, 1863, President Lincoln issued the Emancipation Proclamation, declaring "that all person held as slaves" within the rebellious areas "are, and henceforward shall be free." He hoped not only to inspire all blacks, and slaves in the Confederacy in particular, to support the Union cause, but also to keep England and France from giving political recognition and military aid to the Confederacy.

Because it was a military measure, the Emancipation Proclamation was limited in many ways. It applied only to states that had seceded from the Union, leaving slavery untouched in the loyal border states. It also expressly exempted parts of the Confederacy that had already come under Union control. Most important, the freedom it promised depended upon Union military victory. Although the Emancipation Proclamation did not end slavery in the nation, it fundamentally transformed the war by announcing the acceptance of black troops and expanding the domain of freedom with every advance. As a milestone along the road to slavery's final destruction, it has assumed a place among the great documents of human freedom.

BY THE PRESIDENT OF THE UNITED STATES OF AMERICA:

A PROCLAMATION.

Whereas, on the twenty-second day of September, in the year of our Lord one thousand eight hundred and sixty-two, a proclamation was issued by the President of the United States, containing, among other things, the following, to wit:

"That on the first day of January, in the year of our Lord one thousand eight hundred and sixty-three, all persons held as slaves within any State or designated part of a State, the people whereof shall then be in rebellion against the United States, shall be then, thenceforward, and forever free; and the Executive Government of the United States, including the military and naval authority thereof, will recognize and maintain the freedom of such persons, and will do no act or acts to repress such persons, or any of them, in any efforts they may make for their actual freedom.

"That the Executive will, on the first day of January aforesaid, by proclamation, designate the States and parts of States, if any, in which the people thereof, respectively, shall then be in rebellion against the United States; and the fact that any State, or the people

thereof, shall on that day be, in good faith, represented in the Congress of the United States by members chosen thereto at elections wherein a majority of the qualified voters of such State shall have participated, shall, in the absence of strong countervailing testimony, be deemed conclusive evidence that such State, and the people thereof, are not then in rebellion against the United States."

Now, therefore I, Abraham Lincoln, President of the United States, by virtue of the power in me vested as Commander-in-Chief, of the Army and Navy of the United States in time of actual armed rebellion against the authority and government of the United States, and

"I do order and declare that all persons held as slaves within said designated States, and part of States, are, and henceforward shall be free . . ."

By the President of the United States of America:

A Proclamation.

Whereas, on the twenty-second day of September, in the year of our Lord one thousand eight hundred and sixty-two, a proclamation was issued by the President of the United States, containing, among other things, the following, to wit:

"That on the first day of January, in the year of our Lord one thousand eight hundred and sixty-three, all persons held as slaves within any State or designated part of a State, the people whereof shall then be in rebellion against the United States, shall be then, thenceforward, and forever free; and the Executive Government of the United States, including the military and naval authority thereof, will recognize and maintain the freedom of such persons, and will do no act or acts to repress such persons, or any of them, in any efforts they may make for their actual freedom.

"That the Executive will, on the first day

as a fit and necessary war measure for suppressing said rebellion, do, on this first day of January, in the year of our Lord one thousand eight hundred and sixty-three, and in accordance with my purpose so to do publicly proclaimed for the full period of one hundred days, from the day first above mentioned, order and designate as the States and parts of States wherein the people thereof respectively, are this day in rebellion against the United States, the following, to wit:

Arkansas, Texas, Louisiana, (except the Parishes of St. Bernard, Plaquemines, Jefferson, St. John, St. Charles, St. James Ascension, Assumption, Terrebonne, Lafourche, St. Mary, St. Martin, and Orleans, including the City of New Orleans) Mississippi, Alabama, Florida, Georgia, South Carolina, North Carolina, and Virginia, (except the forty-eight counties designated as West Virginia, and also the counties of Berkley, Accomac, Northampton, Elizabeth City, York, Princess Ann, and Norfolk, including the cities of Norfolk and Portsmouth), and which excepted parts, are for the present, left precisely as if this proclamation were not issued.

And by virtue of the power, and for the purpose aforesaid, I do order and declare that all persons held as slaves within said designated States, and parts of States, are, and henceforward shall be free; and that the Executive government of the United States, including the military and naval authorities thereof, will recognize and maintain the freedom of said persons.

And I hereby enjoin upon the people so declared to be free to abstain from all violence, unless in necessary self-defence; and I recommend to them that, in all cases when allowed, they labor faithfully for reasonable wages.

And I further declare and make known, that such persons of suitable condition, will be received into the armed service of the United States to garrison forts, positions, stations, and other places, and to man vessels of all sorts in said service.

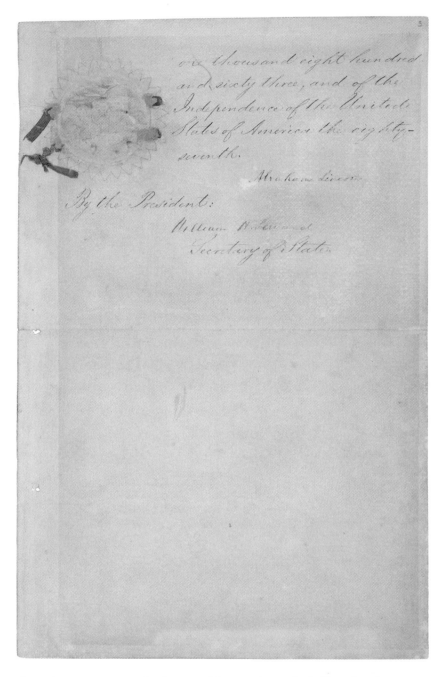

And upon this act, sincerely believed to be an act of justice, warranted by the Constitution, upon military necessity, I invoke the considerate judgment of mankind, and the gracious favor of Almighty God.

In witness whereof, I have hereunto set my hand and caused the seal of the United States to be affixed.

Done at the City of Washington, this first day of January, in the year of our Lord one thousand eight hundred and sixty three, and of the Independence of the United States of America the eighty-seventh.

BY THE PRESIDENT: ABRAHAM LINCOLN

WILLIAM H. SEWARD, SECRETARY OF STATE.

1863

WAR DEPARTMENT GENERAL ORDER 143: CREATION OF THE U.S. COLORED TROOPS

*T*he Civil War set off a rush by free black men to enlist in U.S. military units. They could not qualify, however, because a federal law dating from 1792 barred Negroes from bearing arms for the U.S. Army. The Lincoln administration wrestled with the idea of authorizing the recruitment of black troops, concerned that such a move would prompt the border states to secede. By mid-1862, however, the escalating number of former slaves, the declining number of white volunteers, and the pressing personnel needs of the Union Army forced the government to reconsider the ban. After the Union Army turned back Robert E. Lee's first invasion of the North at Antietam, Maryland, and the Emancipation Proclamation was issued, the Union Army pursued black recruitment in earnest. Volunteers from South Carolina, Tennessee, and Massachusetts filled the first authorized black regiments. In May 1863 the government established the Bureau of Colored Troops to manage the burgeoning numbers of black soldiers.

Nearly forty thousand black soldiers died in the war—thirty thousand of infection or disease. Black soldiers served in artillery and infantry and also performed all noncombat support functions that sustain an army. There were nearly eighty black commissioned officers. Black women, who could not formally join the army, nonetheless served as nurses, spies, and scouts; notable among them was the Underground Railroad leader Harriet Tubman, who scouted for the Second South Carolina Volunteers. Recruitment was slow until black leaders such as Frederick Douglass encouraged black men to become soldiers to ensure eventual full citizenship. (Two of Douglass's own sons contributed to the war effort.) Volunteers began to respond, and in May 1863 the government established the Bureau of Colored Troops to manage the burgeoning numbers of black soldiers.

The Tenth Cavalry, on parade here at Fort Verde, Arizona, in 1886, was formed at Fort Leavenworth, Kansas, twenty years earlier. Commanded by white officers, the "Buffalo Soldiers," as the enlisted men became known, guarded railroad workers, strung miles of new telegraph lines, and built much of Fort Sill. They also patrolled Indian reservations and in 1867–68 joined General William Tecumseh Sherman's campaigns against the Cheyennes, Arapahos, and Comanches.

GENERAL ORDERS, NO. 143

WAR DEPARTMENT,

ADJUNCT GENERAL'S OFFICE,

WASHINGTON, MAY 22, 1863.

I—A Bureau is established in the Adjutant General's Office for the record of all matters relating to the organization of Colored Troops. An officer will be assigned to the charge of the Bureau, with such number of clerks as may be designated by the Adjutant General.

II—Three or more field officers will be detailed as Inspectors to supervise the organization of colored troops at such points as may be indicated by the War Department in the Northern and Western States.

III—Boards will be convened at such posts as may be decided upon by the War Department to examine applicants for commissions to command colored troops, who, on Application to the Adjutant General, may receive authority to present themselves to the board for examination.

"Colored troops may be accepted by com-panies, to be afterward consolidated in battalions and regiments by the Adjutant General."

IV—No persons shall be allowed to recruit for colored troops except specially authorized by the War Department; and no such authority will be given to persons who have not been examined and passed by a board; nor will such authority be given any one person to raise more than one regiment.

V—The reports of Boards will specify the grade of commission for which each candidate is fit, and authority to recruit will be given in accordance. Commissions will be issued from the Adjutant General's Office when the prescribed number of men is ready for muster into service.

VI—Colored troops may be accepted by companies, to be afterward consolidated in battalions and regiments by the Adjutant General. The regiments will be numbered seriatim, in the order in which they are raised, the numbers to be determined by the Adjutant General. They will be designated: "—Regiment of U.S. Colored Troops."

VII—Recruiting stations and depots will be established by the Adjutant General as circumstances shall require, and officers will be detailed to muster and inspect the troops.

VIII—The non-commissioned officers of colored troops may be selected and appointed from the best men of their number in the usual mode of appointing non-commissioned officers. Meritorious commissioned officers will be entitled to promotion to higher rank if they prove themselves equal to it....

BY ORDER OF THE SECRETARY OF WAR:

E.D. TOWNSEND,

ASSISTANT ADJUTANT GENERAL

1863

GETTYSBURG ADDRESS

*A*t the end of the Battle of Gettysburg, which raged from July 1 to 3, 1863, more than fifty-one thousand Confederate and Union soldiers were wounded, missing, or dead. Survivors buried many of the dead in makeshift graves along the battlefield. Pennsylvania Governor Andrew Curtin commissioned a proper burial site for the deceased Union soldiers, and a ceremony dedicated the new cemetery on November 19, 1863. The main speaker for the event was Edward Everett, one of the nation's foremost orators. President Lincoln also was there to speak "as Chief Executive of the nation, formally [to] set apart these grounds to their sacred use by a few appropriate remarks." At the ceremony, Everett's speech lasted for more than two hours. Then President Lincoln spoke for two minutes.

Lincoln gave this brief speech a great deal of thought. His focus was not the specific battle but the larger significance of the war. Invoking the Declaration of Independence and its principles of liberty and equality, Lincoln spoke of "a new birth of freedom" for the nation. The Gettysburg Address reshaped the aims of the war for the American people—transforming it from a war for Union to a war for Union and freedom.

President Lincoln gave this copy of the Gettysburg Address to one of his two private secretaries, John Nicolay; he gave another to John Hay. This one is often called the "first draft" because it is believed to be the earliest copy that exists.

Four score and seven years ago our fathers brought forth, upon this continent, a new nation, conceived in liberty, and dedicated to the proposition that "all men are created equal."

Now we are engaged in a great civil war, testing whether that nation, or any nation so conceived, and so dedicated, can long endure. We are met on a great battle field of that war. We have come to dedicate a portion of it, as a final resting place for those who died here, that the nation might live. This we may, in all propriety do. But, in a larger sense, we can not dedicate—we can not consecrate—we can not hallow, this ground—The brave men, living and dead, who strug-gled here, have hallowed it, far above our poor power to add or detract. The world will little note, nor long remember what we say here; while it can never forget what they *did* here.

It is rather for us, the living, we here be dedicated to the great task remaining before us—that, from these honored dead we take increased devotion to that cause for which they here, gave the last full measure of devotion—that we here highly resolve these dead shall not have died in vain; that the nation, shall have a new birth of freedom, and that government of the people by the people for the people, shall not perish from the earth.

Working for the studio of Alexander Gardner, photographer Timothy O'Sullivan documented the aftermath of the battle at Gettysburg in July 1863. This view of the gateway to Evergreen Cemetery, showing the remains of artillery eathworks, was one of many images by O'Sullivan included in Gardner's Photographic Sketchbook of the War, *published in 1866.*

1864

WADE-DAVIS BILL

*I*n late 1863 President Abraham Lincoln and the Congress began to consider the question of
how the Union would be reunited if the North won the Civil War. In December President
Lincoln proposed a reconstruction program that would allow Confederate states to establish
new state governments after 10 percent of their male population took loyalty oaths and the states
recognized the "permanent freedom of slaves." Several congressional Republicans thought Lincoln's
10 Percent Plan was too mild. Senator Benjamin F. Wade and Representative Henry Winter Davis
proposed a more stringent plan in February 1864. The Wade-Davis Bill required that 50 percent
of a state's white males take an "iron-clad" loyalty oath to be readmitted to the Union. The bill further
required states to give blacks the right to vote.

Congress passed the Wade-Davis Bill, but President Lincoln refused to sign it, killing the bill
with a pocket veto. Lincoln continued to advocate tolerance and speed in plans for the reconstruction
of the Union, in opposition to the stricter approach
of Congress. After Lincoln's assassination in April
1865, however, Congress had the upper hand in
shaping federal policy toward the South and
imposed the harsher reconstruction requirements
that the Wade-Davis Bill had first advocated.

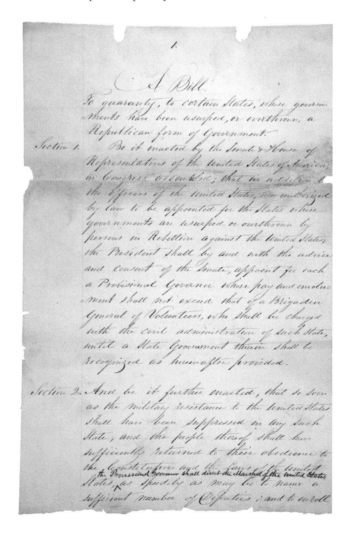

A BILL TO GUARANTEE TO CERTAIN STATES WHOSE
GOVERNMENTS HAVE BEEN USURPED OR OVERTHROWN A
REPUBLICAN FORM OF GOVERNMENT.

Be it enacted by the Senate and House of Representatives of the United States of America in Congress
assembled, That in the states declared in rebellion against
the United States, the President shall, by and with the
advice and consent of the Senate, appoint for each a provisional governor...who shall be charged with the civil
administration of such state until a state government
therein shall be recognized as hereinafter provided.

SEC. 2. And be it further enacted, That so soon as
the military resistance to the United States shall have
been suppressed in any such state, and the people
thereof shall have sufficiently returned to their obedience to the constitution and the laws of the United
States, the provisional governor shall direct the marshal
of the United States, as speedily as may be, to name a
sufficient number of deputies, and to enroll all white
male citizens of the United States, resident in the state
in their respective counties, and to request each one to
take the oath to support the constitution of the United
States, and in his enrollment to designate those who

take and those who refuse to take that oath, which rolls shall be forthwith returned to the provisional governor; and if the persons taking that oath shall amount to a majority of the persons enrolled in the state, he shall, by proclamation, invite the loyal people of the state to elect delegates to a convention charged to declare the will of the people of the state relative to the reestablishment of a state government subject to, and in conformity with, the constitution of the United States.

SEC. 3. And be it further enacted, That the convention shall consist of as many members as both houses of the last constitutional state legislature, apportioned by the provisional governor among the counties, parishes, or districts of the state, in proportion to the white population, returned as electors, by the marshal, in compliance with the provisions of this act....

SEC. 4. And be it further enacted, That the delegates shall be elected by the loyal white male citizens of the United States of the age of twenty-one years...and who shall take and subscribe the oath of allegiance to the United States in the form contained in the act of congress of July two, eighteen hundred and sixty-two;...but no person who has held or exercised any office, civil or military, state or confederate, under the rebel usurpation, or who has voluntarily borne arms against the United States, shall vote, or be eligible to be elected as delegate, at such election. . . .

SEC. 7. And be it further enacted, That the convention shall declare, on behalf of the people of the state, their submission to the constitution and laws of the United States, and shall adopt the following provisions, hereby prescribed by the United States in the execution of the constitutional duty to guarantee a republican form of government to every state, and incorporate them in the constitution of the state, that is to say:

First. No person who has held or exercised any office, civil or military, except offices merely ministerial, and military offices below the grade of colonel, state or confederate, under the usurping power, shall vote for or be a member of the legislature, or governor.

Second. Involuntary servitude is forever prohibited, and the freedom of all persons is guaranteed in said state.

Third. No debt, state or confederate, created by or under the sanction of the usurping power, shall be recognized or paid by the state.

SEC. 8. And be it further enacted, That when the convention shall have adopted those provisions, it shall proceed to reestablish a republican form of government, and ordain a constitution containing those provisions, . . . and if a majority of the votes cast shall be for the constitution and form of government, he shall certify the same, with a copy thereof, to the President of the United States, who, after obtaining the assent of congress, shall, by proclamation, recognize the government so established, and none other, as the constitutional government of the state, and from the date of such recognition, and not before, Senators and Representatives, and electors for President and Vice President may be elected in such state, according to the laws of the state and of the United States....

SEC. 12. And be it further enacted, that all persons held to involuntary servitude or labor in the states aforesaid are hereby emancipated and discharged therefrom, and they and their posterity shall be forever free....

SEC. 14. And be it further enacted, That every person who shall hereafter hold or exercise any office, civil or military, except offices merely ministerial, and military offices below the grade of colonel, in the rebel service, state or confederate, is hereby declared not to be a citizen of the United States.

BY THE PRESIDENT OF THE UNITED STATES:

A PROCLAMATION:...

I, ABRAHAM LINCOLN, President of the United States, do proclaim, declare, and make known, that, while I am (as I was in December last, when by proclamation I propounded a plan for restoration) unprepared by a formal approval of this bill, to be inflexibly committed to any single plan of restoration; and, while I am also unprepared to declare that the free state constitutions and governments already adopted and installed in Arkansas and Louisiana shall be set aside and held for nought, thereby repelling and discouraging the loyal citizens who have set up the same as to further effort, or to declare a constitutional competency in congress to abolish slavery in states, but am at the same time sincerely hoping and expecting that a constitutional amendment abolishing slavery throughout the nation may be adopted, nevertheless I am truly satisfied with the system for restoration contained in the bill as one very proper plan for the loyal people of any state choosing to adopt it, and that I am, and at all times shall be, prepared to give the executive aid and assistance to any such people, so soon as the military resistance to the United States shall have been suppressed in any such state, and the people thereof shall have sufficiently returned to their obedience to the constitution and the laws of the United States, in which cases military governors will be appointed, with directions to proceed according to the bill....

ABRAHAM LINCOLN

1865

PRESIDENT ABRAHAM LINCOLN'S SECOND INAUGURAL ADDRESS

*T*he Civil War began one month after President Lincoln took office and ended five days before he died. It was more bitter and protracted than anyone had predicted, costing more than 600,000 lives. In Lincoln's second inaugural address, delivered in March 1865, just over a month before his death, he spoke about the war as he had come to understand it. He believed the last four years of war were nothing short of God's own punishment for the sins of human slavery. In the speech's closing, he set the tone for his plan for the nation's Reconstruction. "With malice toward none; with charity for all; with firmness in the right, as God gives us to see the right, let us strive on to finish the work we are in; to bind up the nation's wounds; to care for him who shall have borne the battle, and for his widow, and his orphan—to do all which may achieve and cherish a just, and a lasting peace, among ourselves, and with all nations." These immortal words of reconciliation are carved in the walls of the Lincoln Memorial as a permanent reminder of Lincoln's efforts to heal a wounded nation.

President Lincoln delivers his second inaugural address on the east portico of the U.S. Capitol on March 4, 1865.

FELLOW COUNTRYMEN

At this second appearing to take the oath of the presidential office, there is less occasion for an extended address than there was at the first. Then a statement, somewhat in detail, of a course to be pursued, seemed fitting and proper. Now, at the expiration of four years, during which public declarations have been constantly called forth on every point and phase of the great contest which still absorbs the attention, and engrosses the energies of the nation, little that is new could be presented. The progress of our arms, upon which all else chiefly depends, is as well known to the public as to myself; and it is, I trust, reasonably satisfactory and encouraging to all. With high hope for the future, no prediction in regard to it is ventured.

On the occasion corresponding to this four years ago, all thoughts were anxiously directed to an impending civil-war. All dreaded it—all sought to avert it. While the inaugeral [sic] address was being delivered from this place, devoted altogether to saving the Union without war, insurgent agents were in the city seeking to destroy it without war—seeking to dissolve the Union, and divide effects, by negotiation. Both parties deprecated war; but one of them would make war rather than let the nation survive; and the other would accept war rather than let it perish. And the war came.

One eighth of the whole population were colored slaves, not distributed generally over the Union, but localized in the Southern part of it. These slaves constituted a peculiar and powerful interest. All knew that this interest was, somehow, the cause of the war. To strengthen, perpetuate, and extend this interest was the object for which the insurgents would rend the Union, even by war; while the government claimed no right to do more than to restrict the territorial enlargement of it. Neither party expected for the war, the magnitude, or the duration, which it has already attained. Neither anticipated that the cause of the conflict might cease with, or even before, the conflict itself should cease. Each looked for an easier triumph, and a result less fundamental and astounding. Both read the same Bible, and pray to the same God; and each invokes His aid against the other. It may seem strange that any men should dare to ask a just God's assistance in wringing their bread from the sweat of other men's faces; but let us judge not that we be not judged. The prayers of both could not be answered; that of neither has been answered fully. The Almighty has His own purposes. "Woe unto the world because of offences! for it must needs be that offences come; but woe to that man by whom the offence cometh!" If we shall suppose that American Slavery is one of those offences which, in the providence of God, must needs come, but which, having continued through His appointed time, He now wills to remove, and that He gives to both North and South, this terrible war, as the woe due to those by whom the offence came, shall we discern therein any departure from those divine attributes which the believers in a Living God always ascribe to Him? Fondly do we hope—fervently do we pray—that this mighty scourge of war may speedily pass away. Yet, if God wills that it continue, until all the wealth piled by the bond-man's two hundred and fifty years of unrequited toil shall be sunk, and until every drop of blood drawn with the lash, shall be paid by another drawn with the sword, as was said three thousand years ago, so still it must be said "the judgments of the Lord, are true and righteous altogether."

Fellow Countrymen:

At this second appearing to take the oath of the presidential office, there is less occasion for an extended address than there was at the first. Then a statement, somewhat in detail, of a course to be pursued, seemed fitting and proper. Now, at the expiration of four years, during which public declarations have been constantly called forth on every point and phase of the great contest which still absorbs the attention, and engrosses the energies of the nation, little that is new could be presented. The progress of our arms, upon which all else chiefly depends, is as well known to the public as to myself; and it is, I trust, reasonably satisfactory and encouraging to all. With high hope for the future, no prediction in regard to it is ventured.

On the occasion corresponding to this four years ago, all thoughts were anxiously directed to an impending civil war. All dreaded it—all sought to avert it. While the inaugural address was being delivered from this place, devoted altogether to saving the Union without war, insurgent agents were in

With malice toward none; with charity for all; with firmness in the right, as God gives us to see the right, let us strive on to finish the work we are in; to bind up the nation's wounds; to care for him who shall have borne the battle, and for his widow, and his orphan—to do all which may achieve and cherish a just, and a lasting peace, among ourselves, and with all nations.

[Endorsed by Lincoln:]

Original manuscript of second Inaugural presented to Major John Hay.

A. Lincoln

April 10, 1865

1865

ARTICLES OF AGREEMENT RELATING TO THE SURRENDER OF THE ARMY OF NORTHERN VIRGINIA

After four years of unspeakable bloodshed, the Civil War finally ended. Petersburg and Richmond, Virginia, fell to the Union in the spring of 1865, and in early April northern troops surrounded General Robert E. Lee and his soldiers. According to a biographer, Lee said, "[T]here is nothing left for me to do but to go and see General Grant, and I would rather die a thousand deaths." On April 9 Generals Ulysses S. Grant and Robert E. Lee met in the parlor of a house in Appomattox Court House, Virginia, to discuss the surrender of the Army of Northern Virginia. The terms Grant offered his foe were generous: The men of Lee's army could return home in safety if they pledged to end the fighting and deliver their arms to the Union Army. On April 12, 1865, in a quiet but emotional ceremony, the infantry of Lee's army surrendered their arms, folded their battle flags, and received their parole papers, which guaranteed them safe passage home.

General Robert E. Lee (seated, left) surrendered to Union General Ulysses S. Grant in the parlor of Wilmer McLean's home in Appomattox Court House, Virginia.

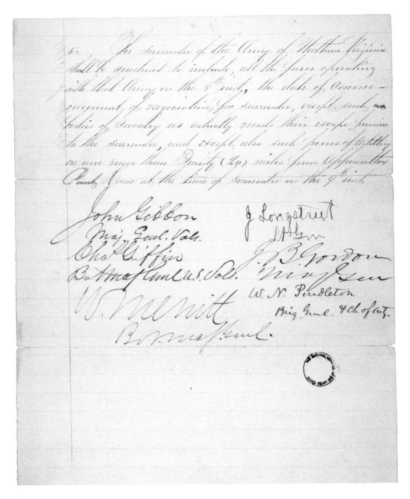

Agreement entered into this day in regard to the surrender of the Army of Northern Virginia to the United States Authorities.

1ST The troops shall march by Brigades and Detachments to a designated point, stock their Arms, deposit their flags, Sabres, Pistols, etc. and from thence march to their homes under charge of their Officers, superintended by their respective Division and Corps Commanders, Officers, retaining their side Arms, and the authorized number of private horses.

2. All public horses and public property of all kinds to be turned over to Staff Officers designated by the United States Authorities.

3. Such transportation as may be agreed upon as necessary for the transportation of the Private baggage of Officers will be allowed to accompany the Officers, to be turned over at the end of the trip to the nearest U.S. Quarter Masters, receipts being taken for the same.

4. Couriers and Wounded men of the artillery and Cavalry whose horses are their own private property will be allowed to retain them.

5. The surrender of the Army of Northern Virginia shall be construed to include all the forces operating with that Army on the 8th inst., the date of commencement of negotiation for surrender, except such bodies of Cavalry as actually made their escape previous to the surrender, and except also such forces of Artillery as were more than Twenty (20) miles from Appomattox Court House at the time of Surrender on the 9th inst.

JOHN GIBBON
MAJOR-GENERAL OF VOLUNTEERS

CHAS. GRIFFIN
BREVET MAJOR-GENERAL, U.S. VOLUNTEERS

W. MERRITT
BREVET MAJOR-GENERAL

J. LONGSTREET
LIEUTENANT-GENERAL

J.B. GORDON
MAJOR-GENERAL

W.N. PENDLETON
BRIGADIER-GENERAL AND CHIEF OF ARTILLERY

1865

THIRTEENTH AMENDMENT TO THE U.S. CONSTITUTION: ABOLITION OF SLAVERY

*I*n 1863 President Lincoln had issued the Emancipation Proclamation declaring "all persons held as slaves within any State, or designated part of a State, the people whereof shall then be in rebellion against the United States, shall be then, thenceforward, and forever free." Nonetheless, Lincoln recognized that the Emancipation Proclamation would have to be followed by a constitutional amendment to guarantee the abolition of slavery. The Thirteenth Amendment, which formally abolished slavery in the United States, passed the Senate on April 8, 1864, and the House on January 31, 1865. The necessary number of states ratified it by December 6, 1865. The Thirteenth Amendment to the United States Constitution provides that "[n]either slavery nor involuntary servitude, except as a punishment for crime whereof the party shall have been duly convicted, shall exist within the United States, or any place subject to their jurisdiction."

Though the Thirteenth Amendment ended slavery, it did not answer all the remaining questions about the status of African Americans. It did not decide whether former slaves were citizens or whether they could vote, nor did it protect them from oppressive working conditions. Nevertheless, it represented a profound shift in the status of black Americans and along with the Fourteenth and Fifteenth Amendments, is one of the trio of Civil War amendments that greatly expanded civil rights in America.

ARTICLE XIII

SECTION 1.
Neither slavery nor involuntary servitude, except as a punishment for crime whereof the party shall have been duly convicted, shall exist within the United States, or any place subject to their jurisdiction.

SECTION 2.
Congress shall have power to enforce this article by appropriate legislation.

The Thirteenth Amendment put out of business such slave traders as Price, Birch & Co. of Alexandria, Virginia.

Thirty-Eighth Congress of the United States of America;

At the Second Session,

Begun and held at the City of Washington, on Monday, the *fifth* day of December, one thousand eight hundred and sixty-*four*

A RESOLUTION

Submitting to the legislatures of the several States a proposition to amend the Constitution of the United States.

Resolved by the Senate and House of Representatives of the United States of America in Congress assembled, (two-thirds of both houses concurring), That the following article be proposed to the legislatures of the several States as an amendment to the Constitution of the United States, which, when ratified by three-fourths of said legislatures shall be valid, to all intents and purposes, as a part of the said Constitution, namely: Article XIII. Section 1. Neither slavery nor involuntary servitude, except as a punishment for crime whereof the party shall have been duly convicted, shall exist within the United States, or any place subject to their jurisdiction. Section 2. Congress shall have power to enforce this article by appropriate legislation.

Schuyler Colfax
Speaker of the House of Representatives.

H. Hamlin
Vice President of the United States
and President of the Senate

Approved February 1. 1865.

Abraham Lincoln

1868

CHECK FOR THE PURCHASE
OF ALASKA

*I*n 1866 the Russian government offered the United States an opportunity to buy the territory *of Alaska. Secretary of State William H. Seward jumped at the chance for American expansion and, with Russian minister to the United States Edouard de Stoeckl, negotiated to pay Russia $7.2 million for the land. The United States thus acquired nearly 600,000 square miles (one-fifth the area of the forty-eight contiguous states combined) for less than 2 cents an acre. Critics of the Alaska Purchase, who called it "Seward's Folly" or "Seward's Icebox," ate their words in 1896 when miners struck gold in the Klondike. Alaska became the forty-ninth state in 1959. Ten years later, prospectors struck oil at the largest North American oil field ever found, which would spark not only an Alaskan economic boom but also controversy over the land rights of native Alaskans and continuing concern for the natural environment.*

The Treaty of Cession, signed by Tzar Alexander II, formally concluded the agreement for the purchase of Alaska from Russia. The transcription comes from the treaty.

ARTICLE I.

His Majesty the Emperor of all the Russias agrees to cede to the United States, by this convention, immediately upon the exchange of the ratifications thereof, all the territory and dominion now possessed by his said Majesty on the continent of America and in the adjacent islands, the same being contained within the geographical limits herein set forth, to

wit: The eastern limit is the line of demarcation between the Russian and the British possessions in North America, as established by the convention between Russia and Great Britain, of February 28–16, 1825, and described in Articles III and IV of said convention, in the following terms:

"Commencing from the southernmost point of the island called Prince of Wales Island, which point lies in the parallel of 54 degrees 40 minutes north latitude, and between the 131st and the 133d degree of west longitude, (meridian of Greenwich,) the said line shall

ascend to the north along the channel called Portland channel, as far as the point of the continent where it strikes the 56th degree of north latitude; from this last-mentioned point, the line of demarcation shall follow the summit of the mountains situated parallel to the coast as far as the point of intersection of the 141st degree of west longitude, (of the same meridian;) and finally, from the said point of intersection, the said meridian line of the 141st degree, in its prolongation as far as the Frozen ocean. . . .

1868

TREATY OF FORT LARAMIE

As more and more speculators and settlers moved west, tensions between them and the Native American tribes living on the land increased. The government set up forts along the Oregon Trail to protect the new settlers. One of these was Fort Laramie, in present-day Wyoming. To provide for a peaceful resolution of increasingly violent conflicts, the U.S. government agreed to reserve a large tract of land for the Lakota peoples, often referred to as the Sioux Nation. In this treaty, signed on April 29, 1868, between the U.S. government and the Sioux, the United States recognized the Black Hills as part of the Great Sioux Reservation, which was set aside for exclusive use by the Sioux people. A few years later, however, when whites discovered gold in the Black Hills, they violated the treaty. Infuriated by this betrayal and the infiltration of what they regarded as sacred ground, Native Americans resisted. Led by Crazy Horse and Sitting Bull, the Lakota and their allies prevailed against General Custer's troops at the Battle of Little Big Horn. Their victory was short-lived, however. To this day, ownership of the Black Hills remains the subject of a legal dispute between the U.S. government and the Sioux.

General William T. Sherman and the American commissioners, formally attired as representatives of the U.S. government, negotiate with the Sioux at Ft. Laramie, Wyoming, around 1867.

ARTICLE I.

From this day forward all war between the parties to this agreement shall forever cease. The government of the United States desires peace, and its honor is hereby pledged to keep it. The Indians desire peace, and they now pledge their honor to maintain it.

If bad men among the whites, or among other people subject to the authority of the United States, shall commit any wrong upon the person or property of the Indians, the United States will...proceed at once to cause the offender to be arrested and punished according to the laws of the United States, and also reimburse the injured person for the loss sustained.

If bad men among the Indians shall commit a wrong or depredation upon the person or property of any one, white, black, or Indian, subject to the authority of the United States, and at peace therewith, the Indians herein named solemnly agree that they will...deliver up the wrongdoer to the United States, to be tried and punished according to its laws....

ARTICLE II.

The United States agrees that the following district of country, to wit, viz: commencing on the east bank of the Missouri river where the 46th parallel of north latitude crosses the same, thence along low-water mark down said east bank to a point opposite where the northern line of the State of Nebraska strikes the river, thence west across said river, and along the northern line of Nebraska to the 104th degree of longitude west from Greenwich, thence north on said meridian to a point where the 46th parallel of north latitude intercepts the same, thence due east along said parallel to the place of beginning; and in addition thereto, all existing reservations of the east back of said river, shall be and the same is, set apart for the absolute and undisturbed use and occupation of the Indians herein named, and for such other friendly tribes or individual Indians as from time to time they may be willing, with the consent of the United States, to admit amongst them; and the United States now solemnly agrees that no persons, except those herein designated and authorized so to do, and except such officers, agents, and employees of the government as may be authorized to enter upon Indian reservations in discharge of duties enjoined by law, shall ever be permitted to pass over, settle upon, or reside in the territory described in this article, or in such territory as may be added to this reservation for the use of said Indians, and henceforth

"[T]he United States now solemnly agrees that no persons, shall ever be permitted to pass over, settle upon, or reside in the territory described in this article, ..."

they will and do hereby relinquish all claims or right in and to any portion of the United States or Territories, except such as is embraced within the limits aforesaid, and except as hereinafter provided....

ARTICLE XI.

In consideration of the advantages and benefits conferred by this treaty and the many pledges of friendship by the United States, the tribes who are parties to this agreement hereby stipulate that they will relinquish all right to occupy permanently the territory outside their reservations as herein defined, but yet reserve the right to hunt on any lands north of North Platte, and on the Republican Fork of the Smoky Hill river, so long as the buffalo may range thereon in such numbers as to justify the chase. And they, the said Indians, further expressly agree:

1ST. That they will withdraw all opposition to the construction of the railroads now being built on the plains....

3D. That they will not attack any persons at home, or travelling, nor molest or disturb any wagon trains, coaches, mules, or cattle belonging to the people of the United States, or to persons friendly therewith.

4TH. They will never capture, or carry off from the settlements, white women or children.

5TH. They will never kill or scalp white men, nor attempt to do them harm.

6TH. They withdraw all pretence of opposition to the construction of the railroad now being built along the Platte river and westward to the Pacific ocean, and they will not in future object to the construction of railroads, wagon roads, mail stations, or other works of utility or necessity, which may be ordered or permitted by the laws of the United States....In testimony of all which, we, the said commissioners, and we, the chiefs and headmen of the Brule band of the Sioux nation, have hereunto set our hands and seals at Fort Laramie, Dakota Territory, this twenty-ninth day of April, in the year one thousand eight hundred and sixty-eight.

Articles of a Treaty made and concluded by and between Lieutenant General William T. Sherman, General William S. Harney, General Alfred H. Terry, General C. C. Augur, J. B. Henderson, Nathaniel G. Taylor, John B. Sanborn and Samuel F. Tappan, duly appointed Commissioners on the part of the United States and the different Bands of the Sioux Nation of Indians by their Chiefs and Head men whose names are hereto subscribed, they being duly authorized to act in the premises.

Article I   From this day forward all war between the parties to this agreement shall forever cease. The Government of the United States desires peace and its honor is hereby pledged to keep it. The Indians desire peace and they now pledge their honor to maintain it.

If bad men among the whites or among other people, subject to the authority of the United States, shall commit any wrong upon the person or property of the Indians, the United States will, upon proof made to the Agent, and forwarded to the Commissioner of Indian Affairs at Washington City, proceed at once to cause the offender to be arrested and punished according to the laws of the United States and also reimburse the injured person for the loss sustained.

If bad men among the Indians shall commit a wrong or depredation upon the person or property of any one, white, black or Indian, subject to the authority of the United States and at peace therewith, the Indians herein named, solemnly agree that they

1868

FOURTEENTH AMENDMENT TO THE U.S. CONSTITUTION: CIVIL RIGHTS

fter the Civil War, the battle over the status of former slaves continued. Southern state governments passed "Black Codes" that reinforced the social and economic oppression of African Americans. As part of their Reconstruction program to guarantee equal civil and legal rights to black citizens, Republicans in Congress submitted to the states three amendments to the Constitution. The major provision of the Fourteenth Amendment was to grant citizenship to "[a]ll persons born or naturalized in the United States," thereby including former slaves. Because it was clear that Southern states would not protect the rights of blacks, the amendment stated that no state shall "deprive any person of life, liberty, or property, without due process of law; nor deny to any person within its jurisdiction the equal protection of the laws."

Although it did not directly grant African Americans the right to vote, it announced that any state that did not grant black men the right to vote would have its representation in Congress reduced. On July 28, 1868, the Fourteenth Amendment was ratified and became part of the supreme law of the land.

With the federal government on their side, black Americans felt newly empowered to stand up for their rights. Although the amendment's promise exceeded its reality, during Reconstruction, citizens used it to press for more complete social, economic, and political equality. Its guarantee of equality under the law for all citizens would be the basis for change and enhancement of civil rights in the twentieth century.

ARTICLE XIV

SECTION 1.

All persons born or naturalized in the United States, and subject to the jurisdiction thereof, are citizens of the United States and of the State wherein they reside. No State shall make or enforce any law which shall abridge the privileges or immunities of citizens of the United States; nor shall any State deprive any person of life, liberty, or property, without due process of law; nor deny to any person within its jurisdiction the equal protection of the laws.

SECTION 2.

Representatives shall be apportioned among the several States according to their respective numbers, counting the whole number of persons in each State, excluding Indians not taxed. But when the right to vote at any election for the choice of electors for President and Vice-President of the United States, Representatives in Congress, the Executive and Judicial officers of a State, or the members of the Legislature thereof, is denied to any of the male inhabitants of such State, being twenty-one years of age, and citizens of the United States, or in any way abridged, except for participation in rebellion, or other crime, the basis of representation therein shall be reduced in the proportion which the number of such male citizens shall bear to the whole number of male citizens twenty-one years of age in such State.

SECTION 3.

No person shall be a Senator or Representative in Congress, or elector of President and Vice-President, or hold any office, civil or military, under the United States, or under any State, who, having previously taken an oath, as a member of Congress, or as an officer of the United States, or as a member of any State legislature, or as an executive or judicial officer of any State, to support the Constitution of the United States, shall have engaged in insurrection or rebellion against the same, or given aid or comfort to the enemies thereof. But Congress may by a vote of two-thirds of each House, remove such disability.

SECTION 4.
The validity of the public debt of the United States, authorized by law, including debts incurred for payment of pensions and bounties for services in suppressing insurrection or rebellion, shall not be questioned. But neither the United States nor any State shall assume or pay any debt or obligation incurred in aid of insurrection or rebellion against the United States, or any claim for the loss or emancipation of any slave; but all such debts, obligations and claims shall be held illegal and void.

SECTION 5.
The Congress shall have the power to enforce, by appropriate legislation, the provisions of this article.

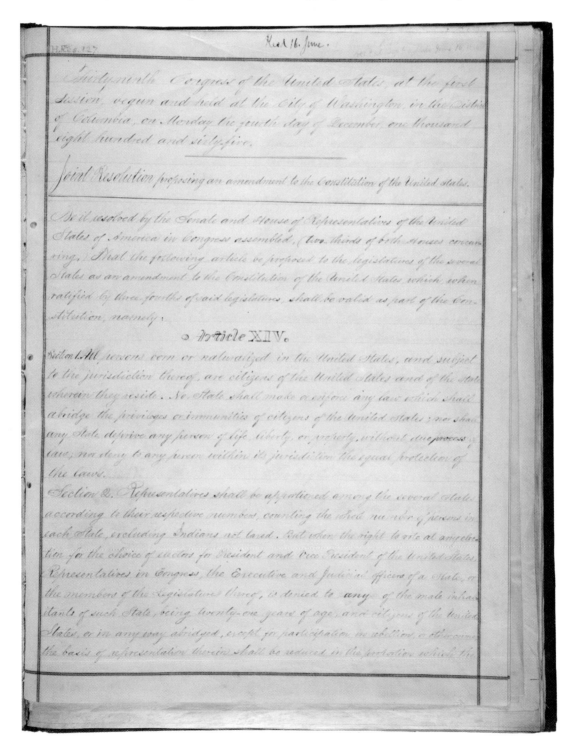

1870

FIFTEENTH AMENDMENT TO THE U.S. CONSTITUTION: VOTING RIGHTS

To former abolitionists and to the Radical Republicans in Congress who fashioned Reconstruction after the Civil War, the Fifteenth Amendment, which became law in 1870, appeared to fulfill all promises to African Americans. The Thirteenth Amendment had freed them, the Fourteenth Amendment had guaranteed citizenship, and now the Fifteenth Amendment granted black males the right to vote. From that point on, the freedmen were generally expected to fend for themselves. In retrospect, the Fifteenth Amendment was only the beginning of a struggle for equality that would continue for more than a century before African Americans began to participate fully in American public and civic life.

African Americans exercised the right to vote and held office in many southern states through the 1880s, but in the early 1890s, these states took steps to ensure subsequent "white supremacy." Literacy tests for the vote, "grandfather clauses" that excluded from voting all whose ancestors could not vote in the 1860s, and other devices to disenfranchise African Americans were written into the constitutions of former Confederate states. Not until a century after the Civil War did the Voting Rights Act of 1965, extended in 1970, 1975, and 1982, finally abolish all remaining deterrents to voting rights for black Americans.

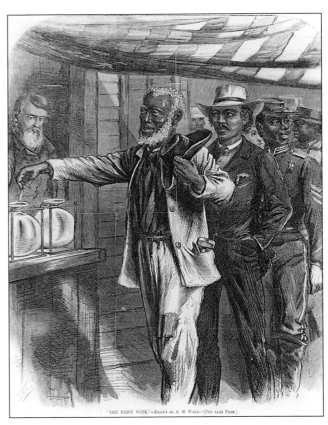

At the head of the line beneath an American flag, a craftsman casts his ballot in the first vote open to black men.

ARTICLE XV.

SECTION 1. The right of citizens of the United States to vote shall not be denied or abridged by the United States or by any State on account of race, color, or previous condition of servitude—

SECTION 2. The Congress shall have the power to enforce this article by appropriate legislation.

Fortieth Congress of the United States of America;

At the *third* Session,

Begun and held at the city of Washington, on Monday, the *seventh* day of *December*, one thousand eight hundred and *sixty-eight*.

A RESOLUTION

Proposing an amendment to the Constitution of the United States.

Resolved *by the Senate and House of Representatives of the United States of America in Congress assembled,* (two-thirds of both Houses concurring) That the following article be proposed to the legislatures of the several States as an amendment to the Constitution of the United States, which, when ratified by three-fourths of said legislatures shall be valid as part of the Constitution, namely:

Article XV.

Section 1. The right of citizens of the United States to vote shall not be denied or abridged by the United States or by any State on account of race, color, or previous condition of servitude —

Section 2. The Congress shall have power to enforce this article by appropriate legislation —

Schuyler Colfax
Speaker of the House of Representatives.

B F Wade
President of the Senate pro tempore.

Attest:
Edw. McPherson
Clerk of House of Representatives.

Geo. C. Gorham
Secy of Senate U.S.

This December 1868 resolution of the Fortieth Congress proposed the amendment that would grant African-American men the right to vote. Congress passed the amendment in February 1869, and it was ratified in February 1870.

1872

ACT ESTABLISHING YELLOWSTONE NATIONAL PARK

After the Civil War, the national government turned more attention to settlement of its western territory and exploitation of the continent's wealth. The government charged explorers with identifying natural resources and assessing the utility of the land for settlement. Explorers disseminated information to the East Coast about western environment and geology by lecturing, publishing in journals both scientific and popular, giving interviews to newspapers, and providing entrepreneurs with images for duplication on stereographic cards and chromolithographic print sets.

American attitudes toward the West shifted from fear to interest. Until the mid-nineteenth century it had been a place to cross over on the way to the Pacific coast or a place of mystery, fearsome in either case. Now it became America's wonderland. Yosemite and Yellowstone became popular vacation destinations, but such popularity quickly came to threaten the survival of the wilderness. Settlement and commercialization of western lands inevitably followed their opening. Leaders of the four great government surveys, while promoting settlement actively, were nonetheless alarmed by

the abuses of settlement: monopoly of water rights, speculation by land rings, and mistreatment of Native Americans on reserved lands. Years before Theodore Roosevelt and the era of Progressives, public servants representing the four great government surveys formulated guidelines for prevention or reformation of environmental abuse, fought for and erected the structures of bureaus and commissions to advance their agenda, and trained experts to be agents of reform.

One of the most imaginative and uniquely American innovations in response to these problems was the national park system. The upper reaches of the Yellowstone River, a

The Hot Springs of Gardiner's River in Yellowstone as painted by Thomas Moran. Ferdinand Hayden reported on his trip in an article in Scribner's Monthly, *which was illustrated by Moran, an artist on the expedition.*

region called Colter's Hell, had profoundly impressed early trappers and army explorers. Ferdinand Hayden surveyed the area in 1871. Upon his return to the East, he campaigned to promote, but also to protect, the natural wonders he had seen. He lobbied members of Congress along with Jay Cooke, the railroad magnate whose lines served the Yellowstone area. On March 1, 1872, Congress passed into law the act creating Yellowstone, "a public park or pleasuring-ground for the benefit and enjoyment of the people."

AN ACT to set apart a certain tract of land lying near the headwaters of the Yellowstone River as a public park.

Be it enacted by the Senate and House of Representatives of the United States of America in Congress assembled, That the tract of land in the Territories of Montana and Wyoming, lying near the headwaters of the Yellowstone River, and described as follows ... is hereby reserved and withdrawn from settlement, occupancy, or sale under the laws of the United States, and dedicated and set apart as a public park or pleasuring-ground for the benefit and enjoyment of the people; and all persons who shall locate or settle upon or occupy the same, or any part thereof, except as hereinafter provided, shall be considered trespassers and removed therefrom.

SEC 2. That said public park shall be under the exclusive control of the Secretary of the Interior, whose duty it shall be, as soon as practicable, to make and publish such rules and regulations as he may deem necessary or proper for the care and management of the same. Such regulations shall provide for the preservation, from injury or spoliation, of all timber, mineral deposits, natural curiosities, or wonders within said park, and their retention in their natural condition. The Secretary may in his discretion, grant leases for building purposes for terms not exceeding ten years, of small parcels of ground, at such places in said park as shall require the erection of buildings for the accommodation of visitors; all of the proceeds of said leases, and all other revenues that may be derived from any source connected with said park, to be expended under his direction in the management of the same, and the construction of roads and bridle-paths therein. He shall provide against the wanton destruction of the fish and game found within said park, and against their capture or destruction for the purposes of merchandise or profit. He shall also cause all persons trespassing upon the same after the passage of this act to be removed therefrom, and generally shall be authorized to take all such measures as shall be necessary or proper to fully carry out the objects and purposes of this act.

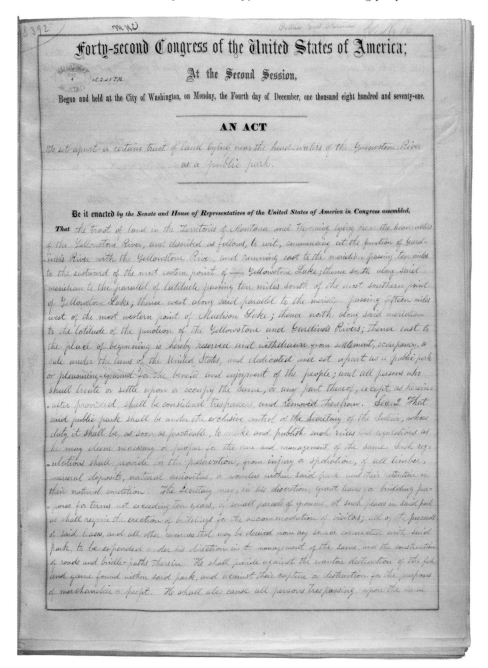

1879

PATENT APPLICATION FOR THE LIGHT BULB

After inventing the phonograph in 1877, Thomas Alva Edison turned to developing another revolutionary product, the light bulb. With financial backing from J. P. Morgan and others, Edison assembled a team of young scientists and technicians and devoted his considerable genius to the challenge of creating a commercially practical long-burning electric lamp. Working in his New Jersey laboratory in Menlo Park, Edison and his team failed thousands of times. But the inventor's determination never wavered. "Genius is 1 percent inspiration and 99 percent perspiration," according to Edison. Finally, in October of 1879, he had a lamp that worked for nearly fifteen hours and gave off a light equal to thirty candles.

The major breakthrough came when Edison switched the filament material from platinum to carbon, which was more effective and significantly cheaper. Carbon had been dismissed earlier as an option because it burns up too quickly. But Edison realized that if he sealed the carbon in a vacuum, such as the inside of a glass bulb, it would not burn out—the oxygen necessary for combustion would be absent. The filament that worked best was a small piece of

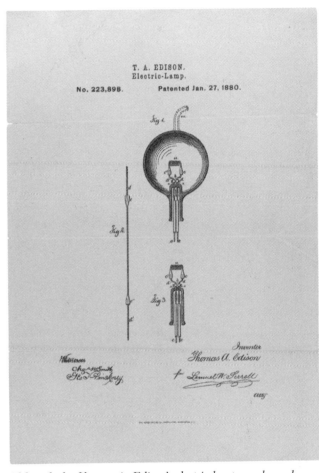

Although the filament in Edison's electric lamp was horseshoe-shaped, the one shown in the patent diagram (a) was made in a spiral form.

cardboard that Edison had baked in an oven. The baking left the cardboard charred, or carbonized. The cardboard filament was then attached to a long thin wire. (Oddly enough, the patent drawing shows the filament in a spiral—the filament in the actual lamp was horseshoe-shaped.) Edison passed an electric current through the wire and when it reached the filament, the filament became incandescent. Edison applied for his patent for the light bulb in 1879 and received it in 1880, making it possible for electric light to begin its spread throughout the country.

TO THE HONORABLE COMMISSIONER OF PATENTS:

Your Petitioner Thomas A. Edison of Menlo Park in the State of New Jersey prays that Letters Patent may be granted to him for the invention of an Improvement in Electric Lamps and in the method of manufacturing the same set forth in the annexed specification. (Case no. 186).

And further prays that you will recognize Lemuel W. Serrell, of the City of New York, N.Y., as his Attorney, with full power of substitution and revocation, to prosecute this application, to make alterations and amendments therein, to receive the Patent, and to transact all business in the Patent Office connected Therewith.

1879

The top of Edison's Patent Application is decorated with an engraving of cherubs using, from left to right, a lever, a hammer, and a crowbar. At the right, an eagle bears a banner that reads ONWARD INVENTIONS, URGE THE WORLD. In the center a monument bears the names of great inventors, including Fulton, Franklin, and Whitney. In the foreground, a mallet, a pulley, hammers, a palette, a T square and various other tools litter the ground; in the background, a horse-drawn plow, a train, a boat, a windmill, and a lighthouse celebrate human ingenuity.

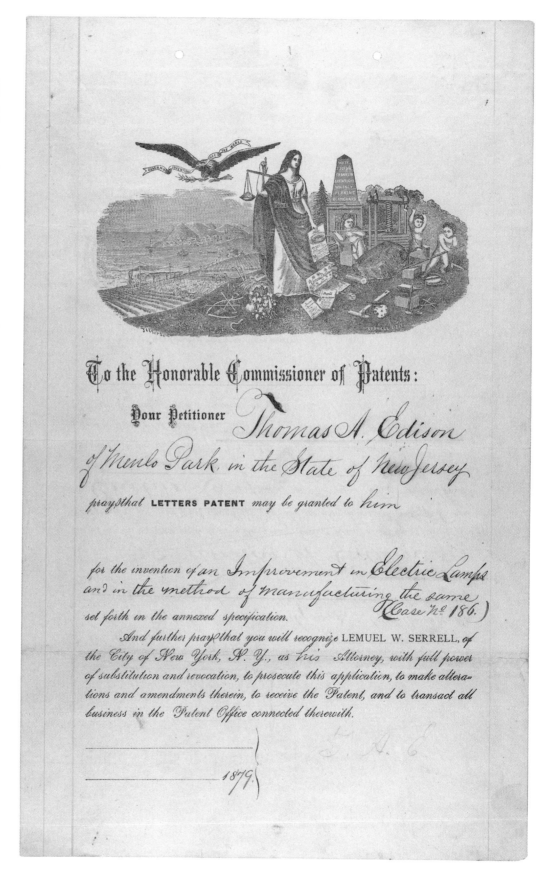

To the Honorable Commissioner of Patents:

Your Petitioner *Thomas A. Edison*

of Menlo Park, in the State of New Jersey

prays that LETTERS PATENT may be granted to *him*

for the invention of *an Improvement in Electric Lamps and in the method of manufacturing the same* set forth in the annexed specification. *(Case No. 186.)*

And further prays that you will recognize LEMUEL W. SERRELL, of the City of New York, N. Y., as *his* Attorney, with full power of substitution and revocation, to prosecute this application, to make altera-tions and amendments therein, to receive the Patent, and to transact all business in the Patent Office connected therewith.

1879.

1882

CHINESE EXCLUSION ACT

*I*n the mid-nineteenth century, the United States welcomed Chinese immigrants as a cheap source of labor for the transcontinental railroad. Many Chinese also sought their fortunes in the Gold Rush of the 1850s. In the western states and especially in California, where the majority of Chinese immigrants settled, tensions soon rose as whites charged that the Chinese were taking away jobs. Violence erupted in several places, and the Chinese daily faced discrimination. Responding to the concerns of whites in western states, in the spring of 1882, Congress passed the Chinese Exclusion Act and President Chester A. Arthur signed it. This act provided a ten-year moratorium on Chinese labor immigration (although it allowed merchants, students, teachers, and other visitors). For the first time, federal law proscribed entry of an ethnic group on the premise that it endangered the peace and order in certain localities. Because the act defined those it excluded as "skilled and unskilled laborers and Chinese employed in mining," very few Chinese could enter the country.

When the exclusion act expired in 1892, Congress extended it for ten years in the form of the Geary Act, which added restrictions by requiring all Chinese residents to register and obtain a certificate of residence. Without a certificate, they faced deportation.

The Geary Act regulated Chinese immigration until the 1920s. With increased postwar immigration, Congress adopted new means for regulation: quotas and requirements pertaining to national origin. By this time, anti-Chinese agitation had quieted. During World War II, when China and the United States were allies, President Franklin D. Roosevelt signed an Act to Repeal the Chinese Exclusion Acts, to Establish Quotas, and for Other Purposes (57 Stat. 600-1). This act of December 13, 1943, also lifted restrictions on naturalization. However, until the Immigration Act of October 1965 (79 Stat. 911), numerous laws continued to restrict Chinese immigration.

Effective July 1, 1968, an annual limit of 170,000 immigrants from outside the Western Hemisphere could enter the United States, with a maximum of 20,000 from any one country. The Immigration Act of 1990 established a flexible worldwide cap on family-based, employment-based, and diversity immigrant visas.

Chun Duck Chin and his seven-year-old son in San Francisco in 1899. Chinese residents often attached such family portraits to various documents filed with the government.

AN ACT TO EXECUTE CERTAIN TREATY STIPULATIONS RELATING TO CHINESE.

Whereas in the opinion of the Government of the United States the coming of Chinese laborers to this country endangers the good order of certain localities within the territory thereof: Therefore, Be it enacted by the Senate and House of Representatives of the United States of America in Congress assembled, That from and after the expiration of ninety days next after the passage of this act, and until the expiration of ten years next after the passage of this act, the coming of Chinese laborers to the United States be, and the same is hereby, suspended; and during such suspension it shall not be lawful for any Chinese laborer to come, or having so come after the expiration of said ninety days to remain within the United States.

SEC. 2. That the master of any vessel who shall knowingly bring within the United States on such vessel, and land or permit to be landed, any Chinese laborer, from any foreign port or place, shall be deemed guilty of a misdemeanor, and on conviction thereof shall be punished by a fine of not more than five hundred dollars for each and every such Chinese laborer so brought, and maybe also imprisoned for a term not exceeding one year.

SEC. 3. That the two foregoing sections shall not apply to Chinese laborers who were in the United States on the seventeenth day of November, eighteen hundred and eighty, or who shall have come into the same before the expiration of ninety days next after the passage of this act, ...

SEC. 4. That for the purpose of properly identifying Chinese laborers who were in the United States on the seventeenth day of November eighteen hundred and eighty, or who shall have come into the same before the expiration of ninety days next after the passage of this act, and in order to furnish them with the proper evidence of their right to go from and come to the United States of their free will and accord, as provided by the treaty between the United States and China dated November seventeenth, eighteen hundred and eighty, the collector of customs of the district from which any such Chinese laborer shall depart from the United States shall, in person or by deputy, go on board each vessel having on board any such Chinese laborers and cleared or about to sail from his district for a foreign port, and on such vessel make a list of all such Chinese laborers, which shall be entered in registry-books to be kept for that purpose, in which shall be stated the name, age, occupation, last place of residence, physical marks of peculiarities, and all facts necessary for the identification of each of such Chinese laborers, which books shall be safely kept in the custom-house....

SEC. 5. That any Chinese laborer mentioned in section four of this act being in the United States, and desiring to depart from the United States by land, shall have the right to demand and receive, free of charge or cost, a certificate of identification....

SEC. 6. That in order to the faithful execution of articles one and two of the treaty in this act before mentioned, every Chinese person other than a laborer who may be entitled by said treaty and this act to come within the United States, and who shall be about to come to the United States, shall be identified as so entitled by the Chinese Government in each case, such identity to be evidenced by a certificate issued under the authority of said government, which certificate shall be in the English language or (if not in the English language) accompanied by a translation into English, stating such right to come, and which certificate shall state the name, title or official rank, if any, the age, height, and all physical peculiarities, former and present occupation or profession, and place of residence in China of the person to whom the certificate is issued and that such person is entitled, conformably to the treaty in this act mentioned to come within the United States. Such certificate shall be prima-facie evidence of the fact set forth therein, and shall be produced to the collector of customs, or his deputy, of the port in the district in the United States at which the person named therein shall arrive.

SEC. 7. That any person who shall knowingly and falsely alter or substitute any name for the name written in such certificate or forge any such certificate, or knowingly utter any forged or fraudulent certificate, or falsely personate any person named in any such certificate, shall be deemed guilty of a misdemeanor; and upon conviction thereof shall be fined in a sum not exceeding one thousand dollars, and imprisoned in a penitentiary for a term of not more than five years....

SEC. 9. That before any Chinese passengers are landed from any such line vessel, the collector, or his deputy, shall proceed to examine such passenger, comparing the certificate with the list and with the passengers; and no passenger shall be allowed to land in the United States from such vessel in violation of law.

SEC. 10. That every vessel whose master shall knowingly violate any of the provisions of this act shall be deemed forfeited to the United States, and shall be liable to seizure and condemnation in any district of the United States into which such vessel may enter or in which she may be found.

SEC. 11. That any person who shall knowingly bring into or cause to be brought into the United States by land, or who shall knowingly aid or abet the same, or aid or abet the landing in the United States from any vessel of any Chinese person not lawfully entitled to enter the United States, shall be deemed guilty of a misdemeanor, and shall, on conviction thereof, be fined in a sum not exceeding one thousand dollars, and imprisoned for a term not exceeding one year.

SEC. 12. That no Chinese person shall be permitted to enter the United States by land without producing to the proper officer of customs the certificate in this act required of Chinese persons seeking to land from a vessel. And any Chinese person found unlawfully within the United States shall be caused to be removed therefrom to the country from whence he came, by direction of the President of the United States, and at the cost of the United States, after being brought before some justice, judge, or commissioner of a court of the United States and found to be one not lawfully entitled to be or remain in the United States.

SEC. 13. That this act shall not apply to diplomatic and other officers of the Chinese Government traveling upon the business of that government....

SEC. 14. That hereafter no State court or court of the United States shall admit Chinese to citizenship; and all laws in conflict with this act are hereby repealed.

SEC. 15. That the words "Chinese laborers", wherever used in this act shall be construed to mean both skilled and unskilled laborers and Chinese employed in mining.

APPROVED, MAY 6, 1882.

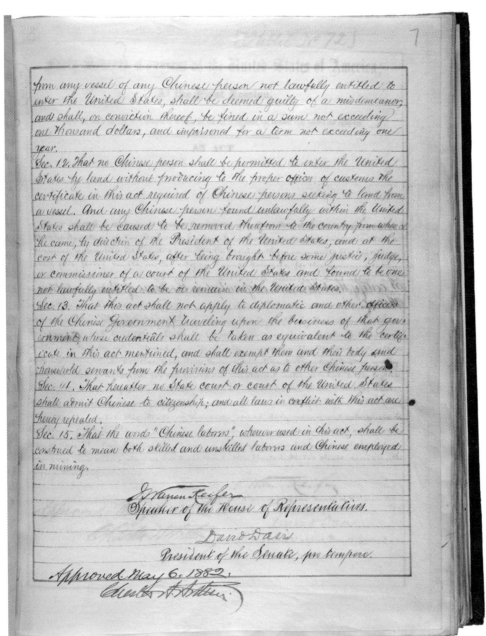

1883

PENDLETON ACT

Although President George Washington made most of his federal appointments based on merit, not strictly along party lines or based on contributions to party coffers, subsequent Presidents began to deviate from this policy. By the time Andrew Jackson was elected President in 1828, the "spoils system," in which political friends and supporters received government positions, was in full force. But in 1881 a disgruntled job seeker assassinated President James A. Garfield, prompting Congress to write a new law that mandated awarding federal government jobs on the basis of merit. Long-time reformer Senator George Hunt Pendleton of Ohio steered the bill through Congress, which passed the Pendleton Act in January 1883. President Chester A. Arthur, who had become an ardent reformer after Garfield's assassination, signed the bill into law.

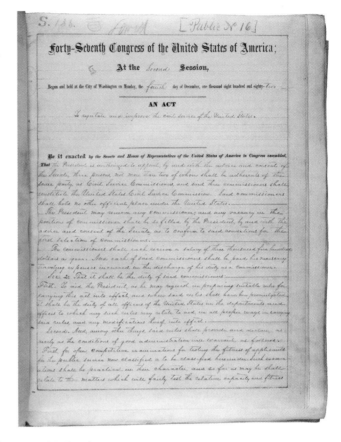

The Pendleton Act provided for the selection of federal government employees through competitive examinations. The act also made it unlawful to fire or demote for political reasons employees whom this law protected. The law further forbade requiring political service or contributions from employees. To enforce this act, the Civil Service Commission was established.

The Pendleton Act transformed the nature of public service. Before the act, new officials inundated government offices after every election, bringing chaos and inexperience to federal service. With the new system, the government was better able to rely on the experience and skills of its workers and to ensure adequate preparation for their jobs. When the Pendleton Act first became law, it covered only 10 percent of the government's 132,000 employees. Today, this number has increased to more than 90 percent of the 2.7 million federal employees.

AN ACT TO REGULATE AND IMPROVE THE CIVIL SERVICE OF THE UNITED STATES.

Be it enacted by the Senate and House of Representatives of the United States of America in Congress assembled, That the President is authorized to appoint, by and with the advice and consent of the Senate, three persons, not more than two of whom shall be adherents of the same party, as Civil Service Commissioners, and said three commissioners shall constitute the United States Civil Service Commission. . . .

SEC. 2. That it shall be the duty of said commissioners:

FIRST. To aid the President, as he may request, in preparing suitable rules for carrying this act into effect, and when said rules shall have been promulgated it shall be the duty of all officers of the United States in the departments and offices to which any such rules may relate to aid, in all proper ways, in carrying said rules, and any modifications thereof; into effect.

SECOND. And, among other things, said rules shall provide and declare, as nearly as the conditions of good administration will warrant, as follows:

First, for open, competitive examinations for testing the fitness of applicants for the public service now classified or to be classified here-under. Such examinations shall be practical in their character, and so far as may be shall relate to those matters which will fairly test the relative capacity and fitness of the persons examined to discharge the duties of the service into which they seek to be appointed.

Second, that all the offices, places, and employments so arranged or to be arranged in classes shall be filled by selections according to grade from among those graded highest as the results of such competitive examinations....

Fourth, that there shall be a period of probation before any absolute appointment or employment aforesaid.

Fifth, that no person in the public service is for that reason under any obligations to contribute to any political fund, or to render any political service, and that he will not be removed or otherwise prejudiced for refusing to do so.

Sixth, that no person in said service has any right to use his official authority or influence to coerce the political action of any person or body....

SEC. 5. That any said commissioner, examiner, copyist, or messenger, or any person in the public service who shall willfully and corruptly, by himself or in co-operation with one or more other persons, defeat, deceive, or obstruct any person in respect of his or her right of examination according to any such rules or regulations, or who shall willfully, corruptly, and falsely mark, grade, estimate, or report upon the examination or proper standing of any person examined hereunder, or aid in so doing, or who shall willfully and corruptly make any false representations concerning the same or concerning the person examined, or who shall willfully and corruptly furnish to any person any special or secret information for the purpose of either improving or injuring the prospects or chances of any person so examined, or to be examined, being appointed, employed, or promoted, shall for each such offense be deemed guilty of a misdemeanor, and upon conviction thereof, shall be punished by a fine of not less than one hundred dollars, nor more than one thousand dollars, or by imprisonment not less than ten days, nor more than one year, or by both such fine and imprisonment....

SEC. 8. That no person habitually using intoxicating beverages to excess shall be appointed to, or retained in, any office, appointment, or employment to which the provisions of this act are applicable.

SEC. 9. That whenever there are already two or more members of a family in the public service in the grades covered by this act, no other member of such family shall be eligible to appointment to any of said grades....

SEC. 10. That no recommendation of any person who shall apply for office or place under the provisions of this act which may be given by any Senator or member of the House of Representatives, except as to the character or residence of the applicant, shall be received or considered by any person concerned in making any examination or appointment under this act.

SEC. 11. That no Senator, or Representative, or Territorial Delegate of the Congress, or Senator, Representative, or Delegate elect, or any officer or employee of either of said houses, and no executive, judicial, military, or naval officer of the United States, and no clerk or employee of any department, branch or bureau of the executive, judicial, or military or naval service of the United States, shall, directly or indirectly, solicit or receive, or be in any manner concerned ill soliciting or receiving, any assessment, subscription, or contribution for any political purpose whatever, from any officer, clerk, or employee of the United States, or any department, branch, or bureau thereof, or from any person receiving any salary or compensation from moneys derived from the Treasury of the United States....

SEC. 13. No officer or employee of the United States mentioned in this act shall discharge, or promote, or degrade, or in manner change the official rank or compensation of any other officer or employee, or promise or threaten so to do, for giving or withholding or neglecting to make any contribution of money or other valuable thing for any political purpose.

SEC. 14. That no officer, clerk, or other person in the service of the United States shall, directly or indirectly, give or hand over to any other officer, clerk, or person in the service of the United States, or to any Senator or Member of the House of Representatives, or Territorial Delegate, any money or other valuable thing on account of or to be applied to the promotion of any political object whatever.

APPROVED, JANUARY SIXTEENTH, 1883.

1887

INTERSTATE COMMERCE ACT

*I*n the years following the Civil War, railroads were privately owned and entirely unregulated. They set prices, excluded competitors, and controlled the market in several geographic areas. By setting guidelines for how the railroads could do business, the Interstate Commerce Act diminished these monopolies. Its passage in 1887 made railroads the first industry subject to federal regulation. The law required "just and reasonable" rate charges and prohibited railroads from granting special deals to high-volume customers. The guidelines helped to protect the interests of farmers along the routes, who depended on the railroads to transport their goods to market. Most important, the law established a five-member Interstate Commerce Commission (ICC).

Years later the ICC became the model for many other regulatory agencies, but in 1887 it was unique. The Interstate Commerce Act challenged the philosophy of laissez-faire economics, which argues that government should stay out of business relationships, by clearly granting Congress the right to regulate private corporations engaged in interstate commerce. The act, with its provision for the ICC, remains a standard for government regulation of private business.

FORTY-NINTH CONGRESS OF THE UNITED STATES OF AMERICA;

AT THE SECOND SESSION,

Begun and held at the City of Washington on Monday, the sixth day of December, one thousand eight hundred and eighty-six

An act to regulate Commerce.

Be it enacted by the Senate and House of Representatives of the United States of America in Congress assembled, That the provisions of this act shall apply to any common carrier or carriers engaged in the transportation of passengers or property wholly by railroad, or partly by railroad and partly by water when both are used, under a common control, management, or arrangement, for a continuous carriage or shipment, from one State or Territory of the United States, or the District of Columbia, to any other State or Territory of the United States, or the District of Columbia, or from any place in the United States to an adjacent foreign country, or from any place in the United States through a foreign country to any other place in the United States.... *Provided, however,* That the provisions of this act shall not apply to the transportation of passengers or property, or to the receiving, delivering, storage, or handling of property, wholly within one State, and not shipped to or from a foreign country from or to any State or Territory as aforesaid....

All charges made for any service rendered or to be rendered in the transportation of passengers or property as aforesaid, or in connection therewith, or for the receiving, delivering, storage, or handling of such property, shall be reasonable and just; and every unjust and unreasonable charge for such service is prohibited and declared to be unlawful....

SEC. 11. That a Commission is hereby created and established to be known as the Inter-State Commerce Commission, which shall be composed of five Commissioners, who shall be appointed by the President, by and with the advice and consent of the Senate. The Commissioners first appointed under this act shall continue in office for the term of two, three, four, five, and six years, respectively, from the first day of January, anno Domini eighteen hundred and eighty-seven, the term of each to be designated by the President; but their successors shall be appointed for terms of six years, except that any person chosen to fill a vacancy shall be appointed only for the unexpired term of the Commissioner whom he shall succeed. Any Commissioner may be removed by the President for inefficiency, neglect of duty, or malfeasance in office. Not more than three of the Commissioners shall be appointed from the same political party. No person in the employ of or holding any official relation to any common carrier subject to the provisions of this act, or owning stock or bonds thereof, or who is in any manner pecuniarily interested therein, shall enter upon the duties of or hold such office. Said Commissioners shall not engage in any other business, vocation,

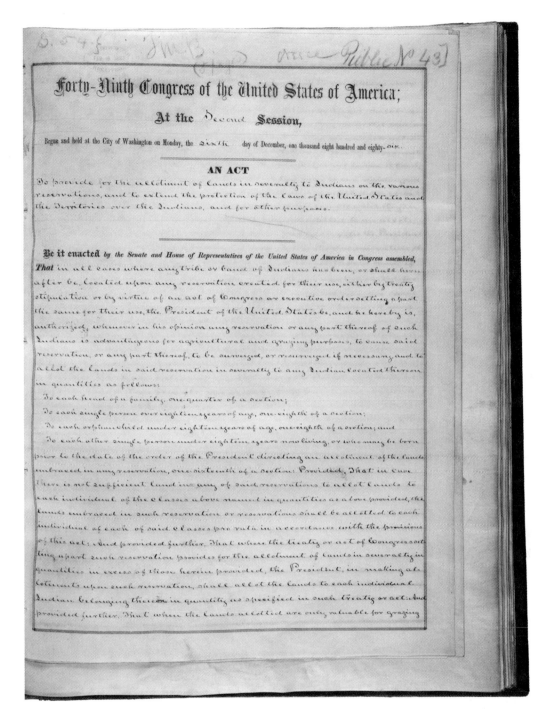

or employment. No vacancy in the Commission shall impair the right of the remaining Commissioners to exercise all the powers of the Commission.

SEC. 12. That the Commission hereby created shall have authority to inquire into the management of the business of all common carriers subject to the provisions of this act, and shall keep itself informed as to the manner and method in which the same is conducted, and shall have the right to obtain from such common carriers full and complete information necessary to enable the Commission to perform the duties and carry out the objects for which it was created; and for the purposes of this act the Commission shall have power to require the attendance and testimony of witnesses and the production of all books, papers, tariffs, contracts, agreements, and documents relating to any matter under investigation, and to that end may invoke the aid of any court of the United States in requiring the attendance and testimony of witnesses and the production of books, papers, and documents under the provisions of this section....

APPROVED, FEBRUARY 4, 1887.

1887

DAWES ACT

ederal Indian policy during the period from 1870 to 1900 marked a departure from earlier policies that focused on removal, treaties, the establishment of reservations, and even war. The new policy aimed specifically to break up reservations by granting land allotments to individual Native Americans. Some people reasoned that if Indians adopted white clothing and ways and were responsible for their own farms, they would gradually drop their Indian-ness and be assimilated into the general population. These individuals hoped that assimilation would bring an end to the U.S. government's paternalistic policies. Ironically, they failed to see the paternalism in their own suggestion.

On February 8, 1887, Congress passed the Dawes Act, named for its author, Senator Henry Dawes of Massachusetts. Also known as the General Allotment Act, the law allowed for the President to break up reservation land, which members of a tribe held in common, into small allotments to parcel out to individuals.

The alleged purpose of the Dawes Act and the subsequent acts that extended its initial provisions was to protect Indian property rights, particularly during the land rushes of the 1890s, but in many instances the results were disastrous. The land that the government allotted to the Indians included desert or near-desert lands unsuitable for farming. In addition, the techniques of self-sufficient farming differed greatly from their tribal way of life. Many Indians did not want to take up agriculture, and those who did want to farm could not afford the tools, animals, seed, and other supplies necessary to get started. Overall, the effect of the Dawes Act was to further crush the morale and the power of Native Americans. Not only did they lose vast amounts of land, because the law allowed for the sale of "surplus" land to whites, but the individualized nature of land ownership established in the Dawes Act struck forcefully at the communal nature of Native American life.

FORTY-NINTH CONGRESS OF THE UNITED STATES OF AMERICA;

AT THE SECOND SESSION,

Begun and held at the City of Washington on Monday, the sixth day of December, one thousand eight hundred and eighty-six.

An Act to provide for the allotment of lands in severalty to Indians on the various reservations, and to extend the protection of the laws of the United States and the Territories over the Indians, and for other purposes.

Be it enacted by the Senate and House of Representatives of the United States of America in Congress assembled, That in all cases where any tribe or band of Indians has been, or shall hereafter be, located upon any reservation created for their use, either by treaty stipulation or by virtue of an act of Congress or executive order setting apart the same for their use, the President

of the United States be, and he hereby is, authorized, whenever in his opinion any reservation or any part thereof of such Indians is advantageous for agricultural and grazing purposes, to cause said reservation, or any part thereof, to be surveyed, or resurveyed if necessary, and to allot the lands in said reservation in severalty to any Indian located thereon in quantities as follows:

To each head of a family, one-quarter of a section;

To each single person over eighteen years of age, one-eighth of a section;

To each orphan child under eighteen years of age, one-eighth of a section; and

To each other single person under eighteen years now living, or who may be born prior to the date of the order of the President directing an allotment of the lands embraced in any reservation, one-sixteenth of a section:

PROVIDED, That in case there is not sufficient land in any of said reservations to allot lands to each individual of the classes above named in quantities as above provided, the lands embraced in such reservation or reservations shall be allotted to each individual of each of said classes pro rata in accordance with the provisions of this act: And provided further, That where the treaty or act of Congress setting apart such reservation provides the allotment of lands in severalty in quantities in excess of those herein provided, the President, in making allotments upon such reservation, shall allot the lands to each individual Indian belonging thereon in quantity as specified in such treaty or act: And provided further, That when the lands allotted are only valuable for grazing purposes, an additional allotment of such grazing lands, in quantities as above provided, shall be made to each individual.

SEC. 2. That all allotments set apart under the provisions of this act shall be selected by the Indians, heads of families selecting for their minor children, and the agents shall select for each orphan child, and in such manner as to embrace the improvements of the Indians making the selection. Where the improvements of two or more Indians have been made on the same legal subdivision of land, unless they shall otherwise agree, a

"[N]othing in this act contained shall be so construed to affect the right and power of Congress to grant the right of way through any lands granted to an Indian, or a tribe of Indians, for railroads or other highways, or telegraph lines, for the public use, . . ."

provisional line may be run dividing said lands between them, and the amount to which each is entitled shall be equalized in the assignment of the remainder of the land to which they are entitled under his act: Provided, That if any one entitled to an allotment shall fail to make a selection within four years after the President shall direct that allotments may be made on a particular reservation, the Secretary of the Interior may direct the agent of such tribe or band, if such there be, and if there be no agent, then a special agent appointed for that purpose, to make a selection for such Indian, which selection shall be allotted as in cases where selections are made by the Indians, and patents shall issue in like manner.

SEC. 3. That the allotments provided for in this act shall be made by special agents appointed by the President for such purpose. . . .

SEC. 8. That the provisions of this act shall not extend to the territory occupied by the Cherokees, Creeks, Choctaws, Chickasaws, Seminoles, and Osage, Miamies and Peorias, and Sacs and Foxes, in the Indian Territory, nor to any of the reservations of the Seneca Nation of New York Indians in the State of New York, nor to that strip of territory in the State of Nebraska adjoining the Sioux Nation on the south added by executive order. . . .

SEC. 10. That nothing in this act contained shall be so construed to affect the right and power of Congress to grant the right of way through any lands granted to an Indian, or a tribe of Indians, for railroads or other highways, or telegraph lines, for the public use, or condemn such lands to public uses, upon making just compensation. . . .

APPROVED, FEBRUARY 8, 1887.

1890

SHERMAN ANTI-TRUST ACT

A *trust was an arrangement by which stockholders in several companies transferred their shares to a single set of trustees. The stockholders received a certificate entitling them to a specified share of the consolidated earnings of the jointly managed companies. During the Gilded Age, trusts came to dominate a number of major industries, including oil, steel, railroads, and tobacco, thereby destroying competition. So-called captains of industry defended consolidation because it improved efficiency. But consolidation also meant long hours and low wages, to which workers objected, and consumers protested against higher prices that resulted from the dearth of competition. Before 1890 several states passed laws to regulate intrastate businesses, prompting the House of Representatives to pass the first federal act that outlawed monopolistic business practices, the Sherman Anti-Trust Act, on June 20, 1890. The act was based on the constitutional power of Congress to regulate interstate commerce, and named for Senator John Sherman of Ohio, who was the chairman of the Senate finance committee and the secretary of the Treasury under President Hayes.*

The Sherman Act authorized the federal government to litigate against trusts to dissolve them and restore competition. However, the law's failure to define such critical terms as "trust," "combination," "conspiracy," and "monopoly" undermined its effectiveness. Nevertheless, Presidents Theodore Roosevelt and William Taft used the Sherman Act with considerable success against the Northern Securities, Standard Oil, and American Tobacco Companies.

Gluttonous, uncouth giants representing the oil, railroad, coal, coffee, meat, and sugar trusts stomp on decent, working "little" people, while the figure representing tobacco pauses to light his cigar with the Declaration of Independence.

invested with jurisdiction to prevent and restrain violations of this act; and it shall be the duty of the several district attorneys of the United States, in their respective districts, under the direction of the Attorney-General, to institute proceedings in equity to prevent and restrain such violations. Such proceedings may be by way of petition setting forth the case and praying that such violation shall be enjoined or otherwise prohibited. When the parties complained of shall have been duly notified of such petition the court shall proceed, as soon as may be, to the hearing and determination of the case, and pending such petition and before final decree, the court may at any time make such temporary restraining order or prohibition as shall be deemed just in the premises.

Sec. 5. Whenever it shall appear to the court before which any proceeding under section four of this act may be pending, that the ends of justice require that other parties should be brought before the court, the court may cause them to be summoned, whether they reside in the district in which the court is held or not, and subpoenas to that end may be served in any district by the marshal thereof.

Sec. 6. Any property owned under any contract or by any combination, or pursuant to any conspiracy (and being the subject thereof,) mentioned in section one of this act, and being in the course of transportion from one State to another, or to a foreign country, shall be forfeited to the United States, and may be seized and condemned by like proceedings as those provided by law for the forfeiture, seizure, and condemnation of property imported into the United States contrary to law.

Sec. 7. Any person who shall be injured in his business or property by any other person or corporation by reason of anything forbidden or declared to be unlawful by this act, may sue therefor in any circuit court of the United States in the district in which the defendant resides or is found, without respect to the amount in controversy, and shall recover three fold the damages by him sustained, and the costs of suit, including a reasonable attorney's fee.

Sec. 8. That the word "person," or "persons," wherever used in this act shall be deemed to include corporations and associations existing under or authorized by the laws of either the United States, the laws of any of the Territories, the laws of any State, or the laws of any foreign country.

Thomas B. Reed
Speaker of the House of Representatives.

Approved July 2d 1890.
Benj Harrison

Levi P. Morton
Vice-President of the United States and
President of the Senate.

FIFTY-FIRST CONGRESS OF THE UNITED STATES OF AMERICA, AT THE FIRST SESSION,

Begun and held at the City of Washington on Monday, the second day of December, one thousand eight hundred and eighty-nine.

An act to protect trade and commerce against unlawful restraints and monopolies.

Be it enacted by the Senate and House of Representatives of the United States of America in Congress assembled,

SEC. 1. Every contract, combination in the form of trust or otherwise, or conspiracy, in restraint of trade or commerce among the several States, or with foreign nations, is hereby declared to be illegal. Every person who shall make any such contract or engage in any such combination or conspiracy, shall be deemed guilty of a misdemeanor, and, on conviction thereof, shall be punished by fine not exceeding five thousand dollars, or by imprisonment not exceeding one year, or by both said punishments, at the discretion of the court.

SEC. 2. Every person who shall monopolize, or attempt to monopolize, or combine or conspire with any other person or persons, to monopolize any part of the trade or commerce among the several States, or with foreign nations, shall be deemed guilty of a misdemeanor, and, on conviction thereof, shall be punished by fine not exceeding five thousand dollars, or by imprisonment not exceeding one year, or by both said punishments, in the discretion of the court.

SEC. 3. Every contract, combination in form of trust or otherwise, or conspiracy, in restraint of trade or commerce in any Territory of the United States or of the District of Columbia, or in restraint of trade or commerce between any such Territory and another, or between any such Territory or Territories and any State or States or the District of Columbia, or with foreign nations, or between the District of Columbia and any State or States or foreign nations, is hereby declared illegal. Every person who shall make any such contract or engage in any such combination or conspiracy, shall be deemed guilty of a misdemeanor, and, on conviction thereof, shall be punished by fine not exceeding five thousand dollars, or by imprisonment not exceeding one year, or by both said punishments, in the discretion of the court.

SEC. 4. The several circuit courts of the United States are hereby invested with jurisdiction to prevent and restrain violations of this act; and it shall be the duty of the several district attorneys of the United States, in their respective districts, under the direction of the Attorney-General, to institute proceedings in equity to prevent and restrain such violations. Such proceedings may be by way of petition setting forth the case and praying that such violation shall be enjoined or otherwise prohibited. When the parties complained of shall have been duly notified of such petition the court shall proceed, as soon as may be, to the hearing and determination of the case; and pending such petition and before final decree, the court may at any time make such temporary restraining order or prohibition as shall be deemed just in the premises.

SEC. 5. Whenever it shall appear to the court before which any proceeding under section four of this act may be pending, that the ends of justice require that other parties should be brought before the court, the court may cause them to be summoned, whether they reside in the district in which the court is held or not; and subpoenas to that end may be served in any district by the marshal thereof.

SEC. 6. Any property owned under any contract or by any combination, or pursuant to any conspiracy (and being the subject thereof) mentioned in section one of this act, and being in the course of transportation from one State to another, or to a foreign country, shall be forfeited to the United States, and may be seized and condemned by like proceedings as those provided by law for the forfeiture, seizure, and condemnation of property imported into the United States contrary to law.

SEC. 7. Any person who shall be injured in his business or property by any other person or corporation by reason of anything forbidden or declared to be unlawful by this act, may sue therefor in any circuit court of the United States in the district in which the defendant resides or is found, without respect to the amount in controversy, and shall recover three fold the damages by him sustained, and the costs of suit, including a reasonable attorney's fee.

SEC. 8. That the word "person," or " persons," wherever used in this act shall be deemed to include corporations and associations existing under or authorized by the laws of either the United States, the laws of any of the Territories, the laws of any State, or the laws of any foreign country.

APPROVED, JULY 2, 1890.

1896

PLESSY V. FERGUSON

*T*he Civil Rights Act of 1875 had made discrimination in public accommodations a federal crime, but in 1883 the Supreme Court struck it down, ruling that the Fourteenth Amendment did not give Congress authority to prevent discrimination by private individuals. The Court told victims of racial discrimination to seek relief not from the federal government but from the states. State governments, unfortunately, were passing legislation that mandated segregation. The Louisiana legislature in 1890 passed a law that required partitioned or separate passenger coaches on trains. The Louisiana State Supreme Court decided, however, that the law was unconstitutional because it applied to interstate travel, over which the state had no jurisdiction. Drawing encouragement from this ruling, a committee of blacks and Creoles supported a test case on intrastate travel. Railroads were on their side, not because they wanted to fight discrimination but because maintaining separate cars was expensive.

With the cooperation of a Louisiana railroad, on June 7, 1892, Homer Plessy, a mulatto, seated himself in a white compartment. A conductor confronted him, and police arrested him, charging him with violation of the state law. When Judge John H. Ferguson ruled against him, Plessy appealed to the State Supreme Court, which upheld the state law but granted a petition that would enable Plessy to appeal the case to the U.S. Supreme Court. That Court upheld the Louisiana law, allowing "equal but separate accommodations for the white, and colored races." Justice Henry Billings Brown delivered the majority opinion. He wrote: "We consider the underlying fallacy of the plaintiff's argument to consist in the assumption that the enforced separation of the two races stamps the colored race with a badge of inferiority. If this be so, it is not by reason of anything found in the act, but solely because the colored race chooses to put that construction upon it."

MR. JUSTICE **BROWN**...**DELIVERED THE OPINION OF THE COURT....**

The constitutionality of this act is attacked upon the ground that it conflicts both with the thirteenth amendment of the constitution, abolishing slavery, and the fourteenth amendment, which prohibits certain restrictive legislation on the part of the states.

1. That it does not conflict with the thirteenth amendment, which abolished slavery and involuntary servitude, except a punishment for crime, is too clear for argument....

2....A statute which implies merely a legal distinction between the white and colored races...has no tendency to destroy the legal equality of the two races, or re-establish a state of involuntary servitude....

The object of the [fourteenth] amendment was undoubtedly to enforce the absolute equality of the two races before the law, but, in the nature of things, it could not have been intended to abolish distinctions based upon color, or to enforce social, as distinguished from political, equality, or a commingling of the two races upon terms unsatisfactory to either. Laws permitting, and even requiring, their separation, in places where they are liable to be brought into contact, do not necessarily imply the inferiority of either race to the other, and have been generally, if not universally, recognized as within the competency of the state legislatures in the exercise of their police power....

So far, then, as a conflict with the fourteenth amendment is concerned, the case reduces itself to the question whether the statute of Louisiana is a reasonable regulation, and with respect to this there must necessarily be a large discretion on the part of the legislature. In determining the question of reasonableness, it is at liberty to act with reference to the established usages, customs, and traditions of the people, and with a view to the promotion of their comfort, and the preservation of the public peace and good order. Gauged by this standard, we cannot say that a law which authorizes or even requires the separation of the two races in public conveyances is unreasonable, or more obnoxious to the fourteenth amendment than the acts of congress requiring separate schools for colored children in the District of Columbia, the constitutionality of which does not seem to have been questioned, or the corresponding acts of state legislatures.

We consider the underlying fallacy of the plaintiff's argument to consist in the assumption that the enforced separation of the two races stamps the colored race with a badge of inferiority. If this be so, it is not by reason of anything found in the act, but solely because the colored race chooses to put that construction upon it.... The argument ... assumes that social prejudices may be overcome by legislation, and that equal rights cannot be secured to the negro except by an enforced commingling of the two races. We cannot accept this proposition. If the two races are to meet upon terms of social equality, it must be the result of natural affinities, a mutual appreciation of each other's merits, and a voluntary consent of individuals.... Legislation is powerless to eradicate racial instincts, or to abolish distinctions based upon physical differences, and the attempt to do so can only result in accentuating the difficulties of the present situation....

The judgment of the court below is therefore affirmed....

MR. JUSTICE HARLAN DISSENTING....

[W]e have before us a state enactment that compels, under penalties, the separation of the two races in railroad passenger coaches, and makes it a crime for a citizen of either race to enter a coach that has been assigned to citizens of the other race....

In respect of civil rights, common to all citizens, the constitution of the United States does not, I think, permit any public authority to know the race of those entitled to be protected in the enjoyment of such rights.... I deny that any legislative body or judicial tribunal may have regard to the race of citizens when the civil rights of those citizens are involved.

The thirteenth amendment ... not only struck down the institution of slavery as previously existing in the United States, but it prevents the imposition of any burdens or disabilities that constitute badges of slavery or servitude. It decreed universal civil freedom in this country....

The white race deems itself to be the dominant race in this country. And so it is, in prestige, in achievements, in education, in wealth, and in power. So, I doubt not, it will continue to be for all time, if it remains true to its great heritage, and holds fast to the principles of constitutional liberty. But in view of the constitution, in the eye of the law, there is in this country no superior, dominant, ruling class of citizens. There is no caste here. Our constitution is color-blind, and neither knows nor tolerates classes among citizens. In respect of civil rights, all citizens are equal before the law.... It is therefore to be regretted that this high tribunal, the final expositor of the fundamental law of the land ... has reached the conclusion that it is competent for a state to regulate the enjoyment by citizens of their civil rights solely upon the basis of race.

In my opinion, the judgment this day rendered will, in time, prove to be quite as pernicious as the decision made by this tribunal in the Dred Scott Case....

The present decision ... will encourage the belief that it is possible, by means of state enactments, to defeat the beneficent purposes which the people of the United States had in view when they adopted the recent amendments of the constitution.... The destinies of the two races, in this country, are indissolubly linked together, and the interests of both require that the common government of all shall not permit the seeds of race hate to be planted under the sanction of law....

We boast of the freedom enjoyed by our people above all other peoples. But it is difficult to reconcile that boast with a state of the law which, practically, puts the brand of servitude and degradation upon a large class of our fellow citizens,—our equals before the law. The thin disguise of 'equal' accommodations for passengers in railroad coaches will not mislead any one, nor atone for the wrong this day done.

1898

DE LÔME LETTER

*A*s Cuba struggled for independence from Spain in the 1890s, the Spanish General Valeriano Weyler y Nicolau adopted a policy in 1896 of incarcerating Cuban civilians in detention centers to prevent them from participating in insurrections against Spanish rule. Because of the reprehensible conditions in the camps, the American press referred to the general as "Butcher" Weyler. Cuban revolutionaries intercepted a letter by Enrique Dupuy de Lôme, the Spanish ambassador to the United States, to Don José Canalejas, the foreign minister of Spain, and released it to the Hearst newspapers, which played a big role in pumping up public support for war. Hearst published the letter in the New York Journal on February 9, 1898. De Lôme's unflattering remarks about President McKinley helped fuel an aggressive, warlike foreign policy and, when the U.S. battleship Maine exploded in Havana harbor, killing 266 American sailors nearly one week later, American public opinion pressured President McKinley to respond.

McKinley obliged by demanding Cuban independence, which Spain refused. Two months later, on April 11, 1898, McKinley delivered a war message to Congress asking for "forcible intervention" by the United States to establish peace in Cuba. Congress officially declared war on April 24, retroactive to April 21. The de Lôme letter had jarred the United States out of its political isolation and onto the world stage.

LEGACION DE ESPAÑA.

WASHINGTON.

HIS EXCELLENCY

DON JOSÉ CANALEJAS.

MY DISTINGUISHED AND DEAR FRIEND: . . .

The situation here remains the same. Everything depends on the political and military outcome in Cuba. The prologue of all this, in this second stage of the war, will end the day when the colonial cabinet shall be appointed and we shall be relieved in the eyes of this country of a part of the responsibility for what is happening in Cuba while the Cubans, whom these people think so immaculate, will have to assume it.

Until then, nothing can be clearly seen, and I regard it as a waste of time and progress, by a wrong road, to be sending emissaries to the rebel camp, or to negotiate with the autonomists who have as yet no legal standing, or to try to ascertain the intentions and plans of this government. The (Cuban) refugees will keep on returning one by one and as they do so will make their way into the sheep-fold, while the leaders in the field will gradually come back. Neither the one nor the other

class had the courage to leave in a body and they will not be brave enough to return in a body. . . .

Besides the ingrained and inevitable rudeness with which is repeated all that the press and public opinion in Spain have said about Weyler, it once more shows what McKinley is, weak and a bidder for the admiration of the crowd besides being a would-be politician who tries to leave a door open behind himself while keeping on good terms with the jingoes of his party. . . .

I am entirely of your opinions; without a military end of the matter nothing will be accomplished in Cuba, and without a military and political settlement there will always be the danger of encouragement being given to the insurgents, by a part of the public opinion if not by the government.

I do not think sufficient attention has been paid to the part England is playing.

Nearly all the newspaper rabble that swarms in your hotels are Englishmen, and while writing for the Journal they are also correspondents of the most influential journals and reviews of London. It has been so ever since this thing began.

As I look at it, England's only object is that the Americans should amuse themselves with us and leave her alone, and if there should be a war, that would the better stave off the conflict which she dreads but which will never come about.

It would be very advantageous to take up, even if only for effect, the question of commercial relations and to have a man of some prominence sent hither, in order that I may make use of him here to carry on a propaganda among the senators and others in opposition to the Junta and to try to win over the refugees.

So, Amblard is coming. I think he devotes himself too much to petty politics, and we have got to do something very big or we shall fail.

Adela returns your greeting, and we all trust that next year you may be a messenger of peace and take it as a Christmas gift to poor Spain.

EVER YOUR ATTACHED FRIEND AND SERVANT,

ENRIQUE DUPUY DE LÔME.

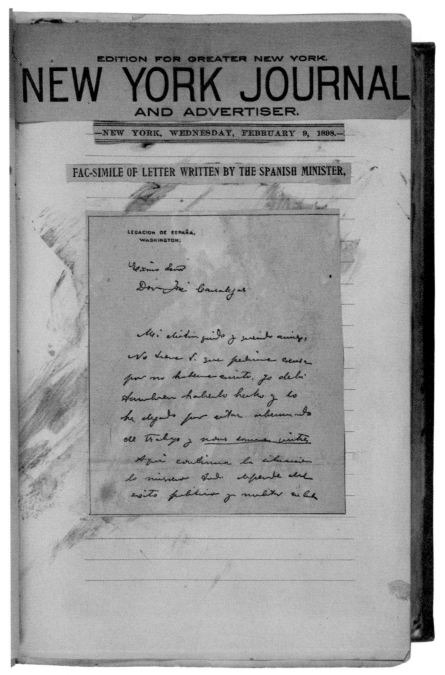

A facsimile of the De Lôme letter was printed in the New York Journal, *published by William Randolph Hearst. The sensational "yellow journalism" of the Hearst papers both increased circulation and helped fuel prowar feeling.*

1898

JOINT RESOLUTION TO PROVIDE FOR ANNEXING THE HAWAIIAN ISLANDS TO THE UNITED STATES

I n the nineteenth century, the United States valued Hawaii for its sugar trade, but the islands became especially attractive in the 1890s as a potential base for political and economic expansion in the Pacific. In 1887 an all-white Hawaiian League forced a constitution on Hawaiian King Kalakaua that substantially weakened his powers. When his successor Queen Liliuokalani challenged this constitution, a small group of American businessmen, with U.S. diplomatic support and military support from the naval base at Pearl Harbor, deposed her. In 1898, President McKinley signed a resolution to annex Hawaii despite Hawaiian wishes for greater autonomy.

In a letter of protest to the U.S. House of Representatives, Queen Liliuokalani wrote: "I . . . do hereby earnestly and respectfully protest against the assertion of ownership by the United States of America of the so-called Hawaiian Crown Islands amounting to about one million acres and which are my property, and I especially protest against such assertion of ownership as a taking of property without due process of law and without just or other compensation. . . . I call upon the President and the National Legislature and the People of the United States to do justice in this matter and to restore to me this property, the enjoyment of which is being withheld from me by your Government under what must be a misapprehension of my right and title." Nevertheless, in 1900 Hawaii officially became a territory of the United States and in 1959 became the fiftieth state.

FIFTY-FIFTH CONGRESS OF THE UNITED STATES OF AMERICA;

AT THE SECOND SESSION,

Begun and held at the City of Washington on Monday, the sixth day of December, one thousand eight hundred and ninety-seven.

Joint Resolution To provide for annexing the Hawaiian Islands to the United States.

Whereas, the Government of the Republic of Hawaii having, in due form, signified its consent, in the manner provided by its constitution, to cede absolutely and without reserve to the United States of America, all rights of sovereignty of whatsoever kind in and over the Hawaiian Islands and their dependencies, and also to cede and transfer to the United States, the absolute fee and ownership of all public, Government, or Crown lands, public buildings or edifices, ports, harbors, military equipment, and all other public property of every kind and description belonging to the Government of the Hawaiian Islands, together with every right and appurtenance thereunto appertaining: Therefore,

Resolved by the Senate and House of Representatives of the United States of America in Congress assembled, That said cession is accepted, ratified, and confirmed, and that the said Hawaiian Islands and their dependencies be, and they are hereby, annexed as a part of the territory of the United States and are subject to the sovereign dominion thereof, and that all and singular the property and rights hereinbefore mentioned are vested in the United States of America.

The existing laws of the United States relative to public lands shall not apply to such lands in the Hawaiian Islands; but the Congress of the United States shall enact special laws for their management and disposition: Provided, That all revenue from or proceeds of the same, except as regards such part thereof as may be used or occupied for the civil, military, or naval purposes of the United States, or may be assigned for the use of the local government, shall be used solely for the benefit of the inhabitants of the Hawaiian Islands for educational and other public purposes.

Until Congress shall provide for the government of such islands all the civil, judicial, and military powers exercised by the officers of the existing government in said islands shall be vested in such person or persons and shall be exercised in such manner as the President of the United states shall direct; and the President shall have power to remove said officers and fill the vacancies so occasioned.

The existing treaties of the Hawaiian Islands with foreign nations shall forthwith cease and determine, being replaced by such treaties as may exist, or as may be hereafter concluded, between the United States and such foreign nations. The municipal legislation of the Hawaiian Islands, not enacted for the fulfillment of the treaties so extinguished, and not inconsistent with this joint resolution nor contrary to the Constitution of the United States nor to any existing treaty of the United States, shall remain in force until the Congress of the United States shall otherwise determine.

Until legislation shall be enacted extending the United States customs laws and regulations to the Hawaiian Islands the existing customs relations of the Hawaiian Islands with the United States and other countries shall remain unchanged.

The public debt of the Republic of Hawaii, lawfully existing at the date of the passage of this joint resolution, including the amounts due to depositors in the Hawaiian Postal Savings Bank, is hereby assumed by the Government of the United States; but the liability of the United States in this regard shall in no case exceed four million dollars. So long, however, as the existing Government and the present commercial relations of the Hawaiian Islands are continued as hereinbefore, provided said Government shall continue to pay the interest on said debt.

There shall be no further immigration of Chinese into the Hawaiian Islands, except upon such conditions as are now or may hereafter be allowed by the laws of the United States; and no Chinese, by reason of anything herein contained, shall be allowed to enter the United States from the Hawaiian Islands.

SEC. 1. The President shall appoint five commissioners, at least two of whom shall be residents of the Hawaiian Islands, who shall, as soon as reasonably practicable, recommend to Congress such legislation concerning the Hawaiian Islands as they shall deem necessary or proper.

SEC. 2. That the commissioners hereinbefore provided for shall be appointed by the President, by and with the advice and consent of the Senate.

SEC. 3. That the sum of one hundred thousand dollars, or so much thereof as may be necessary, is hereby appropriated, out of any money in the Treasury not otherwise appropriated, and to be immediately available, to be expended at the discretion of the President of the United States of America, for the purpose of carrying this joint resolution into effect.

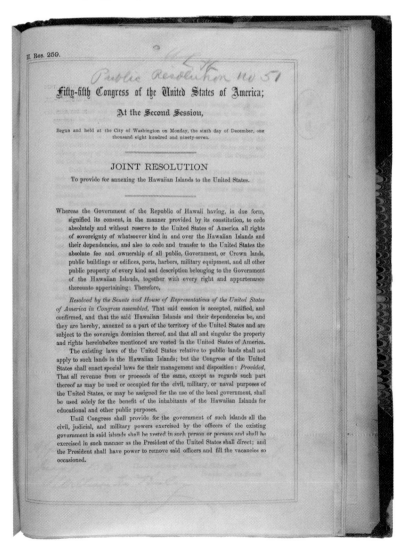

1901

PLATT AMENDMENT

*I*n response to the economic depression of 1893, the U.S. Congress approved a new tariff, which threatened the market for Cuban sugar, increased unemployment on the island, and sparked a rebellion in February 1895 against continued Spanish rule. Americans rallied in support, viewing the insurrection as a war for independence comparable to their own. As public pressure for war mounted, President William McKinley, too, became more bellicose. On April 11, 1898, he asked Congress for authority to

American soldiers land at Baguiri, Cuba, in small boats to begin two years of U.S. military government of the island.

use military force in Cuba to protect American property and trade. Nine days later Congress declared Cuban independence and demanded withdrawal of Spanish troops.

As part of that resolution, Senator Henry M. Teller proposed an amendment, which stated that the United States "hereby disclaims any disposition of intention to exercise sovereignty, jurisdiction, or control over [Cuba] except for pacification thereof, and asserts its determination, when that is accomplished, to leave the government and control of the island to its people." McKinley announced a blockade of Cuba on April 22. Spain responded to this act of war with its own formal declaration of war. Congress issued its war declaration on April 24, but made it retroactive to April 21.

As a result of an armistice, signed on August 12, 1898, Spain withdrew its forces. The United States established a transitional military government and appointed General Leonard Wood as governor. Wood held elections for a constitutional convention, which met in 1900. In July Congress notified the convention that it intended to attach an amendment to the Cuban constitution. The Platt Amendment, named for Senator Orville Platt of Connecticut, prevented Cuba from making treaties with other countries, restricted the size of its national debt, and acknowledged the right of the United States to intervene to preserve Cuban independence and protect individual rights. It also required Cuba to sell or lease lands to the United States for use by the U.S. Navy; this led to the establishment of the Guantanamo Bay naval base. Cubans reluctantly agreed to these demands.

The United States first intervened in 1906 to squelch a rebellion against the new Cuban government. It exercised its prerogative several more times before negotiating a treaty with Cuba in 1934 that repealed the amendment. This shift was consistent with President Franklin D. Roosevelt's "good neighbor" policy toward Latin America, whose purpose was to improve America's relations in the Western Hemisphere. The United States, however, retained its lease on Guantanamo Bay and continues its naval presence on the island.

1.

Whereas the Congress of the United States of America, by an Act approved March 2, 1901, provided as follows: —————

Provided further, That in fulfillment of the declaration contained in the joint resolution approved April twentieth, eighteen hundred and ninety-eight, entitled, "For the recognition of the independence of the people of Cuba, demanding that the Government of Spain relinquish its authority and government in the island of Cuba, and to withdraw its land and naval forces from Cuba and Cuban waters, and directing the President of the United States to use the land

Por cuanto el Congreso de los Estados Unidos de América dispuso, en virtud de una Ley aprobada en Marzo 2 de 1901, lo siguiente: —————

Se dispone además, Que en cumplimiento de la declaración contenida en la resolución conjunta aprobada en 20 de Abril de 1898 bajo el epígrafe "Para reconocer la independencia del pueblo de Cuba exigiendo que el Gobierno de España renuncie á su autoridad y gobierno en la Ysla de Cuba y que retire de Cuba y de las aguas Cubanas sus fuerzas de mar y tierra, y ordenando al Presidente de los Estados Unidos que—para llevar á efecto

Whereas the Congress of the United States of America, by an Act approved March 2, 1901, provided as follows:

Provided further, That in fulfillment of the declaration contained in the joint resolution approved April twentieth, eighteen hundred and ninety-eight, entitled "For the recognition of the independence of the people of Cuba, demanding that the Government of Spain relinquish its authority and government in the island of Cuba, and withdraw its land and naval forces from Cuba and Cuban waters, and directing the President of the United States to use the land and naval forces of the United States to carry these resolutions into effect," the President is hereby authorized to "leave the government and control of the island of Cuba to its people" so soon as a government shall have been established in said island under a constitution which, either as a part thereof or in an ordinance appended thereto, shall define the future relations of the United States with Cuba, substantially as follows:

"**I.** That the government of Cuba shall never enter into any treaty or other compact with any foreign power or powers which will impair or tend to impair the independence of Cuba, nor in any manner authorize or permit any foreign power or powers to obtain by colonization or for military or naval purposes or otherwise, lodgement in or control over any portion of said island."

"**II.** That said government shall not assume or contract any public debt, to pay the interest upon which, and to make reasonable sinking fund provision for the ultimate discharge of which, the ordinary revenues of the island, after defraying the current expenses of government shall be inadequate."

"**III.** That the government of Cuba consents that the United States may exercise the right to intervene for the preservation of Cuban independence, the maintenance of a government adequate for the protection of life, property, and individual liberty, and for discharging the obligations with respect to Cuba imposed by the treaty of Paris on the United States, now to be assumed and undertaken by the government of Cuba."

"**IV.** That all Acts of the United States in Cuba during its military occupancy thereof are ratified and vali-

"Cuba consents that the United States may exercise the right to intervene for the preservation of Cuban independence, the maintenance of a government adequate for the protection of life, property, and individual liberty, and for discharging the obligations with respect to Cuba imposed by the treaty of Paris on the United States. . . ."

dated, and all lawful rights acquired thereunder shall be maintained and protected."

"**V.** That the government of Cuba will execute, and as far as necessary extend, the plans already devised or other plans to be mutually agreed upon, for the sanitation of the cities of the island, to the end that a recurrence of epidemic and infectious diseases may be prevented, thereby assuring protection to the people and commerce of Cuba, as well as to the commerce of the southern ports of the United States and the people residing therein."

"**VI.** That the Isle of Pines shall be omitted from the proposed constitutional boundaries of Cuba, the title thereto being left to future adjustment by treaty."

"**VII.** That to enable the United States to maintain the independence of Cuba, and to protect the people thereof, as well as for its own defense, the government of Cuba will sell or lease to the United States lands necessary for coaling or naval stations at certain specified points to be agreed upon with the President of the United States."

"**VIII.** That by way of further assurance the government of Cuba will embody the foregoing provisions in a permanent treaty with the United States."

THEODORE ROOSEVELT'S COROLLARY TO THE MONROE DOCTRINE

The Monroe Doctrine had sought to prevent European intervention in the Western Hemisphere. In 1902, when British, German, and Italian gunboats blockaded Venezuela's ports because the Venezuelan government had defaulted on its debts to foreign bondholders, Americans worried that this type of European intervention in Latin America would lead to expansion of European empires and undermine U.S. dominance in the region.

To keep other powers out and ensure the financial solvency of the United States' Latin American neighbors, President Theodore Roosevelt issued a corollary to the Monroe Doctrine, stating that the United States was justified in exercising "international police power" to end chronic unrest or wrongdoing in the Western Hemisphere. But whereas the Monroe Doctrine aimed to keep Europe out of the Americas, the Roosevelt Corollary and the President's foreign policy of "walk softly, but carry a big stick" ironically justified American intervention where necessary in the Western Hemisphere. In early 1905, in the most important application of Roosevelt's policy, the Dominican Republic agreed to let the United States install customs collectors, who would distribute 45 percent of revenues to the government for operating expenses and the remaining 55 percent for debt payments. The Senate initially balked but, after the president resorted to executive order, agreed to the arrangement. Roosevelt announced his corollary in his annual message to Congress in December 1904.

Theodore Roosevelt, who had led the Rough Riders during the Spanish-American War, took an active role in foreign affairs when he became President.

The steady aim of this Nation, as of all enlightened nations, should be to strive to bring ever nearer the day when there shall prevail throughout the world the peace of justice. There are kinds of peace which are highly undesirable, which are in the long run as destructive as any war.... The peace of tyrannous terror, the peace of craven weakness, the peace of injustice, all these should be shunned as we shun unrighteous war. The goal to set before us as a nation, the goal which should be set before all mankind, is the attainment of the peace of justice, of the peace which comes when each nation is not merely safe-guarded in its own rights, but scrupulously recognizes and performs its duty toward others.... The eternal vigilance which is the price of liberty must be exercised, sometimes to guard against outside foes; although of course far more often to guard against our own selfish or thoughtless shortcomings.

If these self-evident truths are kept before us, and only if they are so kept before us, we shall have a clear idea of what our foreign policy in its larger aspects should be. It is our duty to remember that a nation has no more right to do injustice to another nation, strong or weak, than an individual has to do injustice to another individual; that the same moral law applies in one case as in the other.... There is as yet no judicial way of enforcing a right in international law. When one nation wrongs another or wrongs many others, there is no tribunal before which the wrongdoer can be brought. Either it is necessary supinely to acquiesce in the wrong, and thus put a premium upon brutality and aggression, or else it is necessary for the aggrieved nation valiantly to stand up for its rights. Until some method is devised by which there shall be a degree of international control over offending nations, it would be a wicked thing for the most civilized powers, for those with most sense of international obligations and with keenest and most generous appreciation of the difference between right and wrong, to disarm. . . . Therefore it follows that a self-respecting, just, and far-seeing nation should on the one hand endeavor by every means to aid in the development of the various movements which tend to provide substitutes for war, which tend to render nations in their actions toward one another, and indeed toward their own peoples, more responsive to the general sentiment of humane and civilized mankind; and on the other hand that it should keep prepared, while scrupulously avoiding wrongdoing itself, to repel any wrong, and in exceptional cases to take action which in a more advanced stage of international relations would come under the head of the exercise of the international police. A great free people owes it to itself and to all mankind not to sink into helplessness before the powers of evil. . . .

It is not true that the United States feels any land hunger or entertains any projects as regards the other nations of the Western Hemisphere save such as are for their welfare. All that this country desires is to see the neighboring countries stable, orderly, and prosperous. . . . Chronic wrongdoing, or an impotence which results in a general loosening of the ties of civilized society, may in America, as elsewhere, ultimately require intervention by some civilized nation, and in the Western Hemisphere the adherence of the United States to the Monroe Doctrine may force the United States, however reluctantly, in flagrant cases of such wrongdoing or impotence, to the exercise of an international police power. . . . Our interests and those of our southern neighbors are in reality identical. They have great natural riches, and if within their borders the reign of law and justice obtains, prosperity is sure to come to them. While they thus obey the primary laws of civilized society they may rest assured that they will be treated by us in a spirit of cordial and helpful sympathy. We would interfere with them only in the last resort, and then only if it became evident that their inability or unwillingness to do justice at home and abroad had violated the rights of the United States or had invited foreign aggression to the detriment of the entire body of American nations. . . .

In asserting the Monroe Doctrine, in taking such steps as we have taken in regard to Cuba, Venezuela,

and Panama, and in endeavoring to circumscribe the theater of war in the Far East, and to secure the open door in China, we have acted in our own interest as well as in the interest of humanity at large. There are, however, cases in which, while our own interests are not greatly involved, strong appeal is made to our sympathies. . . . The cases must be extreme in which such a course is justifiable. . . . What form the action shall take must depend upon the circumstances of the case; that is, upon the degree of the atrocity and upon our power to remedy it. . . . Yet it is not to be expected that a people like ours, which in spite of certain very obvious shortcomings, nevertheless as a whole shows by its consistent practice its belief in the principles of civil and religious liberty and of orderly freedom, a people among whom even the worst crime, like the crime of lynching, is never more than sporadic, so that individuals and not classes are molested in their fundamental rights—it is inevitable that such a nation should desire eagerly to give expression to its horror on an occasion like that of the massacre of the Jews in Kishenef, or when it witnesses such systematic and long-extended cruelty and oppression as the cruelty and oppression of which the Armenians have been the victims, and which have won for them the indignant pity of the civilized world. . . .

1913

SIXTEENTH AMENDMENT TO THE U.S. CONSTITUTION: FEDERAL INCOME TAX

The financial requirements of the Civil War prompted Congress to levy the first American income tax in 1861, a flat 3-percent tax on all incomes larger than $800; the wartime income tax expired in 1872. By the late 1870s, a movement was under way to institute a graduated income tax. Farmers and workers led the movement, arguing that a graduated income tax would reverse the decline in federal revenues, which had resulted from recurring economic depressions, and shift the burden of taxation to the wealthy. In 1894 Congress enacted a 2-percent tax on income over $4,000, affecting only the 2 percent of the population that received a majority of the nation's income. The Supreme Court struck the tax down in a 5–4 decision that focused on property rights and the federal government's limited powers to impose a "direct tax." A general return of prosperity softened the demand for tax reform, but the Democratic party and progressives in the Republican party continued to support the idea in part to address the tremendous disparities of wealth in the country but also to increase revenue for social reforms.

The first Form 1040, introduced in 1913, was a far simpler affair than its equivalent today.

   In 1909 progressives in Congress attached a provision for an income tax to the Payne-Aldrich tariff bill. Conservatives, hoping to kill the idea for good, proposed a constitutional amendment enacting such a tax. They never believed that three-fourths of the states would ratify an amendment. However, Congress approved the bill in July 1909, and the states ratified it by February 1915. In that year less than 1 percent of the population paid income taxes, which the government then assessed at the rate of only 1 percent of net income.

SIXTY-FIRST CONGRESS OF THE UNITED STATES OF AMERICA, AT THE FIRST SESSION,

Begun and held at the City of Washington on Monday, the fifteenth day of March, one thousand nine hundred and nine.

JOINT RESOLUTION

Proposing an amendment to the Constitution of the United States.

   Resolved by the Senate and House of Representatives of the United States of America in Congress assembled (two-thirds of each House concurring therein), That the following article is proposed as an amendment to the Constitution of the United States, which, when ratified by the legislature of three-fourths of the several States, shall be valid to all intents and purposes as a part of the Constitution:

   "ARTICLE XVI. The Congress shall have power to lay and collect taxes on incomes, from whatever source derived, without apportionment among the several States, and without regard to any census or enumeration."

S. J. Res. 40.

Sixty-first Congress of the United States of America;

At the First Session,

Begun and held at the City of Washington on Monday, the fifteenth day of March, one thousand nine hundred and nine.

JOINT RESOLUTION

Proposing an amendment to the Constitution of the United States.

Resolved by the Senate and House of Representatives of the United States of America in Congress assembled (two-thirds of each House concurring therein), That the following article is proposed as an amendment to the Constitution of the United States, which, when ratified by the legislatures of three-fourths of the several States, shall be valid to all intents and purposes as a part of the Constitution:

"ARTICLE XVI. The Congress shall have power to lay and collect taxes on incomes, from whatever source derived, without apportionment among the several States, and without regard to any census or enumeration."

Speaker of the House of Representatives.

Vice-President of the United States and
President of the Senate.

Attest:

Clerk of the House of Representatives.

Charles G. Bennett
Secretary
By Henry H. Gilfry
Chief Clerk

1913

SEVENTEENTH AMENDMENT TO THE U.S. CONSTITUTION: DIRECT ELECTION OF U.S. SENATORS

*A*rticle I, Section 3, of the Constitution ratified in 1788 gives each state equal representation in the Senate. Originally state legislatures elected two senators to six-year terms. Late in the nineteenth century, state legislatures occasionally deadlocked over senatorial elections when different parties controlled different houses of the legislatures; Senate vacancies could last months or years. Progressives advanced a solution called the "Oregon system." Beginning in 1904, the Oregon government asked candidates for the state legislature whether they would support the senatorial candidate who received the most votes in a state primary election. Most agreed to respect the popular vote, significantly reducing the likelihood of bribery and deadlocks. By 1911 more than half of the states had adopted the Oregon system; however, persistent corruption made constitutional reform necessary.

In 1909 and 1910 Senator Joseph L. Bristow of Kansas offered a proposal for direct election of senators. The amendment met strong resistance from southern Democrats, still resentful that the federal government had expanded its authority over elections with the adoption of the Fourteenth and Fifteenth Amendments. Facing likely defeat, Bristow proposed a compromise based on Article 1, Section 2 of the Constitution, which gave the federal government some control but allowed the states discretion in setting criteria for voting. The Senate adopted the proposal in May 1912, and the House accepted the change. Ratification by the states led to formal adoption of the Seventeenth Amendment on April 8, 1913.

SIXTY-SECOND CONGRESS OF THE UNITED STATES OF AMERICA; AT THE SECOND SESSION,

Begun and held at the City of Washington on Monday, the fourth day of December, one thousand nine hundred and eleven.

JOINT RESOLUTION
Proposing an amendment to the Constitution providing that Senators shall be elected by the people of the several States.

Resolved by the Senate and House of Representatives of the United States of America in Congress assembled (two-thirds of each House concurring therein), That in lieu of the first paragraph of section three of Article I of the Constitution of the United States, and in lieu of so much of paragraph two of the same section as relates to the filling of vacancies, the following be proposed as an amendment to the Constitution, which shall be valid to all intents and purposes as part of the Constitution when ratified by the legislatures of three-fourths of the States:

"The Senate of the United States shall be composed of two Senators from each State, elected by the people thereof, for six years; and each Senator shall have one vote. The electors in each State shall have the qualifications requisite for electors of the most numerous branch of the State legislatures.

"When vacancies happen in the representation of any State in the Senate, the executive authority of such State shall issue writs of election to fill such vacancies: Provided, That the legislature of any State may empower the executive thereof to make temporary appointments until the people fill the vacancies by election as the legislature may direct.

"This amendment shall not be so construed as to affect the election or term of any Senator chosen before it becomes valid as part of the Constitution."

Sixty-second Congress of the United States of America;

At the Second Session,

Begun and held at the City of Washington on Monday, the fourth day of December, one thousand nine hundred and eleven.

JOINT RESOLUTION

Proposing an amendment to the Constitution providing that Senators shall be elected by the people of the several States.

Resolved by the Senate and House of Representatives of the United States of America in Congress assembled (two-thirds of each House concurring therein), That in lieu of the first paragraph of section three of Article I of the Constitution of the United States, and in lieu of so much of paragraph two of the same section as relates to the filling of vacancies, the following be proposed as an amendment to the Constitution, which shall be valid to all intents and purposes as part of the Constitution when ratified by the legislatures of three-fourths of the States:

"The Senate of the United States shall be composed of two Senators from each State, elected by the people thereof, for six years; and each Senator shall have one vote. The electors in each State shall have the qualifications requisite for electors of the most numerous branch of the State legislatures.

"When vacancies happen in the representation of any State in the Senate, the executive authority of such State shall issue writs of election to fill such vacancies: *Provided,* That the legislature of any State may empower the executive thereof to make temporary appointments until the people fill the vacancies by election as the legislature may direct.

"This amendment shall not be so construed as to affect the election or term of any Senator chosen before it becomes valid as part of the Constitution."

Champ Clark,
Speaker of the House of Representatives.

J. S. Sherman
Vice President of the United States and
President of the Senate.

1916

KEATING-OWEN CHILD LABOR ACT

oward the end of the nineteenth century, progressive reformers launched campaigns for social justice. Focusing primarily on the needs of groups that lacked political power, their principal concern was the plight of children. The 1900 census revealed that approximately 2 million children were working in mills, mines, fields, factories, and stores and on city streets across the United States. This report strengthened a national movement to end child labor. In 1908 the National Child Labor Committee hired photographer Lewis Hine to travel across the country to create a visual record of the detrimental effects of sweatshop and industrial work on the health and welfare of children. Hine's work succeeded in rallying public opinion to this injustice.

By the turn of the century, many states had adopted child labor laws, but reformers judged them to be ineffective. The Keating-Owen bill, which passed in 1916, was the first federal legislation to curb child labor. Relying on Congress's power to regulate interstate commerce, the law sought to prevent the sale beyond state borders of goods children had produced. The Supreme Court declared the law unconstitutional because it overstepped Congress's power to regulate interstate commerce. A second child-labor bill, which passed into law in December 1918, imposed a 10-percent tax on all products of child labor. The Supreme Court also ruled that this measure was unconstitutional.

In response to public pressure, Congress approved a federal amendment in 1924 to grant itself the power to regulate child labor, but this, too, failed to achieve ratification. Congress finally enforced federal protection of children with its Fair Labor Standards Act in 1938. The Supreme Court upheld this law. Although the Court had quickly ruled the Keating-Owen Child Labor Act unconstitutional, this law set in motion the process that eventually legalized and required protection of children in the workforce.

SIXTY-FOURTH CONGRESS OF THE UNITED STATES OF AMERICA; AT THE FIRST SESSION,

Begun and held at the City of Washington on Monday, the sixth day of December, one thousand nine hundred and fifteen.

AN ACT To prevent interstate commerce in the products of child labor, and for other purposes.

Be it enacted by the Senate and House of Representatives of the United States of America in Congress assembled, That no producer, manufacturer, or dealer shall ship or deliver for shipment in interstate or foreign commerce, any article or commodity the product of any mine or quarry situated in the United States, in which within thirty days prior to the time of the removal of such product therefrom children under the age of sixteen years have been employed or permitted to work, or any article or commodity the product of any mill, cannery, workshop, factory, or manufacturing establishment, situated in the United States, in which within thirty days prior to the removal of such product therefrom children under the age of fourteen years have been employed or permitted to work, or children between the ages of fourteen years and sixteen years have been employed or permitted to work more than eight hours in any day, or more than six days in any week, or after the hour of seven o'clock postmeridian, or before the hour of six o'clock antemeridian: Provided, That a prosecution and conviction of a defendant for the shipment or delivery for shipment of any article or commodity under the conditions herein prohibited shall be a bar to any further prosecution against the same defendant for shipments or deliveries for shipment of any such article or commodity before the beginning of said prosecution.

SEC. 2. That the Attorney General, the Secretary of Commerce and the Secretary of Labor shall constitute a board to make and publish from time to time uniform rules and regulations for carrying out the provisions of this Act.

SEC. 3. That for the purpose of securing proper enforcement of this Act the Secretary of Labor, or any person duly authorized by him, shall have authority to enter and inspect at any time mines, quarries, mills, canneries, workshops, factories, manufacturing establishments, and other places in which goods are produced or held for interstate commerce; and the Secretary of Labor shall have authority to employ such assistance for the purposes of this Act as may from time to time be authorized by appropriation or other law.

SEC. 4. That it shall be the duty of each district attorney to whom the Secretary of Labor shall report any violation of this Act, or to whom any State factory or mining or quarry inspector, commissioner of labor, State medical inspector or school-attendance officer, or any other person shall present satisfactory evidence of any such violation to cause appropriate proceedings to be commenced and prosecuted in the proper courts of the United States without delay for the enforcement of the penalties in such cases herein provided: Provided, That nothing in this Act shall be construed to apply to bona fide boys' and girls' canning clubs recognized by the Agricultural Department of the several States and of the United States.

SEC. 5. That any person who violates any of the provisions of section one of this Act, or who refuses or obstructs entry or inspection authorized by section three of this Act, shall for each offense prior to the first conviction of such person under the provisions of this Act, be punished by a fine of not more than $200, and shall for each offense subsequent to such conviction be punished by a fine of not more than $1,000, nor less than $100, or by imprisonment for not more than three months, or by both such fine and imprisonment, in the discretion of the court: Provided: . . . That no producer, manufacturer, or dealer shall be prosecuted under this Act for the shipment, delivery for shipment, or transportation of a product of any mine, quarry, mill, cannery, workshop, factory, or manufacturing establishment, if the only employment therein within thirty days prior to the removal of such product therefrom, of a child under the age of sixteen years has been that of a child as to whom the producer, or manufacturer has in good faith procured, at the time of employing such child, and has since in good faith relied upon and kept on file a certificate, issued in such form, under such conditions, any by such persons as may be prescribed by the board, showing the child to be of such an age that the shipment, delivery for shipment, or transportation was not prohibited by this Act. Any person who knowingly makes a false statement or presents false evidence in or in relation to any such certificate or application therefor shall be amenable to prosecution and to the fine or imprisonment provided by this section for violations of this Act. . . .

SEC. 6. That the word "person" as used in this Act shall be construed to include any individual or corporation or the members of any partnership or other unincorporated association. The term "ship or deliver for shipment in interstate or foreign commerce" as used in this Act means to transport or to ship or deliver for shipment from any State or Territory or the District of Columbia to or through any other State or Territory or the District of Columbia or to any foreign country; and in the case of a dealer means only to transport or to ship or deliver for shipment from the State, Territory or district of manufacture or production.

SEC. 7. That this Act shall take effect from and after one year from the date of its passage.

APPROVED, SEPTEMBER 1, 1916.

1917

ZIMMERMANN TELEGRAM

*A*s the European nations fought World War I from 1914 to the spring of 1917, the United States remained officially neutral. Americans elected Woodrow Wilson President for a second term in 1916 largely because "[h]e kept us out of war." In January 1917, British cryptographers deciphered a telegram from German foreign minister Arthur Zimmermann to Germany's ambassador to Mexico, offering U.S. territory to Mexico in return for joining the German cause. To protect their intelligence from detection and to capitalize on growing anti-German sentiment in the United States, the British waited for the right moment to present the telegram to President Wilson. Meanwhile, because the British naval blockade was frustrating its efforts, Germany broke its pledge to limit submarine warfare. In protest, the United States severed diplomatic relations with Germany in February 1917.

On February 24 Britain released the Zimmerman telegram to Wilson, and newspapers published the story on March 1. The obvious threats to the United States in the telegram inflamed American public opinion against Germany and helped convince Congress to declare war against Germany and its allies on April 6, 1917.

We intend to begin on the first of February unrestricted submarine warfare. We shall endeavor in spite of this to keep the United States of America neutral. In the event of this not succeeding, we make Mexico a proposal or alliance on the following basis: make war together, make peace together, generous financial support and an understanding on our part that Mexico is to reconquer the lost territory in Texas, New Mexico, and Arizona. The settlement in detail is left to you. You will inform the President of the above most secretly as soon as the outbreak of war with the United States of America is certain and add the suggestion that he should, on his own initiative, invite Japan to immediate adherence and at the same time mediate between Japan and ourselves. Please call the President's attention to the fact that the ruthless employment of our submarines now offers the prospect of compelling England in a few months to make peace.

SIGNED, ZIMMERMANN.

This is one of the worksheets used by British cryptographers as they decoded the Zimmermann telegram.

WESTERN UNION TELEGRAM

NEWCOMB CARLTON, PRESIDENT

MC

Send the following telegram, subject to the terms
on back hereof, which are hereby agreed to

via Galveston

JAN 19 1917

CLASS OF SERVICE DESIRED	
Fast Day Message	✓
Day Letter	
Night Message	
Night Letter	

Patrons should mark an X opposite the class of service desired; OTHERWISE THE TELEGRAM WILL BE TRANSMITTED AS A FAST DAY MESSAGE.

GERMAN LEGATION

MEXICO CITY

130	13042	13401	8501	115	3528	416	17214	6491	11310
18147	18222	21560	10247	11518	23677	13605	3494	14936	
98092	5905	11311	10392	10371	0302	21290	5161	39695	
23571	17504	11269	18276	18101	0317	0228	17694	4473	
23284	22200	19452	21589	67893	5569	13918	8958	12137	
1333	4725	4458	5905	17166	13851	4458	17149	14471	6706
13850	12224	6929	14991	7382	15857	67893	14218	36477	
5870	17553	67893	5870	5454	16102	15217	22801	17138	
21001	17388	7446	23638	18222	6719	14331	15021	23845	
3156	23552	22096	21604	4797	9497	22464	20855	4377	
23610	18140	22260	5905	13347	20420	39689	13732	20667	
6929	5275	18507	52262	1340	22049	13339	11265	22295	
10439	14814	4178	6992	8784	7632	7357	6926	52262	11267
21100	21272	9346	9559	22464	15874	18502	18500	15857	
2188	5376	7381	98092	16127	13486	9350	9220	76036	14219
5144	2831	17920	11347	17142	11264	7667	7762	15099	9110
10482	97556	3569	3670						

BERNSTORFF.

Charge German Embassy.

1917

ADDRESS TO CONGRESS LEADING TO A DECLARATION OF WAR AGAINST GERMANY

When hostilities broke out among European nations in 1914, President Woodrow Wilson announced that the United States would stay neutral. He said that Americans should remain "impartial in thought as well as action." However, events between 1915 and 1917 led the President to alter his position. German submarines sank several ships, including the British liner Lusitania, and killed more than one hundred Americans. After stern warnings from Wilson, the Germans pledged to abide by traditional rules of maritime warfare—to search vessels before sinking them and to avoid civilian casualties. In the meantime, the United States supported the Allies, providing munitions as well as substantial loans. Wilson won a second term in 1916 with the slogan "He Kept Us Out of War," but when Germany resumed unrestricted submarine warfare in early 1917, and the Zimmermann Telegram was released, American attitudes shifted.

On April 2, 1917, Wilson delivered this address to a joint session of Congress, calling for a declaration of war against Germany. Congress complied, and the United States entered World

Congress passed this joint resolution declaring war on Germany after President Wilson called upon it to do so in his address of April 2, 1917.

War I. In his speech, Wilson took the moral high ground and declared that not only had America's rights as a neutral nation been violated but that "[t]he world must be made safe for democracy." Americans must fight "for the rights and liberties of small nations" and "bring peace and safety to make the world itself at last free."

GENTLEMEN OF THE CONGRESS:

I have called the Congress into extraordinary session because there are serious...choices of policy to be made...immediately, which it was neither right nor constitutionally permissible that I should assume the responsibility of making.

On the third of February last I officially laid before you the extraordinary announcement of the Imperial German Government that on and after the first day of February it was its purpose to put aside all restraints of law or of humanity and use its submarines to sink every vessel that sought to approach...any of the ports con-

fol lit
8pt

ADDRESS.

GENTLEMEN OF THE CONGRESS:

¶ I have called the Congress into extraordinary session because there are serious, very serious, choices of policy to be made, and made immediately, which it was neither right nor constitutionally permissible that I should assume the responsibility of making.

On the third of February last I officially laid before you the extraordinary announcement of the Imperial German Government that on and after the first day of February it was its purpose to put aside all restraints of law or of humanity and use its submarines to sink every vessel that sought to approach either the ports of Great Britain and Ireland or the western coasts of Europe or any of the ports controlled by the enemies of Germany within the Mediterranean. That had seemed to be the object of the German submarine warfare earlier in the war, but since April of last year the Imperial Government had somewhat restrained the commanders of its undersea craft in conformity with its promise then given to us that passenger boats should not be sunk and that due warning would be given to all other vessels which its submarines might seek to destroy, when no resistance was offered or escape attempted, and care taken that their crews were given at least a fair chance to save their lives in their open boats. The precautions taken were meagre and haphazard enough, as was proved in distressing instance after instance in the progress of the cruel and unmanly business, but a certain degree of restraint was observed. The new policy has swept every restriction aside. Vessels of every kind, whatever their flag, their character, their cargo, their destination, their errand, have been ruthlessly sent to the bottom without warning and without thought of help or mercy for those on board, the vessels of friendly neutrals along with those of belligerents. Even hospital ships and ships carrying relief to the sorely bereaved and stricken people of Belgium, though the latter were provided with safe conduct through the proscribed areas by the German Government itself and were distinguished by unmistakable marks of identity, have been sunk with the same reckless lack of compassion or of principle.

I was for a little while unable to believe that such things would in fact be done by any government that had hitherto subscribed to the

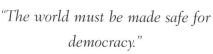

"The world must be made safe for democracy."

trolled by the enemies of Germany.... [S]ince April of last year the Imperial Government had somewhat restrained the commanders of its undersea craft in conformity with its promise then given to us that passenger boats should not be sunk and that due warning would be given to all other vessels which its submarines might seek to destroy when no resistance was offered or escape attempted, and care taken that their crews were given at least a fair chance to save their lives in their open boats.... [A] certain degree of restraint was observed. The new policy has swept every restriction aside.... The present German submarine warfare against commerce is a warfare against mankind.

It is a war against all nations. American ships have been sunk, American lives taken, in ways which it has stirred us very deeply to learn of, but the ships and people of other neutral and friendly nations have been sunk and overwhelmed in the waters in the same way. There has been no discrimination. The challenge is to all mankind....

With a profound sense of the solemn and even tragical character of the step I am taking and of the grave responsibilities which it involves, but in unhesitating obedience to what I deem my constitutional duty, I advise that the Congress declare the recent course of the Imperial German Government to be in fact nothing less than war against the government and people of the United States; that it formally accept the status of belligerent which has thus been thrust upon it, and that it take immediate steps not only to put the country in a more thorough state of defense but also to exert all its power and employ all its resources to bring the Government of the German Empire to terms and end the war....

Our object... is to vindicate the principles of peace and justice... and to set up amongst the really free and self-governed peoples of the world such a concert of purpose and of action as will henceforth insure the observance of those principles. Neutrality is no longer feasible or desirable where the peace of the world is involved and the freedom of its peoples, and the menace to that peace and freedom lies in the existence of autocratic governments backed by organized force which is controlled wholly by their will, not by the will of their people....

[T]he Prussian autocracy... has filled our unsuspecting communities and even our offices of government with spies and set criminal intrigues everywhere afoot against our national unity of counsel, our peace within and without, our industries and our commerce.... [I]ts spies were here even before the war began; and it is... a fact proved in our courts of justice that the intrigues which have more than once come perilously near to disturbing the peace and dislocating the industries of the country have been carried on at the instigation, with the support, and even under the personal direction of official agents of the Imperial Government.... That it means to stir up enemies against us at our very doors the intercepted note to the German Minister at Mexico City is eloquent evidence....

We are glad, now that we see the facts with no veil of false pretense about them to fight thus for the ultimate peace of the world and for the liberation of its peoples, the German peoples included: for the rights of nations great and small and the privilege of men everywhere to choose their way of life and of obedience. The world must be made safe for democracy. Its peace must be planted upon the tested foundations of political liberty. We have no selfish ends to serve....

We are... the sincere friends of the German people, and shall desire nothing so much as the early reestablishment of intimate relations of mutual advantage between us.... We shall, happily, still have an opportunity to prove that friendship in our daily attitude and actions towards the millions of men and women of German birth and native sympathy who live amongst us and share our life.... They are, most of them, as true and loyal Americans as if they had never known any other fealty or allegiance. They will be prompt to stand with us in rebuking and restraining the few who may be of a different mind and purpose. If there should be disloyalty, it will be dealt with with a firm hand of stern repression; but, if it lifts its head at all, it will lift it only here and there and without countenance except from a lawless and malignant few....

[T]he right is more precious than peace, and we shall fight for the things which we have always carried nearest our hearts,—for democracy, for the right of those who submit to authority to have a voice in their own Governments, for the rights and liberties of small nations, for a universal dominion of right by such a concert of free peoples as shall bring peace and safety to all nations and make the world itself at last free....

1918

PRESIDENT WOODROW WILSON'S
FOURTEEN POINTS

*A*nticipating the end of World War I, President Woodrow Wilson created a blueprint *for peace negotiations. In a January 8, 1918, speech on War Aims and Peace Terms, he enumerated fourteen points to ensure world peace. Wilson, who held a Ph.D. in history and political science, based the details of the speech on reports from political and social scientists who had studied and analyzed Allied and American policy in virtually every region of the globe.*

Wilson addressed what he perceived as the causes for the world war, including the practice among European nations of making secret agreements, and offered proposals that he believed would ensure peace in the future. But despite his well-reasoned arguments, most of the Fourteen Points were scuttled when the Allies met with Germany and Austria-Hungary at Versailles to formulate the treaty to end World War I. Wilson discovered that England, France, and Italy were more interested in regaining what they had lost and in punishing Germany. They would not apply his guidelines for peace to Germany. However, his call for a world organization, a League of Nations, to provide a system of collective security was incorporated into the Treaty of Versailles. Wilson launched a campaign for U.S. adoption of the treaty and participation in the league, but the Senate failed to ratify the treaty or approve membership.

The Allied leaders—David Lloyd George of Great Britain, Vittorio Orlando of Italy, Georges Clemenceau of France, and U.S. President Woodrow Wilson—meet at the Paris peace conference in May 1919.

litical and economic independence and territorial integrity of the several Balkan states should be entered into.

XII. The Turkish portions of the present Ottoman Empire should be assured a secure sovereignty, but the other nationalities which are now under Turkish rule should be assured an undoubted security of life and an absolutely unmolested opportunity of autonomous development, and the Dardanelles should be permanently opened as a free passage to the ships and commerce of all nations under international guarantees.

XIII. An independent Polish state should be erected which should include the territories inhabited by indisputably Polish populations, which should be assured a free and secure access to the sea, and whose political and economic independence and territorial integrity should be guaranteed by international covenant.

XIV. A general association of nations must be formed under specific covenants for the purpose of affording mutual guarantees of political independence and territorial integrity to great and small states alike.

In regard to these essential rectifications of wrong and assertions of right we feel ourselves to be intimate partners of all the governments and peoples associated together against the Imperialists. We cannot be separated in interest or divided in purpose. We stand together until the end.

For such arrangements and covenants we are willing to fight and to continue to fight until they are achieved; but only because we wish the right to prevail and desire a just and stable peace such as can be secured only by removing the chief provocations to war, which this programme does remove. We have no jealousy of German greatness, and there is nothing in this programme that impairs it. We grudge her no achievement or distinction of learning or of pacific enterprise such as have made her record very bright and very enviable. We do not wish to injure her or to block in any way her legitimate influence or power. We do not wish to fight her either with arms or with hostile arrangements of trade if she is willing to associate herself with us and the other peace-loving nations of the world in covenants of justice and law and fair dealing. We wish her only to accept a place of equality among the peoples of the world,—the new world in which we now live,—instead of a place of mastery.

Neither do we presume to suggest to her any alteration or modification of her institutions. But it is necessary, we must frankly say, and necessary as a preliminary to any intelligent dealings with her on our part, that we should know whom her spokesmen speak for when they speak to us, whether for the Reichstag majority or for the military party and the men whose creed is imperial domination.

It will be our wish and purpose that the processes of peace, when they are begun, shall be absolutely open and that they shall involve and permit henceforth no secret understandings of any kind. The day of conquest and aggrandizement is gone by; so is also the day of secret covenants entered into in the interest of particular governments and likely at some unlooked-for moment to upset the peace of the world. It is this happy fact, now clear to the view of every public man whose thoughts do not still linger in an age that is dead and gone, which makes it possible for every nation whose purposes are consistent with justice and the peace of the world to avow now or at any other time the objects it has in view.

We entered this war because violations of right had occurred which touched us to the quick and made the life of our own people impossible unless they were corrected and the world secure once for all against their recurrence. What we demand in this war, therefore, is nothing peculiar to ourselves. It is that the world be made fit and safe to live in; and particularly that it be made safe for every peace-loving nation which, like our own, wishes to live its own life, determine its own institutions, be assured of justice and fair dealing by the other peoples of the world as against force and selfish aggression. All the peoples of the world are in effect partners in this interest, and for our own part we see very clearly that unless justice be done to others it will not be done to us. The programme of the world's peace, therefore, is our programme; and that programme, the only possible programme, as we see it, is this:

I. Open covenants of peace, openly arrived at, after which there shall be no private international understandings of any kind but diplomacy shall proceed always frankly and in the public view.

II. Absolute freedom of navigation upon the seas, outside territorial waters, alike in peace and in war, except as the seas may be closed in whole or in part by international action for the enforcement of international covenants.

III. The removal, so far as possible, of all economic barriers and the establishment of an equality of trade conditions among all the nations consenting to the peace and associating themselves for its maintenance.

IV. Adequate guarantees given and taken that national armaments will be reduced to the lowest point consistent with domestic safety.

V. A free, open-minded, and absolutely impartial adjustment of all colonial claims, based upon a strict observance of the principle that in determining all such questions of sovereignty the interests of the populations concerned must have equal weight with the equitable claims of the government whose title is to be determined.

VI. The evacuation of all Russian territory and such a settlement of all questions affecting Russia as will secure the best and freest cooperation of the other nations of the world in obtaining for her an unhampered and unembarrassed opportunity for the independent determination of her own political development and national policy and assure her of a sincere welcome into the society of free nations under institutions of her own choosing; and, more than a welcome, assistance also of every kind that she may need and may herself desire. The treatment accorded Russia by her sister nations in the months to come will be the acid test of their good will, of their comprehension of her needs as distinguished from their own interests, and of their intelligent and unselfish sympathy.

VII. Belgium, the whole world will agree, must be evacuated and restored, without any attempt to limit the sovereignty which she enjoys in common with all other free nations. No other single act will serve as this will serve to restore confidence among the nations in the laws which they have themselves set and determined for the government of their relations with one another. Without this healing act the whole structure and validity of international law is forever impaired.

VIII. All French territory should be freed and the invaded portions restored, and the wrong done to France by Prussia in 1871 in the matter of Alsace-Lorraine, which has unsettled the peace of the world for nearly fifty years, should be righted, in order that peace may once more be made secure in the interest of all.

IX. A readjustment of the frontiers of Italy should be effected along clearly recognizable lines of nationality.

X. The peoples of Austria-Hungary, whose place among the nations we wish to see safeguarded and assured, should be accorded the freest opportunity to autonomous development.

XI. Rumania, Serbia, and Montenegro should be evacuated; occupied territories restored; Serbia accorded free and secure access to the sea; and the relations of the several Balkan states to one another determined by friendly counsel along historically established lines of allegiance and nationality; and international guarantees of the political and economic independence and territorial integrity of the several Balkan states should be entered into.

XII. The Turkish portion of the present Ottoman Empire should be assured a secure sovereignty, but the other nationalities which are now under Turkish rule should be assured an undoubted security of life and an absolutely unmolested opportunity of autonomous development, and the Dardanelles should be permanently opened as a free passage to the ships and commerce of all nations under international guarantees.

XIII. An independent Polish state should be erected which should include the territories inhabited by indisputably Polish populations, which should be assured a free and secure access to the sea, and whose political and economic independence and territorial integrity should be guaranteed by international covenant.

XIV. A general association of nations must be formed under specific covenants for the purpose of affording mutual guarantees of political independence and territorial integrity to great and small states alike....

1920

NINETEENTH AMENDMENT TO THE U.S. CONSTITUTION: WOMEN'S RIGHT TO VOTE

*T**he campaign for woman suffrage officially began in 1848 when activist Elizabeth Cady Stanton organized America's first woman's rights convention in Seneca Falls, New York. Supporters, primarily women, organized, petitioned, and picketed to win the right to vote, but it took them decades to accomplish their purpose. The first proposal for a constitutional amendment dates back to 1868. Between 1878, when California Senator A. A. Sargent, a close friend of Susan B. Anthony, introduced a constitutional amendment to give women the right to vote, and August 18, 1920, when it was ratified, champions of voting rights for*

Suffragettes picket outside the White House on Bastille Day, 1917. Appropriately, their banner reads, "Liberty, Equality, Fraternity."

women worked tirelessly. Some advocates lobbied for suffrage acts in each state—nine western states had adopted woman suffrage legislation by 1912. Others challenged male-only voting laws in the courts. Militant suffragists used tactics such as parades, silent vigils, and hunger strikes and met fierce resistance.

By 1916 most suffrage organizations had united behind the goal of a constitutional amendment. When New York adopted woman suffrage in 1917 and President Wilson changed his position, partly as a result of women's contributions to the nation during the world war, to support a federal amendment in 1918, the political mood began to shift. On May 21, 1919, the House of Representatives passed the amendment, and two weeks later, the Senate followed. After Tennessee became the thirty-sixth state to ratify the amendment, Secretary of State Bainbridge Colby certified the ratification on August 26, 1920. The longest battle over a constitutional amendment had finally won representation for fully half of America's population.

SIXTY-SIXTH CONGRESS OF THE UNITED STATES OF AMERICA; AT THE FIRST SESSION,

Begun and held at the City of Washington on Monday, the nineteenth day of May, one thousand nine hundred and nineteen.

JOINT RESOLUTION
Proposing an amendment to the Constitution extending the right of suffrage to women.

Resolved by the Senate and House of Representatives of the United States of America in Congress assembled (two-thirds of each House concurring therein), That the following article is proposed as an amendment to the Constitution, which shall be valid to all intents and purposes as part of the Constitution when ratified by the legislature of three-fourths of the several States.

"ARTICLE—.

"The right of citizens of the United States to vote shall not be denied or abridged by the United States or by any State on account of sex.

"Congress shall have power to enforce this article by appropriate legislation."

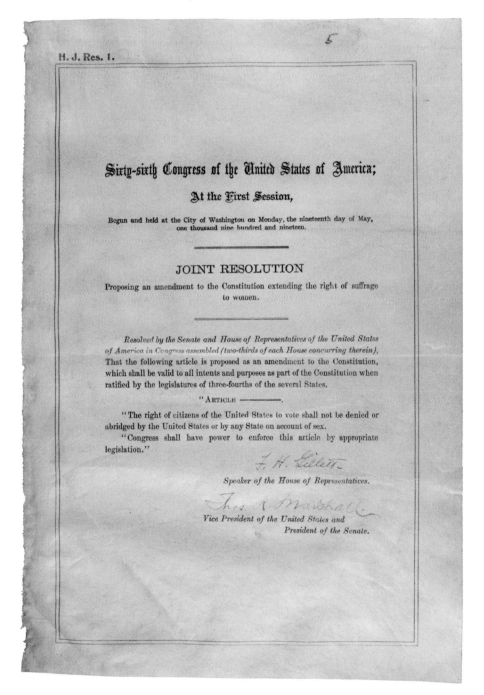

1928

BOULDER CANYON PROJECT ACT

*T*o further their economic development at the beginning of the twentieth century, west-
ern states needed irrigation, electricity, and municipal water supplies. In response, the
Boulder Canyon Project Act of 1928 authorized construction of a dam in Boulder
Canyon and of a canal to connect the Imperial and Coachella Valleys in California with the
Colorado River. The act also divided the waters among Arizona, California, Nevada, New Mexico,
and Utah. In addition and of equal importance, the dam would control flooding of the Colorado
River to preserve the lands along its banks. Construction of the dam began in 1931, and when it
was finished in 1935, it stood 726 feet high, stretched 1,244 feet across at the top, was 660 feet
thick at the base and 45 feet thick at the top, and weighed 6.6 million tons. The enormous dam
generated 2.8 million kilowatts of power and could store up to two years' average flow from the
Colorado River in the newly created Lake Mead.

Congress acknowledged Herbert Hoover's significant role, first as secretary of commerce and
later as President, by renaming the dam in his honor in 1947. Hoover called the dam "the greatest
engineering work of its character ever attempted by the hand of man."

AN ACT To provide for the construction of works for the protection and development of the Colorado River Basin, for the approval of the Colorado River compact, and for other purposes.

Be it enacted by the Senate and House of Representatives of the United States of America in Congress assembled, That for the purpose of controlling the floods, improving navigation and regulating the flow of the Colorado River, providing for storage and for the delivery of the stored waters thereof for reclamation of public lands and other beneficial uses exclusively within the United States, and for the generation of electrical energy as a means of making the project herein authorized a self-supporting and financially solvent undertaking, the Secretary of the Interior, subject to the terms of the Colorado River compact hereinafter mentioned, is hereby authorized to construct, operate, and maintain a dam and incidental works in the main stream of the Colorado River at Black Canyon or Boulder Canyon adequate to create a storage reservoir of a capacity of not less than twenty million acre-feet of water and a main canal and appurtenant structures located entirely within the United States connecting the Laguna Dam, or other suitable diversion dam, which the Secretary of the Interior is hereby authorized to construct if deemed necessary or advisable by him upon engineering or economic con-

siderations, with the Imperial and Coachella Valleys in California, the expenditures for said main canal and appurtenant structures to be reimbursable, as provided in the reclamation law, and shall not be paid out of revenues derived from the sale or disposal of water power or electric energy at the dam authorized to be constructed at said Black Canyon or Boulder Canyon, or for water for potable purposes outside of the Imperial and Coachella Valleys: Provided, however, That no charge shall be made for water or for the use, storage, or delivery of water for irrigation or water for potable purposes in the Imperial or Coachella Valleys; also to construct and equip, operate, and maintain at or near said dam, or cause to be constructed, a complete plant and incidental structures suitable for the fullest economic development of electrical energy from the water discharged from said reservoir; and to acquire by proceedings in eminent domain, or otherwise all lands, rights-of-way, and other property necessary for said purposes....

SEC. 3. There is hereby authorized to be appropriated from time to time, out of any money in the Treasury not otherwise appropriated, such sums of money as may be necessary to carry out the purposes of this Act, not exceeding in the aggregate $165,000,000.

SEC. 4. (a) This Act shall not take effect and no authority shall be exercised hereunder and no work

[PUBLIC No. 642 70th CONGRESS]

Seventieth Congress of the United States of America;
At the Second Session,

Begun and held at the City of Washington on Monday, the third day of
December, one thousand nine hundred and twenty-eight.

AN ACT

To provide for the construction of works for the protection and
development of the Colorado River Basin, for the approval of the
Colorado River compact, and for other purposes.

---

*Be it enacted by the Senate and House of Representatives of the
United States of America in Congress assembled*, That for the purpose of controlling the floods, improving navigation and regulating
the flow of the Colorado River, providing for storage and for the
delivery of the stored waters thereof for reclamation of public lands
and other beneficial uses exclusively within the United States, and for
the generation of electrical energy as a means of making the project
herein authorized a self-supporting and financially solvent undertaking, the Secretary of the Interior, subject to the terms of the Colorado River compact hereinafter mentioned, is hereby authorized to
construct, operate, and maintain a dam and incidental works in the
main stream of the Colorado River at Black Canyon or Boulder
Canyon adequate to create a storage reservoir of a capacity of not
less than twenty million acre-feet of water and a main canal and
appurtenant structures located entirely within the United States connecting the Laguna Dam, or other suitable diversion dam, which the
Secretary of the Interior is hereby authorized to construct if deemed
necessary or advisable by him upon engineering or economic considerations, with the Imperial and Coachella Valleys in California,
the expenditures for said main canal and appurtenant structures
to be reimbursable, as provided in the reclamation law, and shall
not be paid out of revenues derived from the sale or disposal of water
power or electric energy at the dam authorized to be constructed at
said Black Canyon or Boulder Canyon, or for water for potable purposes outside of the Imperial and Coachella Valleys: *Provided, however*, That no charge shall be made for water or for the use, storage,
or delivery of water for irrigation or water for potable purposes in
the Imperial or Coachella Valleys; also to construct and equip,
operate, and maintain at or near said dam, or cause to be constructed,
a complete plant and incidental structures suitable for the fullest
economic development of electrical energy from the water discharged
from said reservoir; and to acquire by proceedings in eminent

Ansel Adams's photograph of Boulder Dam, taken in 1941, reveals the scale of the engineering accomplishment as well as the natural beauty of the setting.

shall be begun and no moneys expended on or in connection with the works or structures provided for in this Act, and no water rights shall be claimed or initiated hereunder, and no steps shall be taken by the United States or by others to initiate or perfect any claims to the use of water pertinent to such works or structures unless and until…the States of Arizona, California, Colorado, Nevada, New Mexico, Utah, and Wyoming shall have ratified the Colorado River compact…and the President by public proclamation shall have so declared….

SEC. 6. That the dam and reservoir provided for by section 1 hereof shall be used: First, for river regulation, improvement of navigation, and flood control; second, for irrigation and domestic uses and satisfaction of present perfected rights in pursuance of Article VIII of said Colorado River compact; and third, for power. The title to said dam, reservoir, plant, and inci-

dental works shall forever remain in the United States, and the United States shall, until otherwise provided by Congress, control, manage, and operate the same, except as herein otherwise provided….

SEC. 18. Nothing herein shall be construed as interfering with such rights as the States now have either to the waters within their borders or to adopt such policies and enact such laws as they may deem necessary with respect to the appropriation, control, and use of waters within their borders, except as modified by the Colorado River compact or other interstate agreement.

APPROVED, DECEMBER 21, 1928.

1933

TENNESSEE VALLEY AUTHORITY ACT

*I*n one of the first efforts of the New Deal aimed at attacking the vicious poverty that affected many rural Americans, President Franklin Roosevelt signed the Tennessee Valley Authority Act on May 18, 1933, establishing the TVA as a federal corporation. The TVA was the first federal agency to address the total resource development needs of a major region (in this case most of Tennessee and parts of Alabama, Mississippi, Kentucky, Virginia, North Carolina, and Georgia). The new agency created flood controls, provided electricity to homes and businesses, and replanted forests. It also sought to improve travel on the Tennessee River by a system of dams and locks, to develop the region's business and farming, and to curtail emigration. The most dramatic change in Valley life resulted from the electricity that hydroelectric dams generated. Electric lights and modern appliances made life easier and farms more productive. Electricity also drew industries to the region, providing desperately needed jobs.

By 2000, TVA was the largest public power company in the United States, producing more than 130 billion kilowatt-hours of electricity a year for 160 power distributors. Its facilities include 29 hydroelectric dams, a pumped-storage plant, 11 coal-fired plants, 3 nuclear plants, and 4 combustion-turbine installations. These facilities provide more than 27,000 megawatts of generating capacity, meeting the energy needs of millions of people in the southeastern United States. The agency manages the nation's fifth-largest river system; it controls flooding, makes river travel easier, provides recreation, and protects water quality.

An Act to Improve the Navigability and to Provide for the Flood Control of the Tennessee River: To Provide for Reforestation and the Proper Use of Marginal Lands in the Tennessee Valley; to Provide for the Agricultural and Industrial Development of Said Valley; to Provide for the National Defense by the Creation of a Corporation for the Operation of Government Properties at and Near Muscle Shoals in the State of Alabama, and for Other Purposes, May 18, 1933.

Be it enacted by the Senate and House of Representatives of the United States of America in Congress assembled, That for the purpose of maintaining and operating the properties now owned by the United States in the vicinity of Muscle Shoals, Alabama, in the interest of the national defense and for agriculture and industrial development, and to improve navigation in the Tennessee River and to control the destructive flood waters in the Tennessee River and Mississippi River Basins, there is hereby created a body corporate by the name of the "Tennessee Valley Authority."...

SEC. 2. (a) The board of directors of the Corporation...shall be composed of three members, to be appointed by the President, by and with the advice and consent of the Senate. In appointing the members of the board, the President shall designate the chairman....

SEC. 4. Except as otherwise specifically provided in this Act, the Corporation—....

(f) May purchase or lease and hold such real and personal property as it deems necessary or convenient in the transaction of its business, and may dispose of any such personal property held by it....

(i) Shall have power to acquire real estate for the construction of dams, reservoirs, transmission lines, power houses, and other structures, and navigation projects at any point along the Tennessee River, or any of its tributaries, and in the event that the owner or owners of such property shall fail and refuse to sell to the Corporation at a price deemed fair and reasonable by the board, then the Corporation may proceed to exercise the right of eminent domain, and to condemn all property that it deems necessary for carrying out the purposes of this Act....

(j) Shall have power to construct dams, reservoirs, power houses, power structures, transmission lines, navigation projects, and incidental works in the Tennessee River and its tributaries, and to unite the various power installations into one or more systems by transmission lines.

SEC. 5. The board is hereby authorized—

(a) To contract with commercial producers for the production of such fertilizers or fertilizer materials as may be needed in the Government's program of development and introduction in excess of that produced by Government plants....

(b) To arrange with farmers and farm organizations for large scale practical use of the new forms of fertilizers under conditions permitting an accurate measure of the economic return they produce....

(d) The board in order to improve and cheapen the production of fertilizer is authorized to manufacture and sell fixed nitrogen, fertilizer, and fertilizer ingredients at Muscle Shoals by the employment of existing facilities, by modernizing existing plants, or by any other process or processes that in its judgment shall appear wise and profitable for the fixation of atmospheric nitrogen or the cheapening of the production of fertilizer....

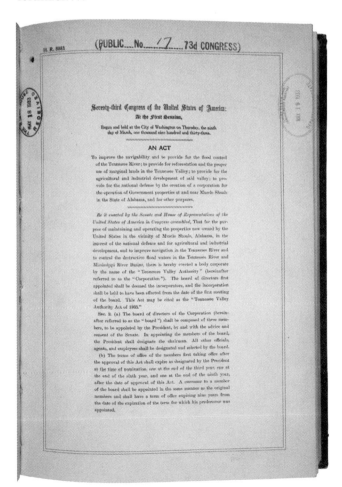

SEC. 10. The board is hereby empowered and authorized to sell the surplus power not used in its operations, and for operation of locks and other works generated by it, to States, counties, municipalities, corporations, partnerships, or individuals....In order to promote and encourage the fullest possible use of electric light and power on farms within reasonable distance of any of its transmission lines the board in its discretion shall have power to construct transmission lines to farms and small villages that are not otherwise supplied with electricity at reasonable rates, and to make such rules and regulations governing such sale and distribution of such electric power as in its judgment may be just and equitable....

SEC. 15. In the construction of any future dam, steam plant, or other facility, to be used in whole or in part for the generation or transmission of electric power the board is hereby authorized and empowered to issue on the credit of the United States and to sell serial bonds not exceeding $50,000,000 in amount....Said bonds shall be issued and sold in amounts and prices approved by the Secretary of the Treasury....

SEC. 20. The Government of the United States hereby reserves the right, in case of war or national emergency declared by Congress, to take possession of all or any part of the property described or referred to in this Act for the purpose of manufacturing explosives or for other war purposes....

SEC. 23. The President shall...recommend to Congress such legislation as he deems proper to carry out the general purposes...(1) the maximum amount of flood control; (2) the maximum development of said Tennessee River for navigation purposes; (3) the maximum generation of electric power consistent with flood control and navigation; (4) the proper use of marginal lands; (5) the proper method of reforestation of all lands in said drainage basin suitable for reforestation; and (6) the economic and social well-being of the people living in said river basin....

SEC. 30. The sections of this Act are hereby declared to be separable, and in the event any one or more sections of this Act be held to be unconstitutional, the same shall not affect the validity of other sections of this Act.

APPROVED, MAY 18, 1933.

1933
NATIONAL INDUSTRIAL RECOVERY ACT

*I*n 1933 Congress enacted the National Industrial Recovery Act (NIRA), one of the measures by which President Franklin D. Roosevelt sought to assist the nation's economic recovery during the Great Depression. The passage of NIRA ushered in a unique experiment in U.S. economic history: the NIRA advocated, and in some cases enforced, an alliance of industries. It suspended antitrust laws and required companies to write industry-wide "codes of fair competition" that effectively fixed prices and wages, established production quotas, and restricted entry of other companies into the alliances. These regulations ran counter to the American ideal of a free market economy.

A separate executive order created the National Recovery Administration (NRA) to implement the act, but from the beginning, the NRA suffered from widespread criticism. Code-drafting businessmen wanted guaranteed profits and security for investment and production; intellectuals wanted central economic planning; and labor union representatives fought with little success for the collective bargaining the NIRA had promised. The codes did little to help recovery, and by raising prices, they actually made the economic situation worse.

NRA did not last long. In 1935, in the case of the Schechter Poultry Corp. v. United States, the U.S. Supreme Court invalidated the compulsory-code system, partly on the grounds that the NIRA improperly delegated legislative powers to the executive.

Businesses that cooperated with the policies of the National Recovery Administration were permitted to display its Blue Eagle emblem. The government hoped that the public would consider support for the NRA's codes to be patriotic, and urged them to boycott businesses that did not display the emblem.

AN ACT

To encourage national industrial recovery, to foster fair competition, and to provide for the construction of certain useful public works, and for other purposes.

Be it enacted by the Senate and House of Representatives of the United States of America in Congress assembled,

TITLE I—INDUSTRIAL RECOVERY

DECLARATION OF POLICY

SECTION 1. A national emergency productive of widespread unemployment and disorganization of industry, which burdens interstate and foreign commerce, affects the public welfare, and undermines the standards of living of the American people, is hereby declared to exist. It is hereby declared to be the policy of Congress to remove obstructions to the free flow of interstate and foreign commerce which tend to diminish the amount thereof; and to provide for the general welfare by promoting the organization of industry for the purpose of cooperative action among trade groups, to induce and maintain united action of labor and management under adequate governmental sanctions and supervision, to eliminate unfair competitive practices, to promote the fullest possible utilization of the present productive capacity of industries, to avoid undue restriction of production (except as may be temporarily required), to increase the consumption of Industrial and agricultural products by increasing purchasing power, to reduce and relieve unemployment, to improve standards of labor, and otherwise to rehabilitate industry and to conserve natural resources.

CODES OF FAIR COMPETITION

SEC. 3. (a) Upon the application to the President by one or more trade or industrial associations or groups the President may approve a code or codes of fair competition for the trade or industry or sub-division thereof, represented by the applicant or applicants, if the President finds (1) that such associations or groups impose no inequitable restrictions on admission to membership therein and are truly representative of such trades or industries or subdivisions thereof, and (2) that such code or codes are not designed to promote monopolies or to eliminate or oppress small enterprises and will not operate to discriminate against them, and will tend to effectuate the policy of this title: Provided, That such code or codes shall not permit monopolies or monopolistic practices....

(b) After the President shall have approved any such code, the provisions of such code shall be the

"It is hereby declared to be the policy of Congress to remove obstructions to the free flow of interstate and foreign commerce which tend to diminish the amount thereof...."

standards of fair competition for such trade or industry or subdivision thereof....

SEC. 7. (a) Every code of fair competition, agreement, and license approved, prescribed, or issued under this title shall contain the following conditions: (1) That employees shall have the right to organize and bargain collectively through representatives of their own choosing, and shall be free from the interference restraint, or coercion of employers of labor, or their agents, in the designation of such representatives or in self-organization or in other concerted activities for the purpose of collective bargaining or other mutual aid or protection; (2) that no employee and no one seeking employment shall be required as a condition of employment to join any company union or to refrain from joining, organizing, or assisting a labor organization of his own choosing; and (3) that employers shall comply with the maximum hours of labor, minimum rates of pay, and other conditions of employment, approved or prescribed by the President.

TITLE II—PUBLIC WORKS AND CONSTRUCTION PROJECTS

FEDERAL EMERGENCY ADMINISTRATION OF PUBLIC WORKS

SECTION 201. (a) To effectuate the purposes of this title, the President is hereby authorized to create a Federal Emergency Administration of Public Works....

SEC. 202. The Administrator, under the direction of the President, shall prepare a comprehensive program of public works, which shall include among other things the following: (a) Construction, repair, and improvement of public highways and park ways, public buildings, and any publicly owned instrumentalities and facilities; (b) conservation and development of natural resources, including control, utilization, and purification of waters, prevention of soil or coastal erosion, development of water power, transmission of electrical energy, and construction of river and harbor improvements and flood control.... (c) any projects of the character heretofore constructed or carried on either directly by public authority or with public aid to serve the interests of the general public; (d) construction, reconstruction, alteration, or repair under public regulation or control of low-cost housing and slum-clearance projects....

SEC. 203. (a) With a view to increasing employment quickly (while reasonably securing any loans made by the United States) the president is authorized and empowered, through the Administrator or through such other agencies as he may designate or create, (1) to construct, finance, or aid in the construction or financing of any public works project included in the program prepared pursuant to section 202; (2) upon such terms as the President shall prescribe, to make grants to States, municipalities, or other public bodies for the construction, repair, or improvement of any such project, but no such grant shall be in excess of 30 per centum of the cost of the labor and materials employed upon such project; (3) to acquire by purchase, or by exercise of the power of eminent domain, any real or personal property in connection with the construction of any such project, and to sell any security acquired or any property so constructed or acquired or to lease any such property with or without the privilege of purchase....

SEC. 204. (a) For the purpose of providing for emergency construction of public highways and related projects, the President is authorized to make grants to the highway departments of the several States in an amount not less than $400,000,000, to be expended by such departments in accordance with the provisions of the Federal Highway Act....

SEC. 205. (a) Not less than $50,000,000 of the amount made available by this Act shall be allotted for (A) national forest highways, (B) national forest roads, trails, bridges, and related projects, (C) national park roads and trails in national parks owned or authorized, (D) roads on Indian reservations, and (E) roads through public lands. . . .

APPROPRIATION

SEC. 220. For the purposes of this Act, there is hereby authorized to be appropriated, out of any money in the Treasury not otherwise appropriated, the sum of $3,300,000,000.

APPROVED, JUNE 16, 1933, 11:55 A.M.

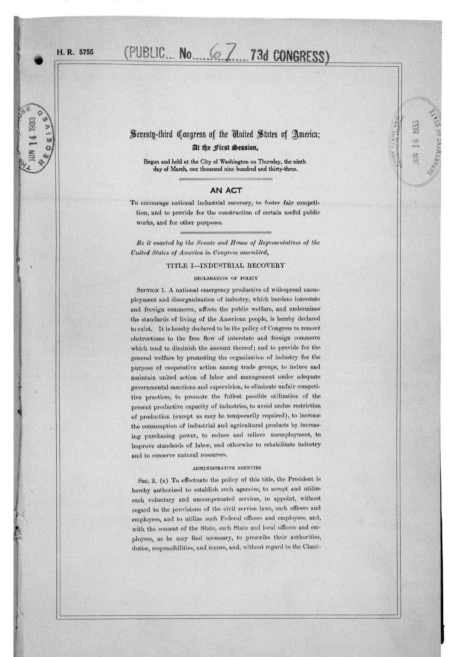

NATIONAL LABOR RELATIONS ACT

During the Great Depression workers had begun to organize militantly in response to employers who had been free to spy on, interrogate, discipline, discharge, and blacklist union members. In 1933 and 1934, a wave of urban general strikes and factory takeovers spread across the nation. Workers trying to form unions and the police and private security forces defending anti-union employers met in violent confrontations.

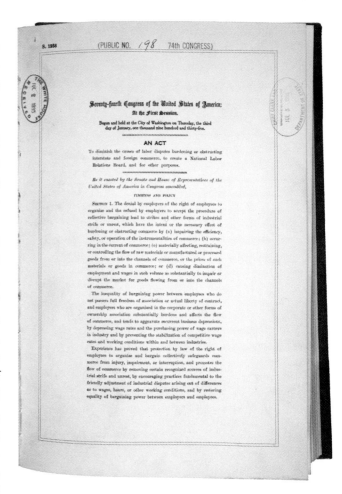

Sympathetic to labor unions, Congress passed the National Labor Relations Act (NLRA) in July 1935. The broad intention of the act, commonly known as the Wagner Act after Senator Robert R. Wagner of New York, was to guarantee employees "the right to self-organization, to form, join, or assist labor organizations, to bargain collectively through representatives of their own choosing, and to engage in concerted activities for the purpose of collective bargaining or other mutual aid and protection." As a result of its passage, union membership surged dramatically; for example, by the end of the 1930s 800,000 women belonged to unions, a threefold increase from 1929. Labor became a formidable political and economic force.

To enforce and maintain the rights it promised, the act included provisions for the National Labor Relations Board (NLRB) to arbitrate deadlocked labor-management disputes, guarantee democratic union elections, and penalize unfair labor practices such as employer interference with the formation of labor unions, encouragement or discouragement of union membership, and refusal to bargain collectively with employee representatives. Congress expanded the provisions of the NLRA under the Taft-Hartley Labor Act of 1957 and the Landrum-Griffin Act of 1959.

AN ACT To diminish the causes of labor disputes burdening or obstructing interstate and foreign commerce, to create a National Labor Relations Board, and for other purposes.

FINDINGS AND POLICIES
SECTION 1. The denial by some employers of the right of employees to organize and the refusal by some employers to accept the procedure of collective bargaining lead to strikes and other forms of industrial strife or unrest, which have the intent or the necessary effect of burdening or obstructing commerce by (a) impairing the efficiency, safety, or operation of the instrumentalities of commerce; (b) occurring in the current of commerce; (c) materially affecting, restraining, or controlling the flow of raw materials or manufactured or processed goods from or into the channels

of commerce, or the prices of such materials or goods in commerce; or (d) causing diminution of employment and wages in such volume as substantially to impair or disrupt the market for goods flowing from or into the channels of commerce.

The inequality of bargaining power between employees who do not possess full freedom of association or actual liberty of contract and employers who are organized in the corporate or other forms of ownership association substantially burdens and affects the flow of commerce, and tends to aggravate recurrent business depressions, by depressing wage rates and the purchasing power of wage earners in industry and by preventing the stabilization of competitive wage rates and working conditions within and between industries.

Experience has proved that protection by law of the right of employees to organize and bargain collectively safeguards commerce from injury, impairment, or interruption, and promotes the flow of commerce by removing certain recognized sources of industrial strife and unrest, by encouraging practices fundamental to the friendly adjustment of industrial disputes arising out of differences as to wages, hours, or other working conditions, and by restoring equality of bargaining power between employers and employees.

Experience has further demonstrated that certain practices by some labor organizations, their officers, and members have the intent or the necessary effect of burdening or obstructing commerce by preventing the free flow of goods in such commerce through strikes and other forms of industrial unrest or through concerted activities which impair the interest of the public in the free flow of such commerce. The elimination of such practices is a necessary condition to the assurance of the rights herein guaranteed....

It is declared to be the policy of the United States to eliminate the causes of certain substantial obstructions to the free flow of commerce and to mitigate and eliminate these obstructions when they have occurred by encouraging the practice and procedure of collective bargaining and by protecting the exercise by workers of full freedom of association, self-organization, and designation of representatives of their own choosing, for the purpose of negotiating the terms and conditions of their employment or other mutual aid or protection....

RIGHTS OF EMPLOYEES
SEC. 7. Employees shall have the right to self-organization, to form, join, or assist labor organizations, to bar-

gain collectively through representatives of their own choosing, and to engage in other concerted activities for the purpose of collective bargaining or other mutual aid or protection, and shall also have the right to refrain from any or all such activities except to the extent that such right may be affected by an agreement requiring membership in a labor organization as a condition of employment as authorized in section 8(a)(3).

UNFAIR LABOR PRACTICES
SEC. 8. (a) It shall be an unfair labor practice for an employer—

(1) to interfere with, restrain, or coerce employees in the exercise of the rights guaranteed in section 7;

(2) to dominate or interfere with the formation or administration of any labor organization or contribute financial or other support to it...;

(3) by discrimination in regard to hire or tenure of employment or any term or condition of employment to encourage or discourage membership in any labor organization...;

(4) to discharge or otherwise discriminate against an employee because he has filed charges or given testimony under this Act;

(5) to refuse to bargain collectively with the representatives of his employees, subject to the provisions of section 9(a).

(b) It shall be an unfair labor practice for a labor organization or its agents—

(1) to restrain or coerce...employees in the exercise of the rights guaranteed in section 7....

(2) to cause or attempt to cause an employer to discriminate against an employee...with respect to whom membership in such organization has been denied or terminated on some ground other than his failure to tender the periodic dues and the initiation fees uniformly required as a condition of acquiring or retaining membership;

(3) to refuse to bargain collectively with an employer, provided it is the representative of his employees subject to the provisions of section 9(a);...

(7) to picket or cause to be picketed, or threaten to picket or cause to be picketed, any employer where an object thereof is forcing or requiring an employer to recognize or bargain with a labor organization as the representative of his employees, or forcing or requiring the employees of an employer to accept or select such labor organization as their collective-bargaining representative, unless such labor organization is currently certified as the representative of such employees....

1935

SOCIAL SECURITY ACT

*L*ocal and state assistance programs made tremendous efforts to meet the demands of older Americans but ultimately failed under the strain of the Great Depression. Nor could the elderly depend on their struggling families in such hard economic times. Populist activists such as the immensely popular Francis E. Townsend and influential Louisiana Senator Huey P. Long put considerable pressure on the Roosevelt administration to address this issue.

In response to this crisis and political pressures, in January 1935 President Franklin Roosevelt asked Congress for "social security" legislation, and Senator Robert Wagner of New York and Representative David Lewis of Maryland introduced bills reflecting the administration's views. The bills encountered opposition from Americans who considered social security a governmental invasion of the private sphere and employers who sought exemption from payroll taxes for having adopted government-approved private pension plans. Eventually compromise legislation passed, and President Roosevelt signed it into law in August 1935.

Best known for providing pensions for retired people, the Social Security Act also established a system of unemployment compensation. State employment offices like this one administered the joint federal-state system.

The act created a uniquely American solution to the problem of old-age pensions. Unlike the system in many European nations—which rely on government funds—taxes on individuals' wages and employers' payrolls support U.S. social security. In addition to insuring retired workers who have contributed to the system over time, the act also instituted vocational training programs and provided funds to assist dependent mothers and children, blind and physically disabled populations, and the unemployed. On signing the act, President Roosevelt said: "We can never insure one-hundred percent of the population against one-hundred percent of the hazards and vicissitudes of life. But we have tried to frame a law which will give some measure of protection to the average citizen and to his family against the loss of a job and against poverty-ridden old age."

AN ACT to provide for the general welfare by establishing a system of Federal old-age benefits, and by enabling the several States to make more adequate provision for aged persons, blind persons, dependent and crippled children, maternal and child welfare, public health, and the administration of their unemployment compensation laws; to establish a Social Security Board; to raise revenue; and for other purposes.

Be it enacted by the Senate and House of Representatives of the United States of America in Congress assembled,

TITLE I—GRANTS TO STATES FOR OLD-AGE ASSISTANCE

SECTION 1. For the purpose of enabling each State to furnish financial assistance, as far as practicable under the conditions in such State, to aged needy individuals, there is hereby authorized to be appropriated for the fiscal year ended June 30, 1936, the sum of $49,750,000, and there is hereby authorized to be appropriated for each fiscal year thereafter a sum sufficient to carry out the purposes of this title....

OLD-AGE BENEFIT PAYMENTS

SEC. 202. (a) Every qualified individual (as defined in section 210) shall be entitled to receive, with respect to the period beginning on the date he attains the age of sixty-five, or on January 1, 1942, whichever is the later, and ending on the date of his death, an old-age benefit (payable as nearly as practicable in equal monthly installments) as follows: (1) If the total wages (as defined in section 210) determined by the Board to have been paid to him, with respect to employment (as defined in section 210) after December 31, 1936, and before he attained the age of sixty-five, were not more than $3,000, the old-age benefit shall be at a monthly rate of one-half of 1 per centum of such total wages; (2) If such total wages were more than $3,000, the old-age benefit shall be at a monthly rate equal to the sum of the following:

(A) One-half of 1 per centum of $3,000; plus

(B) One-twelfth of 1 per centum of the amount by which such total wages exceeded $3,000 and did not exceed $45,000; plus

(C) One-twenty-fourth of 1 per centum of the amount by which such total wages exceeded $45,000.

(b) In no case shall the monthly rate computed under subsection (a) exceed $85....

TITLE III—GRANTS TO STATES FOR UNEMPLOYMENT COMPENSATION ADMINISTRATION

SECTION 301. For the purpose of assisting the States in the administration of their unemployment compensation laws, there is hereby authorized to be appropriated... the sum of $4,000,000, and for each fiscal year thereafter the sum of $49,000,000, to be used as hereinafter provided....

TITLE IV—GRANTS TO STATES FOR AID TO DEPENDENT CHILDREN

SECTION 401. For the purpose of enabling each State to furnish financial assistance, as far as practicable under the conditions in such State, to needy dependent children, there is hereby authorized to be appropriated for the fiscal year ending June 30, 1936, the sum of $24,750,000....

TITLE V—GRANTS TO STATES FOR MATERNAL AND CHILD WELFARE

PART 1—MATERNAL AND CHILD HEALTH SERVICES

SECTION 501. For the purpose of enabling each State to extend and improve, as far as practicable under the conditions in such State, services for promoting the health of mothers and children, especially in rural areas and in areas suffering from severe economic distress, there is hereby authorized to be appropriated for each fiscal year... the sum of $3,800,000....

PART 2—SERVICES FOR CRIPPLED CHILDREN

SEC. 511. For the purpose of enabling each State to extend and improve (especially in rural areas and in areas suffering from severe economic distress), as far as practicable under the conditions in such State, services for locating crippled children and for providing medical, surgical, corrective, and other services and care, and facilities for diagnosis, hospitalization, and aftercare, for children who are crippled or who are suffering from conditions which lead to crippling, there is hereby authorized to be appropriated for each fiscal year... the sum of $2,850,000....

PART 3—CHILD WELFARE SERVICES

SEC. 521. (a) For the purpose of enabling the United States, through the Children's Bureau, to cooperate with State public-welfare agencies establishing, extending, and strengthening, especially in predominantly rural areas, public-welfare services (hereinafter in this section referred to as child-welfare services) for the protection and care of homeless, dependent, and neglected children, and children in danger of becoming delinquent, there is hereby authorized to be appropriated for each fiscal year... the sum of $1,500,000....

PART 4—VOCATIONAL REHABILITAION

SEC. 531. (a) In order to enable the United States to cooperate with the States and Hawaii in extending and strengthening their programs of vocational rehabilitation of the physically disabled... there is hereby authorized to be... the sum of $841,000 for each such fiscal year in addition to the amount of the existing authorization, and for each fiscal year thereafter the sum of $1,938,000....

TITLE VI—PUBLIC HEALTH WORK

SECTION 601. For the purpose of assisting States, counties, health districts, and other political subdivisions of the States in establishing and maintaining adequate public-health services, including the training of personnel for State and local health work, there is hereby authorized to be appropriated for each fiscal year...the sum of $8,000,000....

TITLE VII—SOCIAL SECURITY BOARD ESTABLISHMENT

SECTION 701. There is hereby established a Social Security Board (in this Act referred to as the Board) to be composed of three members to be appointed by the President, by and with the advice and consent of the Senate. During his term of membership on the Board, no member shall engage in any other business, vocation, or employment. Not more than two of the members of the Board shall be members of the same political party.

TITLE VIII—TAXES WITH RESPECT TO EMPLOYMENT

INCOME TAX ON EMPLOYEES

SECTION 801. In addition to other taxes, there shall be levied, collected, and paid upon the income of every individual a tax equal to the following percentages of the wages (as defined in section 811) received by him after December 31, 1936, with respect to employment (as defined in section 811) after such date:

(1) With respect to employment during the calendar years 1937, 1938, and 1939, the rate shall be 1 per centum....

(5) With respect to employment after December 31, 1948, the rate shall be 3 per centum.

DEDUCTION OF TAX FROM WAGES

SEC. 802. (a) The tax imposed by section 801 shall be collected by the employer of the taxpayer by deducting the amount of the tax from the wages as and when paid....

EXCISE TAX ON EMPLOYERS

SEC. 804. In addition to other taxes, every employer shall pay an excise tax, with respect to having individuals in his employ....

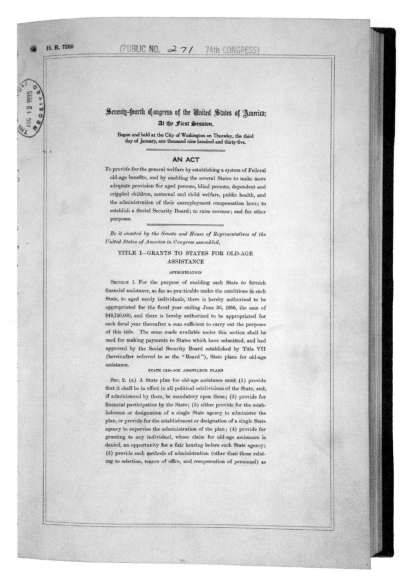

UNEMPLOYMENT TRUST FUND

SEC. 904. (a) There is hereby established in the Treasury of the United States a trust fund to be known as the Unemployment Trust Fund....

TITLE X—GRANTS TO STATES FOR AID TO THE BLIND APPROPRIATION

SECTION 1001. For the purpose of enabling each State to furnish financial assistance, as far as practicable under the conditions in such State, to needy individuals who are blind, there is hereby authorized to be appropriated for the fiscal year ending June 30, 1936, the sum of $3,000,000....

APPROVED, AUGUST 14, 1935.

1936

PRESIDENT FRANKLIN ROOSEVELT'S SPEECH IN DEFENSE OF THE SECOND NEW DEAL

*I*n response to the Great Depression, which disrupted the entire American economy and brought financial ruin to millions, President Franklin D. Roosevelt initiated a wide variety of government programs to reinvigorate the economy, particularly by providing government jobs for the unemployed. Critics charged that the New Deal had not done enough to improve the economy or reduce unemployment. Roosevelt responded to critics in this campaign speech to a crowd of fervent supporters at Madison Square Garden on October 31, 1936, which was also broadcast on the radio.

The President compared the economic achievements of his first term with the "nine crazy years at the ticker and three long years in the breadlines" that had preceded his election in 1932. He also attacked those who accused him of creating "class antagonism" and "destruction of the American system," charging his opponents with "coerc[ing] the votes of the wage earners of this country" and intentionally misinforming workers about New Deal legislation. Roosevelt characterized his government as compassionate to its people and committed to restoring their dignity. Roosevelt defended his Second New Deal, which included the Works Progress Administration (WPA), the National Labor Relations (Wagner) Act, the Social Security Act, and the Wealth Tax Act.

Americans reelected Roosevelt to a second term as President. He took 60 percent of the popular vote, won by a margin of 10 million votes, and carried every state except Maine and Vermont. The coalition he built during this campaign transformed the Democratic Party by broadening its base to include small farmers of the Midwest, urban political bosses, ethnic blue-collar workers, Jews, intellectuals, African Americans, and southern Democrats.

The Works Progress Administration, a New Deal agency, sponsored music and art classes for children. These provided both educational opportunities for the students and employment for the teachers.

Of course we will provide useful work for the needy unemployed; we prefer useful work to the pauperism of a dole.

Here and now I want to make myself clear about those who disparage their fellow citizens on the relief rolls. They say that those on relief are not merely jobless -- that they are worthless. Their solution for the relief problem is to end relief -- to purge the rolls by starvation. To use the language of the stock broker, our needy unemployed would be cared for ~~if, as and when~~ when, as and if, some fairy godmother ~~appeared~~ should happen on the scene.

You and I will continue to refuse to accept that estimate of our unemployed fellow Americans. Your Government is still on the same side of the street with the Good Samaritan and not with those who pass by on the other side.

Again-- what of our objectives?

Of course we will continue our efforts for young men and women so that they may obtain an education and an opportunity to put it to use. Of course, we will continue our help for the crippled, for the blind, for the mothers -- our insurance for the unemployed --

---

On the eve of a national election, it is well for us to stop for a moment and analyze calmly and without prejudice the effect on our Nation of a victory by either of the major political parties....

What was our hope in 1932? Above all other things the American people wanted peace. They wanted peace of mind instead of gnawing fear....

I submit to you a record of peace; and on that record a well-founded expectation for future peace—peace for the individual, peace for the community, peace for the Nation, and peace with the world....

For twelve years this Nation was afflicted with hear-nothing, see-nothing, do-nothing Government. The Nation looked to Government but the Government looked away. Nine mocking years with the golden calf and three long years of the scourge! Nine crazy years at the ticker and three long years in the breadlines! Nine mad years of mirage and three long years of despair!

Powerful influences strive today to restore that kind of government with its doctrine that that Government is best which is most indifferent.

For nearly four years you have had an Administration which instead of twirling its thumbs has rolled up its sleeves. We will keep our sleeves rolled up.

We had to struggle with the old enemies of peace—business and financial monopoly, speculation, reckless banking, class antagonism, sectionalism, war profiteering.

They had begun to consider the Government of the United States as a mere appendage to their own affairs. We know now that Government by organized money is just as dangerous as Government by organized mob. . . .

Here is an amazing paradox! The very employers and politicians and publishers who talk most loudly of class antagonism and the destruction of the American system now undermine that system by this attempt to coerce the votes of the wage earners of this country. It is the 1936 version of the old threat to close down the factory or the office if a particular candidate does not win. It is an old strategy of tyrants to delude their victims into fighting their battles for them. . . .

It is because I have sought to think in terms of the whole Nation that I am confident that today, just as four years ago, the people want more than promises. Our vision for the future contains more than promises. . . .

Of course we will continue to seek to improve working conditions for the workers of America—to reduce hours over-long, to increase wages that spell starvation, to end the labor of children, to wipe out sweatshops. Of course we will continue every effort to end monopoly in business, to support collective bargaining, to stop unfair competition, to abolish dishonorable trade practices.

Of course we will continue to work for cheaper electricity in the homes and on the farms of America, for better and cheaper transportation, for low interest rates, for sounder home financing, for better banking, for the regulation of security issues, for reciprocal trade among nations, for the wiping out of slums. For all these we have only just begun to fight.

Of course we will continue our efforts in behalf of the farmers of America. With their continued cooperation we will do all in our power to end the piling up of huge surpluses which spelled ruinous prices for their crops. We will persist in successful action for better land use, for reforestation, for the conservation of water all the way from its source to the sea, for drought and flood control, for better marketing facilities for farm commodities, for a definite reduction of farm tenancy, for encouragement of farmer cooperatives, for crop insurance and a stable food supply. For all these we have only just begun to fight.

Of course we will provide useful work for the needy unemployed; we prefer useful work to the pauperism of a dole. . . .

Of course we will continue our efforts for young men and women so that they may obtain an education and an opportunity to put it to use. Of course we will continue our help for the crippled, for the blind, for the mothers, our insurance for the unemployed, our security for the aged. Of course we will continue to protect the consumer against unnecessary price spreads, against the costs that are added by monopoly and speculation. We will continue our successful efforts to increase his purchasing power and to keep it constant. . . .

Today there is war and rumor of war. We want none of it. But while we guard our shores against threats of war, we will continue to remove the causes of unrest and antagonism at home which might make our people easier victims to those for whom foreign war is profitable. You know well that those who stand to profit by war are not on our side in this campaign.

"Peace on earth, good will toward men"—democracy must cling to that message. For it is my deep conviction that democracy cannot live without that true religion which gives a nation a sense of justice and of moral purpose. . . .

It is that which makes it possible for government to persuade those who are mentally prepared to fight each other to go on instead, to work for and to sacrifice for each other. That is why we need to say with the Prophet: "What doth the Lord require of thee—but to do justly, to love mercy and to walk humbly with thy God." That is why the recovery we seek, the recovery we are winning, is more than economic. In it are included justice and love and humility, not for ourselves as individuals alone, but for our Nation.

That is the road to peace.

1941

THE FOUR FREEDOMS:
PRESIDENT FRANKLIN ROOSEVELT'S ANNUAL MESSAGE TO CONGRESS

Early in his political career, as state senator and later as governor of New York, Franklin Roosevelt was concerned with human rights in the broadest sense. This concern deepened with the emergence of totalitarian regimes and the eruption of war in Europe in September 1939. In 1940 President Roosevelt held a press conference in which he discussed long-range peace objectives. Subsequently in his Annual Message to Congress on January 6, 1941, he included ideas he had formulated about human rights and freedoms. Referring to events in Europe, he asked Americans to make sacrifices—to engage in the hard work of defense production and to pay higher taxes—to support U.S. allies. In closing, he envisioned a world: founded upon "four essential human freedoms": freedom of speech, freedom of worship, freedom from want, and freedom from fear.

During World War II Norman Rockwell completed a series of paintings portraying the four freedoms as universal goals. The paintings went on a national tour to raise money for the war effort. After the war, the four freedoms appeared again, embedded in the charter of the United Nations and the Declaration of Human Rights that it adopted in 1948. These ideals continue to shape international understandings of basic human rights.

MR. PRESIDENT, MR. SPEAKER, MEMBERS OF THE SEVENTY-SEVENTH CONGRESS:

I address you, the Members of the Seventy-seventh Congress, at a moment unprecedented in the history of the Union. I use the word "unprecedented," because at no previous time has American security been as seriously threatened from without as it is today....

Every realist knows that the democratic way of life is at this moment being directly assailed in every part of the world—assailed either by arms, or by secret spreading of poisonous propaganda by those who seek to destroy unity and promote discord in nations that are still at peace....

Therefore, as your President, performing my constitutional duty to "give to the Congress information of the state of the Union," I find it, unhappily, necessary to report that the future and the safety of our country and of our democracy are overwhelmingly involved in events far beyond our borders....

The need of the moment is that our actions and our policy should be devoted primarily—almost exclusively—to meeting this foreign peril. For all our domestic problems are now a part of the great emergency.

Just as our national policy in internal affairs has been based upon a decent respect for the rights and the dignity of all our fellow men within our gates, so our national policy in foreign affairs has been based on a decent respect for the rights and dignity of all nations, large and small. And the justice of morality must and will win in the end.

Our national policy is this:

FIRST, by an impressive expression of the public will and without regard to partisanship, we are committed to all-inclusive national defense.

SECOND, by an impressive expression of the public will and without regard to partisanship, we are committed to full support of all those resolute peoples, everywhere, who are resisting aggression and are thereby keeping war away from our Hemisphere. By this support, we express our determination that the democratic cause shall prevail; and we strengthen the defense and the security of our own nation.

THIRD, by an impressive expression of the public will and without regard to partisanship, we are committed to the proposition that principles of morality and considerations for our own security will never permit us to acquiesce in a peace dictated by aggressors and sponsored by appeasers. We know that enduring peace cannot be bought at the cost of other people's freedom....

New circumstances are constantly begetting new needs for our safety. I shall ask this Congress for greatly increased new appropriations and authorizations to carry on what we have begun.

I also ask this Congress for authority and for funds sufficient to manufacture additional munitions and war supplies of many kinds, to be turned over to those nations which are now in actual war with aggressor nations.

Our most useful and immediate role is to act as an arsenal for them as well as for ourselves. They do not need man power, but they do need billions of dollars worth of the weapons of defense.

The time is near when they will not be able to pay for them all in ready cash. We cannot, and we will not, tell them that they must surrender, merely because of present inability to pay for the weapons which we know they must have.

I do not recommend that we make them a loan of dollars with which to pay for these weapons—a loan to be repaid in dollars.

I recommend that we make it possible for those nations to continue to obtain war materials in the United States, fitting their orders into our own program. Nearly all their materiel would, if the time ever came, be useful for our own defense.

Taking counsel of expert military and naval authorities, considering what is best for our own security, we are free to decide how much should be kept here and how much should be sent abroad to our friends who by their determined and heroic resistance are giving us time in which to make ready our own defense....

In fulfillment of this purpose we will not be intimidated by the threats of dictators that they will regard as a breach of international law or as an act of war our aid to the democracies which dare to resist their aggression. Such aid is not an act of war, even if a dictator should unilaterally proclaim it so to be....

Their only interest is in a new one-way international law, which lacks mutuality in its observance, and, therefore, becomes an instrument of oppression.

The happiness of future generations of Americans may well depend upon how effective and how immediate we can make our aid felt. No one can tell the exact character of the emergency situations that we may be called upon to meet. The Nation's hands must not be tied when the Nation's life is in danger....

In the future days, which we seek to make secure, we look forward to a world founded upon four essential human freedoms.

The first is freedom of speech and expression—everywhere in the world.

The second is freedom of every person to worship God in his own way—everywhere in the world.

The third is freedom from want—which, translated into world terms, means economic understandings which will secure to every nation a healthy peacetime life for its inhabitants—everywhere in the world.

The fourth is freedom from fear—which, translated into world terms, means a world-wide reduction of armaments to such a point and in such a thorough fashion that no nation will be in a position to commit an act of physical aggression against any neighbor—anywhere in the world....

This nation has placed its destiny in the hands and heads and hearts of its millions of free men and women; and its faith in freedom under the guidance of God. Freedom means the supremacy of human rights everywhere. Our support goes to those who struggle to gain those rights or keep them. Our strength is our unity of purpose. To that high concept there can be no end save victory.

> TO THE CONGRESS OF THE UNITED STATES:
>
> I address you, the Members of the Seventy-Seventh Congress, at a moment unprecedented in the history of the Union. I use the word "unprecedented", because at no previous time has American security been as seriously threatened from without as it is today.
>
> Since the permanent formation of our government under the Constitution, in 1789, most of the periods of crisis in our history have related to our domestic affairs. Fortunately, only one of these — the four year War Between the States — ever threatened our national unity. Today, thank God, one hundred and thirty million Americans, in forty-eight States, have forgotten points of the compass in our national unity.
>
> It is true that prior to 1914 the United States often had been disturbed by events in other Continents. We had even engaged in two wars with European nations and in a number of undeclared wars in the West Indies, in the Mediterranean and in the Pacific for the maintenance of American rights and for the principles of peaceful commerce. In no case, however, had a serious threat been raised against our national safety or our independence.
>
> What I seek to convey is the historic truth that the United States as a nation has at all times maintained opposition to any attempt to lock us in behind an ancient Chinese wall while the procession of civilization went past.

1941

LEND-LEASE ACT

*I*n July 1940, after Britain had lost eleven destroyers to the German navy over a ten-day period, Prime Minister Winston Churchill requested help from President Franklin Roosevelt. Roosevelt responded by exchanging fifty American destroyers for ninety-nine-year leases on British bases in the Caribbean and Newfoundland. This deal led to a major debate over whether the United States should aid Great Britain or maintain strict neutrality. Correctly reading public sentiment, Roosevelt promised during his 1940 presidential campaign to keep America out of the war. Roosevelt, however, wanted to support Britain and believed the United States should serve as a "great arsenal of democracy." In January 1941, honoring both his campaign pledge and the prime minister's appeal for arms, Roosevelt proposed a plan to "lend-lease or otherwise dispose of arms" and other supplies needed by any country whose security was vital to the defense of the United States. In support of the plan, Secretary of War Henry L. Stimson told the Senate Foreign Relations Committee, "We are buying…not lending. We are buying our own security while we prepare." After two months of debate, Congress approved the plan, meeting Great Britain's great need for supplies and allowing the United States to prepare for war while remaining officially neutral.

A BILL Further to promote the defense of the United States, and for other purposes.

Be it enacted by the Senate and House of Representatives of the United States of America in Congress assembled, That this Act may be cited as "An Act to Promote the Defense of the United States."

SEC. 2. As used in this Act—

(a) The term "defense article" means—

(1) Any weapon, munition, aircraft, vessel, or boat;

(2) Any machinery, facility, tool, material, or supply necessary for the manufacture, production, processing, repair, servicing, or operation of any article described in this subsection;

(3) Any component material or part of or equipment for any article described in this subsection;

(4) Any agricultural, industrial or other commodity or article for defense....

SEC. 3. (a) Notwithstanding the provisions of any other law, the President may, from time to time, when he deems it in the interest of national defense, authorize the Secretary Of War, the Secretary of the Navy, or the head of any other department or agency of the Government—

(1) To manufacture in arsenals, factories, and shipyards under their jurisdiction, or otherwise procure, to the extent to which funds are made available therefor, or contracts are authorized from time to time by the Congress, or both, any defense article for the government of any country whose defense the President deems vital to the defense of the United States.

(2) To sell, transfer title to, exchange, lease, lend, or otherwise dispose of, to any such government any defense article, but no defense article not manufactured or procured under paragraph (1) shall in any way be disposed of under this paragraph, except after consultation with the Chief of Staff of the Army or the Chief of Naval Operations of the Navy, or both. The value of defense articles disposed of in any way under authority of this paragraph, and procured from funds heretofore appropriated, shall not exceed $1,300,000,000. The value of such defense articles shall be determined by the head of the department or agency concerned or such other department, agency or officer as shall be designated in the manner provided in the rules and regulations issued hereunder....

(3) To test, inspect, prove, repair, outfit, recondition, or otherwise to place in good working order, to the extent to which funds are made available therefor, or contracts are authorized from time to time by the Congress, or both, any defense article for any such government, or to procure any or all such services by private contract.

(4) To communicate to any such government any defense information pertaining to any defense article

furnished to such government under paragraph (2) of this subsection.

(5) To release for export any defense article disposed of in any way under this subsection to any such government....

(b) The terms and conditions upon which any such foreign government receives any aid authorized under subsection (a) shall be those which the President deems satisfactory, and the benefit to the United States may be payment or repayment in kind or property, or any other direct or indirect benefit which the President deems satisfactory....

(c) After June 30, 1943, or after the passage of a concurrent resolution by the two Houses before June 30, 1943, which declares that the powers conferred by or pursuant to subsection (a) are no longer necessary to promote the defense of the United States, neither the President nor the head of any department or agency shall exercise any of the powers conferred by or pursuant to subsection (a) except that until July 1, 1946, any of such powers may be exercised to the extent necessary to carry out a contract or agreement with such a foreign government made before July 1, 1943, or before

the passage of such concurrent resolution, whichever is the earlier.

(d) Nothing in this Act shall be construed to authorize or to permit the authorization of convoying vessels by naval vessels of the United States.

(e) Nothing in this Act shall be construed to authorize or to permit the authorization of the entry of any American vessel into a combat area in violation of section 3 of the neutrality Act of 1939.

SEC. 4. All contracts or agreements made for the disposition of any defense article or defense information pursuant to section 3 shall contain a clause by which the foreign government undertakes that it will not, without the consent of the President, transfer title to or possession of such defense article or defense information by gift, sale, or otherwise, or permit its use by anyone not an officer, employee, or agent of such foreign government.

SEC. 5. (a) The Secretary of War, the Secretary of the Navy, or the head of any other department or agency of the Government involved shall when any such defense article or defense information is exported, immediately inform the department or agency designated by the President to administer section 6 of the Act of July 2, 1940 (54 Stat. 714) of the quantities, character, value, terms of disposition and destination of the article and information so exported.

(b) The President from time to time, but not less frequently than once every ninety days, shall transmit to the Congress a report of operations under this Act except such information as he deems incompatible with the public interest to disclose. Reports provided for under this subsection shall be transmitted to the Secretary of the Senate or the Clerk of the House of Representatives, as the case may be, if the Senate or the House of Representatives, as the case may be, is not in session....

SEC. 8. The Secretaries of War and of the Navy are hereby authorized to purchase or otherwise acquire arms, ammunition, and implements of war produced within the jurisdiction of any country to which section 3 is applicable, whenever the President deems such purchase or acquisition to be necessary in the interests of the defense of the United States.

APPROVED, MARCH 11, 1941.

77TH CONGRESS
1ST SESSION

H. R. 1776

IN THE HOUSE OF REPRESENTATIVES

JANUARY 10, 1941

Mr. McCORMACK introduced the following bill; which was referred to the Committee on Foreign Affairs

A BILL

Further to promote the defense of the United States, and for other purposes.

1   Be it enacted by the Senate and House of Representa-
2 tives of the United States of America in Congress assembled,
3 That this Act may be cited as "An Act to Promote the
4 Defense of the United States".
5   SEC. 2. As used in this Act—
6   (a) The term "defense article" means—
7   (1) Any weapon, munition, aircraft, vessel, or
8 boat;
9   (2) Any machinery, facility, tool, material, or
10 supply necessary for the manufacture, production, proc-

1941

EXECUTIVE ORDER 8802: PROHIBITION OF DISCRIMINATION IN THE DEFENSE INDUSTRY

*I*n September 1940 A. Philip Randolph, president of the Brotherhood of Sleeping Car Porters, the nation's first predominantly black union, and a delegation of black leaders met with President Franklin Roosevelt to discuss the rankling issue of segregation in the armed services. Despite Roosevelt's graciousness, two weeks later the White House issued a statement making clear that segregation in the military would continue. Convinced that meetings would not achieve his ends, Randolph began to organize a March on Washington to protest discrimination in the defense industries. He was determined that blacks share in the economic oppor-

Eastine Crowner, a waitress before the war, helped build the Liberty Ship SS George Washington Carver, which was launched in May 1943. She was one of nearly 1,000 African-American women employed at Kaiser Shipyards in Richmond, California, during World War II.

tunities arising from wartime production. By May 1941, despite skepticism within the black community and apprehension among white political leaders, Randolph had enlisted 100,000 African Americans to converge on the nation's capital on July 1.

The President called on first lady Eleanor Roosevelt and several members of his administration to confer with Randolph, but eventually he agreed to a personal meeting with the black leader, which occurred on June 18. Randolph, unyielding, warned that blacks would bring "ten, twenty, fifty thousand Negroes on the White House lawn" if the President did not yield to their demands. In response, on June 25, 1941, President Roosevelt issued the first presidential directive on race since Reconstruction. Executive Order 8802 banned discriminatory employment practices by federal agencies and all unions and companies that engaged in war-related work. The order also established the Fair Employment Practices Commission to investigate complaints and redress valid grievances. It would be left to President Harry S Truman, in 1948, to issue an executive order desegregating the military itself.

REAFFIRMING POLICY OF FULL PARTICIPATION IN THE DEFENSE PROGRAM BY ALL PERSONS, REGARDLESS OF RACE, CREED, COLOR, OR NATIONAL ORIGIN, AND DIRECTING CERTAIN ACTION IN FURTHERANCE OF SAID POLICY

JUNE 25, 1941

WHEREAS it is the policy of the United States to encourage full participation in the national defense program by all citizens of the United States, regardless of race, creed, color, or national origin, in the firm belief that the democratic way of life within the Nation can be defended successfully only with the help and support of all groups within its borders; and

WHEREAS there is evidence that available and needed workers have been barred from employment in industries engaged in defense production solely because of considerations of race, creed, color, or national origin, to the detriment of workers' morale and of national unity:

NOW, THEREFORE, by virtue of the authority vested in me by the Constitution and the statutes, and as a prerequisite to the successful conduct of our national defense production effort, I do hereby reaffirm the policy of the United States that there shall be no discrimination in the employment of workers in defense industries or government because of race, creed, color, or national origin, and I do hereby declare that it is the duty of employers and of labor organizations, in furtherance of said policy and of this order, to provide for the full and equitable participation of all workers in defense industries, without discrimination because of race, creed, color, or national origin;

And it is hereby ordered as follows:

1. All departments and agencies of the Government of the United States concerned with vocational and training programs for defense production shall take special measures appropriate to assure that such programs are administered without discrimination because of race, creed, color, or national origin;

2. All contracting agencies of the Government of the United States shall include in all defense contracts hereafter negotiated by them a provision obligating the contractor not to discriminate against any worker because of race, creed, color, or national origin;

3. There is established in the Office of Production Management a Committee on Fair Employment Practice, which shall consist of a chairman and four other

members to be appointed by the President. The Chairman and members of the Committee shall serve as such without compensation but shall be entitled to actual and necessary transportation, subsistence and other expenses incidental to performance of their duties. The Committee shall receive and investigate complaints of discrimination in violation of the provisions of this order and shall take appropriate steps to redress grievances which it finds to be valid. The Committee shall also recommend to the several departments and agencies of the Government of the United States and to the President all measures which may be deemed by it necessary or proper to effectuate the provisions of this order.

FRANKLIN D. ROOSEVELT

THE WHITE HOUSE, JUNE 25, 1941.

1941

ADDRESS TO CONGRESS LEADING TO A DECLARATION OF WAR AGAINST JAPAN

*I*n the early morning of December 7, 1941, the Japanese bombed the U.S. naval base at Pearl Harbor, Hawaii, in a surprise attack. In less than two hours, they devastated the U.S. Pacific Fleet, and more than 3,500 Americans had died or suffered injuries. Early in the afternoon (still morning in Hawaii), President Franklin D. Roosevelt and his chief foreign policy aide, Harry Hopkins, were interrupted by a telephone call from Secretary of War Henry Stimson, who told them of the attack. At about 5 P.M. Eastern Time, following meetings with his military advisers, the President calmly and decisively dictated to his secretary his request to Congress for a declaration of war.

At 12:30 P.M. on December 8, Roosevelt addressed a joint session of Congress and, via radio, the nation. He had made a number of changes on the typewritten draft and continued to make revisions and updates even as he delivered the speech. The speech, a brief, straightforward appeal to Congress and the American people, opened with Roosevelt's description of December 7 as "a date which will live in infamy." The Senate responded to his request with a unanimous vote in support of war; only Montana pacifist Jeanette Rankin dissented in the House. At 4 P.M. that same afternoon, President Roosevelt signed the declaration of war. Furious at the brutal attack and drawing inspiration from Roosevelt's address, the American people united behind a massive mobilization for war.

TO THE CONGRESS OF THE UNITED STATES:

Yesterday, December 7, 1941 — a date which will live in infamy — the United States of America was suddenly and deliberately attacked by naval and air forces of the Empire of Japan.

The United States was at peace with that nation and, at the solicitation of Japan, was still in conversation with its Government and its Emperor looking toward the maintenance of peace in the Pacific. Indeed, one hour after Japanese air squadrons had commenced bombing in Oahu, the Japanese Ambassador to the United States and his colleague delivered to the Secretary of State a formal reply to a recent American message. While this reply stated that it seemed useless to continue the existing diplomatic negotiations, it contained no threat or hint of war or armed attack.

It will be recorded that the distance of Hawaii from Japan makes it obvious that the attack was deliberately planned many days or even weeks ago. During the intervening time the Japanese Government has deliberately sought to deceive the United States by false statements and expressions of hope for continued peace.

The attack yesterday on the Hawaiian Islands has caused severe damage to American naval and military forces. Very many American lives have been lost. In addition American ships have been reported torpedoed on the high seas between San Francisco and Honolulu.

The Japanese bombing of the U.S. naval base at Pearl Harbor destroyed several hundred airplanes, several airfields, and much of the Navy's Pacific Fleet. It also killed 2,390 Americans and propeled the United States into World War II.

MR. VICE PRESIDENT, AND MR. SPEAKER, AND MEMBERS OF THE SENATE AND HOUSE OF REPRESENTATIVES:

Yesterday, December 7, 1941—a date which will live in infamy—the United States of America was suddenly and deliberately attacked by naval and air forces of the Empire of Japan.

The United States was at peace with that Nation and, at the solicitation of Japan, was still in conversation with its Government and its Emperor looking toward the maintenance of peace in the Pacific. Indeed, one hour after Japanese air squadrons had commenced bombing in the American Island of Oahu, the Japanese Ambassador to the United States and his colleague delivered to our Secretary of State a formal reply to a recent American message. And while this reply stated that it seemed useless to continue the existing diplomatic negotiations, it contained no threat or hint of war or of armed attack.

It will be recorded that the distance of Hawaii from Japan makes it obvious that the attack was deliberately planned many days or even weeks ago. During the intervening time the Japanese Government has deliberately sought to deceive the United States by false statements and expressions of hope for continued peace.

The attack yesterday on the Hawaiian Islands has caused severe damage to American naval and military forces. I regret to tell you that very many American lives have been lost. In addition American ships have been reported torpedoed on the high seas between San Francisco and Honolulu.

Yesterday the Japanese Government also launched an attack against Malaya. Last night Japanese forces attacked Hong Kong. Last night Japanese forces attacked Guam. Last night Japanese forces attacked the Philippine Islands. Last night the Japanese attacked Wake Island. And this morning the Japanese attacked Midway Island.

Japan has, therefore, undertaken a surprise offensive extending throughout the Pacific area. The facts of yesterday and today speak for themselves. The people of the United States have already formed their opinions and well understand the implications to the very life and safety of our Nation.

As Commander in Chief of the Army and Navy I have directed that all measures be taken for our defense.

But always will our whole Nation remember the character of the onslaught against us.

No matter how long it may take us to overcome this premeditated invasion, the American people in their righteous might will win through to absolute victory. I believe that I interpret the will of the Congress and of the people when I assert that we will not only defend ourselves to the uttermost but will make it very certain that this form of treachery shall never again endanger us.

Hostilities exist. There is no blinking at the fact that our people, our territory, and our interests are in grave danger.

With confidence in our armed forces—with the unbounding determination of our people—we will gain the inevitable triumph—so help us God.

I ask that the Congress declare that since the unprovoked and dastardly attack by Japan on Sunday, December 7, 1941, a state of war has existed between the United States and the Japanese Empire.

1942

EXECUTIVE ORDER 9066:
JAPANESE RELOCATION ORDER

*M*any Japanese immigrants to the United States settled on the West Coast, cultivating farmlands and fruit orchards, fishing, and operating small businesses. Some state and federal laws and policies restricted citizenship and land ownership. The Japanese attack on Pearl Harbor caused widespread fear in the West and intensified racist attitudes. Contending that circumstances justified unusual security measures, the governors and attorneys general from California, Washington, and Oregon urged the federal government to remove persons of Japanese descent, those born in the United States as well as immigrants, from the West Coast. Department of Justice representatives raised constitutional and ethical objections, so the army was assigned the task instead. However, on February 19, 1942, President Franklin D. Roosevelt issued Executive Order 9066 authorizing the incarceration of Japanese Americans living on the West Coast, and Congress passed the enabling legislation on March 21, 1942.

The Western Defense Command oversaw the removal and detention of 122,000 men, women, and children of Japanese ancestry. Nearly 70,000 of the evacuees were American citizens. They were sent to isolated, fenced, and guarded relocation centers, where they remained for most of the war. The government issued no charges against them, nor could they appeal their incarceration. All lost personal liberties; most lost homes and property. With little success, Japanese Americans challenged the government's actions before the Supreme Court. The last of the camps did not close until 1946.

Serious efforts to seek compensation began in 1980; the Commission on Wartime Relocation and Internment of Civilians held investigations and made recommendations. As a result, Members of Congress introduced several bills from 1984 until 1988, when Congress finally acknowledged the injustice of the internment, apologized for it, and provided for restitution.

Dressed in his World War I uniform, a veteran enters the Santa Anita Park Assembly Center for evacuated people of Japanese ancestry. More than 30,000 Japanese Americans served with distinction during World War II in segregated military units.

AUTHORIZING THE SECRETARY OF WAR TO PRESCRIBE MILITARY AREAS

Whereas the successful prosecution of the war requires every possible protection against espionage and against sabotage to national-defense material, national-defense premises, and national-defense utilities as defined in Section 4, Act of April 20, 1918, 40 Stat. 533, as amended by the Act of November 30, 1940, 54 Stat. 1220, and the Act of August 21, 1941, 55 Stat. 655 (U.S.C., Title 50, Sec. 104);

Now, therefore, by virtue of the authority vested in me as President of the United States, and Commander in Chief of the Army and Navy, I hereby authorize and direct the Secretary of War, and the Military Commanders whom he may from time to time designate, whenever he or any designated Commander deems such action necessary or desirable, to prescribe military areas in such places and of such extent as he or the appropriate Military Commander may determine, from which any or all persons may be excluded, and with respect to which, the right of any person to enter, remain in, or leave shall be subject to whatever restrictions the Secretary of War or the appropriate Military Commander may impose in his discretion. The Secretary of War is hereby authorized to provide for residents of any such area who are excluded therefrom, such transportation, food, shelter, and other accommodations as may be necessary, in the judgment of the Secretary of War or the said Military Commander, and until other arrangements are made, to accomplish the purpose of this order. The designation of military areas in any region or locality shall supersede designations of prohibited and restricted areas by the Attorney General under the Proclamations of December 7 and 8, 1941, and shall supersede the responsibility and authority of the Attorney General under the said Proclamations in respect of such prohibited and restricted areas.

I hereby further authorize and direct the Secretary of War and the said Military Commanders to take such other steps as he or the appropriate Military Commander may deem advisable to enforce compliance with the restrictions applicable to each Military area hereinabove authorized to be designated, including the use of Federal troops and other Federal Agencies, with authority to accept assistance of state and local agencies.

I hereby further authorize and direct all Executive Departments, independent establishments and other Federal Agencies, to assist the Secretary of War or the said Military Commanders in carrying out this Executive Order, including the furnishing of medical aid, hospi-

talization, food, clothing, transportation, use of land, shelter, and other supplies, equipment, utilities, facilities, and services.

This order shall not be construed as modifying or limiting in any way the authority heretofore granted under Executive Order No. 8972, dated December 12, 1941, nor shall it be construed as limiting or modifying the duty and responsibility of the Federal Bureau of Investigation, with respect to the investigation of alleged acts of sabotage or the duty and responsibility of the Attorney General and the Department of Justice under the Proclamations of December 7 and 8, 1941, prescribing regulations for the conduct and control of alien enemies, except as such duty and responsibility is superseded by the designation of military areas hereunder.

FRANKLIN D. ROOSEVELT

THE WHITE HOUSE, FEBRUARY 19, 1942.

1944

GENERAL DWIGHT D. EISENHOWER'S ORDER OF THE DAY

*S*oon after France fell to the Nazis in 1940, the Allies began planning an assault across the English Channel on the German occupying forces. At the Quebec Conference in August 1943, Winston Churchill and Franklin Roosevelt reaffirmed the plan, which was code-named Overlord. Despite serious doubts whether Overload would succeed, Churchill agreed to the operation. Western Allies confirmed the decision to mount the invasion at the Teheran Conference of November and December 1943. Joseph Stalin pressed Roosevelt and Churchill for details. They told him that the invasion "would be possible" by August 1, 1944, but that they had not yet named a supreme commander. To this latter point, the Russian leader pointedly rejoined, "Then nothing will come of these operations." Churchill and Roosevelt acknowledged the need to name the commander without further delay, and Roosevelt appointed Gen. Dwight David Eisenhower soon after the conference.

By May 1944, 2,876,000 Allied troops were amassed in southern England. The largest armada in history, more than 4,000 American, British, and Canadian ships, lay in wait. More than 1,200 planes stood ready to take off. Against a tense backdrop of uncertain weather forecasts, disagreements in strategy, and the need for optimal tidal conditions, Eisenhower decided before dawn on June 5 to proceed with Overlord. Anticipating the D-Day invasion, he had begun drafting his Order of the Day for June 6, 1944, in February. Its purpose was to lift morale and instill a sense of the importance of this operation. The order was distributed to the 175,000-member expeditionary force on the eve of the invasion.

General Eisenhower gives his personal encouragement to paratroopers in England just before they board their airplanes to participate in D-Day, the first assault in the invasion of Europe.

SUPREME HEADQUARTERS
ALLIED EXPEDITIONARY FORCE

Soldiers, Sailors and Airmen of the Allied Expeditionary Force!

You are about to embark upon the Great Crusade, toward which we have striven these many months. The eyes of the world are upon you. The hopes and prayers of liberty-loving people everywhere march with you. In company with our brave Allies and brothers-in-arms on other Fronts, you will bring about the destruction of the German war machine, the elimination of Nazi tyranny over the oppressed peoples of Europe, and security for ourselves in a free world.

Your task will not be an easy one. Your enemy is well trained, well equipped and battle-hardened. He will fight savagely.

But this is the year 1944 ! Much has happened since the Nazi triumphs of 1940-41. The United Nations have inflicted upon the Germans great defeats, in open battle, man-to-man. Our air offensive has seriously reduced their strength in the air and their capacity to wage war on the ground. Our Home Fronts have given us an overwhelming superiority in weapons and munitions of war, and placed at our disposal great reserves of trained fighting men. The tide has turned ! The free men of the world are marching together to Victory !

I have full confidence in your courage, devotion to duty and skill in battle. We will accept nothing less than full Victory !

Good Luck ! And let us all beseech the blessing of Almighty God upon this great and noble undertaking.

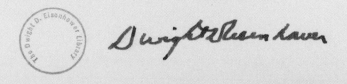

1944

SERVICEMEN'S READJUSTMENT ACT

Fifteen million men and women serving in the armed services would be out of work at the end of World War II, according to Department of Labor estimates. Because widespread unemployment could cause an economic depression, the National Resources Planning Board recommended a series of programs to address the needs of ex-servicemen and -women and, at the same time, strengthen the economy. The American Legion designed the main features of what became the Servicemen's Readjustment Act. Both houses of Congress unanimously passed the bill, and President Franklin Roosevelt signed it into law on June 22, 1944.

American Legion publicist Jack Cejnar called this legislation "the GI Bill of Rights" because it addressed basic needs—hospitalization, loans to purchase or improve homes and businesses, and grants to pay for education—of veterans returning to civilian life. In the long term, the bill not only benefited qualifying individuals but also stimulated the economy. The bill paid for itself in the form of taxes imposed on beneficiaries whose wages increased because of their education or training or whose profits grew from investments they made using government loans.

By 1955 the Veterans Administration had granted 4.3 million home loans, totaling $33 billion. By 1956, when the original law expired, it had disbursed $14.5 billion to veterans for education and training programs. Congress has extended the GI Bill several times. Nearly 2.3 million Korean War–era veterans and more than 8 million Vietnam-era veterans have participated in the program.

TITLE II

CHAPTER IV—EDUCATION OF VETERANS

"(f) Any person who served in the active military of naval forces on or after September 16, 1940, and prior to the termination of hostilities in the present war, shall be entitled to vocational rehabilitation....

"1. Any person who served in the active military or naval service on or after September 16, 1940, and prior to the termination of the present war, and who shall have been discharged or released therefrom under conditions other than dishonorable, and whose education or training was impeded, delayed, interrupted, or interfered with by reason of his entrance into the service, or who desires a refresher or retraining course, and who either shall have served ninety days or more . . . or shall have been discharged or released from active service by reason of an actual service-incurred injury or disability, shall be eligible for and entitled to receive education or training....

"2. Any such eligible person shall be entitled to education or training, or a refresher or retraining course, at an approved educational or training institution, for a period of one year (or the equivalent thereof in continuous part-time study), or for such lesser time as may be required for the course of instruction chosen by him. Upon satisfactory completion of such course of education or training, according to the regularly prescribed standards and practices of the institutions, except a refresher or retraining course, such person shall be entitled to an additional period or periods of education or training, not to exceed the time such person was in the active service on or after September 16, 1940, and before the termination of the war...

"[B]ut in no event shall the total period of education or training exceed four years:...

"3. Such person shall be eligible for and entitled to such course of education or training as he may elect, and at any approved educational or training institution at which he chooses to enroll, whether or not located in the State in which he resides, which will accept or retain him as a student or trainee in any field or branch of knowledge which such institution finds him qualified to undertake or pursue:...

"5. The Administrator shall pay to the educational or training institution, for each person enrolled in full time or part time course of education or training, the customary cost of tuition, and such laboratory, library,

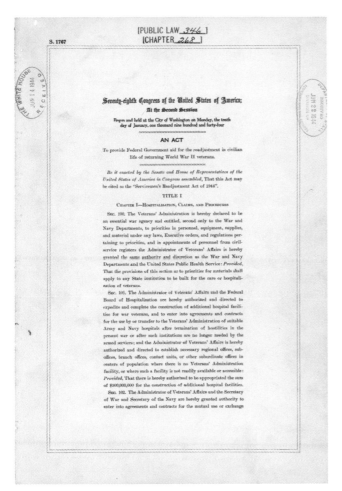

TITLE III—LOANS FOR THE PURCHASE OR CONSTRUCTION OF HOMES, FARMS, AND BUSINESS PROPERTY

CHAPTER V—GENERAL PROVISIONS FOR LOANS

"SEC. 500. (a) Any person who shall have served in the active military or naval service of the United States at any time on or after September 16, 1940, and prior to the termination of the present war and who shall have been discharged or released therefrom under conditions other than dishonorable after active service of ninety days or more, or by reason of an injury or disability incurred in service in line of duty, shall be eligible for the benefits of this title. Any such veteran may apply within two years after separation from the military or naval forces, or two years after termination of the war, whichever is the later date, but in no event more than five years after the termination of the war, to the Administrator of Veterans' Affairs for the guaranty by the Administrator of not to exceed 50 per centum of a loan or loans for any of the purposes specified in sections 501, 502 and 503; *Provided*, That the aggregate amount guaranteed shall not exceed $2,000....

"...That loans guaranteed by the Administrator shall bear interest at a rate not exceeding 4 per centum per annum and shall be payable in full in not more than twenty years....

"SEC. 501. (a) Any application made by a veteran under this title for the guaranty of a loan to be used in purchasing residential property or in constructing a dwelling on unimproved property owned by him to be occupied as his home...

(b) Any application for the guaranty of a loan under this section for the purpose of making repairs, alterations, or improvements in, or paying delinquent indebtedness, taxes, or special assessments on, residential property owned by the veteran and used by him as his home ...

"SEC. 502. Any application made under this title for the guaranty of a loan to be used in purchasing any land, buildings, livestock, equipment, machinery, or implements, or in repairing, altering, or improving any buildings or equipment, to be used in farming operations conducted by the applicant...

"SEC. 503. Any application made under this title for the guaranty of a loan to be used in purchasing any business, land, buildings, supplies, equipment, machinery, or tools, to be used by the applicant in pursuing a gainful occupation...

health, infirmary, and other similar fees as are customarily charged, and may pay for books, supplies, equipment, and other necessary expenses, exclusive of board, lodging, other living expenses, and travel, as are generally required for the successful pursuit and completion of the course by other students in the institution: *Provided*, That in no event shall such payments, with respect to any person, exceed $500 for an ordinary school year:...

"6. While enrolled in and pursuing a course under this part, such person, upon application to the Administrator, shall be paid a subsistence allowance of $50 per month, if without a dependent or dependents, or $75 per month, if he has a dependent or dependents, including regular holidays and leave not exceeding thirty days in a calendar year. Such person attending a course on a part-time basis, and such person receiving compensation for productive labor performed as part of their apprentice or other training on the job at institutions, business or other establishments, shall be entitled to receive such lesser sums, if any, as subsistence or dependency allowances....

1945

MANHATTAN PROJECT NOTEBOOK

The Manhattan Project was the code name for the highly secretive military project that was launched in June 1942 for the purpose of building an atomic bomb. Already engaged in World War II, the United States wanted to develop such a device quickly, before the Germans were able to create one. The federal government handed this task over to a group of distinguished physicists who gathered to work in a top-secret laboratory at the University of Chicago. Under the direction of Nobel Prize–winner Enrico Fermi, the group created the first controlled, self-sustaining nuclear chain reaction on December 2, 1942.

The team of physicists built a pile of graphite and uranium bricks that were precisely arranged to produce a chain reaction. They also inserted cadmium-covered boards into the structure. These boards were the first reactor control rods: they regulated the nuclear reaction and kept it from burning out of control. Once they had succeeded in creating the nuclear reaction, the scientists celebrated with a bottle of Chianti, and each one signed the straw wrapper that came with the bottle. "We're cooking!" was what they recorded in the notebook. Mostly, however, it contains the scientists' mathematical notations. The data shown on these notebook pages record the nuclear reactor's response to the movement of the control rods.

SURRENDER OF GERMANY

*T*he D-Day invasion led to the liberation of Paris on August 25, 1944, and the removal of most German troops from France and Belgium by mid-September. However, the defeat of Germany itself did not come until May 1945. The Allies, with General Eisenhower in command, met strong resistance as they pushed into Central Europe in late 1944; the Soviets began their final assault in January 1945. By mid-April, both armies were moving toward Berlin. Confronting certain defeat, Hitler committed suicide on April 30. On May 2 the Soviets entered Berlin, and German forces in Italy surrendered.

Eisenhower insisted that the Germans surrender to the Western Allies and the Soviets at the same time. Gen. Alfred Jodl, Chief of Staff of the German Army, signed the unconditional surrender of the German Third Reich on May 7, 1945 (which would come to be known as V-E Day, short for Victory in Europe Day), at Supreme Headquarters, Allied Expeditionary Force (SHAEF), in Rheims, France. At the same time, Jodl signed three other surrender documents, one each for Great Britain, France, and the Soviet Union. Lt. Gen. Walter Bedell Smith, SHAEF chief of staff, led the Allied delegation as the representative of General Eisenhower, who refused to meet with the Germans until after the surrender. The Soviets insisted that the official Act of Military Surrender be signed at Berlin on the following day, and the Americans, based on a prior agreement, participated in that ceremony as well. The documents that the Germans signed in Rheims and Berlin, both of which called for unconditional surrender, ended the war in Europe.

ACT OF MILITARY SURRENDER

We the undersigned, acting by authority of the German High Command, hereby surrender unconditionally to the Supreme Commander, Allied Expeditionary Forces and simultaneously to the Soviet High Command all forces on land, sea and in the air who are at this date under German control.

The German High Command will at once issue orders to all German military, naval and air authorities and to all forces under German control to cease active operations at 2301 hours Central European time on 8 May and to remain in the positions occupied at that time. No ship, vessel, or aircraft is to be scuttled, or any damage done to their hull, machinery or equipment.

The German High Command will at once issue to the appropriate commander, and ensure the carrying out of any further orders issued by the Supreme Commander, Allied Expeditionary Force and by the Soviet High Command.

This act of military surrender is without prejudice to, and will be superseded by any general instrument of surrender imposed by, or on behalf of the United Nations and applicable to GERMANY and the German armed forces as a whole.

In the event of the German High Command or any of the forces under their control failing to act in accordance with this Act of Surrender, the Supreme Commander, Allied Expeditionary Force and the Soviet High Command will take such punitive or other action as they deem appropriate.

SIGNED AT RHEIMS AT 0241 ON THE 7TH DAY OF MAY, 1945. FRANCE

ON BEHALF OF THE GERMAN HIGH COMMAND.

JODL

IN THE PRESENCE OF:

ON BEHALF OF THE SUPREME COMMANDER, ALLIED EXPEDITIONARY FORCE.

W. B. SMITH

ON BEHALF OF THE SOVIET HIGH COMMAND

SOUSLOPAROV

F SEVEZ

MAJOR GENERAL, FRENCH ARMY (WITNESS)

At a conference with British prime minister Winston Churchill in Casablanca, Morocco, in January 1943, President Franklin Roosevelt announced that the Allies would accept nothing less than the unconditional surrender of Germany.

1945

UNITED NATIONS CHARTER

*O*n January 1, 1942, twenty-six nations joined in a Declaration of the United Nations, pledging to continue their joint war effort, and promising not to make a separate peace with common enemies. Nearly two years later, the Moscow Declaration, issued on October 30, 1943, by China, Great Britain, the Soviet Union, and the United States, addressed the need for a new international organization. The League of Nations, which the Allies had established in the aftermath of World War I, had been unable to prevent Fascist aggression in the 1930s and ceased to function during the Second World War. Although the League did not officially dissolve until April 18, 1946, its demise opened the way for a new multinational organization to maintain international peace and security and address economic, social, and humanitarian problems.

China, Great Britain, the Soviet Union, and the United States drafted specific proposals for a charter for the new organization when they met at Dumbarton Oaks in Washington in 1944. At the Yalta Conference that convened in February 1945 in the Crimea, they reached further agreement on the framework and structure of the organization. In June representatives from fifty nations attended the founding conference in San Francisco, where they drafted and later signed the UN charter. The UN Charter achieved final ratification on October 24, 1945.

The mission of the UN Security Council and General Assembly is to maintain and restore peace in troubled spots around the globe. Through special agencies, including the World Health Organization (WHO), the International Children's Emergency Fund (UNICEF), and the Educational, Scientific, and Cultural Organization (UNESCO), the UN provides needed assistance to governments and humanitarian aid to millions. Today, nearly two hundred nations are members of the United Nations.

WE THE PEOPLES OF THE UNITED NATIONS DETERMINED to save succeeding generations from the scourge of war, which twice in our lifetime has brought untold sorrow to mankind, and to reaffirm faith in fundamental human rights, in the dignity and worth of the human person, in the equal rights of men and women and of nations large and small, and to establish conditions under which justice and respect for the obligations arising from treaties and other sources of international law can be maintained, and to promote social progress and better standards of life in larger freedom, AND FOR THESE ENDS to practice tolerance and live together in peace with one another as good neighbours, and to unite our strength to maintain international peace and security, and to ensure, by the acceptance of principles and the institution of methods, that armed force shall not be used, save in the common interest, and to employ international machinery for the promotion of the economic and social advancement of all peoples, HAVE RESOLVED TO COMBINE OUR EFFORTS TO ACCOMPLISH THESE AIMS.

Accordingly, our respective Governments, through representatives assembled in the city of San Francisco, who have exhibited their full powers found to be in good and due form, have agreed to the present Charter of the United Nations and do hereby establish an international organization to be known as the United Nations.

CHAPTER I PURPOSES AND PRINCIPLES

ARTICLE 1 The Purposes of the United Nations are: 1. To maintain international peace and security, and to that end: to take effective collective measures for the prevention and removal of threats to the peace, and for the suppression of acts of aggression or other breaches of the peace, and to bring about by peaceful means, and in conformity with the principles of justice and international law, adjustment or settlement of international disputes or situations which might lead to a breach of the peace;

2. To develop friendly relations among nations based on respect for the principle of equal rights and self-determination of peoples, and to take other appropriate measures to strengthen universal peace;

3. To achieve international co-operation in solving international problems of an economic, social, cultural, or humanitarian character, and in promoting and encouraging respect for human rights and for fundamental freedoms for all without distinction as to race, sex, language, or religion; and

4. To be a centre for harmonizing the actions of nations in the attainment of these common ends.

ARTICLE 2 The Organization and its Members, in pursuit of the Purposes stated in Article 1, shall act in accordance with the following Principles.

1. The Organization is based on the principle of the sovereign equality of all its Members.

2. All Members, in order to ensure to all of them the rights and benefits resulting from membership, shall fulfil in good faith the obligations assumed by them in accordance with the present Charter.

3. All Members shall settle their international disputes by peaceful means in such a manner that international peace and security, and justice, are not endangered.

4. All Members shall refrain in their international relations from the threat or use of force against the territorial integrity or political independence of any state, or in any other manner inconsistent with the Purposes of the United Nations.

5. All Members shall give the United Nations every assistance in any action it takes in accordance with the present Charter, and shall refrain from giving assistance to any state against which the United Nations is taking preventive or enforcement action.

6. The Organization shall ensure that states which are not Members of the United Nations act in accordance with these Principles so far as may be necessary for the maintenance of international peace and security.

7. Nothing contained in the present Charter shall authorize the United Nations to intervene in matters which are essentially within the domestic jurisdiction of any state or shall require the Members to submit such matters to settlement under the present Charter; but this principle shall not prejudice the application of enforcement measures under Chapter VII.

CHARTER OF THE UNITED NATIONS

WE THE PEOPLES OF THE UNITED NATIONS DETERMINED

to save succeeding generations from the scourge of war, which twice in our lifetime has brought untold sorrow to mankind, and

to reaffirm faith in fundamental human rights, in the dignity and worth of the human person, in the equal rights of men and women and of nations large and small, and

to establish conditions under which justice and respect for the obligations arising from treaties and other sources of international law can be maintained, and

to promote social progress and better standards of life in larger freedom,

AND FOR THESE ENDS

to practice tolerance and live together in peace with one another as good neighbors, and

to unite our strength to maintain international peace and security, and

to ensure, by the acceptance of principles and the institution of methods, that armed force shall not be used, save in the common interest, and

to employ international machinery for the promotion of the economic and social advancement of all peoples,

HAVE RESOLVED TO COMBINE OUR EFFORTS TO ACCOMPLISH THESE AIMS.

Accordingly, our respective Governments, through representatives assembled in the city of San Francisco, who have exhibited their full powers found to be in good and due form, have agreed to the present Charter of the United Nations and do hereby establish an international organization to be known as the United Nations.

CHAPTER II MEMBERSHIP

ARTICLE 3 The original Members of the United Nations shall be the states which, having participated in the United Nations Conference on International Organization at San Francisco, or having previously signed the Declaration by United Nations of 1 January 1942, sign the present Charter and ratify it in accordance with Article 110.

ARTICLE 4

1. Membership in the United Nations is open to all other peace-loving states which accept the obligations contained in the present Charter and, in the judgment of the Organization, are able and willing to carry out these obligations....

CHAPTER III ORGANS

ARTICLE 7

1. There are established as the principal organs of the United Nations: a General Assembly, a Security Council, an Economic and Social Council, a Trusteeship Council, an International Court of Justice, and a Secretariat. . . .

CHAPTER IV THE GENERAL ASSEMBLY

COMPOSITION

ARTICLE 9

1. The General Assembly shall consist of all the Members of the United Nations. . . .

ARTICLE 11

1. The General Assembly may consider the general principles of co-operation in the maintenance of international peace and security, including the principles governing disarmament and the regulation of armaments, and may make recommendations with regard to such principles to the Members or to the Security Council or to both.

2. The General Assembly may discuss any questions relating to the maintenance of inter-national peace and security brought before it by any Member of the United Nations, or by the Security Council, or by a state which is not a Member of the United Nations. . . .

3. The General Assembly may call the attention of the Security Council to situations which are likely to endanger international peace and security. . . .

ARTICLE 18

1. Each member of the General Assembly shall have one vote.

2. Decisions of the General Assembly on important questions shall be made by a two-thirds majority of the members present and voting. . . .

PROCEDURE

ARTICLE 20

The General Assembly shall meet in regular annual sessions and in such special sessions as occasion may require. . . .

CHAPTER V THE SECURITY COUNCIL

COMPOSITION

ARTICLE 23

1. The Security Council shall consist of fifteen Members of the United Nations. The Republic of China, France, the Union of Soviet Socialist Republics, the United Kingdom of Great Britain and Northern Ireland, and the United States of America shall be permanent members of the Security Council. The General Assembly shall elect ten other Members of the United Nations to be non-permanent members of the Security Council. . . .

2. The non-permanent members of the Security Council shall be elected for a term of two years. . . .

ARTICLE 24

1. In order to ensure prompt and effective action by the United Nations, its Members confer on the Security Council primary responsibility for the maintenance of international peace and security. . . .

ARTICLE 25

The Members of the United Nations agree to accept and carry out the decisions of the Security Council in accordance with the present Charter. . . .

CHAPTER VII ACTION WITH RESPECT TO THREATS TO THE PEACE, BREACHES OF THE PEACE, AND ACTS OF AGGRESSION

ARTICLE 39

The Security Council shall determine the existence of any threat to the peace, breach of the peace, or act of aggression and shall make recommendations, or decide what measures shall be taken in accordance with Articles 4 and 42, to maintain or restore international peace and security. . . .

ARTICLE 41

The Security Council may decide what measures not involving the use of armed force are to be employed to give effect to its decisions, and it may call upon the Members of the United Nations to apply such measures. . . .

ARTICLE 42

Should the Security Council consider that measures provided for in Article 41 would be inadequate or have proved to be inadequate, it may take such action by air, sea, or land forces as may be necessary to maintain or restore international peace and security. . . .

ARTICLE 43

1. All Members of the United Nations, in order to contribute to the maintenance of international peace and security, undertake to make available to the Security Council, on its and in accordance with a special agreement or agreements, armed forces, assistance, and facilities, including rights of passage, necessary for the purpose of maintaining international peace and security. . . .

CHAPTER IX INTERNATIONAL ECONOMIC AND SOCIAL CO-OPERATION

ARTICLE 55

With a view to the creation of conditions of stability and well-being which are necessary for peaceful and friendly relations among nations based on respect for the principle of equal rights and self-determination of peoples, the United Nations shall promote:

tional economic, social, cultural, educational, health, and related matters and may make recommendations with respect to any such matters to the General Assembly, to the Members of the United Nations, and to the specialized agencies concerned.

2. It may make recommendations for the purpose of promoting respect for, and observance of, human rights and fundamental freedoms for all. . . .

CHAPTER XI DECLARATION REGARDING NON-SELF-GOVERNING TERRITORIES

ARTICLE 73 Members of the United Nations which have or assume responsibilities for the administration of territories whose peoples have not yet attained a full measure of self-government recognize the principle that the interests of the inhabitants of these territories are paramount, and accept as a sacred trust the obligation to promote to the utmost, within the system of international peace and security established by the present Charter, the well-being of the inhabitants of these territories. . . .

CHAPTER XV THE SECRETARIAT

ARTICLE 97 The Secretariat shall comprise a Secretary-General and such staff as the Organization may require. The Secretary-General shall be appointed by the General Assembly upon the recommendation of the Security Council. He shall be the chief administrative officer of the Organization. . . .

CHAPTER XVIII AMENDMENTS

ARTICLE 108 Amendments to the present Charter shall come into force for all Members of the United Nations when they have been adopted by a vote of two thirds of the members of the General Assembly and ratified in accordance with their respective constitutional processes by two thirds of the Members of the United Nations, including all the permanent members of the Security Council. . . .

DONE AT THE CITY OF SAN FRANCISCO THE TWENTY-SIXTH DAY OF JUNE, ONE THOUSAND NINE HUNDRED AND FORTY-FIVE.

a. higher standards of living, full employment, and conditions of economic and social progress and development;

b. solutions of international economic, social, health, and related problems; and international cultural and educational co-operation; and

c. universal respect for, and observance of, human rights and fundamental freedoms for all without distinction as to race, sex, language, or religion.

CHAPTER X THE ECONOMIC AND SOCIAL COUNCIL

ARTICLE 61

1. The Economic and Social Council shall consist of fifty-four Members of the United Nations elected by the General Assembly.

FUNCTION AND POWERS

ARTICLE 62

1. The Economic and Social Council may make or initiate studies and reports with respect to interna-

1945
SURRENDER OF JAPAN

The last few months of World War II saw intense fighting in the Pacific. Battles raged in the Philippines and on the islands of Iwo Jima and Okinawa. In July 1945, while attending a summit in Potsdam, Germany, President Harry S Truman learned that American scientists had successfully tested an atomic bomb. Casualty estimates persuaded him that he could avoid a full-scale invasion of the main island of Japan if he ordered the use of this weapon. A vaguely worded ultimatum to Japan elicited no response and, as a result, Truman ordered the bombing, first of Hiroshima, and then of Nagasaki. Emperor Hirohito announced Japan's surrender on August 14, five days after the United States dropped the second atomic bomb. Formal surrender took place on September 2, aboard the USS Missouri in Tokyo Bay.

The official Instrument of Surrender, which the War Department prepared and President Truman then approved, called—in eight short paragraphs—for the complete capitulation of Japan. "We hereby proclaim," the document reads, "the unconditional surrender to the Allied Powers of the Japanese Imperial General Headquarters and of all Japanese armed forces and all armed forces under Japanese control wherever situated." Foreign Minister Mamoru Shigemitsu and General Yoshijiro Umezu signed for Japan. The official time was 4 minutes past 9 o'clock. General Douglas MacArthur, Commander in the Southwest Pacific and Supreme Commander for the Allied Powers, also signed, expressing the hope "that from this solemn occasion a better world shall emerge...a world founded on faith and understanding." One of the Japanese diplomats wondered, perhaps more poignantly, "whether it would have been possible for us, had we been victorious, to embrace the vanquished with a similar magnitude." This surrender ended World War II and set the stage for a democratic government in Japan.

American troops salute as Japanese officials leave the USS Missouri, *anchored in Tokyo Bay, after signing the papers of surrender on September 2, 1945.*

FIRST INSTRUMENT OF SURRENDER

INSTRUMENT OF SURRENDER

We, acting by command of and in behalf of the Emperor of Japan, the Japanese Government and the Japanese Imperial General Headquarters, hereby accept the provisions set forth in the declaration issued by the heads of the Governments of the United States, China, and Great Britain on 26 July 1945 at Potsdam, and subsequently adhered to by the Union of Soviet Socialist Republics, which four powers are hereafter referred to as the Allied Powers.

We hereby proclaim the unconditional surrender to the Allied Powers of the Japanese Imperial General Headquarters and of all Japanese armed forces and all armed forces under the Japanese control wherever situated.

We hereby command all Japanese forces wherever situated and the Japanese people to cease hostilities forthwith, to preserve and save from damage all ships, aircraft, and military and civil property and to comply with all requirements which my be imposed by the Supreme Commander for the Allied Powers or by agencies of the Japanese Government at his direction.

We hereby command the Japanese Imperial Headquarters to issue at once orders to the Commanders of all Japanese forces and all forces under Japanese control wherever situated to surrender unconditionally themselves and all forces under their control.

We hereby command all civil, military and naval officials to obey and enforce all proclamations, and orders and directives deemed by the Supreme Commander for the Allied Powers to be proper to effectuate this surrender and issued by him or under his authority and we direct all such officials to remain at their posts and to continue to perform their non-combatant duties unless specifically relieved by him or under his authority.

We hereby undertake for the Emperor, the Japanese Government and their successors to carry out the provisions of the Potsdam Declaration in good faith, and to issue whatever orders and take whatever actions may be required by the Supreme Commander for the Allied Powers or by any other designated representative of the Allied Powers for the purpose of giving effect to that Declaration.

We hereby command the Japanese Imperial Government and the Japanese Imperial General Headquarters at once to liberate all allied prisoners of war and civilian internees now under Japanese control and to provide for their protection, care, maintenance and immediate transportation to places as directed.

The authority of the Emperor and the Japanese Government to rule the state shall be subject to the Supreme Commander for the Allied Powers who will take such steps as he deems proper to effectuate these terms of surrender.

SIGNED AT TOKYO BAY, JAPAN AT 0904 ON THE SECOND DAY OF SEPTEMBER, 1945

MAMORU SHIGEMITSU
BY COMMAND AND IN BEHALF OF THE EMPEROR OF JAPAN AND THE JAPANESE GOVERNMENT

YOSHIJIRO UMEZU
BY COMMAND AND IN BEHALF OF THE JAPANESE IMPERIAL GENERAL HEADQUARTERS

ACCEPTED AT TOKYO BAY, JAPAN AT 0903 I ON THE SECOND DAY OF SEPTEMBER, 1945, FOR THE UNITED STATES, REPUBLIC OF CHINA, UNITED KINGDOM AND THE UNION OF SOVIET SOCIALIST REPUBLICS, AND IN THE INTERESTS OF THE OTHER UNITED NATIONS AT WAR WITH JAPAN.

DOUGLAS MacARTHUR
SUPREME COMMANDER FOR THE ALLIED POWERS

C.W. NIMITZ
UNITED STATES REPRESENTATIVE

HSU YUNG-CH'ANG
REPUBLIC OF CHINA REPRESENTATIVE

BRUCE FRASER
UNITED KINGDOM REPRESENTATIVE

KUZMA DEREVYANKO
UNION OF SOVIET SOCIALIST REPUBLICS REPRESENTATIVE

THOMAS BLAMEY
COMMONWEALTH OF AUSTRALIA REPRESENTATIVE

L. MOORE COSGRAVE
DOMINION OF CANADA REPRESENTATIVE

JACQUES LE CLERC
PROVISIONAL GOVERNMENT OF THE FRENCH REPUBLIC REPRESENTATIVE

C.E.L. HELFRICH
KINGDOM OF THE NETHERLANDS REPRESENTATIVE

LEONARD M. ISITT
DOMINION OF NEW ZEALAND REPRESENTATIVE

Signed at TOKYO BAY, JAPAN at 0904. I

on the SECOND day of SEPTEMBER ,1945.

重光葵

By Command and in behalf of the Emperor of Japan
and the Japanese Government.

梅津美治郎

By Command and in behalf of the Japanese
Imperial General Headquarters.

Accepted at TOKYO BAY, JAPAN at 0908 I

on the SECOND day of SEPTEMBER ,1945,
for the United States, Republic of China, United Kingdom and the
Union of Soviet Socialist Republics, and in the interests of the other
United Nations at war with Japan.

Douglas MacArthur

Supreme Commander for the Allied Powers.

C.W. Nimitz

United States Representative

徐永昌

Republic of China Representative

Bruce Fraser.

United Kingdom Representative

Union of Soviet Socialist Republics
Representative

T.A. Blamey

Commonwealth of Australia Representative

Dominion of Canada Representative

Provisional Government of the French
Republic Representative

Kingdom of the Netherlands Representative

Dominion of New Zealand Representative

On September 6, 1945, Col. Bernard Thielen brought the surrender document and a second imperial rescript back to Washington, D.C. The following day, Thielen presented the documents to President Truman in a formal White House ceremony. They were then exhibited at the National Archives, and on October 1, they were formally received into the holdings of the National Archives.

1947

TRUMAN DOCTRINE

When World War II ended in 1945, Europe lay in ruins: its cities were shattered; its economies were devastated; its people faced famine. In the two years after the war, the Soviet Union's control of Eastern Europe and fears that communism would gain a foothold in Western Europe—whose countries were either political allies or important trading partners of the United States—heightened the U.S. sense of crisis. Soon after the Nazis withdrew, Greece found itself engaged in a civil war. American policymakers began monitoring that country's crumbling economic and political situation, especially the rise of the Communist-led insurgency known as the National Liberation Front. They feared that further deterioration would lead to an overthrow of the Greek government, which was nominally democratic. The United States had also been following events in Turkey, where a weak government faced Soviet pressure to share control of the strategic Dardanelle Straits. Great Britain, which had been providing financial aid to the free and independent governments of Greece and Turkey, was forced to withdraw it in February 1947 when it could no longer afford the expense. Responsibility for supporting these two governments fell to the United States, the only western democracy with sufficient financial resources at that time.

President Harry S Truman grounded his foreign policy in containing communist expansion in Western Europe. He believed the Soviet Union had to "be faced with an iron fist and strong language."

In a meeting between U.S. Congressmen and State Department officials, Undersecretary of State Dean Acheson articulated what would later become known as the domino theory. He contended that if Greece and Turkey should fall, communism would probably spread south to Iran and as far east as India. To prevent the growth of communism, the legislators agreed to endorse aid on the condition that President Truman explain the severity of the crisis in an address to Congress and in a radio broadcast to the American people.

Speaking to a joint session of Congress on March 12, 1947, President Truman asked for $400 million in military and economic assistance for Greece and Turkey and established the Truman Doctrine, which would guide U.S. diplomacy for the next forty years. Truman declared, "It must be the policy of the United States to support free peoples who are resisting attempted subjugation by armed minorities or by outside pressures." Aid for Greece and Turkey marked the beginning of bipartisan foreign policy aimed at containing communism, a motive that dictated most U.S. actions throughout the Cold War.

MR. PRESIDENT, MR. SPEAKER, MEMBERS OF THE CONGRESS OF THE UNITED STATES:

The gravity of the situation which confronts the world today necessitates my appearance before a joint session of the Congress. The foreign policy and the national security of this country are involved....

The United States has received from the Greek Government an urgent appeal for financial and economic assistance.... [A]ssistance is imperative if Greece is to survive as a free nation.

Greece is not a rich country. Lack of sufficient natural resources has always forced the Greek people to work hard to make both ends meet. Since 1940, this industrious and peace loving country has suffered invasion, four years of cruel enemy occupation, and bitter internal strife....

Greece is today without funds to finance the importation of those goods which are essential to bare subsistence. Under these circumstances the people of Greece cannot make progress in solving their problems of reconstruction. Greece is in desperate need of financial and economic assistance to enable it to resume purchases of food, clothing, fuel and seeds. These are indispensable for the subsistence of its people and are obtainable only from abroad. Greece must have help to import the goods necessary to restore internal order and security, so essential for economic and political recovery.

The Greek Government has also asked for the assistance of experienced American administrators, economists and technicians to insure that the financial and other aid given to Greece shall be used effectively in creating a stable and self-sustaining economy and in improving its public administration.

The very existence of the Greek state is today threatened by the terrorist activities of several thousand armed men, led by Communists, who defy the govern-

ment's authority at a number of points, particularly along the northern boundaries. A Commission appointed by the United Nations Security Council is at present investigating disturbed conditions in northern Greece and alleged border violations along the frontier between Greece on the one hand and Albania, Bulgaria, and Yugoslavia on the other....

The British Government, which has been helping Greece, can give no further financial or economic aid after March 31. Great Britain finds itself under the

---

80TH CONGRESS } HOUSE OF REPRESENTATIVES { DOCUMENT
1st Session   No. 171

RECOMMENDATION FOR ASSISTANCE TO GREECE AND TURKEY

ADDRESS

OF

THE PRESIDENT OF THE UNITED STATES

DELIVERED

BEFORE A JOINT SESSION OF THE SENATE AND THE HOUSE OF REPRESENTATIVES, RECOMMENDING ASSISTANCE TO GREECE AND TURKEY

MARCH 12, 1947.—Referred to the Committee on Foreign Affairs, and ordered to be printed

MR. PRESIDENT, MR. SPEAKER, MEMBERS OF THE CONGRESS OF THE UNITED STATES:

The gravity of the situation which confronts the world today necessitates my appearance before a joint session of the Congress.

The foreign policy and the national security of this country are involved.

One aspect of the present situation, which I wish to present to you at this time for your consideration and decision, concerns Greece and Turkey.

The United States has received from the Greek Government an urgent appeal for financial and economic assistance. Preliminary reports from the American Economic Mission now in Greece and reports from the American Ambassador in Greece corroborate the statement of the Greek Government that assistance is imperative if Greece is to survive as a free nation.

I do not believe that the American people and the Congress wish to turn a deaf ear to the appeal of the Greek Government.

Greece is not a rich country. Lack of sufficient natural resources has always forced the Greek people to work hard to make both ends meet. Since 1940, this industrious and peace-loving country has suffered invasion, 4 years of cruel enemy occupation, and bitter internal strife.

When forces of liberation entered Greece they found that the retreating Germans had destroyed virtually all the railways, roads,

"The seeds of totalitarian regimes are nurtured by misery and want. They spread and grow in the evil soil of poverty and strife. They reach their full growth when the hope of a people for a better life has died. We must keep that hope alive. . . ."

necessity of reducing or liquidating its commitments in several parts of the world, including Greece.

We have considered how the United Nations might assist in this crisis. But the situation is an urgent one requiring immediate action and the United Nations and its related organizations are not in a position to extend help of the kind that is required.

No government is perfect. One of the chief virtues of a democracy, however, is that its defects are always visible and under democratic processes can be pointed out and corrected. The Government of Greece is not perfect. Nevertheless it represents eighty-five per cent of the members of the Greek Parliament who were chosen in an election last year. Foreign observers, including 692 Americans, considered this election to be a fair expression of the views of the Greek people. . . .

Turkey also deserves our attention. . . .

Since the war Turkey has sought financial assistance from Great Britain and the United States for the purpose of effecting that modernization necessary for the maintenance of its national integrity. . . .

The British government has informed us that, owing to its own difficulties it can no longer extend financial or economic aid to Turkey. . . .

We are the only country able to provide that help. . . .

One of the primary objectives of the foreign policy of the United States is the creation of conditions in which we and other nations will be able to work out a way of life free from coercion. . . .

At the present moment in world history nearly every nation must choose between alternative ways of life. The choice is too often not a free one.

One way of life is based upon the will of the majority, and is distinguished by free institutions, representative government, free elections, guarantees of individual liberty, freedom of speech and religion, and freedom from political oppression.

The second way of life is based upon the will of a minority forcibly imposed upon the majority. It relies upon terror and oppression, a controlled press and radio, fixed elections, and the suppression of personal freedoms.

I believe that it must be the policy of the United States to support free peoples who are resisting attempted subjugation by armed minorities or by outside pressures.

I believe that we must assist free peoples to work out their own destinies in their own way.

I believe that our help should be primarily through economic and financial aid which is essential to economic stability and orderly political processes.

The world is not static, and the status quo is not sacred. But we cannot allow changes in the status quo in violation of the Charter of the United Nations by such methods as coercion, or by such subterfuges as political infiltration. In helping free and independent nations to maintain their freedom, the United States will be giving effect to the principles of the Charter of the United Nations.

It is necessary only to glance at a map to realize that the survival and integrity of the Greek nation are of grave importance in a much wider situation. If Greece should fall under the control of an armed minority, the effect upon its neighbor, Turkey, would be immediate and serious. Confusion and disorder might well spread throughout the entire Middle East.

Moreover, the disappearance of Greece as an independent state would have a profound effect upon those countries in Europe whose peoples are struggling against great difficulties to maintain their freedoms and their independence while they repair the damages of war. . . .

I therefore ask the Congress to provide authority for assistance to Greece and Turkey in the amount of $400,000,000 for the period ending June 30, 1948. . . .

The seeds of totalitarian regimes are nurtured by misery and want. They spread and grow in the evil soil of poverty and strife. They reach their full growth when the hope of a people for a better life has died. We must keep that hope alive. . . .

If we falter in our leadership, we may endanger the peace of the world—and we shall surely endanger the welfare of our own nation. . . .

1948

MARSHALL PLAN

*T*o strengthen Western European governments against Soviet influence in the chaos that
followed World War II, Secretary of State George Marshall proposed that European
nations create a plan for their economic reconstruction and that the United States provide economic assistance. In December 1947, President Harry Truman sent Congress a message
based on Marshall's ideas to provide economic aid to Europe. Congress overwhelmingly passed the
Economic Cooperation Act of 1948, and on April 3, 1948, President Truman signed the act, which
became known as the Marshall Plan.

      Over the next four years, Congress appropriated $13.3 billion for West European recovery.
This aid provided much-needed capital and materials that enabled Europeans to rebuild their
national economies. For the United States, the Marshall Plan provided markets for American goods,
created reliable trading partners, and supported the development of stable democratic governments
in Western Europe. Secretary Marshall had proposed the plan in this speech at Harvard University
on June 5, 1947.

I need not tell you gentlemen that the
world situation is very serious. That must be
apparent to all intelligent people. I think
one difficulty is that the problem is one of
such enormous complexity that the very mass
of facts presented to the public by press and
radio make it exceedingly difficult for the
man in the street to reach a clear appraise-
ment of the situation. Furthermore, the
people of this country are distant from the
troubled areas of the earth and it is hard for
them to comprehend the plight and conse-
quent reaction of the long-suffering peoples, and the effect of those reactions on
their governments in connection with our
efforts to promote peace in the world.

      In considering the requirements for the
rehabilitation of Europe the physical loss of
life, the visible destruction of cities, factories,
mines, and railroads was correctly estimated,
but it has become obvious during recent
months that this visible destruction was
probably less serious than the dislocation of
the entire fabric of European economy. For
the past 10 years conditions have been highly
abnormal. The feverish maintenance of the
war effort engulfed all aspects of national economics. Machinery has fallen into disrepair

*The Marshall Plan, whose shield is displayed on the construction sign, helped
finance this housing project in Matera, Italy.*

Congress passed the Economic Cooperation Act of 1948 as a result of Secretary of State George Marshall's proposed plan.

S. 2202

[PUBLIC LAW 472]
[CHAPTER 169]

Eightieth Congress of the United States of America
At the Second Session

Begun and held at the City of Washington on Tuesday, the sixth
day of January, one thousand nine hundred and forty-eight

AN ACT

To promote world peace and the general welfare, national interest,
and foreign policy of the United States through economic, financial,
and other measures necessary to the maintenance of conditions
abroad in which free institutions may survive and consistent with
the maintenance of the strength and stability of the United States.

*Be it enacted by the Senate and House of Representatives of the
United States of America in Congress assembled,* That this Act may be
cited as the "Foreign Assistance Act of 1948".

TITLE I

SEC. 101. This title may be cited as the "Economic Cooperation Act
of 1948".

FINDINGS AND DECLARATION OF POLICY

SEC. 102. (a) Recognizing the intimate economic and other relationships between the United States and the nations of Europe, and
recognizing that disruption following in the wake of war is not contained by national frontiers, the Congress finds that the existing
situation in Europe endangers the establishment of a lasting peace,
the general welfare and national interest of the United States, and
the attainment of the objectives of the United Nations. The restoration or maintenance in European countries of principles of individual
liberty, free institutions, and genuine independence rests largely upon
the establishment of sound economic conditions, stable international
economic relationships, and the achievement by the countries of Europe
of a healthy economy independent of extraordinary outside assistance.
The accomplishment of these objectives calls for a plan of European
recovery, open to all such nations which cooperate in such plan, based
upon a strong production effort, the expansion of foreign trade, the
creation and maintenance of internal financial stability, and the development of economic cooperation, including all possible steps to establish
and maintain equitable rates of exchange and to bring about the progressive elimination of trade barriers. Mindful of the advantages
which the United States has enjoyed through the existence of a large
domestic market with no internal trade barriers, and believing that
similar advantages can accrue to the countries of Europe, it is declared
to be the policy of the people of the United States to encourage these

"[T]he United States should do whatever it is able to do to assist in the return of normal economic health in the world, without which there can be no political stability and no assured peace."

or is entirely obsolete. Under the arbitrary and destructive Nazi rule, virtually every possible enterprise was geared into the German war machine. Long-standing commercial ties, private institutions, banks, insurance companies and shipping companies disappeared, through the loss of capital, absorption through nationalization or by simple destruction. In many countries, confidence in the local currency has been severely shaken. The breakdown of the business structure of Europe during the war was complete. Recovery has been seriously retarded by the fact that 2 years after the close of hostilities a peace settlement with Germany and Austria has not been agreed upon. But even given a more prompt solution of these difficult problems, the rehabilitation of the economic structure of Europe quite evidently will require a much longer time and greater effort than had been foreseen.

There is a phase of this matter which is both interesting and serious. The farmer has always produced the foodstuffs to exchange with the city dweller for the other necessities of life. This division of labor is the basis of modern civilization. At the present time it is threatened with breakdown. The town and city industries are not producing adequate goods to exchange with the food-producing farmer. Raw materials and fuel are in short supply. Machinery is lacking or worn out. The farmer or the peasant cannot find the goods for sale which he desires to purchase. So the sale of his farm produce for money which he cannot use seems to him unprofitable transaction. He, therefore, has withdrawn many fields from crop cultivation and is using them for grazing. He feeds more grain to stock and finds for himself and his family an ample supply of food, however short he may be on clothing and the other ordinary gadgets of civilization. Meanwhile people in the cities are short of food and fuel. So the governments are forced to use their foreign money and credits to procure these necessities abroad. This process exhausts funds which are urgently needed for reconstruction. Thus a very serious situation is rapidly developing which bodes no good for the world. . . .

The truth of the matter is that Europe's requirements for the next 3 or 4 years of foreign food and other essential products—principally from America—are so much greater than her present ability to pay that she must have substantial additional help, or face economic, social, and political deterioration of a very grave character.

The remedy lies in breaking the vicious circle and restoring the confidence of the European people in the economic future of their own countries and of Europe as a whole. . . .

Aside from the demoralizing effect on the world at large and the possibilities of disturbances arising as a result of the desperation of the people concerned, the consequences to the economy of the United States should be apparent to all. It is logical that the United States should do whatever it is able to do to assist in the return of normal economic health in the world, without which there can be no political stability and no assured peace. Our policy is directed not against any country or doctrine but against hunger, poverty, desperation, and chaos. Its purpose should be the revival of working economy in the world so as to permit the emergence of political and social conditions in which free institutions can exist. . . .

It is already evident that, before the United States Government can proceed much further in its efforts to alleviate the situation and help start the European world on its way to recovery, there must be some agreement among the countries of Europe as to the requirements of the situation and the part those countries themselves will take in order to give proper effect to whatever action might be undertaken by this Government. It would be neither fitting nor efficacious for this Government to undertake to draw up unilaterally a program designed to place Europe on its feet economically. This is the business of the Europeans. The initiative, I think, must come from Europe. The role of this country should consist of friendly aid in the drafting of a European program so far as it may be practical for us to do so. The program should be a joint one, agreed to by a number, if not all European nations.

An essential part of any successful action on the part of the United States is an understanding on the part of the people of America of the character of the problem and the remedies to be applied. Political passion and prejudice should have no part. With foresight, and a willingness on the part of our people to face up to the vast responsibilities which history has clearly placed upon our country, the difficulties I have outlined can and will be overcome.

1948

PRESS RELEASE ANNOUNCING U.S. RECOGNITION OF ISRAEL

*I*n 1917 Chaim Weizmann, scientist, statesman, and supporter of the effort to establish a Jewish national homeland, persuaded the British government to issue a statement favoring the establishment of such a homeland in Palestine. The statement, which became known as the Balfour Declaration, was, in part, payment to the Jews for their support of the British against the Turks during World War I. After the war the League of Nations ratified the declaration and in 1922 appointed Britain to rule Palestine.

This course of events made Jews optimistic about the eventual establishment of a homeland, which in turn inspired Jews from many countries—particularly Germany, where Nazi persecution of Jews had begun—to immigrate to Palestine. The arrival of 165,000 Jewish immigrants between 1933 and 1936 awakened Arab fears that Jews would eventually outnumber Palestinians in a representative government. In an attempt at compromise, the British proposed a new constitution and legislative council, but both Palestinians and Jews rejected it because the British would have retained control of the government. By 1936 guerrilla fighting, initially against the British, had also broken out between the Jews and the Arabs. Unable to maintain peace, Britain issued a white paper in 1939 that restricted Jewish immigration into Palestine. The Jews, resenting this betrayal, bitterly opposed the policy and turned to the United States for support.

Although President Franklin D. Roosevelt appeared to sympathize with the Jewish cause, his assurances to the Arabs that the United States would not intervene without consulting both parties caused public uncertainty about his position. When Harry S Truman took office, he made clear that his sympathies were with the Jews. Truman initiated several studies of the Jews' situation, which reinforced the fact of Jewish persecution and made the case for establishing a Jewish homeland. However, throughout the Roosevelt and Truman administrations, the Departments of War and State had advised against American intervention on behalf of the Jews. They feared that such intervention would encourage Arab alliances with the Soviets, whom the United States wished to contain, as well as an Arab restriction on oil supplies to the United States.

In April 1946, an Anglo-American committee recommended that neither Jews nor Arabs dominate Palestine and that 100,000 Jews should be immediately admitted into Palestine. Convinced that attempts to establish either an Arab or a Jewish state would result in civil strife, they proposed that the United Nations establish a trusteeship agreement to bring Jews and Arabs together under a single government. British Foreign Secretary Ernest Bevin flatly rejected the plan, as did both Arabs and Jews.

Britain, anxious to rid itself of the problem, formally requested that the United Nations take over by setting up a Special Committee on Palestine (UNSCOP). This committee recommended an end of the British mandate over Palestine and the partitioning of the territory into two states. Jewish reaction was mixed—some wanted control of all of Palestine; others realized that partition spelled hope for their dream of a homeland. The Arabs opposed the UNSCOP plan, and in October 1947 the Arab League Council directed the governments of its member states to move troops to the Palestine border. Meanwhile, President Truman instructed the State Department to support the UN plan, which it reluctantly did. On November 29, 1947, the UN General Assembly passed the partition plan.

At midnight on May 14, 1948, the Provisional Government of the Jewish homeland proclaimed a new State of Israel. On that same date, in a short press release, President Truman recognized the government. The U.S. delegates to the UN and top-ranking State Department officials were angry that Truman released his recognition statement to the press without notifying them first. On May 15, 1948, the first day of Israeli independence and exactly one year after the establishment of UNSCOP, Arab armies invaded Israel and the first Arab-Israeli war began.

This Government has been informed that a Jewish state has been proclaimed in Palestine, and recognition has been requested by the provisional Government thereof.

The United States recognizes the provisional government as the de facto authority of the new State of Israel.

HARRY TRUMAN

APPROVED, MAY 14, 1948.

6:11

Grateful for the president's recognition of the new state of Israel, its prime minister, David Ben-Gurion (center), and its ambassador to the United States, Abba Eban (right), present Truman with a menorah in the Oval Office.

1948

EXECUTIVE ORDER 9981: DESEGREGATION OF THE ARMED FORCES

Of the 2.5 million African-American males who registered for the draft during World War II, more than one million were inducted into the armed forces. Along with thousands of black women, these inductees served in all branches of the military and in all theaters of operation during World War II. During the war, President Roosevelt had issued an executive order that prohibited discrimination in the defense industries and established a Fair Employment Practices Commission (FEPC) to enforce his directive. Yielding to pressure from Congress, President Truman agreed to shut down the FEPC. However, in December 1946 he appointed a distinguished panel to serve as the President's Commission on Civil Rights. The commission's report, "To Secure These Rights," which the panel issued in October 1947, called for legislation to outlaw lynching and poll taxes, a permanent FEPC, and strengthening of the civil rights division of the Department of Justice.

In February 1948 Truman called on Congress to enact all of these recommendations. Because southern senators immediately threatened a filibuster, he moved ahead on civil rights by using his executive powers. He bolstered the civil rights division, appointed the first African-American judge to the federal bench, named several African Americans to high-ranking positions in his administration, and, most important, issued an executive order abolishing segregation in the armed forces and ordering full integration of all the services.

Executive Order 9981 committed the government to "equality of treatment and opportunity for all persons in the U.S. military without regard to race, color, religion, or national origin." The order established an advisory committee to examine the rules, practices, and procedures of the armed services and to recommend effective methods of desegregation. Despite considerable resistance from the military, by the end of the Korean conflict, almost all the armed forces had achieved integration.

EXECUTIVE ORDER

ESTABLISHING THE PRESIDENT'S COMMITTEE ON EQUALITY OF TREATMENT AND OPPORTUNITY IN THE ARMED SERVICES.

WHEREAS it is essential that there be maintained in the armed services of the United States the highest standards of democracy, with equality of treatment and opportunity for all those who serve in our country's defense:

NOW THEREFORE, by virtue of the authority vested in me as President of the United States, by the Constitution and the statutes of the United States, and as Commander in Chief of the armed services, it is hereby ordered as follows:

1. It is hereby declared to be the policy of the President that there shall be equality of treatment and opportunity for all persons in the armed services without regard to race, color, religion or national origin. This policy shall be put into effect as rapidly as possible, having due regard to the time required to effectuate any necessary changes without impairing efficiency or morale.

"[T]here shall be equality of treatment and opportunity for all persons in the armed services without regard to race, color, religion or national origin."

2. There shall be created in the National Military Establishment an advisory committee to be known as the President's Committee on Equality of Treatment and Opportunity in the Armed Services, which shall be composed of seven members to be designated by the President.

3. The Committee is authorized on behalf of the President to examine into the rules, procedures and practices of the Armed Services in order to determine in what respect such rules, procedures and practices may be altered or improved with a view to carrying out the policy of this order. The Committee shall confer and advise the Secretary of Defense, the Secretary of the Army, the Secretary of the Navy, and the Secretary of the Air Force, and shall make such recommendations to the President and to said Secretaries as in the judgment of the Committee will effectuate the policy hereof.

4. All executive departments and agencies of the Federal Government are authorized and directed to cooperate with the Committee in its work, and to furnish the Committee such information or the services of such persons as the Committee may require in the performance of its duties.

5. When requested by the Committee to do so, persons in the armed services or in any of the executive departments and agencies of the Federal Government shall testify before the Committee and shall make available for use of the Committee such documents and other information as the Committee may require.

6. The Committee shall continue to exist until such time as the President shall terminate its existence by Executive order.

HARRY TRUMAN

THE WHITE HOUSE,
JULY 26, 1948.

EXECUTIVE ORDER

ESTABLISHING THE PRESIDENT'S COMMITTEE ON EQUALITY OF TREATMENT AND OPPORTUNITY IN THE ARMED SERVICES

WHEREAS it is essential that there be maintained in the armed services of the United States the highest standards of democracy, with equality of treatment and opportunity for all those who serve in our country's defense:

NOW, THEREFORE, by virtue of the authority vested in me as President of the United States, by the Constitution and the statutes of the United States, and as Commander in Chief of the armed services, it is hereby ordered as follows:

1. It is hereby declared to be the policy of the President that there shall be equality of treatment and opportunity for all persons in the armed services without regard to race, color, religion or national origin. This policy shall be put into effect as rapidly as possible, having due regard to the time required to effectuate any necessary changes without impairing efficiency or morale.

2. There shall be created in the National Military Establishment an advisory committee to be known as the President's Committee on Equality of Treatment and Opportunity in the Armed Services, which shall be composed of seven members to be designated by the President.

3. The Committee is authorized on behalf of the President to examine into the rules, procedures and practices of the armed services in order to determine in what respect such rules, procedures and practices may be altered or improved with a view to carrying out the policy of this order. The Committee shall confer and advise with the Secretary of Defense, the Secretary

1953

ARMISTICE AGREEMENT FOR THE RESTORATION OF THE SOUTH KOREAN STATE

*A*t the end of World War II, Korea had been divided at the thirty-eighth parallel into American and Soviet occupation zones. North and South established separate communist and noncommunist regimes, and occupation forces then withdrew, giving the impression that the political situation was stable. However, Soviet leader Joseph Stalin encouraged the North to use military force to reunify the country, and on June 25, 1950, North Korean forces invaded the Republic of Korea. President Harry S Truman turned the matter over to the United Nations. The Soviet delegate, boycotting the United Nations because of its refusal to seat Communist China, was not in a position to veto the Security Council's resolution to assist South Korea in repelling the attack. Fourteen nations, including the United States, sent troops; five sent medical units.

Fighting continued until June 1951, when the Soviet delegate to the UN proposed a cease-fire and armistice. Two years and seventeen days later, the truce went into effect. It had taken one-hundred and fifty-eight meetings to negotiate its terms. On July 27, 1953, representatives from the United Nations, North and South Korea, China, and the United States gathered in Panmunjom, just south of the thirty-eighth parallel in the Republic of Korea, to sign the official armistice agreement. The Korean Armistice Agreement, which is still in effect, was not a peace treaty, but a military document whose aim was to suspend hostilities, prevent further confrontations, and provide for the release and repatriation of prisoners of war and victims whom the war had displaced.

President Eisenhower, a key figure in bringing about a cease-fire, announced the armistice to the American people. He observed, "In this struggle we have seen the United Nations meet the challenge of aggression—not with pathetic words of protest, but with deeds of decisive purpose. . . . We have won an armistice on a single battleground—not peace in the world. We may not now relax our guard nor cease our quest." Although the Cold War between communist Russia and capitalist America would continue for nearly four more decades, the Korean War was notable in that both the United States and the Soviet Union recognized the potential for escalation of this conflict and backed away from it.

Agreement between the Commander-in-Chief, United Nations Command, on the one hand, and the Supreme Commander of the Korean People's Army and the Commander of the Chinese People's volunteers, on the other hand, concerning a military armistice in Korea.

PREAMBLE

The undersigned, the Commander-in-Chief, United Nations Command, on the one hand, and the Supreme Commander of the Korean People's Army and the Commander of the Chinese People's Volunteers, on the other hand, in the interest of stopping the Korean conflict, with its great toil of suffering and bloodshed on both sides, and with the objective of establishing an armistice which will insure a complete cessation of hostilities and of all acts of armed force in Korea until a final peaceful settlement is achieved, do individually, collectively, and mutually agree to accept and to be bound and governed by the conditions and terms of armistice set forth in the following articles and paragraphs, which said conditions and terms are intended to be purely military in character and to pertain solely to the belligerents in Korea:

Members of the First Marine Division paid their respects to fallen buddies during memorial services at the division's cemetery at Hamhung, Korea, in 1950.

ARTICLE I
Military Demarcation Line and Demilitarized Zone

1. A military demarcation line shall be fixed and both sides shall withdraw two (2) kilometers from this line so as to establish a demilitarized zone between the opposing forces. A demilitarized zone shall be established as a buffer zone to prevent the occurrence of incidents which might lead to a resumption of hostilities....

6. Neither side shall execute any hostile act within, from, or against the demilitarized zone....

10. Civil administration and relief in that part of the demilitarized zone which is south of the military demarcation line shall be the responsibility of the Commander-in-Chief, United Nations Command; and civil administration and relief in that part of the demilitarized zone which is north of the military demarcation line shall be the joint responsibility of the Supreme Commander of the Korean People's Army and the Commander of the Chinese People's volunteers....

ARTICLE II
Concrete Arrangements for Cease-Fire and Armistice
A. General

12. The Commanders of the opposing sides shall order and enforce a complete cessation of all hostilities in Korea by all armed forces under their control, including all units and personnel of the ground, naval, and air forces, effective twelve (12) hours after this armistice agreement is signed.

13. In order to insure the stability of the military armistice so as to facilitate the attainment of a peaceful settlement through the holding by both sides of a political conference of a higher level, the Commanders of the opposing sides shall:

(a) Within seventy-two (72) hours after this armistice agreement becomes effective, withdraw all of their military forces, supplies, and equipment from the demilitarized zone except as otherwise provided herein....

(b) Within ten (10) days after this armistice agreement becomes effective, withdraw all of their military forces, supplies, and equipment from the rear and the coastal islands and waters of Korea of the other side.

(c) Cease the introduction into Korea of reinforcing military personnel....

(d) Cease the introduction into Korea of reinforcing combat aircraft, armored vehicles, weapons, and ammunition....

(e) Insure that personnel of their respective commands who violate any of the provisions of this armistice agreement are adequately punished....

17. Responsibility for compliance with and enforcement of the terms and provisions of this Armistice Agreement is that of the signatories hereto and their successors in command.

18. The costs of the operations of the Military Armistice Commission and of the Neutral Nations Supervisory Commission and of their Teams shall be shared equally by the two opposing sides....

ARTICLE III
Arrangement Relating to Prisoners of War

51. The release and repatriation of all prisoners of war held in the custody of each side at the time this armistice agreement becomes effective shall be effected in conformity with the following provisions agreed upon by both sides prior to the signing of this armistice agreement.

(a) Within sixty (60) days after this agreement becomes effective each side shall, without offering any hindrance, directly repatriate and hand over in groups all those prisoners of war in its custody who insist on repatriation to the side to which they belonged at the time of capture....

53. All the sick and injured prisoners of war who insist upon repatriation shall be repatriated with priority.

AGREEMENT BETWEEN THE COMMANDER-IN-CHIEF,
UNITED NATIONS COMMAND, ON THE ONE HAND, AND
THE SUPREME COMMANDER OF THE KOREAN PEOPLE'S
ARMY AND THE COMMANDER OF THE CHINESE
PEOPLE'S VOLUNTEERS, ON THE OTHER HAND,
CONCERNING A MILITARY ARMISTICE IN KOREA

PREAMBLE

The undersigned, the Commander-in-Chief, United Nations Command, on the one hand, and the Supreme Commander of the Korean People's Army and the Commander of the Chinese People's Volunteers, on the other hand, in the interest of stopping the Korean conflict, with its great toll of suffering and bloodshed on both sides, and with the objective of establishing an armistice which will insure a complete cessation of hostilities and of all acts of armed force in Korea until a final peaceful settlement is achieved, do individually, collectively, and mutually agree to accept and to be bound and governed by the conditions and terms of armistice set forth in the following Articles and Paragraphs, which said conditions and terms are intended to be purely military in character and to pertain solely to the belligerents in Korea.

-1-

At 10 A.M., in Panmunjom, scarcely acknowledging each other, U.S. Army Lieutenant General William K. Harrison, Jr., and North Korean General Nam Il signed 18 official copies of the tri-language Korean Armistice Agreement.

54. The repatriation of all of the prisoners of war ... shall be completed within a time limit of sixty (60) days after this Armistice Agreement becomes effective. ...

57. (d) (1) A Committee for Assisting the Return of Displaced Civilians is hereby established. ... This committee shall, under the general supervision and direction of the Military Armistice Commission, be responsible for coordinating the specific plans of both sides for assistance to the return of ... civilians. It shall be the duty of this Committee to make necessary arrangements, including those of transportation, for expediting and coordinating the movement of the above-mentioned civilians; to select the crossing point(s) through which the above-mentioned civilians will cross the Military Demarcation Line; to arrange for security at the crossing point(s); and to carry out such other functions as are required to accomplish the return of the above-mentioned civilians. ...

ARTICLE IV
Recommendations to the Governments Concerned on Both Sides

60. In order to insure the peaceful settlement of the Korean question, the military Commanders of both sides hereby recommend to the governments of the countries concerned on both sides that, within three (3) months after the Armistice Agreement is signed and becomes effective, a political conference of a higher level of both sides be held by representatives appointed respectively to settle through negotiation the questions of the withdrawal of all foreign forces from Korea, the peaceful settlement of the Korean question, etc.

ARTICLE V
Miscellaneous. ...

62. The Articles and Paragraphs of this Armistice Agreement shall remain in effect until expressly superseded either by mutually acceptable amendments and additions or by provision in an appropriate agreement for a peaceful settlement at a political level between both sides.

DONE AT PANMUNJOM, KOREA AT 10:00 HOURS ON THE 27TH DAY OF JULY 1953, IN ENGLISH, KOREAN AND CHINESE, ALL TEXTS BEING EQUALLY AUTHENTIC.

NAM IL

GENERAL, KOREAN PEOPLE'S ARMY

SENIOR DELEGATE,

DELEGATION OF THE KOREAN PEOPLE'S ARMY
AND THE CHINESE PEOPLE'S VOLUNTEERS

WILLIAM K. HARRISON, JR.

LIEUTENANT GENERAL, UNITED STATES ARMY

SENIOR DELEGATE,

UNITED NATIONS COMMAND DELEGATION

1954

SENATE RESOLUTION 301:
CENSURE OF SENATOR JOSEPH McCARTHY

*S*oviet aggression in Eastern Europe, the Communist Revolution in China, and the highly publicized trial of Alger Hiss, a former State Department employee and president of the Carnegie Endowment for International Peace who was accused of spying for the Soviet Union, all raised concerns about Communist subversion in the United States. Playing on that fear, Wisconsin's Republican Senator Joseph McCarthy claimed in a speech in Wheeling, West Virginia, in February 1950, that he had a list of 205 State Department employees who were Communists. Although he offered no proof, the media printed his accusations, thereby providing the publicity he craved. In June, Senator Margaret Chase Smith of Maine and six fellow Republicans issued a "Declaration of Conscience," asserting that McCarthy's tactics had "debased [the Senate] to the level of a forum for hate and character assassination." Unchastened, McCarthy continued his attacks and, exploiting public exasperation with the Korean War, marshaled sufficient voter support to unseat several Senate Democrats in the next elections.

When Republicans took control of Congress in 1953, McCarthy became chairman of the Committee on Government Operations and its Subcommittee on Investigations. Exploiting these positions of power, he exercised a veto over all diplomatic nominations and accused government agencies of being "soft" on communism. The State Department responded by purging U.S. Information Agency libraries of books and artwork by Communists and "fellow travelers." President Eisenhower declined to challenge McCarthy publicly. He also issued an executive order revoking safeguards that Truman had built into his internal security program, making it easier to fire federal employees suspected of being "security risks." Democrats, too, were caught up in the hysteria, supported discriminatory legislation and, in the case of Robert Kennedy, even served on McCarthy's staff.

McCarthy's downfall came in 1954 during investigations of alleged security threats in the U.S. Army. McCarthy's bullying of witnesses, which the government televised in one of the first live broadcasts of congressional hearings, turned public opinion against him. Three Republican senators led the move to censure McCarthy.

The Senate began debate on the resolution in July and voted to censure him in December, describing his behavior as "contrary to senatorial traditions." This copy of the resolution records the debate on November 9 as the Senate refined the wording of its resolution. The first count charged McCarthy with failure to cooperate with a Senate subcommittee; it remained unchanged in the final resolution. The second count was replaced by a condemnation of McCarthy's attacks on the very members of the committee that considered his censure.

RESOLVED, That the Senator from Wisconsin, Mr. McCarthy, failed to cooperate with the Subcommittee on Privileges and Elections of the Senate Committee on Rules and Administration in clearing up matters referred to that subcommittee which concerned his conduct as a Senator and affected the honor of the Senate and, instead, repeatedly abused the subcommittee and its members who were trying to carry out assigned duties, thereby obstructing the constitutional processes of the Senate, and that this conduct of the

Senator from Wisconsin, Mr. McCarthy, is contrary to senatorial traditions and is hereby condemned.

SEC. 2. The Senator from Wisconsin, Mr. McCarthy, in writing to the chairman of the Select Committee to Study Censure Charges (Mr. Watkins) after the Select Committee had issued its report and before the report was presented to the Senate charging three members of the Select Committee with "deliberate deception" and "fraud" for failure to disqualify themselves; in stating to the press on November 4, 1954, that the special Senate session that was to begin November 8, 1954, was a "lynch-party"; in repeatedly describing this special Senate session as a "lynch bee" in a nationwide television and radio show on November 7, 1954; in stating to the public press on November 13, 1954, that the chairman of the Select Committee (Mr. Watkins) was guilty of "the most unusual, most cowardly things I've ever heard of" and stating further: "I

expected he would be afraid to answer the questions, but didn't think he'd be stupid enough to make a public statement"; and in characterizing the said committee as the "unwitting handmaiden," "involuntary agent" and "attorneys-in-fact" of the Communist Party and in charging that the said committee in writing its report "imitated Communist methods — that it distorted, misrepresented, and omitted in its effort to manufacture a plausible rationalization" in support of its recommendations to the Senate, which characterizations and charges were contained in a statement released to the press and inserted in the Congressional Record of November 10, 1954, acted contrary to senatorial ethics and tended to bring the Senate into dishonor and disrepute, to obstruct the constitutional processes of the Senate, and to impair its dignity; and such conduct is hereby condemned.

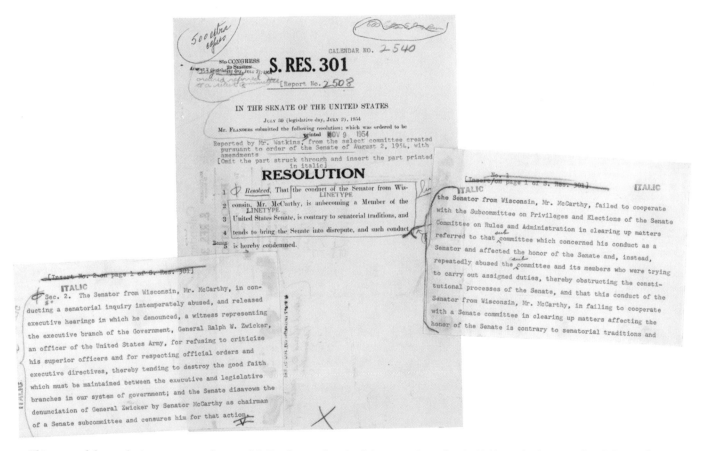

This copy of the resolution to censure Senator McCarthy catches the debate on November 9, 1954, as the Senate refined the wording of its resolution.

1954

BROWN V. BOARD OF EDUCATION

*E*ncouraged by a group of Supreme Court decisions requiring states to admit blacks to graduate and professional schools supported by public funds, the Legal Defense Fund (LDF) of the National Association for the Advancement of Colored People (NAACP), headed by Thurgood Marshall, decided in the early 1950s that the time was right to challenge segregation in public schools.

The Supreme Court agreed to hear five cases. Brown v. Board of Education of Topeka, Kansas, in which the parents of Linda Brown sued to permit her to attend the elementary school nearest her home, appeared first in the alphabetical listing of the case titles. The case revolved to a large extent around the equal protection clause of the Fourteenth Amendment. The issue was not merely whether equality was measured by the physical facilities or the quality of teaching in schools that black children attended but whether segregation itself had a detrimental effect on the education of African-American children.

The lawyers first argued the cases before the Supreme Court in 1952, but the justices, who disagreed over the outcome, decided that anything short of a unanimous decision on this volatile issue could prove disastrous. They scheduled a second hearing in October 1953. In what quickly became a highly controversial approach, the newly appointed chief justice, Earl Warren, relied heavily on psychological evidence that the NAACP had presented: "To separate [black children] from others of similar age and qualifications solely because of their race generates a feeling of inferiority as to their status in the community that may affect their hearts and minds in a way unlikely ever to be undone." Disputing the Court's reasoning in Plessy v. Ferguson, Warren concluded that "in the field of education, the doctrine of 'separate but equal' has no place."

The Court dealt later with the mechanics of implementing desegregation. On May 31, 1955, Warren announced the Court's unanimous decision in Brown II, requiring states to begin formulating plans for desegregation "with all deliberate speed" and assigning federal district court judges the difficult task of evaluating both the plans and the progress of local communities. Southern states and later northern communities cited legal and practical reasons for refusing to comply with the Court's ruling. Despite widespread and persistent opposition to school desegregation, Brown marked a turning point in the civil rights movement and led, eventually, to better educational opportunities for African Americans.

SUPREME COURT OF THE UNITED STATES
Brown v. Board of Education, 347 U.S. 483 (1954) (USSC+)

ARGUED DECEMBER 9, 1952

REARGUED DECEMBER 8, 1953

DECIDED MAY 17, 1954

APPEAL FROM THE UNITED STATES DISTRICT COURT FOR THE DISTRICT OF KANSAS
MR. CHIEF JUSTICE WARREN delivered the opinion of the Court.

These cases come to us from the States of Kansas, South Carolina, Virginia, and Delaware. They are premised on different facts and different local conditions, but a common legal question justifies their consideration together in this consolidated opinion.

In each of the cases, minors of the Negro race, through their legal representatives, seek the aid of the courts in obtaining admission to the public schools of their community on a nonsegregated basis. In each instance, they had been denied admission to schools attended by white children under laws requiring or permitting segregation according to race. This segregation

Supreme Court of the United States

No. 1 ——— , *October Term, 19* 54

Oliver Brown, Mrs. Richard Lawton, Mrs. Sadie Emmanuel et al.,

Appellants,

vs.

Board of Education of Topeka, Shawnee County, Kansas, et al.

Appeal from *the United States District Court for the* ———————————
District of Kansas.

This cause *came on to be heard on the transcript of the record from the United States*
District Court for the ——————— *District of* Kansas, ———————
and was argued by counsel.

On consideration whereof, *It is ordered and adjudged by this Court that the judgment*
of the said District ——————— *Court in this cause be, and the same is*
hereby, reversed with costs; and that this cause be, and the same
is hereby, remanded to the said District Court to take such
proceedings and enter such orders and decrees consistent with
the opinions of this Court as are necessary and proper to admit
to public schools on a racially nondiscriminatory basis with all
deliberate speed the parties to this case.

Per Mr. Chief Justice Warren,

May 31, 1955.

1469

was alleged to deprive the plaintiffs of the equal protection of the laws under the Fourteenth Amendment. In each of the cases other than the Delaware case, a three-judge federal district court denied relief to the plaintiffs on the so-called "separate but equal" doctrine announced by this Court in *Plessy* v. *Ferguson*, 163 U.S. 537. Under that doctrine, equality of treatment is accorded when the races are provided substantially equal facilities, even though these facilities be separate. In the Delaware case, the Supreme Court of Delaware adhered to that doctrine, but ordered that the plaintiffs be admitted to the white schools because of their superiority to the Negro schools.

The plaintiffs contend that segregated public schools are not "equal" and cannot be made "equal," and that hence they are deprived of the equal protection of the laws. Because of the obvious importance of the question presented, the Court took jurisdiction. Argument was heard in the 1952 Term, and reargument was heard this Term on certain questions propounded by the Court.

Reargument was largely devoted to the circumstances surrounding the adoption of the Fourteenth

Amendment in 1868.... This discussion and our own investigation convince us that, although these sources cast some light, it is not enough to resolve the problem with which we are faced. At best, they are inconclusive....

In the first cases in this Court construing the Fourteenth Amendment, decided shortly after its adoption, the Court interpreted it as proscribing all state-imposed discriminations against the Negro race. The doctrine of "separate but equal" did not make its appearance in this Court until 1896 in the case of *Plessy* v. *Ferguson*,... involving not education but transportation. American courts have since labored with the doctrine for over half a century.

In the instant cases, that question is directly presented. Here... there are findings below that the Negro and white schools involved have been equalized, or are being equalized, with respect to buildings, curricula, qualifications and salaries of teachers, and other "tangible" factors. Our decision, therefore, cannot turn on merely a comparison of these tangible factors in the Negro and white schools involved in each of the cases. We must look instead to the effect of segregation itself on public education.

Today, education is perhaps the most important function of state and local governments. Compulsory school attendance laws and the great expenditures for education both demonstrate our recognition of the importance of education to our democratic society. It is required in the performance of our most basic public responsibilities, even service in the armed forces. It is the very foundation of good citizenship. Today it is a principal instrument in awakening the child to cultural values, in preparing him for later professional training, and in helping him to adjust normally to his environment. In these days, it is doubtful that any child may reasonably be expected to succeed in life if he is denied the opportunity of an education. Such an opportunity, where the state has undertaken to provide it, is a right which must be made available to all on equal terms.

We come then to the question presented: Does segregation of children in public schools solely on the basis of race, even though the physical facilities and other "tangible" factors may be equal, deprive the children of the minority group of equal educational opportunities? We believe that it does.

In *Sweatt* v. *Painter*,... in finding that a segregated law school for Negroes could not provide them equal educational opportunities, this Court relied in large part on "those qualities which are incapable of objective measurement but which make for greatness in a law school." In *McLaurin* v. *Oklahoma State Regents*,... the Court, in requiring that a Negro admitted to a white graduate school be treated like all other students, again resorted to intangible considerations: "... his ability to study, to engage in discussions and exchange views with other students, and, in general, to learn his profession." Such considerations apply with added force to children in grade and high schools. To separate them from others of similar age and qualifications solely because of their race generates a feeling of inferiority as to their status in the community that may affect their hearts and minds in a way unlikely ever to be undone....

Segregation of white and colored children in public schools has a detrimental effect upon the colored children. The impact is greater when it has the sanction of the law, for the policy of separating the races is usually interpreted as denoting the inferiority of the negro group. A sense of inferiority affects the motivation of a child to learn. Segregation with the sanction of law, therefore, has a tendency to [retard] the educational and mental development of negro children and to deprive them of some of the benefits they would receive in a racial[ly] integrated school system.

We conclude that, in the field of public education, the doctrine of "separate but equal" has no place. Separate educational facilities are inherently unequal. Therefore, we hold that the plaintiffs and others similarly situated for whom the actions have been brought are, by reason of the segregation complained of, deprived of the equal protection of the laws guaranteed by the Fourteenth Amendment.

Because these are class actions, because of the wide applicability of this decision, and because of the great variety of local conditions, the formulation of decrees in these cases presents problems of considerable complexity. On reargument, the consideration of appropriate relief was necessarily subordinated to the primary question—the constitutionality of segregation in public education. We have now announced that such segregation is a denial of the equal protection of the laws. In order that we may have the full assistance of the parties in formulating decrees, the cases will be restored to the docket, and the parties are requested to present further argument....

It is so ordered.

NATIONAL INTERSTATE AND DEFENSE HIGHWAYS ACT

*A*lthough the Federal Highway Act of 1916 provided matching funds to states to build roads along postal routes, it was not until 1944 that the Federal-Aid Highway Act authorized the designation of 40,000 miles of a "National System of Interstate Highways." This act, however, did not provide special funding for the project or increase the federal share of the construction expense.

When President Dwight D. Eisenhower took office in January 1953, the states had completed 6,500 miles of designated improvements. Between 1954 and 1956, Congress failed on several occasions to pass a national highway bill that would provide a mechanism for funding the interstate system. The main point of contention focused on how the costs would be shared between the federal government and the states. A military man, Eisenhower was well aware of the importance of good roads to national security and, in his 1956 State of the Union Address, renewed his call for a "modern, interstate highway system." Finally persuaded, Congress passed a new Federal-Aid Highway Act later that year. The 1956 act, officially titled the National Interstate and Defense Highways Act, established a 41,000-mile interstate highway system and authorized $25 billion for construction over a 12-year period.

The development of the interstate system not only allowed for more mobility—both for citizens and for the military, if necessary—but it made the automobile central to American culture. Suburbs burgeoned, Americans became commuters, and roadside strip malls, motels, and fast-food restaurants continue to spring up along the highways.

AN ACT

To amend and supplement the Federal-Aid Road Act approved July 11, 1916, to authorize appropriations for continuing the construction of highways; to amend the Internal Revenue Code of 1954 to provide additional revenue from the taxes on motor fuel, tires, and trucks and buses; and for other purposes.

Be it enacted by the Senate and House of Representatives of the United States of America in Congress assembled,

TITLE I—FEDERAL-AID HIGHWAY ACT OF 1956
SEC. 101. SHORT TITLE FOR TITLE I.

This title may be cited as the "Federal-Aid Highway Act of 1956".

SEC. 102. FEDERAL-AID HIGHWAYS.

(a) (1) AUTHORIZATION OF APPROPRIATIONS. —For the purpose of carrying out the provisions of the Federal-Aid Road Act approved July 11, 1916 (39 Stat. 355), and all Acts amendatory thereof and supplementary thereto, there is hereby authorized to be appropriated for the fiscal year ending June 30, 1957, $125,000,000 in addition to any sums heretofore authorized for such fiscal year; the sum of $850,000,000 for the fiscal year ending June 30, 1958; and the sum of $875,000,000 for the fiscal year ending June 30, 1959. The sums herein authorized for each fiscal year shall be available for expenditure as follows:

(A) 45 per centum for projects on the Federal-aid primary highway system.

(B) 30 per centum for projects on the Federal-aid secondary highway system.

(C) 25 per centum for projects on extensions of these systems within urban areas.

(2) APPORTIONMENTS.—The sums authorized by this section shall be apportioned among the several States in the manner now provided by law and in accordance with the formulas set forth in section 4 of

the Federal-Aid Highway Act of 1944; approved December 20, 1944 (58 Stat. 838): Provided, That the additional amount herein authorized for the fiscal year ending June 30, 1957, shall be apportioned immediately upon enactment of this Act.

(b) AVAILABILITY FOR EXPENDITURE.—Any sums apportioned to any State under this section shall be available for expenditure in that State for two years after the close of the fiscal year for which such sums are authorized, and any amounts so apportioned remaining unexpended at the end of such period shall lapse: Provided, That such funds shall be deemed to have been expended if a sum equal to the total of the sums herein and heretofore apportioned to the State is covered by formal agreements with the Secretary of Commerce for construction, reconstruction, or improvement of specific projects as provided in this title and prior Acts: Provided further, That in the case of those sums heretofore, herein, or hereafter apportioned to any State for projects on the Federal-aid secondary highway system, the Secretary of Commerce may, upon the request of any State, discharge his responsibility relative to the plans, specifications, estimates, surveys, contract awards, design, inspection, and construction of such secondary road projects by his receiving and approving a certified statement by the State highway department setting forth that the plans, design, and construction for such projects are in accord with the standards and procedures of such State applicable....

SEC. 108. NATIONAL SYSTEM OF INTERSTATE AND DEFENSE HIGHWAYS.

(a) INTERSTATE SYSTEM.—It is hereby declared to be essential to the national interest to provide for the early completion of the "National System of Interstate Highways", as authorized and designated in accordance with section 7 of the Federal-Aid Highway Act of 1944 (58 Stat. 838). It is the intent of the Congress that the Interstate System be completed as nearly as practicable over a thirteen-year period and that the entire System in all the States be brought to simultaneous completion. Because of its primary importance to the national defense, the name of such system is hereby changed to the "National System of Interstate and Defense Highways". Such National System of Interstate and Defense Highways is hereinafter in this Act referred to as the "Interstate System".

(b) AUTHORIZATION OF APPROPRIATIONS. —For the purpose of expediting the construction, reconstruction, or improvement, inclusive of necessary bridges and tunnels, of the interstate System, including extensions

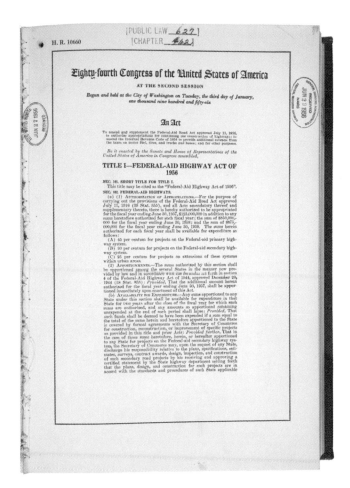

thereof through urban areas, designated in accordance with the provisions of section 7 of the Federal-Aid Highway Act of 1944 (58 Stat. 838), there is hereby authorized to be appropriated the additional sum of $1,000,000,000 for the fiscal year ending June 30, 1957, which sum shall be in addition to the authorization heretofore made for that year, the additional sum of $1,700,000,000 for the fiscal year ending June 30, 1958, the additional sum of $2,000,000,000 for the fiscal year ending June 30, 1959, the additional sum of $2,200,000,000 for the fiscal year ending June 30, 1960, the additional sum of $2,200,000,000 for the fiscal year ending June 30, 1961, the additional sum of $2,200,000,000 for the fiscal year ending June 30, 1962, the additional sum of $2,200,000,000 for the fiscal year ending June 30, 1963, the additional sum of $2,200,000,000 for the fiscal year ending June 30, 1964, the additional sum of $2,200,000,000 for the fiscal year ending June 30, 1965, the additional sum of $2,200,000,000 for the fiscal year ending June 30, 1966, the additional sum of $2,200,000,000 for the fiscal year ending June 30, 1967, the additional sum of $1,500,000,000 for the fiscal year ending June 30, 1968, and the additional sum of $1,025,000,000 for the fiscal year ending June 30, 1969....

1957

EXECUTIVE ORDER 10730:
DESEGREGATION OF
CENTRAL HIGH SCHOOL

On May 17, 1954, the U.S. Supreme Court ruled in Brown v. Board of Education *that segregated schools were "inherently unequal" and in May 1955 ordered the desegregation of public schools "with all deliberate speed." Consistent with that decision, the Little Rock, Arkansas, school board voted unanimously to desegregate the high school in 1957, followed by the junior high schools, and finally the elementary schools. In September 1957 nine African-American students enrolled at Central High School.*

On September 2, the night before the first day of school, Arkansas Governor Orval Faubus ordered the state's National Guard to surround Central High School to prevent any black students from entering. Faubus claimed that he feared pro-testers would turn violent. President Dwight D. Eisenhower met with the governor in person to discuss the situation. Eisenhower, convinced that Faubus had changed his mind and had agreed to allow the African American students to enroll, permitted the troops to remain at Central High to enforce order and protect the students. But a federal district court, taking into account only the governor's determination to keep the students out of the school, found his claims of impending violence to be without merit, and Faubus withdrew the National Guard.

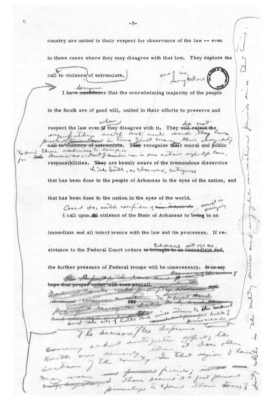

A marked-up page from the third draft of President Eisenhower's Little Rock speech.

A few days later, when nine African American students slipped into the school to enroll, a full-scale riot erupted. Because Faubus failed to check the violence, Eisenhower, as the chief law enforcement officer of the United States, had no choice but to act. He had opposed the Brown decision but in his inaugural oath had sworn to uphold the Constitution. On September 23 he issued an executive order placing the Arkansas National Guard under federal control and sending one thousand U.S. Army paratroopers from the 101st Airborne Division to restore order in Little Rock and enforce the federal court's desegregation order.

At the end of the school year, a federal district court granted the school board's request to postpone desegregation for two and a half years to allow the situation to calm down. The NAACP appealed the decision, and the Supreme Court in Cooper v. Aaron ruled unanimously that desegregation must proceed without delay. The justices emphatically declared that governors and state legislatures must uphold the decisions of the Supreme Court. This was the first significant test of the enforcement of Brown.

EXECUTIVE ORDER

PROVIDING ASSISTANCE FOR THE REMOVAL OF AN OBSTRUCTION

OF JUSTICE WITHIN THE STATE OF ARKANSAS

WHEREAS on September 23, 1957, I issued Proclamation No.

3204 reading in part as follows:

"WHEREAS certain persons in the State of Arkansas, individually and in unlawful assemblages, combinations, and conspiracies, have wilfully obstructed the enforcement of orders of the United States District Court for the Eastern District of Arkansas with respect to matters relating to enrollment and attendance at public schools, particularly at Central High School, located in Little Rock School District, Little Rock, Arkansas; and

"WHEREAS such wilful obstruction of justice hinders the execution of the laws of that state and of the United States, and makes it impracticable to enforce such laws by the ordinary course of judicial proceedings; and

"WHEREAS such obstruction of justice constitutes a denial of the equal protection of the laws secured by the Constitution of the United States and impedes the course of justice under those laws:

"NOW, THEREFORE, I, DWIGHT D. EISENHOWER, President of the United States, under and by virtue of the authority vested in me by the Constitution and statutes of the United States, including Chapter 15 of Title 10 of the United States Code, particularly sections 332, 333 and 334 thereof, do command all persons engaged in such obstruction of justice to cease and desist therefrom, and to disperse forthwith;" and

WHEREAS the command contained in that Proclamation has not

been obeyed and wilful obstruction of enforcement of said court orders

still exists and threatens to continue:

PROVIDING ASSISTANCE FOR THE REMOVAL OF AN OBSTRUCTION OF JUSTICE WITHIN THE STATE OF ARKANSAS

WHEREAS on September 23, 1957, I issued Proclamation No. 3204 reading in part as follows:

"WHEREAS certain persons in the state of Arkansas, individually and in unlawful assemblages, combinations, and conspiracies, have wilfully obstructed the enforcement of orders of the United States District Court for the Eastern District of Arkansas with respect to matters relating to enrollment and attendance at public schools, particularly at Central High School, located in Little Rock School District, Little Rock, Arkansas; and

"WHEREAS such wilful obstruction of justice hinders the execution of the laws of that State and of the United States, and makes it impracticable to enforce such laws by the ordinary course of judicial proceedings; and

"WHEREAS such obstruction of justice constitutes a denial of the equal protection of the laws secured by the Constitution of the United States and impedes the course of justice under those laws:

"NOW, THEREFORE, I, DWIGHT D. EISENHOWER, President of the United States, under and by virtue of the authority vested in me by the Constitution and Statutes of the United States..., do command all persons engaged in such obstruction of justice to cease and desist therefrom, and to disperse forthwith;" and

WHEREAS the command contained in that Proclamation has not been obeyed and wilful obstruction of enforcement of said court orders still exists and threatens to continue:

NOW, THEREFORE, by virtue of the authority vested in me by the Constitution and Statutes of the United States..., It is hereby ordered as follows:

SECTION 1. I hereby authorize and direct the Secretary of Defense to order into the active military service of the United States as he may deem appropriate to carry out the purposes of this Order, any or all of the units of the National Guard of the United States and of the Air National Guard of the United States within the State of Arkansas to serve in the active military service of the United States for an indefinite period and until relieved by appropriate orders.

SEC. 2. The Secretary of Defense is authorized and directed to take all appropriate steps to enforce any orders of the United States District Court for the Eastern District of Arkansas for the removal of obstruction of justice in the State of Arkansas with respect to matters relating to enrollment and attendance at public schools in the Little Rock School District, Little Rock, Arkansas. In carrying out the provisions of this section, the Secretary of Defense is authorized to use the units, and members thereof, ordered into the active military service of the United States pursuant to Section 1 of this Order.

SEC. 3. In furtherance of the enforcement of the aforementioned orders of the United States District Court for the Eastern District of Arkansas, the Secretary of Defense is authorized to use such of the armed forces of the United States as he may deem necessary.

SEC. 4. The Secretary of Defense is authorized to delegate to the Secretary of the Army or the Secretary of the Air Force, or both, any of the authority conferred upon him by this Order.

DWIGHT D. EISENHOWER

THE WHITE HOUSE,

SEPTEMBER 24, 1957.

1961

PRESIDENT DWIGHT D. EISENHOWER'S FAREWELL ADDRESS

*A*s President in the early years of the Cold War, Dwight D. Eisenhower resisted pressure both from the military and the defense industries to increase defense spending. He directed much of his attention as President to peacekeeping efforts. One of his first and most important achievements was the armistice that ended the Korean War. However, he was also convinced that the Soviet Union posed a major threat to the free world, and, for that reason, he agreed to join the arms race. "[W]e can no longer risk emergency improvisation of national defense; we have been compelled to create a permanent armaments industry of vast proportions." "Our arms," he explained, "must be mighty, ready for instant action, so that no potential aggressor may be tempted to risk his own destruction."

At the same time, Eisenhower recognized that the military had formed an alliance with the defense industries and together they could exert tremendous influence over the federal government. He cautioned, "The potential for the disastrous rise of misplaced power exists and will persist," and he warned about the dangers of the "military-industrial complex," a theme that dominated his political farewell to the American people. He delivered the address on January 17, 1961, from the Oval Office of the White House.

MY FELLOW AMERICANS:

Three days from now, after half a century in the service of our country, I shall lay down the responsibilities of office as, in traditional and solemn ceremony, the authority of the Presidency is vested in my successor.

This evening I come to you with a message of leave-taking and farewell, and to share a few final thoughts with you, my countrymen....

Throughout America's adventure in free government, our basic purposes have been to keep the peace; to foster progress in human achievement, and to enhance liberty, dignity and integrity among people and among nations. To strive for less would be unworthy of a free and religious people. Any failure traceable to arrogance, or our lack of comprehension or readiness to sacrifice would inflict upon us grievous hurt both at home and abroad.

Progress toward these noble goals is persistently threatened by the conflict now engulfing the world. It commands our whole attention, absorbs our very beings. We face a hostile ideology—global in scope, atheistic in character, ruthless in purpose, and insidious in method. Unhappily the danger it poses promises to be of indefinite duration. To meet it successfully, there is called for, not so much the emotional and transitory sacrifices of crisis, but rather those which enable us to carry forward steadily, surely, and without complaint the burdens of a prolonged and complex struggle—with liberty at stake. Only thus shall we remain, despite every provocation, on our charted course toward permanent peace and human betterment.

Crises there will continue to be. In meeting them, whether foreign or domestic, great or small, there is a recurring temptation to feel that some spectacular and costly action could become the miraculous solution to all current difficulties. A huge increase in newer elements of our defense; development of unrealistic programs to cure every ill in agriculture; a dramatic expansion in basic and applied research—these and many other possibilities, each possibly promising in itself, may be suggested as the only way to the road we wish to travel.

But each proposal must be weighed in the light of a broader consideration: the need to maintain balance in and among national programs—balance between the private and the public economy, balance between cost and hoped for advantage—balance between the clearly necessary and the comfortably desirable; balance

between our essential requirements as a nation and the duties
imposed by the nation upon the
individual; balance between action
of the moment and the national
welfare of the future. Good judgment seeks balance and progress;
lack of it eventually finds imbal-
ance and frustration.

The record of many decades
stands as proof that our people and
their government have, in the
main, understood these truths and
have responded to them well, in
the face of stress and threat. But
threats, new in kind or degree,
constantly arise. I mention two
only....

Until the latest of our world
conflicts, the United States had no
armaments industry. American
makers of plowshares could, with
time and as required, make swords
as well. But now we can no longer
risk emergency improvisation of
national defense; we have been
compelled to create a permanent
armaments industry of vast proportions. Added to this, three and a half
million men and women are
directly engaged in the defense
establishment. We annually spend
on military security more than the
net income of all United State corporations.

IN THE COUNCILS of government,
we must guard against the acquisition
of unwarranted influence,
whether sought or unsought,
by the military-industrial complex.

The potential for the disastrous
rise of misplaced power
exists and will persist.

WE MUST NEVER let the weight
of this combination endanger
our liberties or democratic processes.

We should take nothing for granted.

15

This conjunction of an immense military establishment and a large arms industry is new in the American
experience. The total influence—economic, political,
even spiritual—is felt in every city, every state house,
every office of the Federal government. We recognize
the imperative need for this development. Yet we must
not fail to comprehend its grave implications. Our toil,
resources and livelihood are all involved; so is the very
structure of our society.

In the councils of government, we must guard
against the acquisition of unwarranted influence,
whether sought or unsought, by the military-industrial
complex. The potential for the disastrous rise of misplaced power exists and will persist.

We must never let the weight of this combination
endanger our liberties or democratic processes. We

should take nothing for granted only an alert and
knowledgeable citizenry can compel the proper mesh-
ing of huge industrial and military machinery of
defense with our peaceful methods and goals, so that
security and liberty may prosper together.

Akin to, and largely responsible for the sweeping
changes in our industrial-military posture, has been the
technological revolution during recent decades.

In this revolution, research has become central; it
also becomes more formalized, complex, and costly. A
steadily increasing share is conducted for, by, or at the
direction of, the Federal government.

Today, the solitary inventor, tinkering in his shop,
has been over shadowed by task forces of scientists in
laboratories and testing fields. In the same fashion, the
free university, historically the fountainhead of free ideas
and scientific discovery, has experienced a revolution

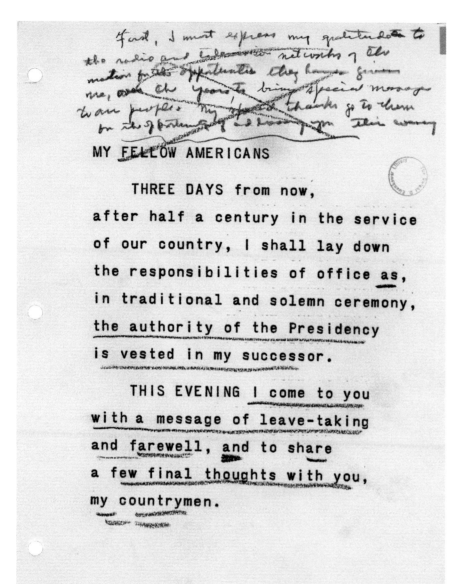

MY FELLOW AMERICANS

THREE DAYS from now,
after half a century in the service
of our country, I shall lay down
the responsibilities of office as,
in traditional and solemn ceremony,
the authority of the Presidency
is vested in my successor.

THIS EVENING I come to you
with a message of leave-taking
and farewell, and to share
a few final thoughts with you,
my countrymen.

in the conduct of research. Partly because of the huge costs involved, a government contract becomes virtually a substitute for intellectual curiosity. For every old blackboard there are now hundreds of new electronic computers.

The prospect of domination of the nation's scholars by Federal employment, project allocations, and the power of money is ever present and is gravely to be regarded.

Yet, in holding scientific research and discovery in respect, as we should, we must also be alert to the equal and opposite danger that public policy could itself become the captive of a scientific-technological elite.

It is the task of statesmanship to mold, to balance, and to integrate these and other forces, new and old, within the principles of our democratic system—ever aiming toward the supreme goals of our free society.

Another factor in maintaining balance involves the element of time. As we peer into society's future, we—you and I, and our government—must avoid the impulse to live only for today, plundering, for our own ease and convenience, the precious resources of tomorrow. We cannot mortgage the material assets of our grandchildren without risking the loss also of their political and spiritual heritage. We want democracy to survive for all generations to come, not to become the insolvent phantom of tomorrow.

Down the long lane of the history yet to be written America knows that this world of ours, ever growing smaller, must avoid becoming a community of dreadful fear and hate, and be, instead, a proud confederation of mutual trust and respect.

Such a confederation must be one of equals. The weakest must come to the conference table with the same confidence as do we, protected as we are by our moral, economic, and military strength....

Disarmament, with mutual honor and confidence, is a continuing imperative. Together we must learn how to compose difference, not with arms, but with intellect and decent purpose....

So—in this my last good night to you as your President—I thank you for the many opportunities you have given me for public service in war and peace. I trust that in that service you find some things worthy; as for the rest of it, I know you will find ways to improve performance in the future....

1961

PRESIDENT JOHN F. KENNEDY'S
INAUGURAL ADDRESS

*J*ohn F. Kennedy assumed the Presidency at the height of the Cold War. Tensions between the two great powers—the United States and Soviet Union—had shaped Dwight Eisenhower's policies and would dominate Kennedy's own short term in office. Well aware that his inaugural address would not only set the tone but, in all probability, chart the course for his administration, Kennedy meticulously crafted a speech that captured his vision for America and the world.

The President began writing in late November, shortly after his election. He wanted this address to focus on foreign policy, on his vision for the country, and to avoid partisan rhetoric. Friends and advisers helped with the speechwriting and made suggestions, but the final result was clearly the work of Kennedy himself.

The inauguration ceremony, held at the Capitol, took place on January 20, 1961. It had snowed eight inches the day before, and 700 plows had cleared the streets on the morning of the inauguration. Despite the freezing temperatures, thousands of people watched as Chief Justice Earl Warren administered the oath of office and then listened to Kennedy's compelling message. Looking beyond the nation's borders, Kennedy called on the United States to combat "tyranny, poverty, disease, and war itself." The memorable climax of the speech came when he said to his fellow Americans, "Ask not what your country can do for you—ask what you can do for your country."

We observe today not a victory of party but a celebration of freedom—symbolizing an end as well as a beginning—signifying renewal as well as change. For I have sworn before you and Almighty God the same solemn oath our forebears prescribed nearly a century and three-quarters ago.

The world is very different now. For man holds in his mortal hands the power to abolish all forms of human poverty and all forms of human life. And yet the same revolutionary beliefs for which our forebears fought are still at issue around the globe—the belief that the rights of man come not from the generosity of the state but from the hand of God.

We dare not forget today that we are the heirs of that first revolution. Let the word go forth from this time and place, to friend and foe alike, that the torch has been passed to a new generation of Americans—born in this century, tempered by war, disciplined by a hard and bitter peace, proud of our ancient heritage—and unwilling to witness or permit the slow undoing of those human rights to which this nation has always been committed, and to which we are committed today at home and around the world.

Let every nation know, whether it wishes us well or ill, that we shall pay any price, bear any burden, meet any hardship, support any friend, oppose any foe to assure the survival and the success of liberty.

This much we pledge—and more.

Chief Justice Earl Warren administers the oath of office to Kennedy, whose wife Jacqueline and predecessor, Dwight Eisenhower, stand just behind Warren.

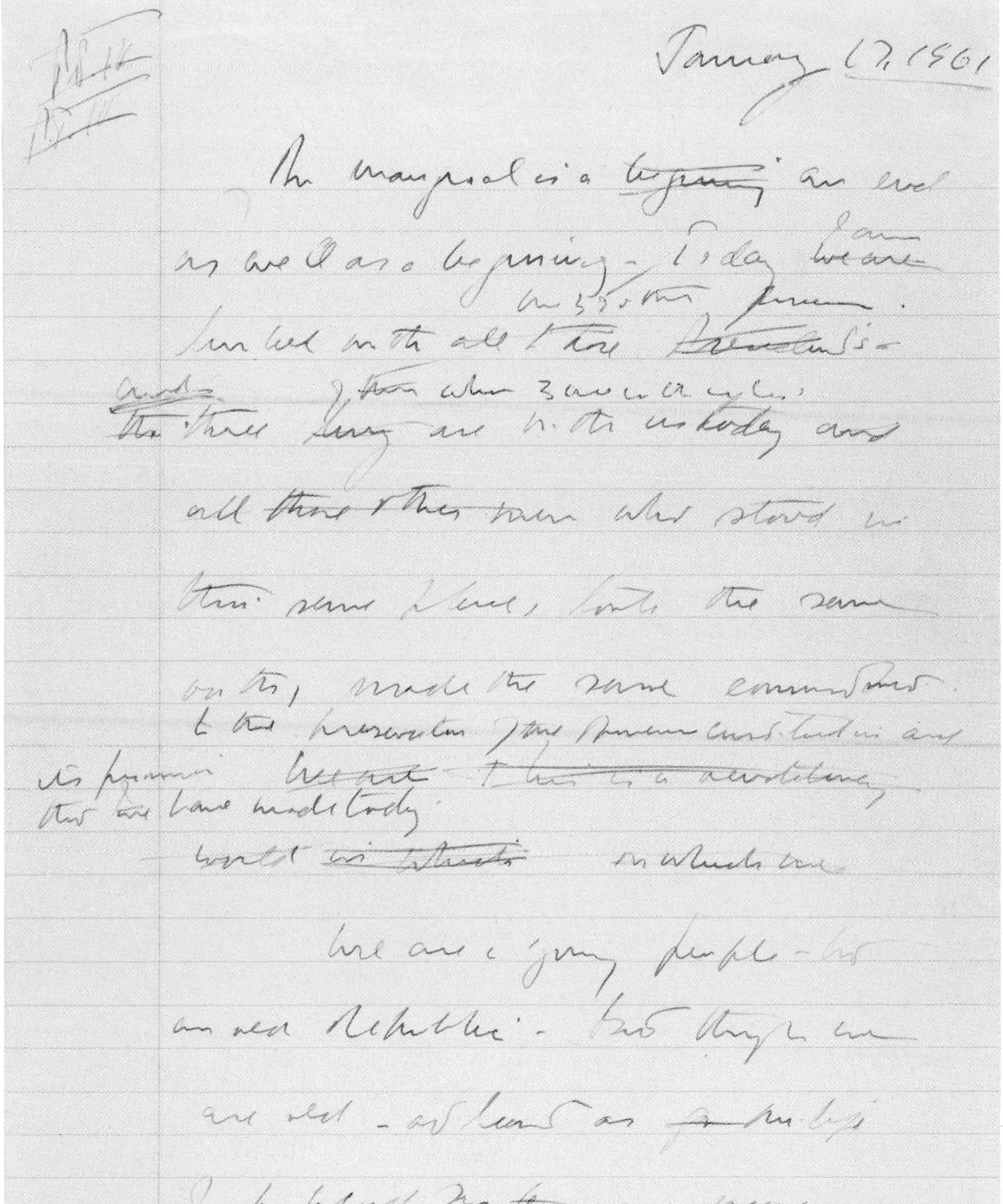

January 17, 1961

The inaugural is a ~~beginning~~ an end
as well as a beginning - Today ~~we are~~ I am
the 35th person
involved with all those [illegible]
and [illegible]
~~the~~ three [illegible] are with us today and
all ~~those other~~ men who stood in
this same place, took the same
oath, made the same commitment
to the preservation of the American constitution and
its promises ~~[illegible]~~ ~~[illegible]~~
that we have made today.
~~world~~ ~~[illegible]~~ [illegible]

We are a young people - but
an old Republic - but though we
are old - at least as ~~[illegible]~~
[illegible] political systems are measured,
we must not forget that we
~~[illegible]~~ ~~[illegible]~~ we are descended
from rebels & traitors - & stand in succession

To those old allies whose cultural and spiritual origins we share, we pledge the loyalty of faithful friends. United there is little we cannot do in a host of cooperative ventures. Divided there is little we can do—for we dare not meet a powerful challenge at odds and split asunder.

To those new states whom we welcome to the ranks of the free, we pledge our word that one form of colonial control shall not have passed away merely to be replaced by a far more iron tyranny. We shall not always expect to find them supporting our view. But we shall always hope to find them strongly supporting their own freedom—and to remember that, in the past, those who foolishly sought power by riding the back of the tiger ended up inside.

To those people in the huts and villages of half the globe struggling to break the bonds of mass misery, we pledge our best efforts to help them help themselves, for whatever period is required—not because the communists may be doing it, not because we seek their votes, but because it is right. If a free society cannot help the many who are poor, it cannot save the few who are rich.

To our sister republics south of our border, we offer a special pledge—to convert our good words into good deeds—in a new alliance for progress—to assist free men and free governments in casting off the chains of poverty. But this peaceful revolution of hope cannot become the prey of hostile powers. Let all our neighbors know that we shall join with them to oppose aggression or subversion anywhere in the Americas. And let every other power know that this Hemisphere intends to remain the master of its own house.

To that world assembly of sovereign states, the United Nations, our last best hope in an age where the instruments of war have far outpaced the instruments of peace, we renew our pledge of support—to prevent it from becoming merely a forum for invective—to strengthen its shield of the new and the weak—and to enlarge the area in which its writ may run.

Finally, to those nations who would make themselves our adversary, we offer not a pledge but a request: that both sides begin anew the quest for peace, before the dark powers of destruction unleashed by science engulf all humanity in planned or accidental self-destruction.

So let us begin anew—remembering on both sides that civility is not a sign of weakness, and sincerity is always subject to proof. Let us never negotiate out of fear. But let us never fear to negotiate.

Let both sides explore what problems unite us instead of belaboring those problems which divide us.

Let both sides, for the first time, formulate serious and precise proposals for the inspection and control of arms—and bring the absolute power to destroy other nations under the absolute control of all nations.

Let both sides seek to invoke the wonders of science instead of its terrors. Together let us explore the stars, conquer the deserts, eradicate disease, tap the ocean depths and encourage the arts and commerce.

And if a beachhead of cooperation may push back the jungle of suspicion, let both sides join in creating a new endeavor, not a new balance of power, but a new world of law, where the strong are just and the weak secure and the peace preserved.

All this will not be finished in the first one hundred days. Nor will it be finished in the first one thousand days, nor in the life of this Administration, nor even perhaps in our lifetime on this planet. But let us begin.

Now the trumpet summons us again—not as a call to bear arms, though arms we need—not as a call to battle, though embattled we are—but a call to bear the burden of a long twilight struggle, year in and year out, "rejoicing in hope, patient in tribulation"—a struggle against the common enemies of man: tyranny, poverty, disease and war itself.

Can we forge against these enemies a grand and global alliance, North and South, East and West, that can assure a more fruitful life for all mankind? Will you join in that historic effort?

In the long history of the world, only a few generations have been granted the role of defending freedom in its hour of maximum danger. I do not shrink from this responsibility—I welcome it. I do not believe that any of us would exchange places with any other people or any other generation. The energy, the faith, the devotion which we bring to this endeavor will light our country and all who serve it—and the glow from that fire can truly light the world.

And so, my fellow Americans: ask not what your country can do for you—ask what you can do for your country.

My fellow citizens of the world: ask not what America will do for you, but what together we can do for the freedom of man.

Finally, whether you are citizens of America or citizens of the world, ask of us here the same high standards of strength and sacrifice which we ask of you. With a good conscience our only sure reward, with history the final judge of our deeds, let us go forth to lead the land we love, asking His blessing and His help, but knowing that here on earth God's work must truly be our own.

1961

EXECUTIVE ORDER 10924:
ESTABLISHMENT OF THE PEACE CORPS

*W*hile campaigning for the Presidency in 1960, Senator John F. Kennedy proposed the idea of a Peace Corps—an organization of volunteers to work in the developing countries of Asia, Africa, and Latin America—to a group of University of Michigan students at a late-night rally. The idea was not new. Senator Hubert Humphrey of Minnesota had proposed establishing a Peace Corps, and his bill had caught the attention of the Massachusetts senator.

Arriving on the Ann Arbor campus at two o'clock in the morning, Kennedy challenged his audience to devote a part of their lives to living and working in Asia, Africa, and Latin America. Within weeks, students organized a petition drive and gathered one thousand signatures in support of the idea. Several hundred others pledged to serve. Enthusiastic letters poured into Democratic Party headquarters, influencing Kennedy's decision to prioritize the establishment of a Peace Corps.

The idea fit well with his vision of a "New Frontier." He sought creative as well as military solutions to the global threat of communism and wanted to improve the image of the United States abroad. Kennedy lost no time in realizing his dream of a Peace Corps. Between his election and inauguration, he asked Sargent Shriver, his brother-in-law, to do a feasibility study. "We received more letters from people offering to work in or to volunteer for the Peace Corps," Shriver recalls, "than for all other existing agencies." Within two months of taking office, Kennedy issued an executive order establishing the Peace Corps and appointed Shriver to head the new agency. In September 1961, with volunteers already in the field, Congress passed legislation establishing the Peace Corps and appropriated funds for its operation.

Since the founding of the Peace Corps, more than 168,000 citizens of all ages and backgrounds have worked in more than 130 countries throughout the world as volunteers in such fields as health, teaching, agriculture, urban planning, skilled trades, forestry, sanitation, and technology.

EXECUTIVE ORDER 10924
ESTABLISHMENT AND ADMINISTRATION OF THE PEACE CORPS IN THE DEPARTMENT OF STATE

By virtue of the authority vested in me by the Mutual Security Act of 1954, as amended, and as President of the United States, it is hereby ordered as follows:

SECTION 1. Establishment of the Peace Corps. The Secretary of State shall establish an agency in the Department of State which shall be known as the Peace Corps. The Peace Corps shall be headed by a Director.

SEC. 2. Functions of the Peace Corps. (a) The Peace Corps shall be responsible for the training and service abroad of men and women of the United States in new programs of assistance to nations and areas of the world, and in conjunction with or in support of existing economic assistance programs of the United States and of the United Nations and other international organizations.

(b) The Secretary of State shall delegate, or cause to be delegated, to the Director of the Peace Corps such of the functions under the Mutual Security Act of 1954, as amended, vested in the President and delegated to the Secretary, or vested in the Secretary, as the Secretary shall deem necessary for the accomplishment of the purposes of the Peace Corps.

SEC. 3. Financing of the Peace Corps. The Secretary of State shall provide for the financing of the

Peace Corps with funds available to the Secretary for the performance of functions under the Mutual Security Act of 1954, as amended.

SEC. 4. Relation to Executive Order No. 10893. This order shall not be deemed to supersede or derogate from any provision of Executive Order No. 10893 of November 8, 1960, as amended, and any delegation made by or pursuant to this order shall, unless otherwise specifically provided therein, be deemed to be in addition to any delegation made by or pursuant to that order.

JOHN F. KENNEDY

THE WHITE HOUSE,

MARCH 1, 1961.

EXECUTIVE ORDER

- - - - - - - - - - - - -

ESTABLISHMENT AND ADMINISTRATION OF THE PEACE CORPS
IN THE DEPARTMENT OF STATE

By virtue of the authority vested in me by the Mutual Security Act of 1954, 68 Stat. 832, as amended (22 U.S.C. 1750 et seq.), and as President of the United States, it is hereby ordered as follows:

Section 1. Establishment of the Peace Corps. The Secretary of State shall establish an agency in the Department of State which shall be known as the Peace Corps. The Peace Corps shall be headed by a Director.

Section 2. Functions of the Peace Corps. (a) The Peace Corps shall be responsible for the training and service abroad of men and women of the United States in new programs of assistance to nations and areas of the world, and in conjunction with or in support of existing economic assistance programs of the United States and of the United Nations and other international organizations.

(b) The Secretary of State shall delegate, or cause to be delegated, to the Director of the Peace Corps such of the functions under the Mutual Security Act of 1954, as amended, vested in the President and delegated to the Secretary, or vested in the Secretary, as the Secretary shall deem necessary for the accomplishment of the purposes of the Peace Corps.

Section 3. Financing of the Peace Corps. The Secretary of State shall provide for the financing of the Peace Corps with funds available

1962

JOHN GLENN'S OFFICIAL COMMUNICATION WITH THE COMMAND CENTER

*S*oviet scientists stunned the world on October 4, 1957, when they launched a 184-pound satellite, Sputnik I, into orbit around the earth. A month later they placed a larger satellite, weighing 1,120 pounds and carrying a dog, into orbit. The military significance of the Soviets' achievement was obvious. If they could send heavy objects into outer space, they could certainly reach the United States with intercontinental missiles carrying nuclear warheads. The Russians' surprising achievement ignited a space race between the United States and the Soviet Union. American scientists then reclaimed some prestige by launching Explorer I, a grapefruit-sized (2.5 pounds) satellite, into orbit on January 31, 1958. Following a series of unmanned launches, the Soviets sent the first man into space on April 12, 1961. Less than a month later, on May 5, Alan B. Shepard, Jr., became the first American in space.

On February 20, 1962, John Glenn became the first astronaut to orbit the earth. Encased in a bulky pressurized suit, strapped into his seat, and crammed into a tiny capsule, Glenn traveled at 17,500 miles per hour, 160 miles above Earth. Two major challenges confronted him during his flight. The autopilot failed, forcing him to fly the plane manually. Then questions arose about whether the capsule's life-saving heat shield would hold during reentry. During the second orbit, a signal warned that the heat shield was loose. Mission Control decided to take no chances and ordered Glenn to retain the retropack to hold the heat shield in place. Under normal conditions, the retropack would have been jettisoned after the rockets were fired to slow the capsule for reentry. While struggling to maintain control of the spacecraft, Glenn watched as huge chunks flew past the window and wondered whether the retropack or the heat shield was breaking up. The heat shield held, and Glenn's capsule splashed down safely after five hours in space.

President John F. Kennedy, responding to the tremendous wave of popular enthusiasm for space exploration that resulted, then proposed a new challenge: to send a man to the Moon.

CC [Capsule Communicator] This is Texas Cap Com, Friendship 7. We are recommending that you leave the retropackage on through the entire reentry. This means that you will have to override the 05g switch which is expected to occur at 04 43 _3. This also means that you will have to manually retract the scope. Do you read?

P This is Friendship 7. What is the reason for this? Do you have any reason? Over.

CC Not at this time; this is the judgement of Cape Flight.

P Ah, Roger. Say again your instructions please. Over.

CC We are recommending that the retropackage not, I say again, not be jettisoned. This means that you will have to override the 05g switch which is expected to occur at 04 43 53. This is approximately 4-1/2 minutes from now. This also means that you will have to retract the scope manually. Do you understand?

P [pilot] Ah, Roger, understand. I will have to make a manual 05g entry when it occurs, and bring the scope in, ah, manually. Is that affirm?

CC That is affirmative, Friendship 7....

In this transcript, column one shows the elapsed time from the launch of the spacecraft in hours, minutes, and seconds. Column two is the duration in seconds of the communication. Column three identifies the communicator as follows: CC is the Capsule (spacecraft) Communicator at the range station; P is the Pilot (astronaut); and CT is the Communications Technician at the range station. Times are expressed in hours, minutes, and seconds (e.g., 04 43 2 means 4 hours, 43 minutes, and 2 seconds from instant of lift-off).

CC Ah, Friendship 7, this is Cape. Over.

P Go ahead, Cape. Friend 7.

CC Ah, recommend you go to reentry attitude and retract the scope manually at this time.

P Ah, Roger, retracting scope manually.

CC While you're doing that, we are not sure whether or not your landing bag has deployed. We feel it is possible to reenter with the retropackage on. Ah, we see no difficulty at this time in that type of reentry. Over....

P This is Friendship 7. I'm on straight manual control at present time. This was, ah, still kicking in and out of orientation mode, mainly in yaw, ah, following retrofire, so I am on straight manual now. I'll back it up—

CC —on reentry....

CC Ah, Seven, this is Cape. The weather in the recovery area is excellent, 3-foot waves, only one-tenth cloud coverage, 10 miles visibility....

P This is Friendship 7. I think the pack just let go.

P This is Friendship 7. A real fireball outside....

P Hello, Cape. Friendship 7. Do you receive? Over.

CC —How do you read? Over.

P Loud and clear; how me?

CC Roger, reading you loud and clear. How are you doing?

---

100   CAL-TEX-3

04 36 56	0.4	CC	Roger.
04 37 00	9.6	P	There is quite a bit of cloud cover down in this area. I can, ah, right on track, I can only see certain areas. I can see quite a bit on up to the north, however.
04 37 18	2.4	P	This is Friendship 7, going to manual control.
04 37 21	1.3	CC	Ah, Roger, Friendship 7.
04 37 23	2.7	P	This is banging in and out here; I'll just control it manually.
04 37 25	0.4	CC	Roger.
04 37 48	3.1	CC	Friendship 7, Guaymas Cap Com, reading you loud and clear.
04 37 51	2.1	P	Roger, Guaymas, read you loud and clear also.

TEXAS

04 38 06	4.0	CT	Friendship 7, Friendship 7, this is Texas Com Tech. Do you read? Over.
04 38 10	1.3	P	Roger, Texas, go ahead.
04 38 13	3.9	CT	Ah, Roger. Reading you 5 square. Standby for Texas Cap Com.
04 38 16	0.4	P	Roger.
04 38 25	23.8	CC	This is Texas Cap Com, Friendship 7. We are recommending that you leave the retropackage on through the entire reentry. This means that you will have to override the 05g switch which is expected to occur at 04 43 3. This also means that you will have to manually retract the scope. Do you read?
04 38 49	4.0	P	This is Friendship 7. What is the reason for this? Do you have any reason? Over.
04 38 53	3.6	CC	Not at this time; this is the judgement of Cape Flight.
04 38 58	2.6	P	Ah, Roger. Say again your instructions please. Over.
04 39 01	22.1	CC	We are recommending that the retropackage not, I say again, not be jettisoned. This means that you will have to override the 05g switch which is expected to occur at 04 43 53. This is approximately 4-1/2 minutes from now. This also means that you will have to retract the scope manually. Do you understand?

P Oh, pretty good.

CC Roger. Your impact point is within one mile of the up-range destroyer....

P Okay, we're through the peak g now.

CC Ah, Seven, this is Cape. What's your general condition? Are you feeling pretty well?

P My condition is good, but that was a real fireball, boy.

P I had great chunks of that retropack breaking off all the way through.

CC Very good; it did break off, is that correct?

P Roger. Altimeter off the peg indicating 80 thousand.

CC Roger, reading you loud and clear.

1962

AERIAL PHOTOGRAPH OF MISSILES IN CUBA

*T*hroughout 1962 American intelligence officials became increasingly suspicious of the movement of Soviet personnel and equipment to Cuba. As a result, U.S. ships and planes began photographing every Cuba-bound Soviet vessel, and U-2 spy planes flew regular reconnaissance over the island, just 90 miles off the coast of Florida. On September 13, President John F. Kennedy warned Soviet Premier Nikita Khrushchev: "If at any time the Communist build-up in Cuba were to endanger or interfere with our security in any way...or if Cuba should ever...become an offensive military base of significant capacity for the Soviet Union, then this

MRBM LAUNCH SITE 2
SAN CRISTOBAL
1 NOVEMBER 1962

FUEL TRAILERS

MISSILE-READY TENT

FORMER LAUNCH POSITIONS

FORMER LOCATION OF MISSILE-READY TENTS

country will do whatever must be done to protect its own security and that of its allies." Despite Kennedy's warnings, the Soviets continued to construct the bases, and the United States continued to monitor their activities.

During the week of October 7, 1962, bad weather prevented American planes from flying over Cuba. However, Sunday morning, October 14, was cloudless, and a U-2 flight crew took photographs that, over the next few days, experts analyzed and reanalyzed. The photos provided positive proof of what the United States had for months suspected: The Soviet Union was installing medium-range nuclear weapons in Cuba. These missiles were capable of striking major American cities and killing millions of Americans within minutes. This discovery led to the first direct confrontation between the two superpowers involving nuclear weapons.

Kennedy relied heavily on members of the Executive Committee (Ex Comm) of the National Security Council throughout the Cuban Missile Crisis. The group assembled on October 16 and met daily—often several times—over the next thirteen days. All recognized the importance of their role as they weighed the alternatives and possible responses.

After consulting with the Ex Comm, President Kennedy decided that he needed to inform the American people of the situation. He laid out the facts in a televised address on October 22, 1962. By that time he had concluded that the best option was a "quarantine," or a limited naval blockade of Cuba. This decision, strengthened by the photographic evidence, received widespread support from Latin America and other U.S. allies.

Despite hopes for avoiding military action, the Pentagon prepared for air strikes and a land invasion. In the meantime the administration communicated almost daily with Soviet Premier Khrushchev. Several Soviet vessels turned back from the quarantine line, and during a televised confrontation with the Soviet Union at the United Nations, the United States presented photographic proof of the missiles.

In public the Soviet leader continued to defend his actions. In private Khrushchev acknowledged the grave danger of the situation and searched for a solution that would preserve his nation's honor. On October 27, Kennedy received a letter from Khrushchev that opened the door for a peaceful resolution. In return for assurances that the United States would not attack Cuba and would lift the blockade, Khrushchev promised to send no more missiles and to remove those that were already in Cuba. A second letter, which arrived the next day, was less accommodating. However, Kennedy, on the advice of his brother Robert, the attorney general, chose to agree to the initial offer. The President also agreed to dismantle several obsolete air and missile bases in Turkey.

Through peaceful negotiations, Kennedy and Khrushchev had averted nuclear war. On November 20, the President announced, "I have today been informed by Chairman Khrushchev that all of the IL-28 bombers in Cuba will be withdrawn in thirty days. . . . I have this afternoon instructed the Secretary of Defense to lift our naval quarantine."

1963
TEST BAN TREATY

*T*he development of atomic and hydrogen bombs and the repeated testing of these devices by nuclear powers raised serious concerns about the harmful effects of radioactive fallout. Over time, knowledge about the nature and effects of fallout increased, making it clear that radioactive debris from nuclear testing would involve every region in the world. Both scientists and the general public expressed fear about contamination of the environment and potential genetic damage.

In May 1955 the Subcommittee of Five (the United States, the United Kingdom, Canada, France, and the Soviet Union) of the United Nations Disarmament Commission began work on an international agreement to end nuclear testing. The agreement took eight years to complete. Committee members had to address complex technical problems regarding verification, reconcile major differences in approaches to arms control and security issues, and cope with regular fluctuations in East-West relationships. The nuclear powers signed the Test Ban Treaty in Moscow on

August 5, 1963; the United States Senate ratified it on September 24, 1963; and the treaty went into effect on October 11, 1963. It prohibits nuclear weapons tests "or any other nuclear explosion" in the atmosphere, in outer space, and under water. Although it does not ban all underground tests, the treaty prohibits such explosions if they cause "radioactive debris to be present outside the territorial limits of the State under whose jurisdiction or control" the explosions were conducted.

The treaty curtailed but did not eliminate nuclear tests. In accepting limitations on testing, the nuclear powers accepted as a common goal "an end to the contamination of man's environment by radioactive substances."

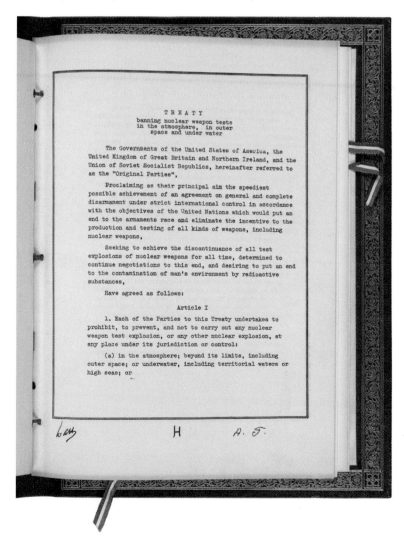

At the Atomic Energy Commission Proving Ground in Nevada, Marines prepare to charge an "objective" seconds after an atomic explosion. This high-security test took place in May 1952.

TREATY BANNING NUCLEAR WEAPON TESTS IN THE ATMOSPHERE, IN OUTER SPACE AND UNDER WATER

The Governments of the United States of America, the United Kingdom of Great Britain and Northern Ireland, and the Union of Soviet Socialist Republics, hereinafter referred to as the "Original Parties,"

Proclaiming as their principal aim the speediest possible achievement of an agreement on general and complete disarmament under strict international control in accordance with the objectives of the United Nations which would put an end to the armaments race and eliminate the incentive to the production and testing of all kinds of weapons, including nuclear weapons,

Seeking to achieve the discontinuance of all test explosions of nuclear weapons for all time, determined to continue negotiations to this end, and desiring to put an end to the contamination of man's environment by radioactive substances,

Have agreed as follows:

ARTICLE I

1. Each of the Parties to this Treaty undertakes to prohibit, to prevent, and not to carry out any nuclear weapon test explosion, or any other nuclear explosion, at any place under its jurisdiction or control:

(a) in the atmosphere; beyond its limits, including outer space; or under water, including territorial waters or high seas; or

(b) in any other environment if such explosion causes radioactive debris to be present outside the territorial limits of the State under whose jurisdiction or control such explosion is conducted. It is understood in this connection that the provisions of this subparagraph are without prejudice to the conclusion of a Treaty resulting in the permanent banning of all nuclear test explosions, including all such explosions underground, the conclusion of which, as the Parties have stated in the Preamble to this Treaty, they seek to achieve.

2. Each of the Parties to this Treaty undertakes furthermore to refrain from causing, encouraging, or in any way participating in, the carrying out of any nuclear weapon test explosion, or any other nuclear explosion, anywhere which would take place in any of the environments described, or have the effect referred to, in paragraph 1 of this Article.

ARTICLE II

1. Any Party may propose amendments to this Treaty. The text of any proposed amendment shall be submitted to the Depositary Governments which shall circulate it to all Parties to this Treaty. Thereafter, if requested to do so by one-third or more of the Parties, the Depositary Governments shall convene a conference, to which they shall invite all the Parties, to consider such amendment.

2. Any amendment to this Treaty must be approved by a majority of the votes of all the Parties to this Treaty, including the votes of all of the Original Parties. The amendment shall enter into force for all Parties upon the deposit of instruments of ratification by a majority of all the Parties, including the instruments of ratification of all of the Original Parties.

ARTICLE III

1. This Treaty shall be open to all States for signature. Any State which does not sign this Treaty before its entry into force in accordance with paragraph 3 of this Article may accede to it at any time.

2. This Treaty shall be subject to ratification by signatory States. Instruments of ratification and instruments of accession shall be deposited with the Governments of the Original Parties—the United States of America, the United Kingdom of Great Britain and Northern Ireland, and the Union of Soviet Socialist Republics—which are hereby designated the Depositary Governments.

3. This Treaty shall enter into force after its ratification by all the Original Parties and the deposit of their instruments of ratification.

4. For States whose instruments of ratification or accession are deposited subsequent to the entry into force of this Treaty, it shall enter into force on the date of the deposit of their instruments of ratification or accession.

5. The Depositary Governments shall promptly inform all signatory and acceding States of the date of each signature, the date of deposit of each instrument of ratification of and accession to this Treaty, the date of its entry into force, and the date of receipt of any requests for conferences or other notices.

6. This Treaty shall be registered by the Depositary Governments pursuant to Article 102 of the Charter of the United Nations.

ARTICLE IV

This Treaty shall be of unlimited duration.

Each Party shall in exercising its national sovereignty have the right to withdraw from the Treaty if it decides that extraordinary events, related to the subject matter of this Treaty, have jeopardized the supreme interests of its country. It shall give notice of such withdrawal to all other Parties to the Treaty three months in advance.

ARTICLE V

This Treaty, of which the English and Russian texts are equally authentic, shall be deposited in the archives of the Depositary Governments. Duly certified copies of this Treaty shall be transmitted by the Depositary Governments to the Governments of the signatory and acceding States.

IN WITNESS WHEREOF THE UNDERSIGNED, DULY AUTHORIZED, HAVE SIGNED THIS TREATY.

DONE IN TRIPLICATE AT THE CITY OF MOSCOW THE FIFTH DAY OF AUGUST, ONE THOUSAND NINE HUNDRED AND SIXTY-THREE.

FOR THE GOVERNMENT OF THE UNITED STATES OF AMERICA

DEAN RUSK

FOR THE GOVERNMENT OF THE UNITED KINGDOM OF GREAT BRITAIN AND NORTHERN IRELAND

SIR DOUGLAS HOME

FOR THE GOVERNMENT OF THE UNION OF SOVIET SOCIALIST REPUBLICS

A. GROMYKO

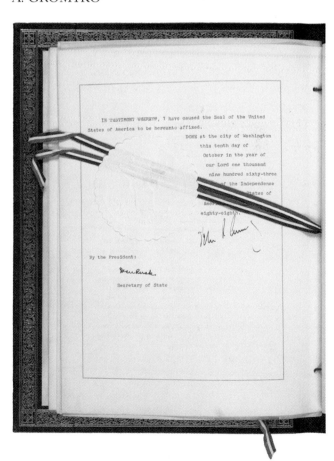

1963

OFFICIAL PROGRAM FOR THE MARCH ON WASHINGTON

*T*he civil rights movement dominated news headlines in 1963. In April police chief "Bull" Connor imprisoned Martin Luther King, Jr., and ordered a brutal attack on nonviolent protestors in Birmingham, Alabama. In June Governor George Wallace barred black students from attending the University of Alabama. President Kennedy, deeply disturbed by these events, decided the time had come to draft federal legislation to guarantee civil rights to all Americans. The night he announced his intentions, a sniper killed NAACP activist Medgar Evers in front of his Mississippi home.

Taking into account the need to win the votes of moderate Republicans, Kennedy's proposal fell short of protecting all the rights of African Americans. Nevertheless, key black leaders welcomed the bill as an important first step but were uncertain whether Congress would pass the law. A. Philip Randolph and Bayard Rustin, longtime activists, decided to organize a March on Washington for Jobs and Freedom. The original plan called for a sit-in at the Capitol until Congress enacted a satisfactory bill. The administration opposed this scheme and pressured civil rights leaders to limit their demonstration to a single day of activities, to culminate in a walk from the Washington Monument to the Lincoln Memorial and a program of speeches and singing. Many, including John Lewis, chairman of the Student Nonviolent Coordinating Committee (SNCC), resented the government's interference.

On August 28, 250,000 Americans assembled on the National Mall. Martin Luther King, Jr., gave the most stirring speech, adding to his prepared remarks a powerful rendition of his dream for America. "I have a dream," he said, "that one day this nation will rise up and live out the true mean-

ing of its creed: 'We hold these truths to be self-evident—that all men are created equal.'" The day ended with a meeting between the march leaders and President Kennedy at the White House. John Lewis recalled: "[W]e met briefly with Kennedy, posed for several

A. Philip Randolph, Bayard Rustin, John Lewis, and other prominent civil rights leaders headed the March on Washington, where thousands of African Americans and white supporters rallied in favor of first-class citizenship for African Americans.

MARCH ON WASHINGTON FOR JOBS AND FREEDOM
AUGUST 28, 1963

LINCOLN MEMORIAL PROGRAM

1. The National Anthem — *Led by* Marian Anderson.

2. Invocation — The Very Rev. Patrick O'Boyle, *Archbishop of Washington.*

3. Opening Remarks — A. Philip Randolph, *Director March on Washington for Jobs and Freedom.*

4. Remarks — Dr. Eugene Carson Blake, *Stated Clerk, United Presbyterian Church of the U.S.A.; Vice Chairman, Commission on Race Relations of the National Council of Churches of Christ in America.*

5. Tribute to Negro Women Fighters for Freedom — Mrs. Medgar Evers
  Daisy Bates
  Diane Nash Bevel
  Mrs. Medgar Evers
  Mrs. Herbert Lee
  Rosa Parks
  Gloria Richardson

6. Remarks — John Lewis, *National Chairman, Student Nonviolent Coordinating Committee.*

7. Remarks — Walter Reuther, *President, United Automobile, Aerospace and Agricultural Implement Wokers of America, AFL-CIO; Chairman, Industrial Union Department, AFL-CIO.*

8. Remarks — James Farmer, *National Director, Congress of Racial Equality.*

9. Selection — Eva Jessye *Choir*

10. Prayer — Rabbi Uri Miller, *President Synagogue Council of America.*

11. Remarks — Whitney M. Young, Jr., *Executive Director, National Urban League.*

12. Remarks — Mathew Ahmann, *Executive Director, National Catholic Conference for Interracial Justice.*

13. Remarks — Roy Wilkins, *Executive Secretary, National Association for the Advancement of Colored People.*

14. Selection — Miss Mahalia Jackson

15. Remarks — Rabbi Joachim Prinz, *President American Jewish Congress.*

16. Remarks — The Rev. Dr. Martin Luther King, Jr., *President, Southern Christian Leadership Conference.*

17. The Pledge — A Philip Randolph

18. Benediction — Dr. Benjamin E. Mays, *President, Morehouse College.*

"WE SHALL OVERCOME"

photographs . . . and exchanged a couple of words each with the President. . . . As for the subject at hand, the civil rights bill . . . the President was noncommittal."

The March on Washington would be remembered as perhaps the most triumphant moment of the civil rights movement. Not only was it the largest demonstration for human rights in United States history, but it also occasioned a rare display of unity among the various civil rights organizations. Although the march did not achieve its immediate goal of passage of civil rights legislation—it would be another year before such legislation was approved—it was a landmark event. On a single summer afternoon, several generations of black leaders representing a spectrum of organizations and viewpoints shared their common commitment to achieving social and political equality, and in doing so, they inspired a nation.

The crowds filled the entire mall from the Capitol to the Lincoln Memorial, which is dwarfed in the background by the Washington Monument.

1964

CIVIL RIGHTS ACT

*P*ersistent, widespread, and often violent resistance to the civil rights movement led President John F. Kennedy to share his concerns with the nation in a televised address on June 6, 1963. "The heart of the question," he asserted, "is whether all Americans are to be afforded equal rights and equal opportunities." By the end of the month, the administration had drafted civil rights legislation that addressed voting rights, public accommodations, school desegregation, and nondiscrimination in federally assisted programs. The bill was modest, its conciliatory

Senator Richard Russell and other Southerners were able to block effective civil rights legislation until 1964, but they were no match for Lyndon Johnson.

goal to win the support of moderate Republicans. Conservatives from both parties led the opposition. In the House of Representatives, the Rules Committee refused to release the bill for consideration by the entire membership. Senate opponents resorted to filibuster.

Following Kennedy's assassination at the end of November, President Johnson exercised his considerable influence over Congress to secure passage of the Civil Rights Act. A native of Texas, Lyndon Johnson had observed racial discrimination firsthand and was committed to ending it. After the House passed the bill in February by a vote of 290 to 130, Johnson turned his attention to moderate Senate Republicans. The support of Senate Minority Leader Everett Dirksen, a moderate Republican from Illinois, was necessary to end the filibuster in the Senate. With the assistance of Democratic Senator Hubert Humphrey of Minnesota, Johnson worked diligently to persuade Dirksen to support the Civil Rights Act. Dirksen exacted concessions, but in early summer finally agreed to back the bill. The final Senate passed it by a vote of 73 to 27, and Johnson signed the act on July 2, 1964.

Reminiscent of the Civil Rights Act of 1875, this law prohibits discrimination in public accommodations, including restaurants, hotels, and theaters. It outlaws job discrimination on the basis of race, gender, religion, and nationality; forbids discrimination by employers and contractors in federally funded programs; and empowers the Equal Employment Opportunity Commission to monitor discrimination in the workplace. The act also authorizes the Justice Department to initiate suits to challenge segregation in schools and other public facilities and to protect the voting rights of blacks.

AN ACT

To enforce the constitutional right to vote, to confer jurisdiction upon the district courts of the United States to provide injunctive relief against discrimination in public accommodations, to authorize the Attorney General to institute suits to protect constitutional rights in public facilities and public education, to extend the Commission on Civil Rights, to prevent discrimination in federally assisted programs, to establish a Commission on Equal Employment Opportunity, and for other purposes.

Be it enacted by the Senate and House of Representatives of the United States of America in Congress assembled, That this Act may be cited as the "Civil Rights Act of 1964".

TITLE I—VOTING RIGHTS

"(2) No person acting under color of law shall—

"(A) in determining whether any individual is qualified under State law or laws to vote in any Federal election, apply any standard, practice, or procedure different from the standards, practices, or procedures applied under such law or laws to other individuals within the same county, parish, or similar political subdivision who have been found by State officials to be qualified to vote;

"(B) deny the right of any individual to vote in any Federal election because of an error or omission on any record or paper relating to any application, registration, or other act requisite to voting, if such error or omission is not material in determining whether such individual is qualified under State law to vote in such election; or

"(C) employ any literacy test as a qualification for voting in any Federal election unless (i) such test is administered to each individual and is conducted wholly in writing, and (ii) a certified copy of the test and of the answers given by the individual is furnished to him within twenty-five days of the submission of his request made within the period of time during which records and papers are required to be retained and preserved pursuant to title III of the Civil Rights Act of 1960. . . ."

TITLE II—INJUNCTIVE RELIEF AGAINST DISCRIMINATION IN PLACES OF PUBLIC ACCOMMODATION

SEC. 201. (a) All persons shall be entitled to the full and equal enjoyment of the goods, services, facilities, and privileges, advantages, and accommodations of any place of public accommodation, as defined in this section, without discrimination or segregation on the ground of race, color, religion, or national origin. . . .

(d) Discrimination or segregation by an establishment is supported by State action within the meaning of this title if such discrimination or segregation (1) is carried on under color of any law, statute, ordinance, or regulation; or (2) is carried on under color of any custom or usage required or enforced by officials of the State or political subdivision thereof; or (3) is required by action of the State or political subdivision thereof.

(e) The provisions of this title shall not apply to a private club or other establishment not in fact open to the public. . . .

TITLE III—DESEGREGATION OF PUBLIC FACILITIES

SEC. 301. (a) Whenever the Attorney General receives a complaint in writing signed by an individual to the effect that he is being deprived of or threatened with the loss of his right to the equal protection of the laws . . . and the Attorney General believes the complaint is meritorious and certifies that the signer or signers of such complaint are unable, in his judgment, to initiate and maintain appropriate legal proceedings for relief . . . the Attorney General is authorized to institute for or in the name of the United States a civil action in any appropriate district court of the United States against such parties and for such relief as may be appropriate. . . .

TITLE IV—DESEGREGATION OF PUBLIC EDUCATION

SURVEY AND REPORT OF EDUCATIONAL OPPORTUNITIES

SEC. 402. The Commissioner [of Education] shall conduct a survey and make a report to the President and the Congress, within two years of the enactment of this title, concerning the lack of availability of equal educational opportunities for individuals by reason of race, color, religion, or national origin in public educational institutions at all levels in the United States, its territories and possessions, and the District of Columbia. . . .

TITLE V—COMMISSION ON CIVIL RIGHTS

"DUTIES OF THE COMMISSION

"SEC. 104. (a) The Commission shall—

"(1) investigate allegations in writing under oath or affirmation that certain citizens of the United States are being deprived of their right to vote and have that vote counted by reason of their color, race, religion, or national origin . . . ;

"(6) Nothing in this or any other Act shall be construed as authorizing the Commission, its Advisory

Committees, or any person under its supervision or control to inquire into or investigate any membership practices or internal operations of any fraternal organization, any college or university fraternity or sorority, any private club or any religious organization."...

TITLE VII—EQUAL EMPLOYMENT OPPORTUNITY

DISCRIMINATION BECAUSE OF RACE, COLOR, RELIGION, SEX, OR NATIONAL ORIGIN

SEC. 703. (a) It shall be an unlawful employment practice for an employer—

(1) to fail or refuse to hire or to discharge any individual, or otherwise to discriminate against any individual with respect to his compensation, terms, conditions, or privileges of employment, because of such individual's race, color, religion, sex, or national origin; or

(2) to limit, segregate, or classify his employees in any way which would deprive or tend to deprive any individual of employment opportunities or otherwise adversely affect his status as an employee, because of such individual's race, color, religion, sex, or national origin....

(c) It shall be an unlawful employment practice for a labor organization—

(1) to exclude or to expel from its membership, or otherwise to discriminate against, any individual because of his race, color, religion, sex, or national origin;

(2) to limit, segregate, or classify its membership, or to classify or fail or refuse to refer for employment any individual, in any way which would deprive or tend to deprive any individual of employment opportunities, or would limit such employment opportunities or otherwise adversely affect his status as an employee or as an applicant for employment, because of such individual's race, color, religion, sex, or national origin; or

(3) to cause or attempt to cause an employer to discriminate against an individual in violation of this section....

EQUAL EMPLOYMENT OPPORTUNITY COMMISSION

SEC. 705. (a) There is hereby created a Commission to be known as the Equal Employment Opportunity Commission, which shall be composed of five members, not more than three of whom shall be members of the same political party, who shall be appointed by the President by and with the advice and consent of the Senate....

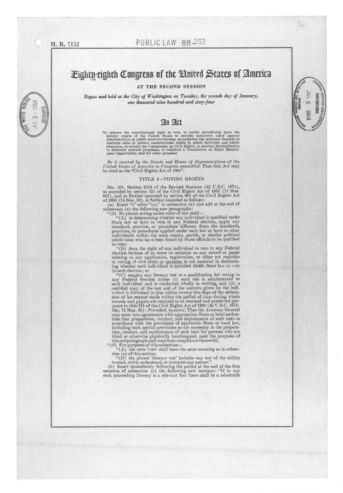

PREVENTION OF UNLAWFUL EMPLOYMENT PRACTICES

SEC. 706. (a) Whenever it is charged in writing under oath...that an employer, employment agency, or labor organization has engaged in an unlawful employment practice, the Commission shall furnish such employer, employment agency, or labor organization... with a copy of such charge and shall make an investigation of such charge.... If the Commission shall determine, after such investigation, that there is reasonable cause to believe that the charge is true, the Commission shall endeavor to eliminate any such alleged unlawful employment practice by informal methods of conference, conciliation, and persuasion....

SEC. 707. (a) Whenever the Attorney General has reasonable cause to believe that any person or group of persons is engaged in a pattern or practice of resistance to the full enjoyment of any of the rights secured by this title,...the Attorney General may bring a civil action in the appropriate district court of the United States....

APPROVED JULY 2, 1964.

1964

TONKIN GULF RESOLUTION

*A*merican involvement in the Vietnam War increased steadily under President Johnson. A critical event leading to this large-scale escalation came on August 2, 1964, when the U.S. destroyer Maddox engaged in a brief naval battle in the Gulf of Tonkin. North Vietnamese patrol boats retaliated. Johnson sent a second destroyer, the C. Turner Joy, into the Gulf, and on August 4, blips on the ship's radar screen seemed to indicate enemy fire. Although there was no evidence of damage to either ship, and the commander raised doubts as to whether an attack had actually occurred, Johnson ordered a major air attack on North Vietnamese torpedo boats and nearby oil storage dumps.

The President's action came in the midst of a political campaign in which his Republican opponent, Senator Barry Goldwater, was charging that he had not adopted a strong enough policy against the communist threat in Southeast Asia. Though they lacked verification, Johnson used these events to ask Congress to authorize him as commander-in-chief to use "all necessary measures" to "repel any armed attacks against the forces of the United States and to prevent further aggression"

in the region. After a brief debate and with only two dissenting votes in the Senate, Congress approved the resolution. Johnson never asked Congress for a formal declaration of war against North Vietnam, but instead relied on the Gulf of Tonkin Resolution as authority for expanding the U.S. role in that conflict. President Nixon, too, claimed that this resolution provided the legal basis for his military policies in Vietnam.

With public opposition to the Vietnam War growing, members of Congress decided to reconsider and, in January 1971, to repeal the Gulf of Tonkin Resolution. In 1973 Congress passed the War Powers Act in an attempt to restrict the President's authority to commit U.S. troops to an extended conflict without congressional approval.

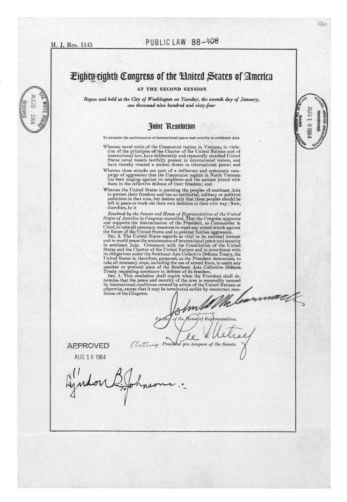

EIGHTY-EIGHTH CONGRESS OF THE UNITED STATES OF AMERICA

AT THE SECOND SESSION

Begun and held at the City of Washington on Tuesday, the seventh day of January, one thousand nine hundred and sixty-four

JOINT RESOLUTION

To promote the maintenance of international peace and security in southeast Asia.

Whereas naval units of the Communist regime in Vietnam, in violation of the principles of the Charter of the United Nations and of international law, have deliberately and repeatedly attacked United Stated naval vessels lawfully present in international waters, and have thereby created a serious threat to international peace; and

Whereas these attackers are part of a deliberate and systematic campaign of aggression that the Communist regime in North Vietnam has been waging against its neighbors and the nations joined with them in the collective defense of their freedom; and

Whereas the United States is assisting the peoples of southeast Asia to protest their freedom and has no territorial, military or political ambitions in that area, but desires only that these people should be left in peace to work out their destinies in their own way: Now, therefore be it

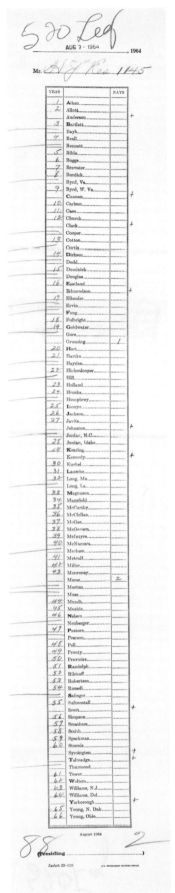

Resolved by the Senate and House of Representatives of the United States of America in Congress assembled, That the Congress approves and supports the determination of the President, as Commander in Chief, to take all necessary measures to repel any armed attack against the forces of the United States and to prevent further aggression.

SECTION 2. The United States regards as vital to its national interest and to world peace the maintenance of international peace and security in southeast Asia. Consonant with the Constitution of the United States and the Charter of the United Nations and in accordance with its obligations under the Southeast Asia Collective Defense Treaty, the United States is, therefore, prepared, as the President determines, to take all necessary steps, including the use of armed force, to assist any member or protocol state of the Southeast Asia Collective Defense Treaty requesting assistance in defense of its freedom.

SECTION 3. This resolution shall expire when the President shall determine that the peace and security of the area is reasonably assured by international conditions created by action of the United Nations or otherwise, except that it may be terminated earlier by concurrent resolution of the Congress.

The tally sheet for the Senate roll call on the Tonkin Gulf Resolution, which took place on August 7, 1964, shows the progress of the voting. Only Senators Wayne Morse and Ernest Gruening dissented.

1965

SOCIAL SECURITY ACT AMENDMENTS

*B*uilding on the success of the 1935 Social Security Act, President Harry Truman proposed legislation to establish a plan for national health insurance. However, the American Medical Association strongly opposed government administration of a health insurance plan, and Congress acquiesced to its warnings of the dangers of "socialized medicine" by refusing to pass the measure. The basic problem did not go away. In fact, statistics showed that the need for national health insurance was increasing. According to the 1950 census, the number of senior citizens in the United States had grown from 3 million in 1900 to 12 million in 1950. Two-thirds of older Americans had incomes of less than $1,000 annually, and only one in eight had health insurance. Between 1950 and 1963, the number of older Americans grew from 12 million to 17.5 million, or from 8.1 to 9.4 percent of the population. During that same period, the cost of hospital care rose at a rate of about 6.7 percent a year, meaning that it was well beyond the means of most older Americans.

President Johnson made health insurance for the elderly a priority and relied on the solid Democratic majority in Congress to secure passage of the legislation to fund it. Medicare, financially supported by an increase in both employer and employee contributions, subsidizes the cost of hospitalization, usually for one hundred days, for most people older than 65. It also includes a voluntary program, paid for jointly by the government and Medicare recipients, which covers the cost of X-ray diagnostic tests, up to one hundred home-nurse visits, and certain doctors' and surgical fees.

House Ways and Means Committee Chairman Wilbur Mills, a Democrat from Arkansas, led a move to insure others in need: individuals on welfare, the blind and disabled, the elderly who do not qualify for Social Security, and families with dependent children. In contrast to Medicare, Medicaid is an "entitlement": if the state provides matching funds, the federal government guarantees annual assistance to program recipients. In signing the Medicare bill, President Johnson observed, "No longer will illness crush and destroy the savings that [older Americans] have so carefully put away over a lifetime so that they might enjoy dignity in their later years."

TITLE I—HEALTH INSURANCE FOR THE AGED AND MEDICAL ASSISTANCE...

SEC. 100. This title may be cited as the "Health Insurance for the Aged Act".

PART 1—HEALTH INSURANCE BENEFITS FOR THE AGED
ENTITLEMENT TO HOSPITAL INSURANCE BENEFITS

SEC. 101. Title II of the Social Security Act is amended by adding at the end thereof the following new section:
"ENTITLEMENT TO HOSPITAL INSURANCE BENEFITS
"**SEC. 226.** (a) Every individual who—

"(1) has attained the age of 65, and (2) is entitled to monthly insurance benefits under section 202 or is a qualified railroad retirement beneficiary, shall be entitled to hospital insurance benefits under part A of title XVIII for each month for which he meets the condition specified in paragraph (2), beginning with the first month after June 1966 for which he meets the conditions specified in paragraphs (1) and (2)....

HOSPITAL INSURANCE BENEFITS AND SUPPLEMENTARY MEDICAL INSURANCE BENEFITS

SEC. 102. (a) The Social Security Act is amended by adding after title XVII the following new title:

"**TITLE XVIII—HEALTH INSURANCE FOR THE AGED**
"PROHIBITION AGAINST ANY FEDERAL INTERFERENCE

"**SEC. 1801.** Nothing in this title shall be construed to authorize any Federal officer or employee to exercise any supervision or control over the practice of medicine or the manner in which medical services are provided, or over the selection, tenure, or compensation of any officer or employee of any institution, agency, or person providing health services; or to exercise any supervision or control over the administration or operation of any such institution, agency, or person.

"FREE CHOICE BY PATIENT GUARANTEED

"SEC. 1802. Any individual entitled to insurance benefits under this title may obtain health services from any institution, agency, or person qualified to participate under this title if such institution, agency, or person undertakes to provide him such services....

"PART A—HOSPITAL INSURANCE BENEFITS FOR THE AGED

"DESCRIPTION OF PROGRAM

"SEC. 1811. The insurance program for which entitlement is established by section 226 provides basic protection against the costs of hospital and related post-hospital services in accordance with this part for individuals who are age 65 or over and are entitled to retirement benefits under title II of this Act or under the railroad retirement system.

"SCOPE OF BENEFITS

"SEC. 1812. (a) The benefits provided to an individual by the insurance program under this part shall consist of entitlement to have payment made on his behalf (subject to the provisions of this part)...
"No Payments to Federal Providers of Services

"(c) No payment may be made under this part (except under subsection (d)) to any Federal provider of services, except a provider of services which the Secretary determines is providing services to the public generally as a community institution or agency; and no such payment may be made to any provider of services for any item or service which such provider is obligated by a law of, or a contract with, the United States to render at public expense.

"Payments for Emergency Hospital Services

"(d) Payments shall also be made to any hospital for inpatient hospital services or outpatient hospital diagnostic services furnished, by the hospital or under arrangements (as defined in section 1861 (w)) with it, to an individual entitled to hospital insurance benefits under section 226 even though such hospital does not have an agreement in effect under this title if (A) such services were emergency services and (B) the Secretary would be required to make such payment if the hospital had such an agreement in effect and otherwise met the conditions of payment hereunder....

"ELIGIBLE INDIVIDUALS

"SEC. 1836. Every individual who—
"(1) has attained the age of 65, and
"(2) (A) is a resident of the United States, and is either (i) a citizen or (ii) an alien lawfully admitted for permanent residence who has resided in the United States continuously during the 5 years immediately preceding the month in which he applies for enrollment under this part, or (B) is entitled to hospital insurance benefits under part A, is eligible to enroll in the insurance program established by this part....

TITLE II—OTHER AMENDMENTS RELATING TO HEALTH CARE

PART 1—MATERNAL AND CHILD HEALTH AND CRIPPLED CHILDREN'S SERVICES

INCREASE IN MATERNAL AND CHILD HEALTH SERVICES...

(b) SECTION 504 of such Act is amended by adding at the end thereof the following new subsection:

"(d) Notwithstanding the preceding provisions of this section, no payment shall be made to any State thereunder for any period after June 30, 1966, unless it makes a satisfactory showing that the State is extending the provision of maternal and child health services in the State with a view to making such services available by July 1, 1975, to children in all parts of the State."

1965

VOTING RIGHTS ACT

*T*he Fifteenth Amendment to the Constitution, ratified in 1870, guarantees that the right to vote cannot be withheld "on account of race, color, or previous condition of servitude." Despite that constitutional mandate, African Americans found themselves essentially disenfranchised by the end of the nineteenth century. Poll taxes, literacy tests, and "grandfather" clauses —which decreed that only men whose grandfathers had been eligible to vote on January 1, 1867, were permitted to vote—prevented blacks from exercising their political rights. Those who attempted to register or cast a ballot risked harassment, intimidation, economic reprisals, and physical violence.

Recognizing the power of the ballot box, civil rights leaders made voting rights a key item on their agendas. Violence against voting-rights activists in 1964 brought the issue to national attention. Working together, President Lyndon Johnson and Congress drafted voting rights legislation that included powerful tools for enforcement.

President Johnson signed the Voting Rights Act on August 6, 1965. The Twenty-Fourth Amendment, which Congress ratified in 1964, had abolished poll taxes, but the Voting Rights Act empowered the attorney general to enforce it. The act outlawed literacy tests and required specified jurisdictions to obtain "pre-clearance" from the attorney general or a federal district judge for any new voting practices and procedures. The law also provided for the appointment of federal examiners and gave them power to register qualified citizens.

The Voting Rights Act of 1965 faced numerous challenges in the courts. Between 1965 and 1969, the Supreme Court issued several key decisions upholding the constitutionality of federal oversight of voting procedures. By the end of 1965, a quarter of a million new black voters had been registered, one-third by federal examiners. By the end of 1966, more than 50 percent of African Americans were registered to vote in nine out of thirteen southern states, and by 1968 nearly 400 blacks held elective office in the South. Congress readopted and strengthened the expired Voting Rights Act in 1970, 1975, and 1982.

AN ACT To enforce the fifteenth amendment to the Constitution of the United States, and for other purposes.

Be it enacted by the Senate and House of Representatives of the United States of America in Congress assembled, That this Act shall be known as the "Voting Rights Act of 1965."

SEC. 2. No voting qualification or prerequisite to voting, or standard, practice, or procedure shall be imposed or applied by any State or political subdivision to deny or abridge the right of any citizen of the United States to vote on account of race or color.

SEC. 3. (a) Whenever the Attorney General institutes a proceeding...the court shall authorize the appointment of Federal examiners by the United States Civil Service Commission...to serve for such period of time and for such political subdivisions as the court shall determine is appropriate to enforce the guarantees of the fifteenth amendment....

(b) If in a proceeding instituted by the Attorney General under any statute to enforce the guarantees of the fifteenth amendment in any State or political subdivision the court finds that a test or device has been used for the purpose or with the effect of denying or abridging the right of any citizen of the United States to vote on account of race or color, it shall suspend the use of tests and devices in such State or political subdivisions as the court shall determine is appropriate and for such period as it deems necessary.

(c) If in any proceeding instituted by the Attorney General ...the court finds that violations of the fifteenth amendment justifying equitable relief have occurred within the territory of such State or political subdivision, the court...shall retain jurisdiction for such period as it may deem appropriate and during such period no voting qualification or prerequisite to voting, or standard, practice, or procedure with respect to voting different from that in force or effect at the time the proceeding was commenced shall be enforced unless and until the court finds that such qualification, prerequisite, standard, practice, or procedure does not have the purpose and will not have the effect of denying or abridging the right to vote on account of race or color....

SEC. 4. (a) To assure that the right of citizens of the United States to vote is not denied or abridged on account of race or color, no citizen shall be denied the right to vote in any Federal, State, or local election because of his failure to comply with any test or device in any State....

(c) The phrase "test or device" shall mean any requirement that a person as a prerequisite for voting or registration for voting (1) demonstrate the ability to read, write, understand, or interpret any matter, (2) demonstrate any educational achievement or his knowledge of any particular subject, (3) possess good moral character, or (4) prove his qualifications by the voucher of registered voters or members of any other class....

(e)(1) Congress hereby declares that to secure the rights under the fourteenth amendment of persons educated in American-flag schools in which the pre-

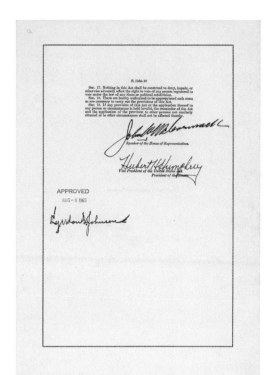

dominant classroom language was other than English, it is necessary to prohibit the States from conditioning the right to vote of such persons on ability to read, write, understand, or interpret any matter in the English language....

SEC. 10. (a) The Congress finds that the requirement of the payment of a poll tax as a precondition to voting (i) precludes persons of limited means from voting or imposes unreasonable financial hardship upon such persons as a precondition to their exercise of the franchise, (ii) does not bear a reasonable relationship to any legitimate State interest in the conduct of elections, and (iii) in some areas has the purpose or effect of denying persons the right to vote because of race or color. Upon the basis of these findings, Congress declares that the constitutional right of citizens to vote is denied or abridged in some areas by the requirement of the payment of a poll tax as a precondition to voting....

SEC. 11. (a) No person acting under color of law shall fail or refuse to permit any person to vote who is entitled to vote under any provision of this Act or is otherwise qualified to vote, or willfully fail or refuse to tabulate, count, and report such person's vote.

(b) No person, whether acting under color of law or otherwise, shall intimidate, threaten, or coerce, or attempt to intimidate, threaten, or coerce any person for voting or attempting to vote, or intimidate, threaten, or coerce, or attempt to intimidate, threaten, or coerce any person for urging or aiding any person to vote or attempt to vote, or intimidate, threaten, or coerce any person for exercising any powers or duties under section 3(a), 6, 8, 9, 10, or 12(e).

(c) Whoever knowingly or willfully gives false information as to his name, address, or period of residence in the voting district for the purpose of establishing his eligibility to register or vote, or conspires with another individual for the purpose of encouraging his false registration to vote or illegal voting, or pays or offers to pay or accepts payment either for registration to vote or for voting shall be fined not more than $10,000 or imprisoned not more than five years, or both....

APPROVED AUGUST 6, 1965.

Further Reading

America's Documents

Bredhoff, Stacey, and John W. Carlin. *American Originals*. Seattle: University of Washington Press, 2001.

Carlton, David L., and Samuel T. McSeveney. *Reading America's History: Selected Historical Documents*. 4th ed. New York: Bedford/St. Martin's, 2000.

Commager, Henry Steele, and Milton Cantor. *Documents of American History*. 10th ed. Englewood Cliffs, N.J.: Prentice Hall, 1988.

Grafton, John. *The Declaration of Independence and Other Great Documents of American History, 1175–1865*. Mineola, N.Y.: Dover, 2000.

Henretta, James A., David Brody, Susan Ware, and Marilynn S. Johnson. *America's History*. 4th ed. New York: Bedford/St. Martin's, 2000.

Levy, Peter B. *100 Key Documents in American Democracy*. Westport, Conn.: Greenwood, 1993.

Miller, Marilyn. *Words That Built a Nation: A Young Person's Collection of Historic American Documents*. New York: Scholastic, 1999.

Lee Resolution and Declaration of Independence

Bullock, Steven C. *The American Revolution: A History in Documents*. New York: Oxford University Press, 2003.

Countryman, Edward. *The American Revolution*. 2nd ed. New York: Hill and Wang, 2003.

Greene, Jack P., and J. R. Pole, eds. *The Blackwell Encyclopedia of the American Revolution*. Cambridge: Blackwell, 1991.

Maier, Pauline. *American Scripture: Making the Declaration of Independence*. New York: Vintage, 1988.

Wills, Garry. *Inventing America: Jefferson's Declaration of Independence*. Boston: Houghton Mifflin, 2002.

Wood, Gordon. *The Creation of the American Republic, 1776–1787*. Chapel Hill: University of North Carolina Press, 1998.

Articles of Confederation

Morris, Richard. *The Forging of the Union, 1781–1789*. New York: HarperCollins, 1988.

Onuf, Peter. *The Origins of the Federal Republic: Jurisdictional Controversies in the United States, 1775–1787*. Philadelphia: University of Pennsylvania Press, 1983.

Rakove, Jack N. *The Beginnings of National Politics: An Interpretive History of the Continental Congress*. Baltimore: Johns Hopkins University Press, 1979.

Treaty of Alliance with France

Hoffman, Ronald, and Peter J. Albert, eds. *Diplomacy and Revolution: The Franco-American Alliance of 1778*. Charlottesville: University Press of Virginia for the United States Capitol Historical Society, 1981.

Stinchcombe, William C. *The American Revolution and the French Alliance*. Syracuse, N.Y.: Syracuse University Press, 1969.

Treaty of Paris

Dull, Jonathan R. *A Diplomatic History of the American Revolution*. New Haven: Yale University Press, 1985.

Hoffman, Ronald, and Peter J. Albert, eds. *Peace and the Peacemakers: The Treaty of 1783*. Charlottesville: University Press of Virginia for the United States Capitol Historical Society, 1986.

Morris, Richard B. *The Peacemakers; The Great Powers and American Independence*. New York: Harper & Row, 1965.

Northwest Ordinance

Onuf, Peter. *Statehood and Union: A History of the Northwest Ordinance*. Midwest History and Culture. Bloomington: Indiana University Press, 1992.

Taylor, Robert M. Jr. *The Northwest Ordinance, 1787: A Bicentennial Handbook*. Indianapolis: Indiana Historical Society, 1987.

Williams, Frederick D., ed. *The Northwest Ordinance: Essays on Its Formation, Provisions, and Legacy*. East Lansing, Mich.: Michigan State University Press, 1989.

Virginia Plan and U.S. Constitution

Beard, Charles A. *An Economic Interpretation of the Constitution*. Union, N.J.: Lawbook Exchange, 2000.

Beeman, Richard, et al., eds. *Beyond Confederation: Origins of the Constitution and American National Identity*. Chapel Hill: University of North Carolina Press, 1987.

Berns, Walter. *Taking the Constitution Seriously*. New York: Simon & Schuster, 1987.

Bernstein, Richard B., with Kym S. Rice. *Are We to Be a Nation?: The Making of the Constitution*. Cambridge, Mass.: Harvard University Press, 1987.

Bowen, Catherine D. *Miracle at Philadelphia: The Story of the Constitutional Convention, May to September 1787*. Boston: Little, Brown, 1986.

Garraty, John A., ed. *Quarrels That Have Shaped the Constitution*. New York: Perennial Library, 1987.

Handlin, Oscar, and Jack Rakove. *James Madison and the Creation of the American Republic*. Boston: Longman, 2001.

Rutland, Robert Allen. *The Ordeal of the Constitution: The Antifederalists and the Ratification Struggle of 1787–1788*. Boston: Northeastern University Press, 1983.

Wood, Gordon. *The Creation of the American Republic, 1776–1787*. Chapel Hill: University of North Carolina Press, 1998.

Federal Judiciary Act

Marcus, Maeva, ed. *Origins of the Federal Judiciary: Essays on the Judiciary Act of 1789*. New York: Oxford University Press, 1992.

Bill of Rights

Bodenhamer, David J., and James W. Ely, eds. *The Bill of Rights in Modern America: After 200 Years*. Bloomington: Indiana University Press, 1993.

Cogan, Neil H., ed. *The Complete Bill of Rights: The Drafts, Debates, Sources, and Origins*. New York: Oxford University Press, 1997.

Cushman, Robert F., ed. *Leading Constitutional Decisions*. 18th ed. Englewood Cliffs, N.J.: Prentice Hall, 1992.

Hentoff, Nat. *The First Freedom: The Tumultuous History of Free Speech in America*. New York: Delacorte, 1988.

Levy, Leonard W. *Origins of the Bill of Rights*. New Haven: Yale University Press, 1999.

Patrick, John J. *The Bill of Rights: A History in Documents*. New York: Oxford University Press, 2003.

George Washington/Farewell Address

Alden, John. *George Washington: A Biography*. Baton Rouge: Louisiana State University Press, 1984.

Smith, Richard Norton. *Patriarch: George Washington and the New American Nation*. New York: Mariner Books, 1997.

Spalding, Matthew, et al. *A Sacred Union of Citizens: George Washington's Farewell Address and the American Character*. Lanham, Md.: Rowman and Littlefield, 1998.

Patent for the Cotton Gin

Green, Constance McLaughlin. *Eli Whitney and the Birth of American Technology*. 1956. Reprint, New York: Longman, 1997.

North, Douglass C. *The Economic Growth of the United States, 1790–1860*. New York: W.W. Norton, 1966.

ALIEN AND SEDITION ACTS 1798

Levy, Leonard. *Legacy of Suppression; Freedom of Speech and Press in Early American History*. Cambridge, Mass.: Belknap Press of Harvard University Press, 1964.

Rosenberg, Norman. *Protecting the "Best Men": An Interpretive History of the Law of Libel*. Chapel Hill: University of North Carolina Press, 1990.

Smith, James Morton. *Freedom's Fetters: The Alien and Sedition Laws and American Civil Liberties*. Ithaca: Cornell University Press, 1956.

LOUISIANA PURCHASE

De Conde, Alexander. *This Affair of Louisiana*. New York: Scribners, 1976.

Fleming, Thomas J. *The Louisiana Purchase*. Hoboken, N.J.: John Wiley, 2003.

Horsman, Reginald. *Expansion and American Indian Policy*. East Lansing: Michigan State University Press, 1967.

Kastor, Peter J., ed. *The Louisiana Purchase: Emergence of an American Nation*. Washington, D.C.: CQ Press, 2002.

Kennedy, Roger G. *Mr. Jefferson's Lost Cause: Land, Farmers, Slavery, and the Louisiana Purchase*. New York: Oxford University Press, 2003.

Labbe, Dolores Egger. *The Louisiana Purchase and Its Aftermath*. Lafayette, La.: University of Southwestern Louisiana, 1998.

Peterson, Merrill. *Thomas Jefferson and the New Nation*. New York: Oxford University Press, 1970.

LEWIS AND CLARK

Ambrose, Stephen E. *Undaunted Courage; Meriwether Lewis, Thomas Jefferson, and the Opening of the American West*. New York: Simon & Schuster, 1996.

Betts, Robert B. *In Search of York: The Slave Who Went to the Pacific with Lewis and Clark*. Boulder: University Press of Colorado, Lewis and Clark Trail Heritage Foundation, 2000.

Moulton, Gary E., ed. *The Journals of the Lewis and Clark Expedition*. 13 vols. Lincoln: University of Nebraska Press, 1983–2001.

Ronda, James. *Lewis and Clark Among the Indians*. Lincoln: University of Nebraska Press, 1984.

Stephanson, Anders. *Manifest Destiny: American Expansionism and the Empire of Right*. New York: Hill and Wang, 1995.

Stuart, Reginald C. *United States Expansionism and British North America, 1775–1871*. Chapel Hill: University of North Carolina Press, 1988.

MARBURY V. MADISON

Clinton, Robert L. Marbury *v.* Madison *and Judicial Review*. Lawrence: University Press of Kansas, 1989.

Hobson, Charles F. *The Great Chief Justice: John Marshall and the Rule of Law*. Lawrence: University Press of Kansas, 1996.

Nelson, William. Marbury *v.* Madison: *The Origins and Legacy of Judicial Review*. Lawrence: University Press of Kansas, 2000.

Newmyer, R. Kent. *John Marshall and the Heroic Age of the Supreme Court*. Baton Rouge: Louisiana State University Press, 2001.

Simon, James. *What Kind of Nation: Thomas Jefferson, John Marshall, and the Epic Struggle to Create a United States*. New York: Simon & Schuster, 2002.

White, G. Edward, with Gerald Gunther. *The Marshall Court and Cultural Change, 1815–1835*. New York: Oxford University Press, 1991.

TREATY OF GHENT

Hickey, Donald. *The War of 1812: A Forgotten Conflict*. Urbana: University of Illinois Press, 1989.

Rutland, Robert. *The Presidency of James Madison*. Lawrence: University Press of Kansas, 1990.

Stagg, J. C. A. *Mr. Madison's War; Politics, Diplomacy, and Warfare in the Early American Republic, 1783–1830*. Princeton, N.J.: Princeton University Press, 1983.

Watts, Steven. *The Republic Reborn: War and the Making of Liberal America, 1790–1820*. Baltimore: Johns Hopkins University Press, 1987.

McCULLOCH V. MARYLAND

Gunther, Gerald, ed. *John Marshall's Defense of* McCulloch *v.* Maryland. Stanford, Calif.: Stanford University Press, 1969.

Newmyer, R. Kent. *John Marshall and the Heroic Age of the Supreme Court*. Baton Rouge: Louisiana State University Press, 2001.

White, G. Edward, with Gerald Gunther. *The Marshall Court and Cultural Change, 1815–1835*. New York: Oxford University Press, 1991.

MISSOURI COMPROMISE

Fehrenbacher, Don Edward. *Sectional Crisis and Southern Constitutionalism*. Baton Rouge: Louisiana State University Press, 1995.

Freehling, William W. *The Road to Disunion: Secessionists at Bay, 1776–1854*. New York: Oxford University Press, 1990.

Moore, Glover. *The Missouri Controversy, 1819–1821*. Lexington: University of Kentucky Press, 1953.

Morrison, Michael A. *Slavery and the American West: The Eclipse of Manifest Destiny and the Coming of the Civil War*. Chapel Hill: University of North Carolina Press, 1997.

Ransom, Roger. *Conflict and Compromise: The Political Economy of Slavery, Emancipation, and the American Civil War*. New York: Cambridge University Press, 1989.

Remini, Robert. *Henry Clay: Statesman for the Union*. New York: W. W. Norton, 1991.

MONROE DOCTRINE

Ammon, Harry. *James Monroe: The Quest for National Identity*. Charlottesville: University Press of Virginia, 1990.

Cunningham, Noble E. Jr. *The Presidency of James Monroe*. Lawrence: University Press of Kansas, 1996.

May, Ernest R. *The Making of the Monroe Doctrine*. Cambridge, Mass.: Belknap Press of Harvard University Press, 1975.

Perkins, Dexter. *Hands Off: A History of the Monroe Doctrine*. Boston: Little, Brown, 1941.

Smith, Gaddis. *The Last Years of the Monroe Doctrine, 1945–1993*. New York: Hill and Wang, 1994.

GIBBONS V. OGDEN

Baxter, Maurice G. *The Steamboat Monopoly:* Gibbons v. Ogden *1824*. New York: Knopf, 1972.

Friedman, Lawrence M. *A History of American Law*. New York: Simon & Schuster, 1985.

Levinson, Isabel Simone. Gibbons v. Ogden: *Controlling Trade Between States*. Springfield, N.J.: Enslow, 1999.

Newmyer, R. Kent. *The Supreme Court under Marshall and Taney*. Arlington Heights, Ill.: Harlan Davidson, 1986.

White, G. Edward, with Gerald Gunther. *The Marshall Court and Cultural Change, 1815–1835*. New York: Oxford University Press, 1991.

ANDREW JACKSON AND INDIAN REMOVAL

Anderson, William L., ed. *Cherokee Removal: Before and After*. Athens: University of Georgia Press, 1991.

Ehle, John. *Trail of Tears: The Rise and Fall of the Cherokee Nation*. New York: Doubleday, 1988.

McLoughlin, William. *Cherokees and Missionaries, 1789–1839*. New Haven: Yale University Press, 1984.

Remini, Robert. *Life of Andrew Jackson*. New York: Penguin Books, 1990.

Wallace, Anthony F. C. *The Long, Bitter Trail: Andrew Jackson and the Indians*. New York: Hill and Wang, 1993.

Treaty of Guadalupe Hidalgo

Eisenhower, John S. D. *So Far from God: The U.S. War with Mexico 1846–1848*. New York: Random House, 1989.

Limerick, Patricia Nelson. *The Legacy of Conquest: The Unbroken Past of the American West*. New York: W. W. Norton, 1987.

Marovina, Timothy M. *Tejano Religion and Ethnicity: San Antonio, 1821–1860*. Austin: University of Texas Press, 1995.

Robinson, Cecil. *The View from Chapultepec: Mexican Writers on the Mexican-American War*. Tucson: University of Arizona Press, 1989.

Compromise of 1850

Ashworth, John. *Slavery, Capitalism, and Politics in the Antebellum Republic: Commerce and Compromise, 1820–1850*. New York: Cambridge University Press, 1995.

Johanssen, Robert W. *The Frontier, the Union, and Stephen A. Douglas*. Urbana: University of Illinois Press, 1989.

Sewall, Richard. *A House Divided: Sectionalism and Civil War, 1848–1865*. Baltimore: Johns Hopkins University Press, 1988.

Stegmaier, Mark J. *Texas, New Mexico, and the Compromise of 1850: Boundary Dispute & Sectional Crisis*. Kent, Ohio: Kent State University Press, 1996.

Kansas-Nebraska Act

Foner, Eric. *Free Soil, Free Labor, Free Men: The Ideology of the Republican Party Before the Civil War*. New York: Oxford University Press, 1995.

Gienapp, William E. *The Origins of the Republican Party, 1852–1856*. New York: Oxford University Press, 1987.

Morrison, Michael A. *Slavery and the American West: The Eclipse of Manifest Destiny and the Coming of the Civil War*. Chapel Hill: University of North Carolina Press, 1999.

Scott v. Sanford

Fehrenbacher, Donald. *Slavery, Law, and Politics: The Dred Scott Case in Historical Perspective*. New York: Oxford University Press, 1981.

Fehrenbacher, Donald. *The Dred Scott Case: Its Significance in American Law and Politics*. New York: Oxford University Press, 2001.

Kaufman, Kenneth. *Dred Scott's Advocate: A Biography of Roswell M. Field*. Columbia: University of Missouri Press, 1996.

Stampp, Kenneth. *America in 1857: A Nation on the Brink*. New York: Oxford University Press, 1990.

The Civil War and Fort Sumter

Barney, William L. *The Civil War and Reconstruction: A Student Companion*. New York: Oxford Univesrity Press, 2001.

Detzer, David. *Allegiance: Fort Sumter, Charleston, and the Beginning of the Civil War*. New York: Harcourt, 2002.

Klein, Maury. *Days of Defiance: Sumter, Secession, and the Coming of the Civil War*. New York: Vintage, 1999.

McPherson, James. *Battle Cry of Freedom: The Civil War Era*. New York: Oxford University Press, 1988.

Seidman, Rachel Filene. *The Civil War: A History in Documents*. New York: Oxford University Press, 2001.

Morrill Act

Cross, Coy F. II. *Justin Smith Morrill: Father of the Land-Grant Colleges*. East Lansing, Mich.: Michigan State University Press, 1999.

Eddy, Edward Danforth. *Colleges for Our Land and Time: The Land-Grant Idea in American Education*. New York: Harper, 1957.

Williams, Roger L. *The Origins of Federal Support for Higher Education: George W. Atherton and the Land-Grant College Movement*. University Park: Pennsylvania State University Press, 1991.

Homestead Act

Gates, Paul W. *History of Public Land Law Development*. New York: Arno Press, 1979.

Opie, John. *The Law of the Land: 200 Years of American Farmland Policy*. Lincoln: University of Nebraska Press, 1994.

Emancipation Proclamation

Burlingame, Michael. *The Inner World of Abraham Lincoln*. Urbana: University of Illinois Press, 1994.

Donald, David Herbert. *Lincoln*. New York: Simon & Schuster, 1995.

Gienapp, William E. *Abraham Lincoln and Civil War America: A Biography*. New York: Oxford University Press, 2002.

Jones, Howard. *Abraham Lincoln and a New Birth of Freedom: The Union and Slavery in the Diplomacy of the Civil War*. Lincoln: University of Nebraska Press, 1999.

Klingaman, William K. *Abraham Lincoln and the Road to Emancipation, 1861–1865*. New York: Viking, 2001.

Peterson, Merrill D. *Lincoln in American Memory*. New York: Oxford University Press, 1994.

Regosin, Elizabeth. *Freedom's Promise: Ex-slave Families and Citizenship in the Age of Emancipation*. Charlottesville: University Press of Virginia, 2002.

Gettysburg Address

Gramm, Kent. *November: Lincoln's Elegy at Gettysburg*. Bloomington: Indiana University Press, 2001.

Hess, Earl J. *Pickett's Charge: The Last Attack at Gettysburg*. Chapel Hill: University of North Carolina Press, 2001.

Wills, Garry. *Lincoln at Gettysburg: The Words That Remade America*. New York: Simon & Schuster, 1992.

The Civil War and U.S. Colored Troops

Berlin, Ira, et al. *Slaves No More: Three Essays on Emancipation and the Civil War*. New York: Cambridge University Press, 1992.

Duncan, Russell. *Where Death and Glory Meet: Colonel Robert Gould Shaw and the 54th Massachusetts Infantry*. Athens: University of Georgia Press, 1999.

Frankel, Noralee. *Break Those Chains at Last: African Americans 1860–1880*. New York: Oxford University Press, 1996.

Hollandsworth, James G. Jr. *The Louisiane Native Guards: The Black Military Experience During the Civil War*. Baton Rouge: Louisiana State University Press, 1995.

Miller Edward A. Jr. *The Black Civil War Soldiers of Illinois: The Story of the Twenty-Ninth U.S. Colored Infantry*. Columbia: University of South Carolina Press, 1998.

Washington, Versalle F. *Eagles on Their Buttons: A Black Infantry Regiment in the Civil War*. Columbia: University of Missouri Press, 1999.

Wade-Davis Bill

Abbott, Richard H. *The Republican Party and the South, 1855–1877*. Chapel Hill: University of North Carolina Press, 1986.

Bond, James E. *No Easy Walk to Freedom: Reconstruction and the Ratification of the Fourteenth Amendment*. Westport, Conn.: Praeger, 1997.

Carter, Dan T. *When the War Was Over: The Failure of Self-Reconstruction in the South*. Baton Rouge: Louisiana State University Press, 1985.

Foner, Eric. *Reconstruction: America's Unfinished Revolution, 1863–1877*. New York: HarperCollins, 1989.

Saville, Julia. *The Work of Reconstruction: From Slave to Wage Laborer in South Carolina, 1860–1870*. New York: Cambridge University Press, 1996.

LINCOLN'S SECOND INAUGURAL ADDRESS
White Ronald C., Jr. *Lincoln's Greatest Speech: The Second Inaugural.* New York: Simon & Schuster, 2002.

ARTICLES OF AGREEMENT RELATING TO THE SURRENDER OF THE ARMY OF NORTHERN VIRGINIA
Hendrickson, Robert. *The Road to Appomattox.* New York: Wiley, 1998.

Lowry, Don. *Towards an Indefinite Shore: The Final Months of the Civil War, December 1864–May 1865.* New York: Hippocrene, 1995.

Marvel, William. *A Place Called Appomattox.* Chapel Hill: University of North Carolina Press, 2000.

THIRTEENTH, FOURTEENTH, AND FIFTEENTH AMENDMENTS
Bernstein, Richard B., with Jerome Agel. *Amending America: If We Love the Constitution So Much, Why Do We Keep Trying to Change It?* New York: Times Books, 1993.

Kyvig, David E. *Explicit and Authentic Acts: Amending the U.S. Constitution.* Lawrence: University Press of Kansas, 1996.

Maltz, Earl M. *Civil Rights, the Constitution, and Congress, 1863–1869.* Lawrence: University Press of Kansas, 1990.

Richards, David A. J. *Conscience and the Constitution: History, Theory, and Law of the Reconstruction Amendments.* Princeton: Princeton University Press, 1993.

Vorenberg, Michael. *Final Freedom: The Civil War, the Abolition of Slavery, and the Thirteenth Amendment.* New York: Cambridge University Press, 2001.

PURCHASE OF ALASKA
Kushner, Howard I. *Conflict on the Northwest Coast: American-Russian Rivalry in the Pacific Northwest, 1790–1867.* Westport, Conn.: Greenwood, 1975.

Mayer, Melanie J., and Robert N. DeArmond. *Staking Her Claim: The Life of Belinda Mulrooney, Klondike and Alaska Entrepreneur.* Athens: Swallow Press/Ohio University Press, 2000.

Naske, Claus-M., and Herman E. Slotnick. *Alaska: A History of the 49th State.* Grand Rapids, Mich.: Eerdmans, 1979.

PATENT APPLICATION FOR THE LIGHTBULB
Adair, Gene. *Thomas Alva Edison: Inventing the Electric Age.* New York: Oxford University Press, 1996.

DE LÔME LETTER
Brands, H.W. *The Reckless Decade: America in the 1890s.* Chicago: University of Chicago Press, 2002.

Gould, Lewis L. *The Spanish-American War and President McKinley.* Lawrence: University Press of Kansas, 1982.

Milton, Joyce. *The Yellow Kids: Foreign Correspondents in the Heyday of Yellow Journalism.* New York: Harper & Row, 1989.

Trask, David. *The War with Spain in 1898.* Lincoln: University of Nebraska Press, 1996.

PLATT AMENDMENT
Perez, Luis, Jr. *Cuba Under the Platt Amendment, 1902–1934.* Pittsburgh: University of Pittsburgh Press, 1986.

THEODORE ROOSEVELT/FOREIGN POLICY
Collin, Richard H. *Theodore Roosevelt, Culture, Diplomacy, and Expansion: A New View of American Imperialism.* Baton Rouge: Louisiana State University Press, 1985.

Gould, Lewis L. *The Presidency of Theodore Roosevelt.* Lawrence: University Press of Kansas, 1991.

McCullough, David. *Mornings on Horseback.* New York: Simon & Schuster, 1981.

Morris, Edmund. *Theodore Rex.* New York: Random House, 2001.

SIXTEENTH AMENDMENT
Brownlee, Elliott. *Federal Taxation in America: A Short History.* New York: Cambridge University Press, 1996.

Buenker, John D. *The Income Tax and the Progressive Era.* New York: Garland, 1985.

Witte, John. *The Politics and Development of the Federal Income Tax.* Madison: University of Wisconsin Press, 1985.

SEVENTEENTH AMENDMENT
Hoebeke, C. H. *The Road to Mass Democracy: Original Intent and the Seventeenth Amendment.* New Brunswick, N.J.: Transaction, 1995.

Rossum, Ralph A. *Federalism, the Supreme Court, and the Seventeenth Amendment: The Irony of Constitutional Democracy.* Lanham, Md.: Lexington Books, 2001.

KEATING-OWEN CHILD LABOR ACT
Diner, Steven J. *A Very Different Age: Americans of the Progressive Era.* New York: Hill and Wang, 1998.

Hindman, Hugh D. *Child Labor: An American History.* Armonk, N.Y.: M. E. Sharpe, 2002.

Trattner, Walter I. *Crusade for the Children: The National Child Labor Committee and Child Labor Reform in America.* Chicago, Quadrangle Books, 1970.

ZIMMERMAN TELEGRAM
Gannon, James. *Stealing Secrets, Telling Lies: How Spies and Codebreakers Helped Shape the Twentieth Century.* Washington, D.C.: Brassey's, 2001.

Kahn, David. *The Codebreakers.* New York: Simon & Schuster, 1996.

Tuchman, Barbara. *The Zimmermann Telegram.* New York: Random House, 1985.

WOODROW WILSON'S FOURTEEN POINTS
Ambrosius, Lloyd E. *Woodrow Wilson and the American Diplomatic Tradition: The Treaty Fight in Perspective.* Cambridge: Cambridge University Press, 1987.

Knock, Thomas J. *To End All Wars: Woodrow Wilson and the Quest for a New World Order.* New York: Oxford University Press, 1992.

Ninkovich, Frank. *The Wilsonian Century: U.S. Foreign Policy Since 1900.* Chicago: University of Chicago Press, 1999.

Steigerwald, David. *Wilsonian Idealism in America.* Ithaca, N.Y.: Cornell University Press, 1994.

NINETEENTH AMENDMENT
Barry, Kathleen. *Susan B. Anthony: A Biography of a Singular Feminist.* New York: Ballantine Books, 1990.

Deutsch, Sarah Jane. *From Ballots to Breadlines: American Women 1920–1940.* New York: Oxford University, 1994.

DuBois, Ellen Carol. *Harriot Stanton Blatch and the Winning of Woman Suffrage.* New Haven: Yale University Press, 1997.

Griffith, Elisabeth. *In Her Own Right: The Life of Elizabeth Cady Stanton.* New York: Oxford University Press, 1985.

Lunardi, Christine A. *From Equal Suffrage to Equal Rights: Alice Paul and the National Woman's Party, 1912–1928.* New York: New York University Press, 1986.

Muncy, Robyn. *Creating a Female Dominion in American Reform, 1890–1935.* New York: Oxford University Press, 1991.

BOULDER CANYON PROJECT ACT
Armstrong, Ellis. *History of Public Works in the United States, 1776–1976.* Kansas City, Mo.: American Public Works Association, 1976.

TENNESSEE VALLEY ACT
Grant, Nancy L. *TVA and Black Americans: Planning for the Status Quo.* Philadelphia: Temple University Press, 1990.

McDonald, Michael J., and John Muldowny. *TVA and the Resettlement of Population in the Norris Dam Area.* Knoxville: University of Tennessee Press, 1982.

Nurick, Aaron J. *Participation in Organizational Change: The TVA Experiment.* New York: Praeger, 1985.

Talbert, Roy, Jr. *FDR's Utopian: Arthur Morgan of the TVA.* Jackson: University Press of Mississippi, 1987.

NATIONAL RECOVERY ACT

Bellush, Bernard. *The Failure of the NRA.* New York: W. W. Norton, 1975.

Kennedy, David. *Freedom from Fear: The American People in Depression and War, 1929–1945.* New York: Oxford University Press, 1999.

McElvaine, Robert. *The Great Depression: America, 1929–1941.* New York: Times Books, 1985.

McElvaine, Robert: *The Depression and New Deal: A History in Documents.* New York: Oxford University Press, 2000.

Romasco, Albert. *The Politics of Recovery: Roosevelt's New Deal.* New York: Oxford University Press, 1983.

Waldrep, G. C. III. *Southern Workers and the Search for Community: Spartanburg County, South Carolina.* Urbana: University of Illinois Press, 2000.

NATIONAL LABOR RELATIONS ACT

Derber, Milton. *The American Ideal of Industrial Democracy, 1865–1965.* Urbana: University of Illinois Press, 1970.

Huthmacher, J. Joseph. *Senator Robert Wagner and the Rise of Urban Liberalism.* New York: Scribners, 1968.

Irons, Peter. *The New Deal Lawyers.* Princeton: Princeton University Press, 1982.

SOCIAL SECURITY ACT

Achenbaum, W. Andrew. *Social Security: Visions and Revisions.* New York: Cambridge University Press, 1986.

Haber, Carole, and Brian Gratton. *Old Age and the Search for Security: An American Social History.* Bloomington: Indiana University Press, 1994.

Lobove, Roy. *The Struggle for Social Security.* Pittsburgh: University of Pittsburgh Press, 1986.

SECOND NEW DEAL

Gordon, Colin. *New Deals: Business, Labor, and Politics in America, 1920–1935.* New York: Cambridge University Press, 1994.

Leuchtenburg, William E. *The FDR Years: On Roosevelt and His Legacy.* New York: Columbia University Press, 1995.

Schwarz, Jordan. *The New Dealers: Power Politics in the Age of Roosevelt.* New York: Vintage, 1994.

LEND LEASE ACT

Dallek, Robert. *Franklin D. Roosevelt and American Foreign Policy, 1932–1945.* New York: Oxford University Press, 1979.

Dobson, Alan P. *U.S. Wartime Aid to Britain, 1940–1946.* New York: St. Martin's Press, 1986.

Kimball, Warren. *The Most Unsordid Act: Lend Lease, 1939–1941.* Baltimore: Johns Hopkins University Press, 1969.

Kimball, Warren. *Forged in War: Roosevelt, Churchill, and the Second World War.* New York: Morrow, 1997.

EXECUTIVE ORDER 8802: PROHIBITION OF DISCRIMINATION IN THE DEFENSE INDUSTRY

Anderson, Jervis. *A Philip Randolph.* New York: Harcourt Brace, 1973.

Wynn, Neil. *The Afro-American and the Second World War.* London: P. Elek, 1976.

DECLARATION OF WAR AGAINST JAPAN

Prange, Gordon W. *Pearl Harbor: The Verdict of History.* New York: McGraw-Hill, 1986.

Prange, Gordon W. *December 7, 1941: The Day the Japanese Attacked Pearl Harbor.* New York: McGraw-Hill, 1988.

Prange, Gordon W., with Donald M. Goldstein and Katherine V. Dillon. *At Dawn We Slept: The Untold Story of Pearl Harbor.* New York: Viking, 1991.

Slackman, Michael. *Target: Pearl Harbor.* Honolulu: University of Hawaii Press, Arizona Memorial Museum Association, 1990.

Satterfield, Archie. *The Day the War Began.* Westport, Conn.: Praeger, 1992.

EXECUTIVE ORDER 9066/JAPANESE RELOCATION

Daniels, Roger. *Prisoners Without Trial: Japanese Americans in World War II.* New York: Hill and Wang, 1993.

Irons, Peter. *Justice at War: The Story of the Japanese American Internment Cases.* Berkeley: University of California Press, 1993.

Robinson, Greg. *By Order of the President: FDR and the Internment of Japanese Americans.* Cambridge, Mass.: Harvard University Press, 2001.

Smith, Page. *Democracy on Trial: The Japanese American Evacuation and Relocation in World War II.* New York: Simon & Schuster, 1995.

EISENHOWER'S ORDER OF THE DAY

Hastings, Max. *Overlord: D-Day and the Battle for Normandy.* New York: Simon and Schuster, 1984.

Hastings, Max. *Victory in Europe: D-day to V-E Day.* Boston: Little, Brown, 1985.

Lewis, Adrian R. *Omaha Beach: A Flawed Victory.* Chapel Hill: University of North Carolina Press, 2001.

SERVICEMEN'S READJUSTMENT ACT

Bennett, Michael J. *When Dreams Came True: The G.I. Bill and the Making of Modern America.* Dulles, Va.: Brassey's, 1996.

Olson, Keith. *The G.I, Bill, the Veterans, and the Colleges.* Lexington: University Press of Kentucky, 1974.

MANHATTAN PROJECT NOTEBOOK

Cooper, Dan. *Enrico Fermi and the Revolutions of Modern Physics.* New York: Oxford University Press, 1999.

Herkan, Gregg. *Brotherhood of the Bomb: The Tangled Lives and Loyalties of Robert Oppenheimer, Ernest Lawrence, and Edward Teller.* New York: Henry Holt, 2002.

Kurzman, Dan. *Day of the Bomb: Countdown to Hiroshima.* New York: McGraw-Hill, 1986.

Rhodes, Richard. *The Making of the Atomic Bomb.* New York: Simon & Schuster, 1986.

Schweber, Silvan S. *In the Shadow of the Bomb: Bethe, Oppenheimer, and the Moral Responsibility of the Scientist.* Princeton, N.J.: Princeton University Press, 2000.

SURRENDER OF GERMANY

Ambrose, Stephen A. *Eisenhower and Berlin, 1945: The Decision to Halt at the Elbe.* New York: W. W. Norton, 1967.

Casey, Steven. *Cautious Crusade: Franklin D. Roosevelt, American Public Opinion, and the War Against Nazi Germany.* New York: Oxford University Press, 2001.

Offner, Arnold A., and Theodore A. Wilson. eds. *Victory in Europe, 1945: From World War to Cold War.* Lawrence: University Press of Kansas, 2000.

Ryan, Cornelius. *The Last Battle.* New York: Simon & Schuster, 1966.

Toland, John. *The Last 100 Days.* New York: Random House, 1966.

SURRENDER OF JAPAN

Brooks, Lester. *Behind Japan's Surrender: The Secret Struggle that Ended an Empire.* New York: McGraw-Hill, 1968.

Dower, John. *Embracing Defeat: Japan in the Wake of World War Two.* New York: W. W. Norton, 1999.

Sigal, Leon V. *Fighting to a Finish: The Politics of War Termination in the United States and Japan, 1945.* Ithaca: Cornell University Press, 1988.

Toland, John. *Rising Sun: The Decline and Fall of the Japanese Empire.* New York; Random House, 1970.

TRUMAN DOCTRINE

Blum, Robert M. *Drawing the Line: The Origin of the American Containment Policy in East Asia.* New York: W. W. Norton, 1982.

Freeland, Richard M. *The Truman Doctrine and the Origins of McCarthyism: Foreign Policy, Domestic Politics, and Internal Security, 1946–1948.* New York: New York University Press, 1985.

Leffler, Melvyn P. *The Specter of Communism: The United States and the Origins of the Cold War, 1917–1953.* New York: Hill and Wang, 1994.

McCullough, David. *Truman.* New York: Simon & Schuster, 1992.

Offner, Arnold A. *Another Such Victory: President Truman and the Cold War, 1945–1953.* Stanford: Stanford University Press, 2002.

MARSHALL PLAN

Cray, Ed. *General of the Army: George C. Marshall, Soldier and Statesman.* New York: W. W. Norton, 1990.

Donovan, Robert J. *The Second Victory: The Marshall Plan and the Postwar Revival of Europe.* New York: Madison Books, 1987.

Eichengreen, Barry, ed. *Europe's Post-War Recovery.* New York: Cambridge University Press, 1995.

Hogan, Michael J. *The Marshall Plan: America, Britain, and the Reconstruction of Western Europe, 1947–1952.* New York: Cambridge University Press, 1987.

Hoffman, Stanley, and Charles Maier, eds. *The Marshall Plan: A Retrospective.* Boulder, Colo.: Westview, 1984.

Milwad, Alan S., *The Reconstruction of Western Europe 1945–51.* London: Methuen, 1984.

Pisani, Sallie. *The CIA and the Marshall Plan.* Lawrence: University Press of Kansas, 1991.

U.S. RECOGNITION OF ISRAEL

Benson, Michael T. *Harry S. Truman and the Founding of Israel.* Westport, Conn.: Praeger, 1997.

Ben-Zvi, Abraham. *Decade of Transition: Eisenhower, Kennedy, and the Origins of the American-Israeli Alliance.* New York: Columbia University Press, 1998.

Christison, Kathleen. *Perceptions of Palestine: Their Influence on U.S. Middle East Policy.* Berkeley: University of California Press, 2000.

Cohen, Michael. *Truman and Israel.* Berkeley: University of California Press, 1990.

DESEGREGATION OF THE ARMED FORCES

Dalfiume, Richard M. *Desegregation of the U.S. Armed Forces; Fighting on Two Fronts, 1939–1953.* Columbia: University of Missouri Press, 1969.

King, Desmond. *Separate and Unequal: Black Americans and the US Federal Government.* New York: Oxford University Press, 1995.

CENSURE OF JOSEPH MCCARTHY

Fried, Richard M., *Men Against McCarthy.* New York: Columbia University Press, 1976.

Fried, Richard M. *Nightmare in Red: The McCarthy Era in Perspective.* New York: Oxford University Press, 1990.

Griffith, Robert. *The Politics of Fear: Joseph R. McCarthy and the Senate.* 2nd ed. Amherst: University of Massachusetts Press, 1987.

Herman, Arthur. *Joseph McCarthy: Reexamining the Life and Legacy of America's Most Hated Senator.* New York: Free Press, c2000.

Oshinsky, David M. *A Conspiracy So Immense: The World of Joe McCarthy.* New York: Free Press, 1983.

Schrecker, Ellen. *Many Are the Crimes: McCarthyism in America.* Boston: Little, Brown, 1998.

Steinberg, Peter L. *The Great "Red Menace": United States Prosecution of American Communists, 1947–1952.* Westport, Conn.: Greenwood Press, 1984.

ARMISTICE AGREEMENT FOR THE RESTORATION OF THE SOUTH KOREAN STATE

Blair, Clay. *The Forgotten War: America in Korea, 1950–1953.* New York: New York Times Books, 1987.

Foot, Rosemary. *A Substitute for Victory: The Politics of Peacemaking at the Korean Armistice Talks.* Ithaca, N.Y.: Cornell University Press, 1990.

Lowe, Peter. *The Korean War.* New York: St. Martin's, 2000.

Pierpaoli, Paul G. Jr. *Truman and Korea: The Political Culture of the Early Cold War.* Columbia: University of Missouri Press, 1999.

Wainstock, Dennis D. *Truman, MacArthur, and the Korean War.* Westport, Conn.: Greenwood Press, 1999.

Whelan, Richard. *Drawing the Line: The Korean War, 1950–1953.* Boston: Little, Brown, 1990.

BROWN V. BOARD OF EDUCATION

Armor, David J. *Forced Justice: School Desegregation and the Law.* New York: Oxford University Press, 1995.

Berman, Daneil M. *It Is So Ordered: The Supreme Court Rules on School Segregation.* New York: W. W. Norton, 1966.

Kluger, Richard. *Simple Justice: The History of* Brown v. Board of Education *and Black America's Struggle for Equality.* New York: Vintage, 1976

Patterson, James T. Brown v. Board of Education: *A Civil Rights Milestone and Its Troubled Legacy.* New York: Oxford University Press, 2001.

Sarat, Austin, ed. *Race, Law, and Culture: Reflections on* Brown v. Board of Education. New York: Oxford University Press, 1997.

Wilkinson, J. Harvie III. *From* Brown to Bakke: *The Supreme Court and School Integration, 1954–1978.* New York: Oxford University Press, 1981.

Wilson, Paul E. *A Time to Lose: Representing Kansas in* Brown v. Board of Education. Lawrence: University Press of Kansas, 1995.

NATIONAL INTERSTATE AND DEFENSE HIGHWAY ACT

Rose, Mark H. *Interstate: Express Highway Politics, 1939–1989.* Knoxville: University of Tennessee Press, 1990.

Seely, Bruce E. *Building the American Highway System.* Philadelphia: Temple University Press, 1987.

PRESIDENT EISENHOWER AND DESEGREGATION OF CENTRAL HIGH SCHOOL, LITTLE ROCK

Branch, Taylor. *Parting the Waters: America in the King Years 1954–1973.* New York: Simon & Schuster, 1988.

Duram, James. *Moderate Among Extremists: Dwight D. Eisenhower and the School Desegregation Crisis.* Chicago: Nelson-Hall, 1981.

Huckaby, Elizabeth. *Crisis at Central High, Little Rock, 1957–58.* Baton Rouge: Louisiana State University Press, 1980.

Raines, Howell. *My Soul Is Rested: Movement Days in the Deep South Remembered.* New York: Penguin Books, 1983.

EISENHOWER'S FAREWELL ADDRESS

Bowie, Robert R., and Richard H. Immerman. *Waging Peace: How Eisenhower Shaped an Enduring Cold War Strategy.* New York: Oxford University Press, 1998.

Hooks, Gregory. *Forging the Military-Industrial Complex: World War II's Battle of the Potomac.* Urbana: University of Illinois Press, 1991.

Perret, Geoffrey. *Eisenhower.* New York: Random House, 1999.

KENNEDY'S INAUGURAL ADDRESS

Bernstein, Irving. *Promises Kept: John F. Kennedy's New Frontier.* New York: Oxford University Press, 1991.

Brown, Thomas. *JFK: History of an Image.* Bloomington: Indiana University Press, 1988.

Burner, David. *John F. Kennedy and a New Generation.* New York: HarperCollins, 1988.

Dallek, Robert. *An Unfinished Life: John F. Kennedy, 1917–1963.* New York: Little, Brown, 2003.

Parmet, Herbert. *J.F.K: The Presidency of John F. Kennedy.* New York: Dial, 1983.

Reeves, Richard. *President Kennedy: Profile of Power.* New York: Simon & Schuster, 1993.

White, Mark J., ed. *Kennedy: the New Frontier Revisited.* New York: New York University Press, 1998.

ESTABLISHMENT OF THE PEACE CORPS

Fischer, Fritz. *Making Them Like Us: Peace Corps Volunteers in the 1960s.* Washington D.C.: Smithsonian Institution Press, 1998.

Hoffman, Elizabeth Cobbs. *All You Need Is Love: The Peace Corps and the Spirit of the 1960s.* Cambridge, Mass.: Harvard University Press, 1998

Latham, Michael E. *Modernization as Ideology: American Social Science and "Nation Building" in the Kennedy Era.* Chapel Hill: University of North Carolina Press, 2000.

Rice, Gerald. *The Bold Experiment: JFK's Peace Corps.* Notre Dame, Ind.: University of Notre Dame Press, 1985.

TRANSCRIPT OF JOHN GLENN'S OFFICIAL COMMUNICATION

Bilstein, Roger E. *Flight in America: From the Wrights to the Astronauts.* Baltimore: Johns Hopkins University Press, 1994.

Lewis, Richard S. *Appointment on the Moon; The Full Story of Americans in Space from Explorer 1 to the Lunar Landing and Beyond.* New York: Ballantine Books, 1969.

McDougall, Walter. *The Heavens and the Earth: A Political History of the Space Age.* New York: Basic Books, 1985.

AERIAL PHOTOGRAPH OF CUBA

Beschloss, Michael. *The Crisis Years: Kennedy and Krushchev.* New York: Edward Burlingame Books, 1991.

Chayes, Abram. *The Cuban Missile Crisis.* New York: Oxford University Press, 1974.

Higgins, Trumbull. *The Perfect Failure: Kennedy, Eisenhower, and the C.I.A. at the Bay of Pigs.* New York: W. W. Norton, 1987.

May, Ernest R., and Philip D. Zelikow, eds. *The Kennedy Tapes; Inside the White House During the Cuban Missile Crisis.* Cambridge, Mass.: Harvard University Press, 1997.

Scott, L.V. *Macmillan, Kennedy, and the Cuban Missile Crisis: Political, Military, and Intelligence Aspects.* New York: St. Martin's Press, 1999.

Thompson, Robert Smith. *The Missiles of October: The Declassified Story of John F. Kennedy and the Cuban Missile Crisis.* New York: Simon & Schuster, 1992.

TEST BAN TREATY

Divine, Robert A. *Blowing on the Wind: The Nuclear Test Ban Debate 1954–1960.* New York: Oxford University Press, 1978.

Seaborg, Glenn T., with Benjamin S. Loeb. *Kennedy, Khrushchev, and the Test Ban.* Berkeley: University of California Press, 1981.

PROGRAM FOR THE MARCH ON WASHINGTON/CIVIL RIGHTS ACT/VOTING RIGHTS ACT

Bloom, Jack. *Class, Rights, and the Civil Rights Movement.* Bloomington: Indiana University Press, 1987.

Collier-Thomas, Bettye, and V. P. Franklin. *Sisters in the Struggle: African American Women in the Civil Rights–Black Power Movement.* New York: New York University Press, 2001.

Foster, Lorn S., ed. *The Voting Rights Act: Consequences and Implications.* Westport, Conn.: Praeger, 1985.

Garrow, David. *Protest at Selma: Martin Luther King, Jr., and the Voting Rights Act of 1965.* New Haven: Yale University Press, 1980.

Levy, Peter B. *The Civil Rights Movement.* Westport, Conn.: Greenwood Press, 1998.

Loevy, Robert D. ed. *The Civil Rights Act of 1964: The Passage of the Law That Ended Racial Segregation.* Albany: State University of New York Press, 1997.

Riches, William T. Martin. *The Civil Rights Movement: Struggle and Resistance.* New York: St. Martin's Press, 1997.

Stern, Mark. *Calculating Visions: Kennedy, Johnson, and Civil Rights.* Piscataway, N.J.: Rutgers University Press, 1992.

TONKIN GULF RESOLUTION

Appy, Christian. *Working Class War: American Combat Soldiers and Vietnam.* Chapel Hill: University of North Carolina Press, 1993.

Gardner, Lloyd C. *Pay Any Price: Lyndon Johnson and the Wars for Vietnam.* Chicago: Elephant Paperbacks, 1997.

Moïse, Edwin E. *Tonkin Gulf and the Escalation of the Vietnam War.* Chapel Hill: University of North Carolina Press, 1996.

Siff, Ezra Y. *Why the Senate Slept: The Gulf of Tonkin Resolution and the Beginning of America's Vietnam War.* Westport, Conn.: Praeger, 1999.

Young, Marilyn B., John J. Fitzgerald, and Tom Grunfeld. *The Vietnam War: A History in Documents.* New York: Oxford University Press, 2002.

SOCIAL SECURITY ACT AMENDMENTS

Achenbaum, W. Andrew. *Social Security: Visions and Revisions.* New York: Cambridge University Press, 1986.

Schieber, Sylvester J., and John B. Shoven. *The Real Deal: The History and Future of Social Security.* New Haven: Yale University Press, 1999.

Tynes, Sheryl R. *Turning Points in Social Security: From "Cruel Hoax" to "Sacred Entitlement."* Stanford, Calif.: Stanford University Press, 1996.

DOCUMENT CITATIONS

p. 10: "The Lee Resolution for Independence, June 7, 1776," *Papers of the Continental Congress, 1774–1783, Records of the Continental and Confederation Congresses and the Constitutional Convention, 1774–89, RG 360, National Archives.

p. 12: "Engrossed copy of the Declaration of Independence, August 2, 1776," *Miscellaneous Papers of the Continental Congress, 1774–89, Records of the Continental and Confederation Congresses and the Constitutional Convention, 1774–89, RG 360, National Archives.

p. 15: "Engrossed and corrected copy of the Articles of Confederation, showing amendments adopted, November 15, 1777," *Papers of the Continental Congress, 1774–89, Records of the Continental and Confederation Congresses and the Constitutional Convention, 1774–89, RG 360; National Archives.

p. 17: "Treaty of Alliance with France, 1778," *International Treaties and Related Records, 1778–1974, General Records of the United States Government, RG 11, National Archives.

p. 21: "Treaty of Paris, 1783," *International Treaties and Related Records, 1778–74, General Records of the United States Government, RG 11, National Archives.

p. 24: "Virginia (Randolph) Plan as Amended" (National Archives Microfilm Publication M866, roll 1); *The Official Records of the Constitutional Convention, Records of the Continental and Confederation Congresses and the Constitutional Convention, 1774–89, RG 360, National Archives.

p. 27: "Northwest Ordinance, July 13, 1787" (National Archives Microfilm Publication M332, roll 9), *Miscellaneous Papers of the Continental Congress, 1774–89, Records of the Continental and Confederation Congresses and the Constitutional Convention, 1774–89, RG 360, National Archives.

p. 30: "Signed Copy of the Constitution of the United States," *Miscellaneous Papers of the Continental Congress, 1774–89, Records of the Continental and Confederation Congresses and the Constitutional Convention, 1774–89, RG 360, National Archives.

p.37: Madison, James. *Federalist* No. 10, "The Same Subject Continued: The Union as a Safeguard Against Domestic Faction and Insurrection." *New York Daily Advertiser,* November 22, 1787.

p. 37: Hamilton, Alexander, or James Madison. *Federalist* No. 51: "The Structure of the Government Must Furnish the Proper Checks and Balances Between the Different Departments." *New York Packet,* February 8, 1788.

p. 41: "President George Washington's First Inaugural Address, April 30, 1789," (SEN 1A-E1), *Records of the United States Senate, RG 46, National Archives.

p. 42: "Engrossed Judiciary Act, September 24, 1789, First Congress," *Enrolled Acts and*

*Resolutions, General Records of the United States Government, RG 11, National Archives.

p. 45: "Engrossed Bill of Rights, September 25, 1789," *General Records of the United States Government, RG 11, National Archives.

p. 46: "Eli Whitney's Patent for the Cotton Gin, March 14, 1794," *Records of the Patent and Trademark Office, RG 241, National Archives.

p. 48: "Washington's farewell address," New York, New York Public Library, 1935. pp. 105, 136. Courtesy of the Milstein Division of United States History, Local History & Genealogy, The New York Public Library, Astor, Lenox, and Tilden Foundations.

p. 50: "The Alien Act, July 6, 1798," Fifth Congress, *Enrolled Acts and Resolutions, General Records of the United States Government, RG 11, National Archives.

p. 52: "President Thomas Jefferson's confidential message to Congress concerning relations with the Indians, January, 18, 1803," RG 233, *Records of the United States House of Representatives, H.R. 7A-D1; National Archives.

p. 55: "Louisiana Purchase Treaty, April 30, 1803," *General Records of the United States Government, RG 11, National Archives.

p. 57: "Show-cause order served on James Madison, Secretary of State, 1802," *Records of the Supreme Court of the United States, RG 267, National Archives.

p. 60: "Treaty of Ghent, 1814," *International Treaties and Related Records, 1778–1974, General Records of the United States Government, RG 11, National Archives.

p. 62: "*McCulloch v. Maryland* decision, March 6, 1819," *Minutes of the Supreme Court of the United States, RG 267, National Archives.

p. 65: "Conference committee report on the Missouri Compromise, March 1, 1820," *Joint Committee of Conference on the Missouri Bill, 03/01/1820–03/06/1820, Records of Joint Committees of Congress, 1789–1989, RG 128, National Archives.

p. 67: "Message of President James Monroe at the commencement of the first session of the Eighteenth Congress (The Monroe Doctrine)," 12/02/1823, *Presidential Messages of the 18th Congress, ca. 12/02/1823–ca. 03/03/1825 (SEN 18A-E1); 18th Congress; Records of the United States Senate, 1789-1990, RG 46, National Archives.

p. 69: "Supreme Court Decree in *Gibbons v. Ogden, 1824,*" *Records of the Supreme Court of the United States, RG 267, National Archives.

p. 70: "President Jackson's Message to Congress 'On Indian Removal,'" December 6, 1830, *Records of the United States Senate, 1789–1990, RG 46, National Archives.

p. 73: "Treaty of Guadalupe-Hidalgo [Exchange copy]," February 2, 1848, *Perfected Treaties, 1778–1945, General Records of the United States Government, 1778–1992, RG 11, National Archives.

p. 74: "Resolution introduced by Senator Henry Clay in relation to the adjustment of all existing questions of controversy between the states arising out of the institution of slavery" (the resolu-

tion later became known as the Compromise of 1850), January, 29, 1850, *Senate Simple Resolutions, Motions, and Orders of the 31st Congress, ca. 03/1849–ca. 03/1851 (SEN 31A-B3), Records of the United States Senate, 1789–1990, RG 46, National Archives.

p. 78: "An Act to Organize the Territories of Nebraska and Kansas, 1854," *Records of the Interior and Insular Affairs Committee and Its Predecessors, 1805–1988, General Records of the United States Government, RG 11, National Archives.

p. 80: "Judgment in the U.S. Supreme Court Case *Dred Scott v. John F. A. Sanford,* March 6, 1857," *Case Files 1792–1995, Records of the Supreme Court of the United States, RG 267, National Archives.

p. 82: "Telegram from Maj. Robert Anderson to Hon. Simon Cameron, Secretary, announcing his withdrawal from Fort Sumter, April 18, 1861," Records of the Adjutant General's Office, 1780's-1917, RG 94; National Archives.

p. 83: "Act of May 20, 1862 (Homestead Act)," Public Law 37-64, 05/20/1862, *General Records of the United States Government, RG 11, National Archives.

p. 85: "Pacific Railway Act, July 1, 1862," *Enrolled Acts and Resolutions of Congress, 1789–1996, General Records of the United States Government, RG 11, National Archives.

p. 87: "Act of July 2, 1862 (Morrill Act)," Public Law 37-108, which established land grant colleges, 07/02/1862, *Enrolled Acts and Resolutions of Congress, 1789–1996, General Records of the United States Government, RG 11, National Archives.

pp. 89–90: "Emancipation Proclamation, January 1, 1863," *Presidential Proclamations, 1791–1991, General Records of the United States Government, RG 11, National Archives.

p. 92: "General Order No. 143, May 22, 1863," *Orders and Circulars, 1797–1910, Records of the Adjutant General's Office, 1780's-1917, RG 94, National Archives.

p. 93: "Abraham Lincoln, Draft of the Gettysburg Address," Nicolay Copy, November 1863, Series 3, General Correspondence, 1837–97, *The Abraham Lincoln Papers at the Library of Congress, Manuscript Division (Washington, D. C.: American Memory Project, [2000–2002]), http://memory.loc.gov/ammem/alhtml/alhome. html.

p. 95: "Handwritten copy of Wade-Davis Bill as originally submitted 1864," *Records of Legislative Proceedings, (HR 35A-B1); Records of the United States House of Representatives 1789–1946, RG 233, National Archives.

p. 98: "Abraham Lincoln, Second Inaugural Address," endorsed by Lincoln, April 10, 1865, March 4, 1865; Series 3, General Correspondence, 1837–1897, *The Abraham Lincoln Papers at the Library of Congress, Manuscript Division (Washington, D.C.: American Memory Project, [2000–2002]), http://memory.loc.gov/ammem/alhtml/alhome. html.

p. 100: "Articles of Agreement in Regard to the Surrender of the Army of Northern Virginia under Gen. Robert E. Lee, April 10, 1865," War Department, Record and Pension Office, 1892–1904, *Records of the Adjutant General's Office, 1780's–1917*, RG 94, National Archives.

p. 102: "The House Joint Resolution proposing the 13th amendment to the Constitution, March 2, 1861," *Enrolled Acts and Resolutions of Congress, 1789–1999, General Records of the United States Government*, RG 11, National Archives.

p. 103: "Cancelled check in the amount of $7.2 million, for the purchase of Alaska, issued August 1, 1868," *Records of the Accounting Officers of the Department of the Treasury*, RG 217, National Archives. "The Russian exchange copy of the Treaty of Cession, March 30, 1867," *General Records of the United States Government*, RG 11, National Archives.

p. 106: "Treaty with the Sioux-Brule, Oglala, Miniconjou, Yanktonai, Hunkpapa, Blackfeet, Cuthead, Two Kettle, San Arcs, and Santee-and Arapaho, 4/29/1868," *General Records of the United States Government*, RG 11, National Archives.

p. 108: "The Joint Resolution proposing the 14th amendment to the Constitution, June 16, 1866," *Enrolled Acts and Resolutions of Congress, 1789–1999, General Records of the United States Government* RG 11, National Archives.

p. 110: "The Joint Resolution proposing the 15th amendment to the Constitution, December 7, 1868," *Enrolled Acts and Resolutions of Congress, 1789–1999, General Records of the United States Government*, RG 11, National Archives.

p. 112: "Act creating Yellowstone National Park, March 1, 1872," *Enrolled Acts and Resolutions of Congress, 1789–1996, General Records of the United States Government*, RG 11, National Archives.

p. 114: "Thomas Edison's patent drawing for an improvement in electric lamps, patented January 27, 1880," *Records of the Patent and Trademark Office*, RG 241; National Archives.

p. 117: "An act to execute certain treaty stipulations relating to the Chinese, May 6, 1882," *Enrolled Acts and Resolutions of Congress, 1789–1996, General Records of the United States Government*, RG 11, National Archives.

p. 118: "An Act to regulate and improve the civil service of the United States, January 16, 1883," *Enrolled Acts and Resolutions of Congress, 1789–1996, General Records of the United States Government*, RG 11, National Archives.

p. 121: "Act of February 4, 1887 (Interstate Commerce Act), Public Law 49-41, February 4, 1887," *Enrolled Acts and Resolutions of Congress, 1789–, General Records of the United States Government, 1778–1992*, RG 11, National Archives.

p. 123: "An Act to Provide for the Allotment of Lands in Severalty to Indians on the Various Reservations (General Allotment Act or Dawes Act)," Statutes at Large 24, 388–91, NADP Document A1887.

p. 125: "Act of July 2, 1890 (Sherman Anti-Trust Act), July 2, 1890," *Enrolled Acts and Resolutions of Congress, 1789–1992, General Records of the United States Government*, RG11, National Archives.

p. 127: "*Plessy* v. *Ferguson*, Judgment, Decided May 18, 1886," *Records of the Supreme Court of the United States*, RG 267, *Plessy* v. *Ferguson*, 163, #15248, National Archives.

p. 130: "Page from *New York Journal* containing the 'Facsimile of Letter Written by the Spanish Minister,' February 9, 1898," *Notes from the Spanish Legation in the U.S. to the Department of State, 1790–1906*, RG 59, National Archives.

p. 132: "Joint Resolution to Provide for Annexing the Hawaiian Islands to the United States, July 7, 1898," *Enrolled Acts and Resolutions of Congress, General Records of the United States Government, 1778–1992*, RG 11, National Archives.

p. 134: "An Act Making appropriations for the support of the Army for the fiscal year ending June thirtieth, nineteen hundred and two, March 2, 1901," *Enrolled Acts and Resolutions of Congress, 1789–1996, General Records of the United States Government*, RG 11, National Archives.

p. 137: "Theodore Roosevelt's Annual Message to Congress for 1904," December 6, 1904 (HR 58A-K2), *Records of the U.S. House of Representatives*, RG 233, Center for Legislative Archives, National Archives.

p. 139: "The 16th Amendment, March 15, 1913," *Ratified Amendments, 1795–1992, General Records of the United States Government*, RG 11, National Archives.

p. 141: "Joint Resolution proposing 17th amendment, 1913," *Enrolled Acts and Resolutions of Congress, 1789–, General Records of the U.S. Government*, RG 11, National Archives.

p. 142: "An act to prevent interstate commerce in the products of child labor, and for other purposes, September 1, 1916," *Enrolled Acts and Resolutions of Congress, 1789–1996, General Records of the United States Government*, RG 11, National Archives.

pp. 144, 145: "Zimmermann Telegram, 1917," *Decimal File, 1910–29*, 862.20212/82A (1910–29), and "Decoded Zimmermann Telegram, 1917," *Decimal File, 1910–1929*, 862.20212/69, *General Records of the Department of State*, RG 59, National Archives.

p. 147: "President Wilson's Declaration of War Message to Congress, April 2, 1917," *Records of the United States Senate*, RG 46, National Archives.

p. 150: "President Wilson's Message to Congress, January 8, 1918," *Records of the United States Senate*, RG 46, National Archives.

p. 153: "Joint Resolution of Congress proposing a constitutional amendment extending the right of suffrage to women, May 19, 1919," *Ratified Amendments, 1795–1992, General Records of the United States Government*, RG 11, National Archives.

p. 155: "An Act to provide for the construction of works for the protection and development of the Colorado River Basin, for the approval of the Colorado River compact, and for other purposes, December 21, 1928," *Enrolled Acts and*

Resolutions of Congress, 1789–1996, *General Records of the United States Government*, RG 11, National Archives.

p. 158: "An Act to improve the navigability and to provide for the flood control of the Tennessee River; to provide for reforestation and the proper use of marginal lands in the Tennessee Valley; to provide for the agricultural and industrial development of said valley; to provide for the national defense by the creation of a corporation for the operation of Government properties at and near Muscle Shoals in the State of Alabama, and for other purposes, May 18, 1933," *Enrolled Acts and Resolutions of Congress, 1789–1996, General Records of the United States Government*, RG 11, National Archives.

p. 161: "An Act to encourage national industrial recovery, to foster fair competition, and to provide for the construction of certain useful public works, and for other purposes, June 16, 1933," *Enrolled Acts and Resolutions of Congress, 1789–1996, General Records of the United States Government*, RG 11, National Archives.

p. 162: "An act to diminish the causes of labor disputes burdening or obstructing interstate and foreign commerce, to create a National Labor Relations Board, and for other purposes, July 5, 1935," *General Records of the United States Government*, RG 11, National Archives.

p. 166: "An act to provide for the general welfare by establishing a system of Federal old-age benefits, and by enabling the several States to make more adequate provision for aged persons, blind persons, dependent and crippled children, maternal and child welfare, public health, and the administration of their unemployment compensation laws; to establish a Social Security Board; to raise revenue; and for other purposes, August 14, 1935," *Enrolled Acts and Resolutions of Congress, 1789–1996, General Records of the United States Government*, RG 11, National Archives.

p. 168: "Campaign Address at Madison Square Garden, New York City, October 31, 1936," *Speeches of President Franklin D. Roosevelt, 1933–1945*, Collection FDR-PPF: *Papers as President, President's Personal File, 1933–1945*, Franklin D. Roosevelt Library, National Archives and Records Administration.

p. 171: "Franklin D. Roosevelt Annual Message to Congress, January 6, 1941," (SEN 77A-H1), *Records of the United States Senate*, RG 46, National Archives.

p. 173: "Lend Lease Bill, dated January 10, 1941," *(HR 77A-D13), Records of the U.S. House of Representatives*, HR 77A-D13, RG 233, National Archives.

p. 175: "Executive Order 8802 dated June 25, 1941," *General Records of the United States Government*, RG 11, National Archives.

p. 176: "'Day of Infamy' Speech by Franklin D. Roosevelt, December 8, 1941," (SEN 77A-H1), *Records of the United States Senate*, RG 46, National Archives.

p. 179: "Executive Order 9066, February 19, 1942," *General Records of the United States Government*, RG 11, National Archives.

p. 181: "D-day statement to soldiers, sailors, and airmen of the Allied Expeditionary Force, June 1944," Collection DDE-EPRE: Eisenhower, Dwight D: Papers, Pre-Presidential, 1916-1952; Dwight D. Eisenhower Library; National Archives and Records Administration.

p. 183: "An act to provide Federal Government aid for the readjustment in civilian life of returning World War II veterans, June 22,1944," *Enrolled Acts and Resolutions of Congress, 1789–1996, General Records of the United States Government*, RG 11, National Archives.

p. 184: "Notebook recording the first controlled, self-sustaining nuclear chain reaction, December 2, 1942," *Records of the Atomic Energy Commission*, RG 326, National Archives.

p. 185: "Act of Military Surrender (Reims) 1944," *Records of the U.S. Joint Chiefs of Staff*, RG 218, National Archives.

p. 188: "First and signature pages of the United Nations Charter, June 26, 1945," *General Records of the United States Government*, RG 11, National Archives.

p. 193: "Instrument of Surrender, September 2, 1945," *Records of the U.S. Joint Chiefs of Staff*, RG 218, National Archives.

p. 195: "President Truman's Message to Congress, March 12, 1947," Document 171, 80th Congress, 1st Session, *Records of the United States House of Representatives*, RG 233, National Archives.

p. 198: "Act of April 3, 1948, European Recovery Act [Marshall Plan]," *Enrolled Acts and Resolutions of Congress, 1789–1996, General Records of the United States Government*, RG 11, National Archives.

p. 200: "President Truman's statement recognizing the State of Israel, May 14, 1948," *Charles Ross Papers, 1904–1967*, Alphabetical Correspondence File: "Handwriting of the President," Harry S. Truman Library, National Archives and Records Administration.

p. 203: "Executive Order 9981, July 26, 1948," *General Records of the United States Government*, RG 11, National Archives.

p. 206: "Korean War Armistice Agreement, July 27, 1953," *Treaties and Other International Agreements Series #2782, General Records of the United States Government*, RG 11, National Archives.

p. 208: "Senate Resolution 301, December 2, 1954," (SEN 83A-B4), *Records of the United States Senate*, RG 46, National Archives.

p. 210: "*Brown* v. *Board of Education of Topeka*, Judgment," *Records of the Supreme Court of the United States*, RG 267, National Archives.

p. 213: "An act to amend and supplement the Federal-Aid Road Act approved July 11, 1916, to authorize appropriations for continuing the construction of highways; to amend the Internal Revenue Code of 1954 to provide additional revenue from the taxes on motor fuel, tires and trucks and buses; and for other purposes, June 29, 1956," *Enrolled Acts and Resolutions of Congress, 1789–1996, General Records of the United States Government*, RG 11, National Archives.

p. 215: "Executive Order 10730, September 23, 1957 (Little Rock Crisis)," *General Records of the United States Government*, RG 11, National Archives.

pp. 219: "Farewell address by President Dwight D. Eisenhower, January 17, 1961, Final TV Talk 1/17/61 (1)," Box 38, Speech Series, *Papers of Dwight D. Eisenhower as President, 1953–61*, Eisenhower Library, National Archives and Records Administration.

p. 221: "Inaugural Address, Kennedy Draft, 01/17/1961," *Papers of John F. Kennedy, President's Office Files, 01/20/1961–11/22/1963*, John F. Kennedy Library, National Archives and Records Administration.

p. 224: "Executive Order 10924, Establishment and Administration of the Peace Corps in the Department of State, March 1, 1961," *General Records of the United States Government*, RG 11, National Archives.

p. 226: "Transcription of John Glenn's Flight Communications, February 28, 1962," *Records of the National Aeronautics and Space Administration*, RG 255, National Archives and Records Administration—Southwest Region (Fort Worth, Tex.).

p. 227: "Photograph, MRBM Lauch Site 2, San Cristobal, 1 November 1962," United States Department of Defense: Cuban Missile Crisis, 10/1962-11/1962, PX 66-20-91, ARC# 193933, John F. Kennedy Library, National Archives and Records Administration.

pp. 229–31: "Nuclear Test Ban Treaty, July 26, 1963," *Treaties and Other International Agreements Series #5433, General Records of the U.S. Government*, RG 11, National Archives.

p. 233: "March on Washinton (Program), 08/28/1963," Bayard Rustin Papers, John F. Kennedy Library, National Archives and Records Administration.

p. 237: "An act to enforce the constitutional right to vote, to confer jurisdiction upon the district courts of the United States, to provide injunctive relief against discrimination in public accommodations, to authorize the Attorney General to institute suits to protect constitutional rights in public facilities and public education, to extend the Commission on Civil Rights, to prevent discrimination in federally assisted programs, to establish a Commission on Equal Employment Opportunity, and for other purposes, July 2, 1964," *Enrolled Acts and Resolutions of Congress, 1789–1996, General Records of the United States Government*, RG 11, National Archives.

pp. 238–39: "Tonkin Gulf Resolution," Public Law 88-408, 88th Congress, August 7, 1964, (SEN 88A-M1), *General Records of the United States Government*, RG 11, National Archives.

p. 239: "Tonkin Gulf Resolution, Senate roll call tally sheet," 08/07/1964; (SEN 88-AM1), Misc Roll Calls, 88th Congress, 2nd Session; *Records of the U.S. Senate*, RG 46, National Archives.

p. 241: "An act to provide a hospital insurance program for the aged under the Social Security Act with a supplementary medical benefits program and an expanded program of medical assistance, to increase benefits under the Old-Age, Survivors, and Disability Insurance System, to improve the Federal-State public assistance programs, and for other purposes, July 30, 1965," *Enrolled Acts and Resolutions of Congress, 1789–1996, General Records of the United States Government*, RG 11, National Archives.

pp. 242–43: "An act to enforce the fifteenth amendment to the Constitution of the United States and for other purposes, August 6, 1965," *Enrolled Acts and Resolutions of Congress, 1789–1996, General Records of the United States Government*, RG 11, National Archives.

PICTURE CREDITS

Index

MICHAEL BESCHLOSS is a member of the Foundation for the National Archives' board of directors. As a historian, he has brought important American documents to life in his books and lectures and has always stressed the importance of such records as the enduring foundation of democracy. His most recent book is the acclaimed *New York Times* bestseller *The Conquerors: Roosevelt, Truman and the Destruction of Hitler's Germany.*

JOHN W. CARLIN was appointed eighth Archivist of the United States by President Bill Clinton in 1995. As Archivist, he has focused the National Archives and Records Administration on providing ready access to essential evidence by improving the management of federal records, ensuring their preservation, and increasing their accessibility. He is the former Speaker of the House and a two-term governor of Kansas.

THE NATIONAL ARCHIVES AND RECORDS ADMINISTRATION (NARA), an independent federal agency, is America's national record keeper. Its mission is to ensure ready access to the essential evidence that documents the rights of American citizens, the actions of federal officials, and the national experience. To do this, NARA establishes policies and procedures for managing U.S. government records. It assists and trains federal agencies in documenting their activities, administering records-management programs, scheduling records, and retiring noncurrent records to regional records services facilities for cost-effective storage. NARA appraises, accessions, arranges, describes, preserves, and makes available to the public the historically valuable records of the three branches of government. NARA manages a nationwide system of Presidential libraries, records centers, and regional archives. The agency administers the Information Security Oversight Office and makes grants to non-federal institutions to support historical documentation through the National Historical Publications and Records Commission. NARA publishes the *Federal Register, Statutes at Large,* government regulations, and Presidential and other public documents. Every day NARA serves a broad spectrum of American society—from genealogists to veterans to historians to journalists to public officials to students and teachers and many more—all seeking answers from the records the agency preserves. To learn more about the National Archives, go to *www.archives.gov.*

NATIONAL HISTORY DAY is not just one day, but a year-long history education program that is transforming the way history and civics are taught and learned by helping teachers meet educational standards; disseminating high-quality curriculum materials; and sponsoring challenging contests that promote knowledge and skills that enrich the lives of students in school and beyond. The NHD program received the Charles Frankel Prize for Public Programming from the National Endowment for the Humanities and was recognized by President George W. Bush, U.S. Secretary of Education Rod Paige, and historian David McCullough for its profound impact on history education throughout the nation.

At the core of the program is a national contest, similar to a science fair, in which students in grades 6 through 12 conduct extensive research related to an annual theme and present their findings in the form of museum-like exhibits, multimedia documentaries, dramatic performances, or research papers. Educators integrate the contest as part of their curriculum and use the program as a performance assessment tool. To learn more about the program and receive free materials, go to *www.nationalhistoryday.org* or call 301-314-9739.

www.ourdocuments.gov is the official Web site of *Our Documents: A National Initiative on American History, Civics, and Service,* an effort to promote public understanding of how rights and responsibilities have taken shape over time. *Our Documents* began as an initiative of the National Archives and Records Administration and National History Day in cooperation with the Corporation for National and Community Service and the USA Freedom Corps. *Our Documents* invites all Americans to participate in a series of events and programs to initiate thinking, talking, and teaching about the rights and responsibilities of citizens in our American democracy. At the heart of this initiative are 100 milestone documents of U.S. history. These documents reflect America's diversity and unity, past and future, and mostly its commitment as a nation to continue to strive to "form a more perfect union." *Our Documents* wants all Americans to read these milestone documents, consider their meaning, discuss them, and decide which are the most significant and why. The Web site *www.ourdocuments.gov* has further information on the 100 documents featured in this book, extensive transcriptions, resources for teachers, and information on how to participate in this initiative.